An Introduction to the

Study of Education

THIRD EDITION

Edited by David Matheson

 Routledge
Taylor & Francis Group

LONDON AND NEW YORK

First published in Great Britain in 1999 by David Fulton Publishers Ltd
Second Edition 2004
Reprinted 2005
Third Edition published 2008
by Routledge
2 Park Square, Milton Park, Abingdon, Oxon, OX14 4RN

Simultaneously published in the USA and Canada
by Routledge
270 Madison Ave, New York NY 10016

Routledge is an imprint of the Taylor & Francis Group, an informa business

Transferred to Digital Printing 2010

Typeset in Garamond by Prepress Projects Ltd, Perth, UK

British Library Cataloguing-in-Publication Data
A catalogue record for this book is available from the British Library

Library of Congress Cataloging in Publication Data
An Introduction to the Study of Education/edited by David Matheson. – 3rd ed.

p.cm.

ISBN 978-0-415-45365-3 (pbk.)

1. Education—Great Britain. 2. Education—Study and teaching (Higher)—Great Britain. 3. Education—Social aspects—Great Britain. I. Matheson, David 1957–

LA632.158 2008

370.941—dc22

2007042491

ISBN 13: 978-0-415-45365-3 (pbk)
ISBN 10: 0-415-45365-8 (pbk)

Dedicated to the memory of

John Marr (1956–2004)

Soledad Perez (1958–2004)

Estelle Brisard (1973–2006)

Lillian Matheson (1954–2008)

Contents

Figures

Tables

Contributors

Estelle Brisard, late of the University of Paisley.

Professor Trevor Corner, Middlesex University.

Dr Reg Dennick, University of Nottingham.

Professor Nigel Grant, late of the University of Glasgow.

Dr Mary Kellett, Open University.

Graham A. Martin, University of Chester.

Dr Jane Martin, Institute of Education, London.

Dr Catherine Matheson, City University.

Dr David Matheson, University of Nottingham.

Professor Ian Menter, University of Glasgow.

Dr Graham Mitchell, University of Northampton.

Professor John Nisbet, University of Aberdeen.

Dr John Stanley, Instituto superior de Maia, Portugal.

Heather Rai, University of Nottingham.

Professor J. Eric Wilkinson, University of Glasgow.

Dr Michael Wyness, University of Warwick.

What is education?

David Matheson

> Education is what survives when what has been learnt has been forgotten.
> (B. F. Skinner)

Introduction

THERE ARE SOME CONCEPTS that most of us *think* we know, and we assume that others share the same or similar ideas. These can include notions such as fairness, equality and justice. They are terms that are easy to use and to feel that we understand what we mean by them but notoriously difficult to explain to others, other than by appealing to common sense and asserting that 'everyone' knows what justice, fairness, equality and so on actually are.

Among these slippery concepts is the concept of education. Education is what Winch and Gingell (1999) term an essentially contested concept. It is one that has a vast range of definitions, none of which is totally satisfactory. For example, we have the common equation between education and school. In this case, what about higher education? Where does further education fit in? And, for that matter, where do we place things we teach ourselves? We can discuss education that includes all of these arenas for learning or we can exclude at least some of them. We may even do as Abbs does and claim that 'education and school can refer, and often do refer, to antithetical activities' (1979: 90). Or we can go even further and align ourselves with Illich (1986) and assert not only that school is the antithesis of education but that its main function is to provide custodial day care for young people.

This chapter has its function to consider what education might be. I intend to do this by considering a well-known attempt at defining education. I will then consider some of the things that education can be for and, lastly, I will consider what it might mean to be educated before briefly considering Education Studies itself.

Defining education

The literature is replete with attempts at defining education and so, at most, I will succeed here in merely scratching the surface. Firstly, there is what we might term the 'elastic' sense of education. This is one in which, in a manner akin to the manner in which Lewis Carroll's Humpty Dumpty ascribes any meaning he wants to a word, education means precisely what the speaker, though within limits unknown to Humpty, wants it to mean. This approach capitalises on the kudos attached to the term *education* and seeks to ascribe it to whatever the speaker wants to give it. The result is a very loose approach wherein terms like *education* and *learning* are used interchangeably and the whole notion of education gets diluted to vanishing point. Despite this, as Lawson (1975) says, to call an activity or process 'educational' is typically to vest it with considerable status.

It is a commonplace that humans are learning machines. As Malcolm Tight puts it, 'Learning, like breathing, is something everyone does all of the time' (Tight 1996: 21). A first step then in trying to get a definition of education that is worth the bother is to exclude some activities. Unfortunately this is exactly where the problems start. As soon as we exclude activities from the list of what constitutes education we have to exercise a value judgment and we have to find a good reason for doing so. Nonetheless, at least by going about it this way, if we do decide that education equals school – an all too common assumption – then we may hope to have begun with a definition of education into which school fits, rather than beginning with school and making our definition of education fit into it.

The synonymous use of school and education is, however, hardly surprising when we consider that most of us will have experienced in schools what is arguably the most important part of our formal education. After all, it is there that we tend to have learned to read, we have developed our skills in social interaction, we have encountered authority that does not derive from a parent and we have been required to conform to sets of rules, some of which may have been explained, some of which may not. School leaves its mark on us and on our personal conception of education but this risks rendering us at least myopic to other possibilities.

One of the most popular approaches to the definition of education, at least in Anglophone countries, is that proposed by Richard Peters. Peters' contention is that 'education implies that something worthwhile is being or has been intentionally transmitted in a morally acceptable manner' (1966: 25). He manages to encompass two significant components: there is not only the end product, there is also the means adopted to achieve it.

Peters' definition suggests several areas for exploration:

1 intentionality and the 'something';
2 the notion of transmission;
3 the criteria for ascertaining whether the something is worthwhile;
4 the basis upon which moral acceptability is to be judged.

Intentionality and the 'something'

For Peters, education cannot come about by accident. In this he concurs with Hamm's claim that 'learning is an activity that one engages in with purpose and intention to come up to a certain standard' (1989: 91). This implies, *inter alia*, that those things which we learn incidentally cannot count. Equally it implies that the person fulfilling the function of teacher has some clear notion of what is to be transmitted to the learners.[1] This may take the form of some specific material to be learned or it may take the form of attitudes to be acquired and opinions to be formed. A question to be asked concerns whether we can ever separate what is being transmitted from the manner in which the transmission occurs. In other words, can the message stand alone from the medium that carries it? Or is the case, as Marshall Mcluhan (1967) claimed, that the medium *is* the message?[2]

For Peters, the 'something' refers to knowledge and understanding (and this can reasonably be extended to include skills and attitudes).[3] This in turn leads to several other questions, not least of which is to consider exactly what we mean by knowledge. Knowledge consists of several components. Most notably these consist, in their turn, of knowing *how* to do things (procedural knowledge) and knowing *that* (prepositional knowledge) certain things exist or are true or have happened and so on. There is also the rather thorny question of how we know that we know something and just what knowledge is, but this is perhaps beyond the scope of this book.[4]

Understanding is important for Peters, since this takes us beyond simply knowing and into the realms where we become better equipped to grasp underlying principles, and are consequently able to explain why things are the way they are or why they happen the way they do, and so on. The role of knowledge and

---

[1] It also implies some sort of examination to see if the learner has come up to the 'standard'. Examination may of course be self-examination, rather than some of sort test imposed or conducted by a third party.

[2] A master of aphorisms and puns, Mcluhan deliberately entitled his book on this subject *The Medium is the Massage*.

[3] Indeed, if one follows Bloom's (1969) *Taxonomy of Educational Objectives*, then one has to include at least some skills since the hierarchy of cognitive objectives is as follows and the last three listed are clearly skills to be acquired.

- Knowledge
- Comprehension
- Application
- Analysis
- Synthesis
- Evaluation
- Similarly, following Bloom's affective objectives will mean including attitudes in our 'something.'

[4] For discussion of the nature of knowledge, the reader is referred to the *Blackwell Companion to Epistemology*. For a counter-argument to the commonly held belief that knowledge is justified, true belief (JTB), see the Gettier Problem (http://en2.wikipedia.org/wiki/Gettier_problem), which tackles the inconsistency in the JTB approach with humour and panache.

understanding in defining education becomes even more crucial when one considers Peters' view on what it means to be educated (see Barrow and Woods 1995: ch. 1). According to Peters, becoming educated is an asymptotic process: we can move towards it but we can never fully attain it. For Peters, 'this understanding should not be too narrowly specialised' (1970: 4). Just how narrow is too narrow is open to speculation but this is a point best dealt with later as we consider what it means to be educated.

Transmission

'Transmission' creates in the mind an image of something passing from one place to another. However, we have to take care to understand just what Peters means by the term. In an age dominated by broadcast media, there is a tendency to equate 'broadcast' with 'transmission'; in other words, one may transmit but we never know who will receive or indeed exactly what they will receive. If Peters equates 'transmission' with 'broadcast' then clearly he is referring to teaching rather than to learning. On the other hand, if by transmission he actually means what we might nowadays term 'successful transmission' (i.e. when the message sent is equal to the message received), then he refers to both teaching *and* learning. Indeed the etymology of 'transmission' would clearly indicate the latter. We need only look at the manner in which 'transmission' was employed in the days before our present media age (in terms, for example, of a vehicle's transmission – which transfers movement from the engine to the wheels – which certainly brooks no ambiguity as to the 'message' sent being the same as the 'message' received) to see the justification for this claim. Nonetheless we do live in a media age; transmission has adopted a range of meanings; and so perhaps Peters' definition might be better altered to use the term 'successful transmission'.

In any case the need for transmission in Peters' definition of education brings with it the idea that, first, one cannot educate oneself by means of discovery, although one can by means of educational materials such as books, since in this latter case it is the ideas of the writer of the book that are being transmitted via the book. Second, there is an implication of a deficiency model of education whereby the teacher has 'something' that the learner does not and hence the teacher's task is, at least in part, to remedy deficiencies on the part of the learner.[5] This is a view of education that stands at odds with Freire (1972) and Rogers and Freiberg (1993), who see personal growth *from within* as a central tenet of education and for

[5] Being unable to educate oneself by means of discovery stands at odds with Donald Schön's (1984) work on the Reflective Practitioner, which has been extremely influential in the United Kingdom in terms of how not only teachers but also medical practitioners, engineers, architects and various other professionals are trained. Schön discusses, among other things, the development of the expert touch, that tacit knowledge that allows us to make adjustments to our practice on the hoof. It is a type of knowing that we see in every skilled craftsperson who knows by apparent intuition just what to do in a given situation. It is a skill that, like any skill, is learned but, although a teacher may help one on one's way, one essentially teaches oneself.

whom 'transmission' of any 'something' is in effect anathema. For each of these writers, an educator may facilitate learning but nothing more.

Worthwhile and useless knowledge

There are various criteria we might use to mark out *educationally* worthwhile or valuable knowledge from that which is worthless. We might do this in terms of need but in doing so one must take care not to confuse *needs* with *wants*. What I want is not necessarily what I need and vice versa; this goes for everything I could possibly want or need, and that includes knowledge. Again, it is a matter of perspective and relative importance. With this in mind, needs can be defined in terms of societal needs or individual needs. The question arises whether the needs of society are necessarily compatible with the needs of the individual. The answer one gives is very much contingent on one's view of the social goal of education and whether one views society as composed of individuals or sees individuals subsumed into society.

There is also the cultural aspect to knowledge to consider. Whether we seek cultural replication, maintenance or renovation, or even replacement, will play a major role in one's definition of educationally worthwhile knowledge. Our view, not only of the society we have now, but also of the society we want to have, is critical both in determining educationally worthwhile knowledge and in determining what counts as knowledge at all. This is exemplified, in all too many parts of the world, by the way in which some minority (and sometimes even majority[6]) languages have been proscribed in schools. This happened, for example, to Welsh, Scottish Gaelic, Scots, Swiss and French patois, Breton and Catalan, to name but a few cases in Europe. These languages were effectively designated as educationally (and often politically) unacceptable knowledge in often vicious bids to extirpate them.

Moral acceptability

Peters contends that education must be conducted in a morally acceptable manner. If there were consensus about what constitutes morality then this exigency would present few, if any, problems. Unfortunately in our present society we see what are termed moral values being challenged on a regular basis. No longer is the teacher seen, if ever s/he were, as an absolute authority on moral matters, and this is the

---

[6] 'Majority' is a very relative term. In the UK, English speakers are in the majority, but they are very much in the minority in Europe, however we want to define Europe – for this too is a relative term: do we mean the European Union? If so, then what about Switzerland and Norway? If Europe is that part of the world west of the Urals which sits on the European Continental Shelf (a traditional definition of Europe) then what about Iceland? The Icelanders consider themselves European and yet their country is a volcanic island in the middle of the Atlantic and very definitely not on the European Continental Shelf. Similarly, minority is relative. Both terms can also be considered in terms of power.

case across the whole range of teaching and learning. Our society increasingly recognises itself as multicultural (as indeed it has been in reality since the dawn of recorded history – see Grant 1997) and, as such, acknowledges that there can exist a multiplicity of value systems within one society. This poses the major problem of defining 'morally acceptable'. There are, however, some points of agreement within our society that certain 'educational' methods are simply unacceptable. At the extreme this precludes inflicting physical pain as a means of encouraging learning. Yet it was only in 1985 that corporal punishment was finally outlawed in state schools in the UK. Although in theory in its latter years this punishment was reserved for recalcitrant miscreants, in practice it could be used, and was used, as an 'aid' to learning whereby, for example, a pupil might be hit for not spelling a word correctly.[7] Moral torture in the form of denigration, however officially decried, still continues as a not uncommon means of pupil regulation. This can range from sarcasm to denigration of speech patterns and the learners' cultural roots.

The literature, however, tends to highlight *indoctrination* as an immoral means of encouraging learning. Indoctrination is defined as the intentional implantation of unshakeable beliefs regardless of appeals to evidence (Barrow and Woods 1995). Indoctrination is seen as running counter to the very idea of education as it 'necessarily involves lack of respect for an individual's rationality [and hence] is morally unacceptable' (Barrow and Woods 1995: 80). These same writers illustrate their opposition to indoctrination by means of an imaginary Catholic school where all the teachers endeavour to have the pupils wholeheartedly and unequivocally share their belief in Catholicism. The fact that Barrow and Woods demonstrate some remarkable ignorance about Catholicism[8] is beside the point. Their focus is on major areas of belief, on whole-life beliefs, on what one might term *macro*-beliefs. What about the lesser ones, the *meso*-beliefs and the *micro*-beliefs? How did we learn that science is objective? That experts are to be trusted? That reading is a necessary prerequisite for any modern society? It does not demand much imagination to determine a welter of beliefs that we usually hold unshakeably and that have been intentionally transmitted to us. There is also the question of the level at which intentionality occurs. Although a teacher may not intend to indoctrinate his/her learners, it is quite conceivable and indeed likely that the socio-political system within which that teacher operates demands that certain values and beliefs be transmitted (this is a theme returned to in the next chapter). If we are not only indoctrinated but also conditioned then perhaps the very thoughts we are capable of thinking are restrained and constrained.[9]

---

[7] This was the standard practice in the primary school I attended in the 1960s.
[8] This they do by, among other things, insisting that Catholics believe that the Pope is infallible (p. 70). The reality is that the Pope is held under the doctrine of infallibility to be able to make infallible statements under certain circumstances and only on matters of doctrine.
[9] See Matheson and Matheson (2000) for a discussion of discourse and the limitations that language can set on our thinking.

In Chapter 5 of this volume Trevor Corner and Nigel Grant remind us that we are generally better at identifying when others are indoctrinating. When it happens in our own education system we are more liable to call it 'moral education' or 'citizenship'. The question of moral (un)acceptability remains unanswered.

Perhaps a better question to ask is whether one can avoid *all* indoctrination in an educational process. Can one always present a learner with rationales for why things are as we say they are? Will one always have learners who are capable of understanding such rationales? How does one rationalise to a 3-year-old that to stick one's finger in the fire is not a good idea? By explaining the basic theories of thermodynamics and the interaction between skin and hot surfaces? By slightly scorching the child's finger? By telling the child that it will hurt and hope that one's authority as an adult/parent will be enough to have the child always believe that sticking a finger in the fire is not a good idea? Simply presenting notions as truth is much simpler than explaining them and may be greatly preferable to demonstrating possible consequences of an action that one wishes the learner to avoid. Explanation demands a level of understanding that may simply not exist in the learner. However, even rationalising everything might be construed as 'indoctrination', in that one is presenting the learner and encouraging in him/her a pattern of behaviour and hence beliefs about its acceptability. One's force of argument may give one such an advantage over the learner that the latter simply succumbs to the belief being proposed. As a teacher one may feel that the learner has agreed with the reasonableness of the belief and has agreed to share it. As a learner one might just feel ground down.

In passing, it can be worth reminding ourselves that 'acquiring a belief is like catching a cold' (Heil 1999: 47). No matter how I might contrive to 'catch' whatever metaphorical virus transmits a belief, no matter how I might believe myself willing to acquire the said belief, it is only when conditions are just right that I will acquire it. However, repetition and reinforcement that the proposed belief is true will help enormously in engendering these conditions. This point is illustrated by the way in which media stories can achieve a life of their own, regardless of how true they are and frequently in the face of powerful evidence to the contrary (Miller *et al.* 1998; Moore 2002).

It seems that the teacher is in a cleft stick if s/he decides to avoid *all* indoctrination. Giving no teaching implies to budding learners either that learning has a low value or that they themselves have. If we offer teaching, we are offering a complete package of beliefs that go with it and implying, if not insisting upon, its acceptability and desirability and hence 'indoctrinating' (Sutherland 1994).

On the other hand, perhaps there is a major argument in favour of critical thinking. Indeed, if one's position is that indoctrination *in all its forms and regardless of the intent* is immoral (i.e. if one accepts that Peters' definition of what constitutes education is valid at least in this respect) then the encouragement of critical thinking is essential. Expressed at its least subtle we have Postman and

Weingartner's notion of 'crap-detection' whereby the 'crap detector . . . is not completely captivated by the arbitrary abstractions of the community in which he [*sic*] happened to grow up' (1976: 18). In other words, the crap detector is able to look past the symbolism and theatricals of his/her society and adopt a critical perspective. This is a notion that is most often associated with Paulo Freire and his idea of conscientisation. In dealing with Freire a word of caution is needed: Freire wrote in Portuguese and used the term *consciencização*, which, since the Portuguese words for conscience and consciousness are the same, could be translated into English as either *conscience-raising* or *consciousness-raising*, so there is an element of ambiguity about the concept. However, Freire, a gifted linguist, was probably aware of this and hence the double meaning is very likely to be deliberate.

Conscientisation is a means of empowerment by which the learner decides what is to be learned and does so in terms of what is meaningful to his/her own existence. The goal of this education is to make the learner more critically aware of the area under discussion, and hence more critically aware of him/herself and his/her environment. The political implications of such an educational goal and its associated pedagogy are immense. In this view of education, there is no received wisdom and everything is open to question. Nonetheless, the quandary outlined above remains, whereby offering teaching in any shape or form, or not at all, constitutes indoctrination; but perhaps the development of the critical faculty is the most moral of options in that it encourages the learner to question even the basic premise upon which the learning experience is based (Akkari and Perez 2000).

What is education for?

What education is for is clearly dependent on how we choose to define education and how we determine the relationship between education and the society in which it operates. For the purposes of this section, in which we look at some of the social goals of education, we shall concentrate on the formal domain. Formal education is above all associated with school, further education and higher education. It tends to aim, at least at some levels, at a qualification and is often associated in the public mind with younger people. Non-formal education requires no entrance qualifications (such as schools certificates or degrees, but it may require a certain level of knowledge and/or expertise in the domain in question), may result in no exit qualifications and is more usually associated with adults. The boundaries between formal and non-formal education were never very strict and are becoming even more blurred as time goes on.

Since time immemorial, formal education has been used with a social goal in mind. Every society seeks to replicate itself and finds ways of transmitting what it considers worthwhile to its young and sometimes its not-so-young citizens. In

Ancient Greece, for example, the Spartans used a formal school system to instil into their young men the ideas of absolute obedience to their military commanders, extreme courage and resistance to pain as well as what were for the time some of the most advanced notions of military strategy. The young women were trained in domestic arts and motherhood. By the same token, it was not uncommon for commentators to complain, as did Seneca during the Roman Empire, that 'we are training children for school, not for life.'[10] From this it becomes clear that it has been held for a very long time that school *ought* to have a social function and that this social function has not always been clear and well-defined.

Since the Reformation, at least, the idea that formal education can be used to reproduce society, mould society or create a new society has been widely discussed and written about in the West. The Reformers sought to create a society based around the *reading* of the Bible, which distinguished them from their Roman Catholic predecessors, who emphasised the *interpretation* of the Bible given by the Old Church. The social upheaval of the Reformation was accompanied by attempts to literally create a new society based on a literate population. To this end, John Knox *et al.* (1560), in their *First Book of Discipline*, proposed the creation of schools in every centre of population, whose aims would be not only to teach basic skills such as reading and writing but also to act as a means whereby the more able boys and girls would learn sufficiently to allow entry to higher education. In this way, the intelligentsia would be kept in contact with the rest of the population and the upper echelons of society would be revitalised by new blood.

This idea of using education for social engineering has echoes in Robert Owen, who states in his *New View of Society* (1835) that:

> Any general character, from the best to the worst, from the most ignorant to the most enlightened, may be given to any community, even to the world at large, by the application of proper means; which means are to a great extent at the command and under the control of those who have influence in the affairs of men
>
> (Owen [1835] 1965: 85)

It is important to underline here that *character* refers not to individuals but to the communities that they form. The essential point however is that for Owen education had the power to shape collections of individuals into communities and to determine the nature of those communities. In other words, education has a major socialising function. This theme is taken up by Durkheim, for whom 'education consists of the methodical socialisation of the young generation' (Durkheim 1956: 71). Durkheim also sees education as a means for social reproduction:

---

[10] *Non vitae sed scholae discimus.*

> Education, far from having as its unique or principle object the individual and his interests, is above all the means by which society perpetually recreates the conditions of its existence.
>
> (Durkheim 1956: 123)

Part of the recreation of itself is the need for economic sustenance if not growth. However, until recently there seemed to be a certain coyness about openly espousing the view that 'the economic aims of education are as legitimate as any other' (Winch 2002: 101). Yet, if education – whether a lifelong activity or, as Winch puts it, 'broadly but not exclusively concerned with preparation for life' (ibid.) – does not have economic aims, then why is so much money spent on it? In point of fact, it is fairly easy to establish that the economic aims of education are paramount, *especially* when education is viewed as a preparation for life or as a means of coping with changes in one's economic circumstances.

Formal education serves many functions besides those outlined above. It contains examinations and assessments of various kinds that serve to decide, in part at least, the choice of next destinations to which the learner can move on. Depending on one's perspective, these can be seen as an opportunity for social mobility or as a means for further entrenching social divides and further ossifying the existing social structure. Formal education may liberate or enslave, expand horizons or confirm feelings of personal failure. But let us note that formal education is seen as a right but seldom as a privilege, despite general consensus that it is essential in order for a person to learn how to function within our society.

What does it mean to become educated?

Becoming educated carries with it a number of notions such as the acquisition of *depth* whereby a person understands (increasingly) the underlying principles within an 'area of knowledge'. The educated person will acquire *breadth* in the sense that s/he will develop a cognitive perspective *within* an area of knowledge and *between* areas of knowledge. This implies the creation of linkages across the area of knowledge and into areas which may adjoin or not. This not only serves to distinguish knowledge from information but serves to encourage the adoption of differing perspectives on the same domain (an almost essential prerequisite to creative problem-solving). Indeed for Peters, 'being educated is incompatible with being narrowly specialised' (1970: 4).

An area of knowledge is, by definition, not an amorphous mass but has certain rules that bind it together. In this view of education, the educated person has to abide by these rules when acquiring knowledge, when handling knowledge and when using knowledge. To take one example, when learning another language, one accepts that the grammar and syntax of that language are rules to be obeyed (as best one can) if one wishes to actually communicate in that language. Failure to obey the rules will make communication difficult, if not altogether impossible. Against this has to be set the notion that fundamental creativity often comes about when the accepted rules in an area of knowledge are bent or ignored and a new, revised set has to be put in place.[11]

In our culture we are used to measuring 'being educated' against, for example, level of qualification or extent of acquaintance with some domain or other. In this way, the capacity to expound upon and employ the literary canon, or some other set of knowledge, may be the scale against which one's being educated is measured. Barrow (1999) draws this together with the development of criticality mentioned above and states that 'it is to have a developed mind, which means a mind that has developed understanding such that it can discriminate between logically different kinds of questions and exercise judgment, critically and creatively, in respect of important matters' (p. 139). Such discrimination and judgment inevitably need to be based upon a significant amount of knowledge. Just how much is significant and about what sort of knowledge we are talking is, of course, open to debate and will vary according to circumstances. My being educated in horticulture may be of little use when faced with a burst pipe in my living room.

All this implies that, while we may wax lyrical about general education, the sheer scope of knowledge and skills which are there to be acquired, at least in theory, is such that we must forcibly remain uneducated in at least some, if not many, domains. However, Barrow's argument, in company with many others, implies very strongly that education is the antithesis of indoctrination, although, as suggested above, education must perforce contain elements of indoctrination, if only to convince some learners of its own worth.

Education suffers from a variety of definitional problems, not least of which is the frequently false equation between education and studying (compounded by a similarly false equation between learning and studying). Studying implies some sort of examination, if only of oneself. Learning does not. Whether education makes a similar implication is dependent on how one chooses to define it. However, we might do well to distinguish between *education* and *being educated*. If *education* runs into such problems through its being simultaneously a process and a product then why not dispense with the one and concentrate on the other? In this way, discussion of what it means *to be educated* can potentially be more fruitful since the term implies not a process (with all the pitfalls and traps that await even the more astute, such as Richard Peters) but rather a product. In this way, it is immaterial how we have acquired the components of being educated; what counts is that we have indeed acquired them.

---

[11] One can also contrast the way adults tend to learn languages with the way children do. Adults aim more for accuracy in grammar etc., children for communication in just the same way as they learned their native tongue. Children use a new language for the purpose for which language was intended (i.e. to communicate) and only as a secondary consideration do they learn how to structure it. Compare the success rates of children and adults in language acquisition to judge the relative efficacy of the two approaches.

With this idea in mind, it is worth taking a moment to consider those things that, in your opinion, every person should know and those things that every person should be able to do. Should we value some knowledge and skills over others? If so, which ones? And, as importantly, why should these knowledge and skills be more important than others? By asking questions such as this, we can begin to establish a canon of basic knowledge – which might be quite sophisticated – as well as establishing a hierarchy of knowledge. Critical in this venture, though, is establishing the rationale for such a set of affairs. In the end we may arrive at the same conclusion as Maskell (1999), who argues that those whom we might term 'educated' are all too often themselves in want of an education, suffering as they do from limited horizons and narrow ranges of knowledge.

We might even arrive at the notion of the *educated public*, which notion, as Wain (1994) tells us, can take a variety of forms but in all of them seems to imply some sort of community of persons endowed not just with knowledge and understanding across a wide range of spheres but with criticality and a capacity to communicate effectively with each other.

What is the study of education?

Education is unlike most other academic disciplines in that there is no agreement what it actually is. In consequence the study of education is somewhat diverse. It begins inevitably from the concept of education held by those directing the study – whether through their role as course managers, as researchers or as funders of research projects.

From the student's point of view?

If one succumbs to the notion that education equals school, then one's view of what constitutes knowledge of education worthy of study (for who really wants to study useless knowledge?) will be somewhat different from knowledge considered worthwhile by one who believes that education is a lifelong process. Unfortunately, there is a widespread tendency to do just that, despite the fact that it closes one's mind to the educational experiences that occur in the longer part of one's life. The excuse given, as Gutmann reminds us, is that 'an exhaustive study of the other potential educational agencies in society would be exhausting if not impossible' (cited in Wain 1994: 155). This is doubtless true but one could just pick and choose, as has occurred in the present text, and try at least to be representative of what is available.

At least one attempt has been made to establish what students of Education Studies might study. This was undertaken for the Quality Assurance Agency for Higher Education. The result is the benchmark statements for Education Studies

(QAA 2000), which seek to state what a student completing a single Honours programme in the subject will be capable of. Joint and Combined Honours students would be expected to show capability in a relevant selection of the areas.

The benchmark statements represent a compromise between those who argue that Education Studies is a discipline in its own right[12] and those who see it as an offshoot of teacher training. Equally the statements have to accommodate those who emphasise one methodological approach, be this sociological, historical, psychological, philosophical, some combination of these or some other approach entirely.

> Education Studies is concerned with understanding how people develop and learn throughout their lives. It facilitates a study of the nature of knowledge, and a critical engagement with a variety of perspectives, and ways of knowing and understanding, drawn from a range of appropriate disciplines. There is diversity in Education Studies courses at undergraduate level but all involve the intellectually rigorous study of educational processes, systems and approaches, and the cultural, societal, political and historical contexts within which they are embedded.
>
> (QAA 2000: 4)

What is perhaps most remarkable is that, other than the definition given above, the statements never explicitly state what topics need be studied. This should come as no surprise: if there can be no consensus on what constitutes education, there can surely be none on what constitutes Education Studies.

Despite this, Education Studies is perhaps unique among academic disciplines in that all students can bring directly to bear their own experiences and their own process of education. Since we have all found ourselves in situations that involve teaching and learning (and in studying Education Studies we are continuing to do so), then we all have experience that is relevant. In this respect, perhaps the only other domain that comes close in terms of universalised experience is Medicine, since we have all been ill at least once in our lives.

From the researcher's point of view?

The various chapters of this book, including this one, together with their references lists, give some indication of the wide diversity of subjects studied by researchers in Education Studies. Fundamentally, one can say that if a topic involves teaching or learning in any shape or form whatsoever, whether in a classroom or in the school of life or wherever, then it is fair game to be researched. Not that one would necessarily get funding, of course.

---

[12] I once heard Education Studies being described as parasitic and proud of it!

Like research in any academic discipline, research in Education Studies goes through trends, as John Nisbett shows us in Chapter 16 in this volume. Topics come and topics go. Presently, for example, we see much ink being spilt on the apparent under-achievement of boys. In a few years this may have vanished from the agenda. Likewise for notions of teaching and learning. We have seen a growth in recent years of work looking at issues arising out of our multicultural and multiethnic society. We have even seen research being conducted on educational research (Ofsted 2000).

Conclusion

In essence, this chapter has been about ideas regarding education and its purpose, as well as briefly considering Education Studies. Ideas when formalised into practice naturally have material impacts and some of these are picked up in later chapters. A negative perspective on such an impact is given by Common, who presents us with perhaps the most cynical view of formal education as social control:

> We learn reading and boredom, writing and boredom, arithmetic and boredom, and so on according to the curriculum, till in the end it is quite certain you can put us in the most boring job there is and we'll endure it.
>
> (Common in Meighan 1986: 75)

Suggested further reading

There is a vast literature concerning the topics we have discussed in this chapter. However a few texts stand out as especially suitable for the debutant. On the philosophical side there are Barrow and Woods (1995) and Walker and Soltis (1992), who introduce the reader to a wide variety of concepts in the philosophy of education without getting lost in jargon. Freire (1972) is a clear and lucid account of the ideas behind conscientisation, and Akkari and Perez (2000) offer a critique of Freire and his ideas. Maskell (1999) presents a strong argument in favour of revising what it is to be educated and advocates an emphasis on great literature. Worth reading, given our increasingly technological society, is Snow's (1959) *Two Cultures*, where he decries the breakdown in communication between the sciences and the humanities, which extends to almost deliberate ignorance of things scientific by those 'into' literature and vice versa.

Sociologically two texts stand out. Meighan and Siraj-Blatchford (2004) adopt a themed approach whereas Blackledge and Hunt (1993) arrange their material according to major theories and theorists and take the reader from Durkheim through various Marxisms to the micro-interpretive approach.

References

Abbs, P. (1979) *Reclamations*. London: Heinemann.

Akkari, A. and Perez, S. (2000) 'Education and Empowerment', in Matheson, C. and Matheson, D. (eds) *Educational Issues in the Learning Age*. London: Continuum.

Barrow, R. (1999) 'The Higher Nonsense: Some Persistent Errors in Educational Thinking', *Journal of Curriculum Studies*. **31** (2), 131–142.

Barrow, R. and Woods, R. (1995) *An Introduction to the Philosophy of Education*. London: Routledge.

Blackledge, D. and Hunt, B. (1993) *Sociological Interpretations of Education*. London: Routledge.

Bloom, B. S. and associates (1969) *Taxonomy of Educational Objectives: The Classification of Educational Goals*. London: Longman.

Durkheim, E. (1956) *Education and Sociology*. New York: The Free Press.

Freire, P. (1972) *The Pedagogy of the Oppressed*. Harmondsworth: Penguin.

Grant, N. (1997) 'Intercultural Education in the United Kingdom', in Woodrow, D., Verma, G., Rocho-Trindade, M., Campani, G. and Bagley, C. *Intercultural Education: Theories, Policies and Practice*. Aldershot: Ashgate.

Hamm, C. (1989) *Philosophical Issues in Education: An Introduction*. London: Falmer.

Heil, J. (1999) 'Belief', in Dancy, J. and Sosa, E. (eds) *A Companion to Epistemology*. Oxford: Blackwell.

Illich, I. (1986) *Deschooling Society*. Harmondsworth: Pelican.

Knox, J., Douglas, J., Row, J., Spottiswoode, J., Willock, J. and Winram, J. (1560) *The [First] Book of Discipline*. Available at www.swrb.com/newslett/actualNLs/bod_ch00.htm (accessed 21 November 2007).

Lawson, K. H. (1975) *Philosophical Concepts and Values in Adult Education*. Nottingham: University of Nottingham.

Mcluhan, M. (1967) *The Medium is the Massage*. New York: Bantam Books.

Maskell, D. (1999) 'What has Jane Austen to Teach Tony Blunkett?', *Journal of Philosophy of Education*. **33** (2), 157–174.

Matheson, C. and Matheson, D. (2000) 'Educational Spaces and Discourses', in Matheson, C. and Matheson, D. (eds) *Educational Issues in the Learning Age*. London: Continuum.

Meighan, R. (1986) *A Sociology of Educating*, 2nd edn. London: Cassell.

Meighan, R. and Siraj-Blatchford, I. (2004) *A Sociology of Educating*, 4th edn. London: Continuum.

Miller, D., Kitzinger, J. and Williams, K. (1998) *The Circuit of Mass Communication: Media Strategies, Representation and Audience Reception in the AIDS Crisis*. Thousand Oaks, CA: SAGE.

Moore, M. (2002) *Bowling for Columbine*. Dog Eat Dog Films Production.

Ofsted (2000) *Educational Research: A Critique*. London: Ofsted.

Owen, R. [1835](1965) *A New View of Society and Report to the County of Lanark*, ed. V. A. C. Gatrell. Harmondsworth: Pelican.

Peters, R. S. (1966) *Ethics and Education*. London: Allen and Unwin.

Peters, R. S. (1970) 'Education and the Educated Man', *Journal of Philosophy of Education*. **4,** 5–20.

Postman, N. and Weingartner, C. (1976) *Teaching as a Subversive Activity*. Harmondsworth: Pelican.

Quality Assurance Agency for Higher Education (2000) *Education Studies*. Available at www.qaa.ac.uk/academicinfrastructure/benchmark/honours/education.pdf (accessed 21 November 2007).

Rogers, C. and Freiberg, H. J. (1993) *Freedom to Learn*, 3rd edn. New York: Merrill.

Schön, D. (1984) *The Reflective Practitioner: How Professionals Think in Action.* New York: Basic Books.

Snow, C. P. (1959) *The Two Cultures and the Scientific Revolution*. London: Canto.

Sosa, E. and Greco, J. (eds) (1998) *Blackwell Guide to Epistemology.* London: Blackwell.

Sutherland, M. (1994) *Theory of Education*. Harlow: Longman.

Tight, M. (1996) *Key Concepts in Adult Education and Training*. London: Routledge.

Wain, K. (1994) 'Competing Conceptions of the Educated Public', *Journal of Philosophy of Education.* **28** (2), 149–159.

Walker, D. F. and Soltis, J. F. (1992) *Curriculum and Aims*. New York: Teachers' College Press.

Winch, C. (2002) 'The Economic Aims of Education', *Journal of Philosophy of Education.* **36** (1), 101–117.

Winch, C. and Gingell, J. (1999) *Key Concepts in the Philosophy of Education.* London: Routledge.

2

Ideology in education in the United Kingdom

Catherine Matheson

To *idéologues* one must attribute all the misfortunes which have befallen France.
   Do you know what fills me most with wonder? The powerlessness of force to establish anything . . . In the end the sword is always conquered by the mind.

(Napoleon Bonaparte)

Introduction

EVERY CONCEPT IN EDUCATION has varying and various interpretations but perhaps none more so than ideology. As this chapter will show, it is used in a variety of senses and to a variety of ends. To do this, we begin with a discussion of the concept of ideology and show how it has had multiple meanings from the time it was first coined. We then move on to discuss ideology in education and show some of the types of ideology that are used in understanding education, before illustrating some of these types.

The concept of ideology

Ideology is a 'highly ambiguous concept' (Meighan and Siraj-Blatchford 1998: 179), a 'most equivocal and elusive concept' (Larrain 1979: 13) which has many meanings and usages and can be conceived either negatively and critically as a 'false consciousness' or positively as a 'world view'. The former has a restricted meaning and tends to be used in a pejorative manner to describe a set of undesirable and even distorted beliefs; the latter has a looser meaning and is used by philosophers and social scientists in neutral and analytical ways. Ideology can also be viewed as a subjective psychological phenomenon emphasising the role of individuals and groups or as a more objective social phenomenon 'impregnating the basic structure of society' (Larrain 1979: 14). Ideology can also be seen either restrictively, as part of, or more loosely, as equal to, the whole of the cultural sphere or ideological superstructure of society.

The word 'ideology' originated with that group of *savants* or intellectuals in the French Revolution who were entrusted by the Convention of 1795 with the founding and management of a new centre of revolutionary thought. These people were located within the newly established *Institut de France*, which was committed to the ideas of the French Enlightenment and thus the practical realisation of freedom of thought and expression (Lichtheim 1967).

In its original sense, the word 'ideology' was first used in 1796 by the French philosopher Destutt de Tracy, a member of the *Institut de France* and one of the directors of the highly influential French literary review *Mercure de France*. It was, in the words of one of the *Mercure*'s regular contributors, Joseph-Jérôme Le François de Lalande, nothing more than a name for the 'science of ideas, their rules and their origins' (Lalande in Rey and Rey-Debove 1990: 957). Deriving ideas from sensations, Destutt de Tracy undertook to study the 'natural history of ideas' in his *Eléments d'idéologie* (1801–15). He wanted to unmask the historicity of ideas by tracing their origins and setting aside metaphysical and religious prejudices but also wanted this unmasking to reveal a true and universal knowledge of human nature (Hall 1978). Ideology was presented as a science and set in opposition to prejudice and false beliefs because scientific progress was possible only if these could be avoided.

From the start, however, ideology was to have pejorative connotations, one reason being because de Tracy and those who practised it, the ideologues or *idéologistes*, were concerned with two logically incompatible concepts of 'ideology': the relation between history and thought, and the promotion of 'true' ideas which would be true regardless of the historical context. Following Helvétius, who believed that education could do everything, the ideologues shared his enthusiasm for education (Larrain 1979). After the years of revolution they wanted to educate the French people and above all the young people so that a just and happy society could be established. De Tracy wanted his book to be a study programme for youngsters and explicitly acknowledged that a motive for writing it was the new law (1801) introducing public education.

The other reason for the pejorative connotation of ideology was Napoleon, who was the first to use 'ideology' in a truly negative sense. Initially he shared the objectives and goals of the *Institut de France* and even became an honorary member in 1797 (Lichtheim 1967). The *Institut* then facilitated Bonaparte's accession to power, which he achieved in 1799, by helping him win the support of the educated middle class (Hall 1978). However, he abandoned the ideologues in 1803 when he signed his Concordat with the Church and deliberately set out to destroy the core of the *Institut*, the liberal and republican ideas of which greatly influenced the educational establishment. From then on the *idéologistes* were ridiculed as utopian visionaries under the name of *idéologues* (Dancy and Sosa 1993: 191). After the defeat in Russia in 1812, Napoleon turned on them forcefully and attributed all of France's misfortune to the ideologists or *idéologues* as he disparagingly called them (Lichtheim 1967), whom he considered unrealistic, doctrinaire and ignorant of political practice. (It is worth noting that English language has reversed the pejorative and non-pejorative use of the terms.) Nonetheless, after Napoleon's demise the Comte de Tracy, who became a well-known personality inside and outside France, held an influential salon where writers and scientists met.

It is from this pejorative use of ideology as an undesirable or misguided set of ideas that many modern uses of the word have grown. Continuing this tendency, Marx and Engels used ideology pejoratively to mean a false belief or illusion. In *The German Ideology*, written in 1845–7 but not published until 1927, Marx and Engels, although not clearly defining the concept, use 'ideology' to deride the proposition of the belief in the power of ideas to determine reality. For Marx (and Marxists) ideology was thus often seen as an attempted justification of a distorted set of ideas which consciously and/or unconsciously concealed contradictions in the interests of the dominant class or of a group and served to maintain disproportionate allocation of economic and political power to the ruling class or dominant groups (Marx and Engels [1845–7] 1970). Elsewhere Marx uses the term less pejoratively and gives a sociological interpretation of ideology (Marx [1859] in Meighan and Siraj-Blatchford 1998) in which ideology can be defined as a broad interlocked set of ideas and beliefs about the world held by a group of people operating at various levels in society and in various contexts and that is demonstrated in their behaviour. This adds to the ambiguity of the concept of ideology not only because of the competing definitions but also because the set of beliefs operates with several layers of meaning (Meighan and Siraj-Blatchford 1998).

After a period of disuse the word was revived with the publication in 1927 of Marx and Engels' previously unpublished *German Ideology*, which reinforced the Marxist and central sociological tradition view of ideology as 'distortion of reality' (Bullock et al. 1988). The classical Marxist position claims that ideological misconceptions cannot be dispelled by confronting those under their spell with the 'truth', since ideologies contain standards of evidence and argumentation that prevent the recognition of reality as it is (Dancy and Sosa 1993). For Gramsci and other Marxists, however, ideology is explained in terms of its social role; it is neither true nor false but 'the "cement" which holds together the structure [in which economic class struggle takes place] and the realm of the complex superstructures' (Hall 1978: 53). In other words, ideologies are those beliefs that are generated by a particular mode of production or economic structure. For Althusser, ideologies are non-scientific beliefs related more closely to social practice than to theoretical enquiry (Summer 1979). Lack of space precludes discussion of scientific beliefs as being the only true beliefs and hence free from ideological constraints. More recently, the concept of ideology has seen a renewed (implicit rather than explicit) interest, particularly in feminism, cultural studies and post-modernism in general, for the 'unmasking relations of power and domination implicit in culturally dominant forms of theoretical and social discourse' (Dancy and Sosa 1993: 193).

For my purposes I shall consider ideology in its broad sense of set of beliefs as opposed to the narrow sense of a set of undesirable or misguided beliefs. Within contemporary sociology one distinguishes between 'particular' ideologies concerning specific groups and 'total' ideologies concerning a total commitment to a way of life. Every ideology is composed of three ingredients: an invariable mythological structure, an alternating set of philosophical beliefs and a historically determined chosen group of people (Feuer 1975). Where ideologies exist in competition there are several outcomes: domination, incorporation and legitimisation. In the first instance, we have cultural domination or hegemony. In the second, we have radical ideas incorporated into the traditional ideology. In the last instance, an ideology may achieve acceptance of its beliefs by direct repression or by more indirect means of institutional control such as those of the media, education, religion, law or economy (Meighan and Siraj-Blatchford 1998).

Ideology, knowledge and the curriculum

A curriculum as a package of ideas, together with the manner in which it is delivered (its pedagogy), certainly fits the bill as an ideology. Curriculum heritage is the product of a philosophical tradition that can be traced through historical and contemporary curriculum practice, and in which we find the European triad of humanism (Plato, Erasmus and Locke), rationalism (Plato and Descartes) and naturalism (Rousseau). The first two elements of the triad underline respectively the importance of the human character and especially the feelings and the importance of reason, but with both understanding is sought by submission of the individual to an external body of knowledge, while the third seeks understanding in the private, concrete and the natural (McLean 1995). As is the case with much in ideology, the triad's elements are not mutually exclusive.

It is these first two approaches that have dominated curriculum development across Europe, and, as a consequence of European influence, across much of the world. In France there is the rational encyclopaedic educational ideology with state prescription of national occupational needs (McLean 1995). In this collectivist tradition upper secondary schooling is subordinated to economic and social planning and general and vocational education are linked in content and control (collectivism). In the pluralist tradition we move towards the individualist and humanist approach such as exists in the UK and Germany with a clear separation between general education and vocational training, but in Germany the curriculum is more infiltrated with rational encyclopaedic ideology than in the UK. We also have generalism (as in France and Germany) versus specialism or, some say, élitism in England and to a lesser extent in Scotland (McLean 1995). Naturalism, however, as we shall shortly see, is very present and has been highly influential, especially in primary schools.

Educational ideologies

An educational ideology is any package of educational ideas held by a group of people about formal arrangements for education, typically expressed by contrasting two patterns of opposed assumptions such as teacher-centred and child-centred methods (the Plowden Report, DES 1967) or traditional and progressive methods (Bennett 1976). Going beyond dichotomies, Davies (1969) and Cosin (1972) outline four ideologies of education: conservative or elitist, which maintains cultural hegemony; revisionist or technocratic, which is concerned with vocational relevance; romantic or individualist or psychological, which focuses on individual development and derives from the work of Pestalozzi, Froebel, Herbart, Montessori and Piaget; and democratic socialist or liberal tradition or egalitarian, which seeks equality of opportunity and the progressive elimination of élitist values (Meighan and Siraj-Blatchford 1998). These categories are not hermetically sealed, nor are they entirely mutually exclusive; they overlap, and indeed an educational ideology might belong to several categories simultaneously. Assuming one accepts these categories as valid at all, the category(ies) to which a particular ideology might be assigned will often be a matter of perspective.

Any ideology can be compared with others on the basis of a series of theories functioning as part of an aspect of knowledge, learning, teaching resources, organisation, assessments and aims. The concept of ideology can be used as an analytical tool to compare various patterns of education. Ideologies operate at different conceptual levels and, if categorised into levels of operations, can be compared along the lines of whole education systems, competing ideologies within a national system, ideologies within formal education and ideologies of classroom practice. Ideologies are usually linked with, for example, ideologies of classroom practice being linked to other parts of the educational and political network. The levels at which ideologies operate can be seen nationally in terms of Education Acts; regionally in terms of Local Education Authorities; locally at the levels of educational establishments, rival groups within educational establishment, classroom, teacher–learner interaction, and rival groups within classroom (Meighan and Siraj-Blatchford 1998).

One could also distinguish between ideologies of legitimisation or implementation, the former concerning goals, values and ends and the latter the means, and it can be a worthwhile exercise to consider the ideologies outlined below in this light.

Educational ideologies and politics

By definition, education is a political activity in the broad sense, although this does not necessarily mean that it is a party political activity. Politics has to do with power and the distribution of power. Education has to do with knowledge (whether in terms of knowing that or knowing how). If knowledge is power, then education is political. If Gramsci's theory of hegemony (see Chapter 1) is accurate, then politics is an educational activity and education is a political activity. All educators have an ideology, whether formally articulated or not, and whether or not they are aware of having an ideology. To subscribe to a particular view of the aims of education is to subscribe to an educational ideology. Debate about the nature and purpose of education is therefore 'bound to be not only ideological but, in the broad sense, political as well' (Winch and Gingell 1999: 111).

Often people think that it would seem that there is a correlation between political views and educational views. The correlation is usually that left-wing political views and support for child-centred or progressive education go hand in hand. This may have been more true at particular times, but it need not be so. Three examples illustrate the fact that political and educational ideologies cannot necessarily be subsumed into each other, although they certainly overlap.

The first example concerns two Labour personalities who had different educational ideologies. In his Ruskin College speech of 1976 (see Chapter 12) the Labour Prime Minister, James Callaghan, acknowledged his indebtedness to R. H. Tawney, who had been one of the originators of the Labour Party programme on education many years previously. Ironically, Callaghan and Tawney had very different views on most educational issues. Tawney defended liberal values, teacher autonomy and social democratic meritocracy. Callaghan in his speech advocated greater state control, teacher accountability and parentocracy; that is, more power to parents and less to the teachers. Callaghan aimed at increasing state control over education and over the curriculum whereas Tawney had fought to remove central government hold on the curriculum. He feared that government might abuse its power over the curriculum to serve the interests of industry or political ideologies instead of serving the interest of the pupils, who were best served by the professional judgment of the teachers. Callaghan questioned the power of the teachers over the curriculum and thought that teachers should be more accountable to parents and to industry (Brooks 1991).

The second example is that of a Marxist who had nothing but contempt for progressive educational ideologies. Antonio Gramsci, who thought that education had the power to affect political consciousness, advocated conservative schooling for radical politics (Entwistle 1979) and there could be no time for what he considered to be the playful experimentation approach of progressive educational methods. Instead, as much as possible of literacy, numeracy, history, politics and economics, and science had to be learned as quickly as possible. In order to be in a position to counteract the dominant hegemony one had to learn what the dominant hegemony learned through education and much more. Learning had to be done in a concentrated, systematic and disciplined intellectual way. Incidentally, the surfeit of playful experimentation and the opening up the imagination was one the major reasons behind the erstwhile Soviet Union abandoning in 1931 the very progressive and child-centred Dalton Plan that had been introduced from the USA shortly after the Russian Revolution. The Soviet Union needed to industrialise rapidly, and discovery methods with self-directed learning were simply not delivering the expertise quickly enough (Grant 1979).

A third example is that a form of selective secondary schooling for all, introduced by a Labour government after the Second World War, is currently associated with right-of-centre politics. Over the last couple of decades the Conservative Party has greatly criticised comprehensive education, which was widely introduced from the end of the 1960s onwards, replacing state-funded selective schooling in many areas but not all. The Conservative government did not stop the spread of comprehensive schools but rather accelerated it. In 1967, the Conservative Party leader, Edward Heath, could state that 'it has never been a Conservative principle that in order to achieve (selection or grouping by ability) children have to be segregated in different institutions' (Heath in Finn *et al.* 1978: 176).

Political ideas and ideologies evolve and their expression in educational circumstances evolves too. Indeed the apparently same educational ideology can be adopted simultaneously or consecutively by different political ideologies. This is the case not only with selective and comprehensive schools but also with standards and achievement (see Chapters 13 and 14) or equality of opportunity (see Chapters 6, 7, 8 and 9) and more recently the application of market principles to education and the idea of 'privatisation' not only not rejected by Labour but taken even further (see Chapter 14).

Some examples of educational ideologies

An élitist ideology: the public school ethos

'There is perhaps no better illustration of an élitist educational ideology than that which is held to underpin the education of the ruling class in a country' (Matheson and Limond 1999: 20). This kind of ideology is important not only for the way in which it might be held to form the ideas and behaviour of the ruling class but also for the influence it has on the education of the non-ruling class (Matheson and Limond 1999).

Everyone knows something of the public school ethos or public school spirit. The largely autobiographical novel *Tom Brown's Schooldays*, whether faithful portrayal or 'romantic fiction and expurgated fact' (Chandos 1984: 45), has helped reinforce the mystique of the public school ethos: the 'pragmatic, almost unsupervised, trial-and-error, sink-or-swim test for survival in a self-governing community of male juveniles' (Chandos 1984: 38).

Its principal values are those of character over intellect and the importance of physicality. School is a place to train character. It is what came to distinguish the English public school from all other Western approaches to education or educational institutions. It is what 'impresses and amazes foreigners' (Gathorne-Hardy 1977: 75). In France, Germany and even Scotland, schools not only drew from a wider social spectrum but were academic institutions and character was left to the family (Vaizey 1977). Examples of the public school ethos can be found in *Tom Brown's Schooldays*. The first example is from the point of view of Tom's father:

> Shall I tell him to mind his work, and say he's sent to school to make himself a good scholar? Well, but he isn't in school for that – at any rate, not for that mainly. I don't care a straw for Greek particles, or the digamma, no more does his mother. What is he sent to school for? . . . If only he'll turn out a brave, helpful, truth-telling Englishman, and a gentleman, and a Christian, that's all I want
>
> (Hughes [1857] 1963: 71–72)

The second example demonstrates that Tom himself seems to have fully internalised the importance of physicality and that character matters more than intellectual achievement, these being the fundamental values of the public school ethos: 'I want to be A1 at cricket and football, and all the other games, and to make my hands keep my head against any fellow, lout or gentleman . . . I want to carry away just as much Latin and Greek as will take me through Oxford respectably' (Hughes [1857] 1963: 262).

The public schools pre-date the emergence of the British Empire. The most distinguished date to the High Medieval period. The public school ethos is therefore a package of ideas, values and associated practices that have grown up over time. However it was in the imperial period that their role, nature and ethos became most clearly defined (Matheson and Limond 1999). The main aim of the education of those who attended public schools was to develop a certain sort of character. This would be one in which self-control and 'stiff upper lip' would be of great importance as it gave clear imperial advantage. It was well suited to the needs of the army but equally suited to other forms and aspects of imperial service from missionary work to exploration and administration (Matheson and Limond 1999).

Henry Newbolt's poem 'Vitai Lampada' from *Poems: Old and New* (1912) linked together Empire and public school.

> The sand of the desert is sodden –
> Red with the wreck of a square that broke;

The river of death has brimmed his banks,

. . .

But the voice of the schoolboy rallies the ranks:

'Play up! Play up! and play the game'.

The Empire is no longer but the public school ethos endures, albeit in modified form. *Tom Brown's Schooldays* gave rise to the public school novel and the public school memoirs. The magic derives from the myth and the myth derives from literature. The public school ethos survives not just because the public school mystique has a firm hold on popular imagination but especially because the public schools continue to educate the ruling class (Matheson and Limond 1999).

The Clarendon Commission (1864), an investigation of the nine leading public schools, found that:

> The average school boy was almost ignorant of geography and of the history of his own country, unacquainted with any modern language but his own and hardly competent to write English correctly, to do a simple sum; a total stranger to the laws which govern the physical world.
>
> (quoted in Martin 1979: 60)

Nonetheless the public schools were praised for 'their public spirit, their vigour and manliness of character' as well as 'their love of healthy sport and exercise' and above all the fact that 'they have had perhaps the largest share in moulding the character of an English gentleman' (quoted in Martin 1979: 65).

Today the public school ethos endures, not only in about the tenth or so of English schools that are independent schools, both day and boarding schools, and are thus not financed by the state, but it also permeates to some extent the whole of the English education system. More particularly the public school ethos endures in what is allegedly 'education's best kept secret' (Hackett 2001: 10), that there remain in England about thirty-six state boarding schools where one can get what amounts to a public school place for between a third and a half of what it would cost to send one's child(ren) to an independent school. The government pays for the teaching and the parents pay a mere £4,500 to £6,000 for food and accommodation. Such schools are praised and prized for their discipline, the importance given to team sports, and excellent exam results (Hackett 2001). Such importance given to academic achievement is a more recent development within the ideology of the public school ethos.

Some romantic or psychological ideologies

The romantic or psychological ideology, derived from the naturalism of Rousseau, was central to the establishment of progressive schools and has had considerable influence on some forms of curriculum revision and on the primary schools. Working within this ideology was perhaps the greatest influence upon the modern primary school curriculum: John Dewey, who argued against the subservice of the child to a curriculum devised for him/her by adults with its logical division of subject matters and little notice taken of the child's interest. For him, 'the child is the starting point, the centre, the end. His[/her] development, his[/her] growth, is the ideal' (Dewey 1906: 21 in Curtis 1965: 162). This centrality of the child to the schooling process can perhaps be said to have reached its peak in the United Kingdom and especially in England with the Plowden Report (DES 1967).

In its own terms, Plowdenism emphasises such things as 'Learning . . . [but] not [by] . . . direct teaching . . . [and] working harmoniously according to an unfolding rather than a preconceived plan' (Maclure 1973: 313). Plowden's was the pedagogy of learning by doing and following one's interests or enthusiasms (Matheson and Limond 1999). It was influenced by developmental psychology such as that of Piaget, Dewey and Montessori. A long time before Plowden it had been officially approved as an educational ideology in England. The Report of the Consultative Committee on *The Primary School* (1931) backed the idea that 'the curriculum is to be thought in terms of activity and experience, rather than of knowledge to be acquired and facts to be stored' (HMSO 1931: 75). The aim of education was to open up the imagination. The cramming of factual or propositional knowledge (knowing that) was condemned, but experience and activity or procedural knowledge (knowing how) were advocated instead. Schooling would be based on scientific ideas of how the child grows and changes. The purpose was to meet the needs of those processes because anything else would be counterproductive in practice if not also morally wrong (Matheson and Limond 1999). Just as the Reports of the Consultative Committee on *The Primary School* (1931) and on *The Nursery School* (1933) were full of metaphors about growth and nurture and psychological needs, so was the Plowden Report, which stressed that education should foster flexibility and adaptability to an economically changing world. Such an ideology saw the aims of education as psychological harmony, and intellectualism as detrimental to that psychological harmony. The importance of getting on with others and understanding them as well as of psychological balance was stressed: 'They will need as always to be able to live with their fellows, appreciating and respecting their differences, understanding and sympathizing with their feelings. [. . .] They will need to be well-balanced, with neither the emotions nor the intellect giving ground to each other' (DES 1967, sections 494, 496).

In the 1960s there was an increasing commitment to child-centred education as local authorities moved away from the 11+ examinations and the number of comprehensive schools increased (Brooks 1991). The Plowden Report deplored that some teachers 'still used books of English exercises and of mechanical computation' (DES 1967 quoted in Brooks 1991: 92). In 1971 two academics, Brian Cox and A. E. Dyson, began a backlash against child-centred teaching methods, standards and behaviour in comprehensive schools, in what became known as the Black Papers. Particularly condemned was William Tyndale School in Islington, where the headteacher ran the school as a co-operative and told a governor he did not care about what parents wanted. The Black Papers paved the way for general media criticism of child-centred education and culminated in the 1976 Ruskin Speech, when James Callaghan underlined that there was unease felt by parents and industry about the new informal methods of teaching (Woodward 2001). The Prime Minister seemed to have accepted much of the Black Papers' propaganda about declining standards, but the ideology promulgated in Plowden was far from being what was actually happening in English schools (Brooks 1991).

Although often half-heartedly implemented, Plowdenism can nevertheless be seen as the British, or more specifically English, culmination of the romantic or individualist/psychological tradition (Matheson and Limond 1999). So Plowden had arguably a non-negligible influence in British primary classrooms until the advent in England and Wales of the National Curriculum with its emphasis on cognitive performance. To its critics it is misguided and even a libertarian charter that promulgates the pursuit of 'relevance' to oneself as the essential criterion of intellectual worth. To its supporters it is 'a truth which has never been fully tested in practice because it has often been misunderstood or overlaid only very thinly as a veneer on existing practices and principles' (Matheson and Limond 1999: 22).

In all, Plowdenism bears a striking resemblance to Montessorism, the theories of Maria Montessori articulated in *The Montessori Method* (1912) and *The Advanced Montessori Method* (1917). The former deals with what were known as mentally or socially handicapped children and the latter applies the deriving principles to normal children. In other words, Maria Montessori advocates a psychological method, implying that 'the educative process is adapted to the stage of mental development of the child, and to his/her interests and is not wholly subordinated to the necessities of a curriculum or to the teacher's scheme of work' (Rusk 1954: 262). Like that of Plowdenism, Montessori's own child-centred progressive pedagogy with emphasis on freedom and auto-education is associated with the names of Rousseau, Pestalozzi, Froebel, Herbart, Dewey and Piaget. Such a pedagogy aims to replace traditional pedagogy, whereby the teacher maintains discipline and immobility and engages in loud and continual discourse, 'by didactic material which contains within itself the control of errors' and thus 'makes auto-education possible to each child' (Montessori 1912: 371). She later added that, 'to make the process one of self-education, it is not enough that the stimulus should call forth activity, it must also direct it' (Montessori 1917: 71).

Montessori's emphasis on interest as a driving force for the learner finds a modern echo in Malcolm Knowles' (1998) idea of andragogy (although, unlike

Montessori, Knowles thought primarily of adult learners). Interest as a motivator has, however, a much longer heritage and was defined as 'the doctrine of interest' by Herbart, who derived the idea from Rousseau but expanded upon it (Herbart 1816 in Rusk 1954: 210).

Herbart asserts that 'that which is too simple must be avoided' and 'instruction must be comprehensible and yet difficult rather than easy, otherwise it causes *ennui* [boredom]' (Herbart 1901 quoted in Rusk 1954: 225). Herbart further asserts that 'the principle of interest braces [pupils] up to endure all manner of drudgery and hard work', the idea being 'of making drudgery tolerable by giving it a meaning' (Adams quoted in Rusk 1954: 225). The doctrine of interest is to be found in Plato's *Republic*, Rousseau's *Emile* and Pestalozzi's correspondence. Herbart also advocated the principle of recapitulation or spiral curriculum, which is a doctrine common to many educators from Plato to Montessori and Dewey. For Herbart, there is no education without instruction and conversely no instruction that does not educate (Rusk 1954). Paradoxically, for an educational ideologist in the romantic tradition, Herbart ascribes to the teacher a centrality that is largely absent from those whose ideas derived from his (Dewey 1923).

A revisionist ideologist: Herbert Spencer

Herbert Spencer challenged the traditional curriculum and 'liberal education' by classifying the subjects with scientific subjects being seen as most important 'because the knowledge which enables one to earn a living should come first in the curriculum and literary subjects should occupy the lowest place on the scale' (Curtis 1965). Spencer further asserted that 'education of whatever kind, has for its proximate end to prepare a child for the business of life – to produce a citizen who, while he[/she] is well conducted, is also able to make his[/her] way in the world' (Spencer 1911 in Curtis 1965: 154).

Spencer presents several facets of the doctrine of relevancy (i.e. relevant to the economy and relevant to the learner's future quality of life). The importance of this former facet in educational and economic debate should not be understated. Other than its returning to the forefront of debates with great frequency (e.g. in Callaghan's 1976 Ruskin College speech), the doctrine suggests a great number of questions. How might it be determined *how* a learner is going to earn his/her living? How can we know what economic needs there will be in the future? To what extent does formal education not already instil *pre*-vocational skills? Spencer wrote at a time of economic stability when the future appeared largely to be a direct continuation of the past. Our future now appears much more uncertain but is this reason sufficient to discard Spencer's ideas? Even relevancy to the economy is relative, as is discussed at length by White (1997). There are also questions that arise out of the second facet: the business of life also appears to be in mutation but are there underlying skills and values that the learner needs to acquire in order to be successful (by some measure or other) in the ways of the world? We no longer have the consensual moral frameworks that we arguably had at times in the past. Therefore what skills or values need the learner acquire? And who is to decide these? In sum, to apply the doctrine of relevance, be it to the economy's future (or actual) needs or to the learner's future (or actual) needs, we are obliged to decide who is to decide these needs, on what basis (i.e. on what criteria) and to what end(s). Fundamentally, we need to decide what education is for.

Liberal or egalitarian ideology

The democratic intellect

The philosophical underpinning of the Scottish education system appears to stand in opposition to the English education system. Both ideologies associated with the dominant values of each system are linked to the history of education in each country. For Scots of the nineteenth century, education had become a badge of national identity, instead of being associated with the privileged ruling class. Education was 'a potent symbol of Scottishness and one of the ways in which a sense of nationhood was preserved without in any way threatening the basic structure of the union with England' (Devine 1999: 389). This 'national' education system had been proposed by John Knox and his fellow reformers in the *Book of Discipline* in the sixteenth century. Its ideology remained a guiding principle for Scottish education. It was not only meritocratic but, according to some, even egalitarian, resting on a ladder of opportunity going from parish schools to burgh schools and then universities, although burgh schools could be bypassed and it was possible for a boy who had talent to go from the parish school to university after he had been given some post-elementary education in mathematics and Latin by the parish schoolmaster (Stephens 1998: 1)

Although not an autobiographical novel as was *Tom Brown's School Days*, Ian Maclaren's novel *Beside the Bonnie Briar Bush* exemplifies and reinforces an educational tradition and hence its ideology. The teacher who 'could detect a scholar in the egg, and prophesied Latinity from a boy who was only fit to be a cowherd' (Maclaren [1894] 1940: 8) is the leader of the local community. His function is to spot likely talent for intellectual endeavour and then persuade the family to live frugally to save up and the better-off members of the community to give their help to put together the money for the university fees.

The term 'democratic intellectualism' was coined in 1919 by Walter Elliot, then Conservative Secretary of State for Scotland, and is associated with the works of George Elder Davie (Matheson and Limond 1999). The term is used to characterise Scotland's post-Reformation and Enlightenment history (Davie 1961: 75) in terms of thoughtful citizenship, reasoned participation and thriving intellectual debate, derived from the fact that, until the middle of the nineteenth century, Scottish universities nurtured and promoted a set of highly distinctive academic values (Matheson and Limond 1999). The main mechanism of this nurturing and promotion was their concentration on teaching philosophy in a system that went into decline only when forced to change, starting in the 1840s and 1850s (Bell and Grant 1977).

Davie was a lecturer in philosophy at Edinburgh University. He argued that the true nature of Scotland's educational tradition was democratic intellectualism and deplored the way this true nature had been eroded by closer contact with England (Davie 1993). He argued that Scotland's educational ideology fitted broadly within a European tradition of generalist curriculum and philosophy-centred higher education. This was contrasted with the insular and eccentric English narrowness of curriculum and specialised 'Honours' courses. Not only was there a wider access to universities in Scotland but also a wider and more balanced curriculum with the study of philosophy firmly at its centre (Bell 2000). To understand this point fully it is necessary to think of philosophy not as an academic subject but as a way of encouraging students to inquire into issues and ideas, morals and metaphysics. In English universities (and at the start of the nineteenth century England had only two, while Scotland, with a tenth of the population, had four) the emphasis was on teaching a precise grasp of Latin and Greek grammar through studying Greek and Latin authors (Matheson and Limond 1999). In Scotland by contrast the emphasis was more on understanding what these authors had said rather than how they expressed themselves. (It was thus far more acceptable in Scottish universities to read classical authors in translation.) The ideas expressed in their words were of greater importance than the words themselves, thus the Scottish interest was philosophical rather than literary (Matheson and Limond 1999). The common sense of the subject was put before questions of detail. An understanding of ancient civilization was preferable to textual study (Davie 1961). Asking and answering philosophical questions was always of prime importance, as was enlightenment over erudition, hence more morals and metaphysics than literature and language (Beveridge and Craig 1989). There was specific teaching of philosophy as a compulsory subject in its own right, but the weaving of philosophical concerns into all other subjects was of far greater significance (Matheson and Limond 1999).

Social democracy

In the period 1944 to 1970 educational policy was based upon the ideology of 'social democracy' constructed by three social groups who formed a coalition: the Labour Party (although supported in much of this by the Conservative Party), educationalists working in sociology and economics, and the teaching profession. The key features of the ideology of 'social democracy' were a commitment to educational progress through state policy and a concern with access and equality of opportunity. Reform was via the state (the state being seen as neutral) and was for the benefit of all sections of society, especially the underprivileged. A focus of attention in social democracy was working-class under-achievement and wastage of ability; as a consequence, the idea of non-selective comprehensive schools slowly emerged. Teachers, for their part, pursued professional status and demanded autonomy and control of the curriculum. The notion was promoted, and accepted, that teachers knew best what was best for their pupils.

A clarion call of social democracy was equality of opportunity in education, a notion fraught with conceptual difficulties. In a simple form, equality of opportunity can be seen as open and fair competition for economic rewards and social privileges. The problems arise when one tries to determine what is open and fair. The way in which this meaning shifted in the UK is demonstrated by the move by socialists from supporting selective secondary schools in the 1940s and 1950s to calling for a total end to selection for secondary school from the 1960s onwards. Both the generalisation of and the abolition of selective secondary schools were justified on the grounds of equality of opportunity. However, coupled with equality of opportunity was also equality per se (Finn *et al*. 1978). Arguably, equality of opportunity equalises the chances people have to become unequal. It is therefore incompatible with any notion of equality as reducing privilege, except perhaps privilege of birth. Equality of opportunity does however give rise to the notion of the meritocracy whereby everyone has, in theory, the same chances to go as far as their talents will take them. As this inevitably leads to the creation or at least the sustenance of an élite, it is perhaps best described as an élitist ideology hiding away in an apparently egalitarian one. This only goes to show the lack of mutual exclusivity of the four categories of educational ideology mentioned above.

In the 1970s the ideology of social democracy was finally challenged largely because of its failure to promote economic growth and growing concerns about falling standards and indiscipline in schools. James Callaghan's 1976 speech in Ruskin College, Oxford, effectively sounded the death knell for social democracy in education. Callaghan called for more control of teachers and more accountability from schools. Education, he claimed, should be seen as a means for training young people for work. The effect was the official beginning of the process that led to the National Curriculum in England and Wales with its concomitant national testing, Ofsted and the full trappings of direct state control over school (Chitty 1993).

The best of all worlds or neither one thing nor another

The Third Way

In 1998 Anthony Giddens came up with a new political ideology, the Third Way. (He borrowed much of his ideas from the New Democrats in the United States, who a few years before New Labour wanted to be seen to have moved away from the left and towards the right to attract votes.) Giddens' book provoked a storm of interest and controversy (Giddens 1998). He wrote a response to his critics two years later (Giddens 2000).

The Third Way is an attempt to find a path between the New Right and the Old Left as there is a need to move away from the sterile debate between left and right, or between those who favour either the state or the free market doing everything. It was brought about by the realities of the modern world; that is, the dissolution of the welfare consensus, the rapid technological changes of the Information Age, globalisation and the discrediting of Marxism. It aims to combine social solidarity with a dynamic economy, to stress equality of opportunity, not of outcome, and to concentrate on the creation of wealth and not its redistribution (Giddens 1998). What does this really mean in theory and in practice? Its critics say it is an empty concept without any real content, an intellectual cover for those whose principles are sufficiently flexible to accommodate any type of wealth creation and a betrayal of left-wing ideals.

In terms of education, this new ideology is based on the idea that there is no viable alternative to the market economy. So the Third Way is really social democracy because social justice and equality of opportunity are encouraged but, instead of the state paying the full cost of this, market principles are necessary to lessen state ownership, state funding and state intervention, and to encourage private initiatives to play their part in the educational process. The Third Way wants to encourage the less talented to succeed, as the exclusion of the less able is feared as much as the withdrawal of the most able. This has to be prevented by improving education to such an extent with the help of market forces that someone with money will choose not to pay for their child(ren)'s education. The critics have ridiculed this idea by underlining that this would mean that the state must take a great deal in tax from everyone so it can afford to offer a state education that would attract those who previously chose to send their child(ren) to independent schools and who now would therefore become a burden to the taxpayer by no longer doing this!

Conclusion

This has been only a brief look at the role of ideology in education and, of necessity, it has been an eclectic look. There are a multitude of other educational ideologies that might equally merit inclusion, but space does not permit this. I have not specifically discussed the ideological precepts that underpin the National Curriculum; some of these are dealt with in other chapters. I have omitted the ideology of the market, which has set schools and universities in competition with each other in a bid to attract students and other sources of funding. I have not considered the ideology of 'privatisation'. Other chapters in this volume take up again the theme of ideology in education under different guises. There are educational ideologies based on gender, 'race', social class, age, culture, the nature of learning itself, to name but a few that are touched upon.

It is, however, worth remembering that few, if any, ideologies actually bear the name openly. Rather we have various collections of notions, ideas and beliefs, which may apply better to one level of education than to another (and this can mean, for example, applying better to a macro-perspective than to a micro-perspective or applying better to one level than to another) by which not only is behaviour influenced or even determined, but the very ways in which we think about phenomena may themselves be set. In this light, it can be worth wondering why comprehensive *secondary* school can rouse so much passion but comprehensive *primary* school never has. Is this through a rational choice on our part or is it through our internalising of an ideological precept that precludes the stimulation of heated debates over the possibility of non-comprehensive primary school?

Ideologies are not static. They evolve and they may expire, as did Scottish democratic intellectualism, although arguably until the re-establishment of the Scottish Parliament in 1999 this ideology had a few remaining vestiges such as the Scottish Ordinary degree, which, unlike its English counterpart, is not (usually) a failed Honours degree but a general, as opposed to a specialised, degree. One of the first concerns of the Scottish Parliament was to set out to abolish university fees, as these were seen to go against a tradition and ideology articulated within a country that not only was proud of having a wider social intake in higher education than England, but wanted to be seen to promote the accessibility of higher education better than England. The more important role of the teacher within democratic intellectualism can also be seen in the fact that the Scottish Parliament decided to substantially increase teachers' salaries.

In terms of the public school ethos, the discourse of excellence and achievement – or rather of 'league tables' and 'exam results' – is more marketable and resonates better than that of character. The importance of character formation gave way to psychological well-being, which was the cornerstone of progressive education. Recently there has been a revival of character education in Britain. The White Paper *Schools: Achieving Success* (DES 2001) talked of 'education with character' and linked this with the promotion of citizenship education.

Whether any of these, or the other ideologies mentioned, were ever true (or valid, as the case may be) is another issue but one we shall not pursue. Truth/validity depends on perspective. What is important in all these ideologies is not their truth or validity but rather the impact they have had and in some cases continue to have.

Suggested further reading

A good further introduction to educational ideologies is to be found in Meighan and Siraj-Blatchford (1998). Blackledge and Hunt (1985) detail and critique various sociological perspectives and the ideologies within they function. For more on the 'public school ethos' see Gathorne-Hardy (1977) and Walford (1986). For gender balance Walford (1993) and Avery (1991) should be read. For more on the 'democratic intellect' consult McCrone (1992), who gives a good understanding of the background for this ideology. Davie (1961) is essential for a good understanding of his ideas and Lockhart Walker (1994) is also extremely useful. For an examination of the present government's educational ideologies in its first four years in office, see Paterson (2003).

References

Avery, G. (1991) *The Best Type of Girl*. London: Andre Deutsch.

Bell, R. (2000) 'Scottish Universities', *Comparative Education*, **36** (2), 163–175.

Bell, R. and Grant, N. (1977) *Patterns of Education in the British Isles*. London: Unwin Education Books.

Bennett, S. N. (1976) *Teaching Styles and Pupils' Progress*. London: Open Books.

Beveridge, C. and Craig, R. (1989) *The Eclipse of Scottish Culture*. Edinburgh: Polygon.

Billig, M., Condor, S., *et al.* (1988) *Ideological Dilemmas: A Social Psychology of Everyday Life*. London: Sage Publications.

Blackledge, D. and Hunt, B. (1985) *Sociological Interpretations of Education*. London: Routledge.

Brooks, R. (1991) *Contemporary Debates in Education: A Historical Perspective*. London: Longman.

Bullock, A., Stallybrass, O., Trombley, S. (eds) (1988) *The Fontana Dictionary of Modern Thought*. London: Fontana Press.

Chandos, J. (1984) *Boys Together: English Public Schools 1800–1864*. Newhaven, CT: University Press.

Clarendon Commission (1864) *On the Principal Public Schools*. London: HMSO.

Chitty, C. (1993) *The Education System Transformed*. London: Baseline Books.

Cosin, B. (1972) *Ideology*. Milton Keynes: Open University Press.

Curtis, S. J. (1965) *Introduction to the Philosophy of Education*. Foxton: University Tutorial Press.

Dancy, J. and Sosa, E. (eds) (1993) *A Companion to Epistemology*. Oxford: Blackwell.

Davie, G. E. (1961) *The Democratic Intellect: Scotland and her Universities in the Nineteenth Century*. Edinburgh: Edinburgh University Press.

Davie, G. E. (1993) 'The Importance of the Ordinary MA', *Edinburgh Review*, **90**, 61–69.

Davies, I. (1969) 'Education and Social Science', *New Society*, 8 May.

Department of Education and Science (DES) (1967) *Children and their Primary Schools (The Plowden Report)*. London: HMSO.

Department for Education and Skills (2001) *Schools: Achieving Success*. London: The Stationery Office.

Destutt de Tracy, A. (1801–15) *Éléments d'idéologie*. Paris: Lévi.

Devine, T. (1999) *The Scottish Nation 1700–2000*. London: Penguin.

Dewey, J. (1906) *The School and the Child*. Glasgow: Blackie.

Dewey, J. (1923) *Democracy and Education*. New York: Macmillan.

Entwistle, H. (1979) *Conservative Schooling for Radical Politics*. London: Routledge.

Feuer, L. S. (1975) *Ideology and the Ideologists*. Oxford: Basil Blackwell.

Finn, D., Grant, N., Johnson, R. (1978) 'Social Democracy, Education and the Crisis', in Centre for Contemporary Cultural Studies (ed.) *On Ideology*. London: Hutchinson.

Forgacs, D. (ed.) (1988) *A Gramsci Reader*. London: Lawrence & Wishart.

Gathorne-Hardy, J. (1977) *The Public School Phenomenon 597–1977*. London: Hodder and Stoughton.

Giddens, A. (1998) *The Third Way: The Renewal of Social Democracy*. Cambridge: Polity Press.

Giddens, A. (2000) *The Third Way and its Critics*. Cambridge: Polity Press.

Grant, N. (1979) *Soviet Education*. Harmondsworth: Penguin.

Hackett, G. (2001) 'Boarders on a Budget', *Sunday Times*, 23 September, 10–11.

Hall, S. (1978) 'The Hinterland of Science: Ideology and the "Sociology of Knowledge" ', in Centre for Contemporary Cultural Studies (ed.) *On Ideology*. London: Hutchinson.

Hughes, T. [1857] (1963) *Tom Brown's Schooldays*. London: Collins.

Husén, T. (1974) *The Learning Society*. London: Methuen.

Knowles, M. (1998) *The Adult Learner*. Houston, TX: Gulf Publishing.

Larrain, J. (1979) *The Concept of Ideology*. London: Hutchinson University Library.

Lichtheim J. (1967) *The Concept of Ideology and Other Essays*. New York: Vintage.

Lockhart Walker, A. (1994) *The Revival of the Democratic Intellect*. Edinburgh: Polygon.

McCrone, D. (1992) *Understanding Scotland: The Sociology of a Stateless Nation*. London: Routledge.

Maclaren, I. [1894] (1940) *Beside the Bonnie Briar Bush*. New York: Dodd, Mead and Co.

McLean, M. (1995) *Education Traditions Compared*. London: David Fulton.

Maclure, J. S. (1973) *Educational Documents England and Wales 1816 to the Present Day*. London: Methuen.

Marx, K. and Engels, F. [1845–7] (1970) *The German Ideology*. London: Lawrence & Wishart.

Martin, C. (1979) *A Short History of English Schools 1750–1965*. Hove: Wayland.

Matheson, C. and Limond, D. (1999) 'Ideology in Education in the UK', in D. Matheson and I. Grosvenor (eds) *An Introduction to the Study of Education*, 1st edn. London: David Fulton

Meighan, R. and Siraj-Blatchford, I. (1998) *A Sociology of Educating*, 3rd edn. London: Cassell.

Montessori, M. (1912) *The Montessori Method*. London: Heinemann.

Montessori, M. (1917) *The Advanced Montessori Method*. London: Heinemann.

Newbolt, H. (1912), *Poems: Old and New*. London: John Murray.

Paterson, L. (2003) 'The Three Educational Ideologies of the British Labour Party, 1997–2001', *Oxford Review of Education*. **29** (2), 165–185.

Report of the Hadow Consultative Committee (1931) *The Primary School*. London: Her Majesty's Stationery Office.

Report of the Hadow Consultative Committee (1933) *Infant and Nursery Schools*. London: Board of Education.

Rey, A. and Rey-Debove, J. (1990) *Le petit Robert*. Paris: Dictionnaires Le Robert.

Rusk, R. R. (1954) *The Doctrines of the Great Educators*. London: Macmillan.

Stephens, W. B. (1998) *Education in Britain 1750–1914*. London: Macmillan.

Summer, C. (1979) *Reading Ideologies*. London: Academic Press.

Vaizey, L. (1977) 'Facts, Theories and Emotions', in G. Macdonald-Fraser (ed.) *The World of the Public School*. London: Weidenfeld and Nicholson.

Walford, G. (1986) *Life in Public Schools*. London: Methuen.

Walford, G. (ed.) (1993) *The Private Schooling of Girls: Past and Present*. London: Woburn Press.

White, J. (1997) *Education and the End of Work*. London: Cassell.

Winch, C. and Gingell, J. (1999) *Key Concepts in the Philosophy of Education*. London: Routledge.

Woodward, W. (2001) 'What's New?', *The Guardian*, 16 October.

3

Theories of learning

Constructive experience

Reg Dennick

There is nothing more practical than a good theory.
(Lewin 1951)

Introduction and outline

THIS CHAPTER FIRST OF all outlines what is meant by 'theory' in the context of education and learning and then describes some of the major theories. In addition it attempts to make connections between what are often seen as separate theoretical areas by identifying some unifying concepts and relationships. By doing so a synthesis will be revealed giving these areas a coherence that will be practically useful for teachers and educators.

I propose to briefly describe the nature of scientific theory and its relationship to educational/sociological theory. I will then examine a number of key educational theories in more detail, explaining their origins, assumptions and structure. I will look firstly at constructivist theories of learning, as I believe they have the widest application to all modes of learning whether in the classroom, the lecture theatre, online or in the workplace. Next I will examine theories associated with experiential learning, as they have particular relevance to learning in professional, working, environments. Both of these two theories are strongly associated with the scientific method and I will attempt to unify these theories by showing that the way the scientific community creates new knowledge, in its broadest and multidisciplinary sense, is mirrored in the cognitive processes of the individual. Finally I will outline how humanistic theories of the individual learner can connect to and support these learning theories.

When describing and explaining the above three theories I will make connections to a variety of other educational frameworks, which will be briefly mentioned, and attempt to show that they are all related to elements of the main theories. Finally

I will attempt to synthesise these theories into what I will term 'constructive experience'. I will outline connections between all these theoretical frameworks by demonstrating that the mechanism of experiential learning is consistent with a constructivist model of learning and that humanistic theories of the individual can underpin both of these models. A unifying principle will be the scientific method in its broadest aspect, encompassing the hard and social sciences, which not only socially creates new knowledge but from a constructivist perspective is arguably a model of the learning process in the individual.

What is a theory?

In common usage the term 'theory' is often merely used to refer to a conjecture or idea used to explain an event or situation. In addition it frequently has the connotation of something which is not necessarily true, as in 'it's only a theory'. However, the concept of a theory has a deeper meaning in the context of scientific thinking (Chalmers 1999). Scientific usage implies a much more elaborate framework, often constructed after a whole series of hypotheses have been proposed, tested and supported by empirical evidence. This produces a set of concepts, ideas and facts that together provide a coherent framework for describing and predicting the properties and behaviour of some specified phenomena or domain of reality. A theory has often been derived via empirical observation and deliberate experimentation and its presentation is sometimes formalised by mathematical notation. A theory is therefore much more than just an idea.

Importantly a theory can be disproved. Nevertheless, because many theories have stood the test of time, for example quantum theory, relativity theory, evolutionary theory, they do achieve a high truth status. This status is achieved by virtue of the fact that each theory more or less corresponds to an area of reality and is capable of explaining and predicting it, frequently with great accuracy. A theory's ability to explain and predict provides support to the view that somehow it is mirroring 'reality'. One commonly held interpretation of the scientific method and the epistemology of science assumes that there is a real, objective world 'out there' that can be understood and modelled by scientific theories. Their truth value is measured by how well they map onto the reality they purport to describe but they can be falsified and refuted by the presence of observations and anomalies that contradict or do not fit their predictions, or by rational and logical analysis. As will be explained, a feature of a 'good' scientific theory is that it should be capable of refutation or falsification by rational or empirical evidence.

The domain of education and learning, however, is predominantly the realm of the social sciences; conventional scientific theories, as described above, do not necessarily map onto the facts, experiences and relationships found in these areas. Many of the assumptions underpinning the scientific method itself are seen as problematic. For example the very existence of an objective, social and interpersonal world that exists independently of our assumptions, prejudices and biases is called into question, as is the idea that observations of social systems can be carried out objectively. In addition, in many cases it is impossible to manipulate and experiment on social systems in the way that the natural sciences might do, as there are profound methodological differences and ethical difficulties to consider. This does not prevent the creation of social and educational theories but the criteria used to determine their validity and truth value do not have the same 'objective' status as those used for scientific theories. Some of the more extreme versions of social theorising such as might be found in 'critical theory' and postmodernism may not even be related to any form of empirical observations or evidence at all. (For a useful review of contemporary sociology theorising see Benton and Craib 2001.)

There is no unifying theory of education or learning[1] and different areas are explored and studied by different disciplines. Useful general references for exploring educational theory are Curzon (1997), Jarvis *et al.* (1998), Knowles *et al.* (1998), Jarvis (2006), Merriam *et al.* (2007). Unlike the 'hard' sciences, in which theories are abandoned once they have been refuted by empirical evidence and become of interest only to historians of science, educational theories largely do not undergo this culling process, leading to a plurality of competing and complementary frameworks that co-exist. Elements from a variety of educational theories and their associated practices are frequently combined to help understand and optimise learning in many areas of teaching. It also seems to be the case that educational theories sometimes appear to be created by people in different disciplines or different educational traditions and are then developed in isolation from each other. Some theories are virtually identical to other theories and yet the authors appear to be oblivious of each other's work. Other theories appear to be outgrowths or extensions of elements in another theory, again without the authors necessarily acknowledging this. Consequently educational 'theory' contains a spectrum of frameworks ranging from the more empirical behaviourist theories through developmental and constructivist psychology and humanistic interpersonal frameworks to the unempirical and epistemologically relative end of the social sciences. However, if learning ultimately takes place in the brain, it has to be acknowledged that we are still a long way from providing a theory that connects overt human behaviour with 'objective' neurophysiology. The theories of learning described here use concepts and structures in a metaphorical way, their connections to underlying cerebral anatomy and processes as yet undefined.

Educational theories can be used to explain the structure of the curriculum and how it can be designed, whether for children or focused on higher education. There are also theories explaining how social, cultural and political factors influence the types of education existing in the world today in different countries

---

[1] The website http://tip.psychology.org/ lists over fifty.

and societies. The main theories described and explained here all have practical uses in the classroom, in the lecture theatre, in working environments and in adult education. A feature of these particular theories is that they make predictions about what teachers and learners should do in order to optimise learning in given situations.

Constructivist models of learning

As the name implies the constructivist view of learning is concerned with how learners *build* an understanding of the world. Implicit in the concept is that meaning and understanding are built up in a process that depends on the specific knowledge foundations and cognitive operations of each individual and the learning activities they engage in. Genuine understanding cannot be simply transmitted or copied from one brain to another without the receiving brain actively engaging in the process. Experience must be filtered through the learner's own personal knowledge constructs, to be assimilated into their conceptual frameworks in a process that enables the individual to find meaning in the world. Crucially this process also involves modifying, demolishing and accommodating mental frameworks that no longer provide an adaptive advantage. Constructivist theory is associated with an evolutionary perspective that sees learning and the creation of mental models as an adaptation to the environment. Useful general references for exploring constructivist theory are Waltzlawick (1984), Tobin (1993), Fensham *et al.* (1994), Philips (1995) and Steffe and Gale (1995).[2]

In order to understand the nature of constructivist theory it is necessary to briefly describe the history of epistemology, that branch of philosophy that deals with the nature of knowledge. By understanding the origins of constructivist ideas in their historical context it will be seen that some of its underlying assumptions and concepts still play a very important role in contemporary educational theory.

Philosophical background

Two important epistemological strands can be traced back to the Greeks (Kelly 1986). Plato taught that true knowledge was located in, and could be generated by, the rational, thinking mind. He postulated that our minds were born with ideal 'forms' of knowledge and that the aim of human development was to understand these ideal and universal forms in areas such as beauty, truth, goodness, and geometrical and logical reasoning. Reason was seen as a higher faculty than emotions or feelings. The world of sensory experiences, by contrast, was seen as a world of error, incompleteness and uncertainty, and knowledge derived from it

---

[2] http://carbon.cudenver.edu/~mryder/itc_data/constructivism.html presents a comprehensive overview of Constructivism.

was not to be trusted. This conception, that our minds contain innate knowledge and that new knowledge can be created by means of reason alone, is known as *Rationalism*.

The other major strand, which can be traced back to Aristotle and his interest in the natural world, stressed the senses as the ultimate origin of knowledge and is known as *Empiricism*.

These two epistemological theories became prominent by coming into conflict in the seventeenth and eighteenth centuries when the Christian world view in Western civilization, with its political and religious dogma, started to break down and fragment, owing in part to the empirical discoveries of Kepler, Copernicus, Galileo and ultimately Newton. During this period, known as the Enlightenment, Empiricist philosophers such as Locke and Hume asserted that the mind was a *tabula rasa*, a blank slate written on by sensory experience. Empiricists asserted that there was nothing in the mind that was not previously presented to the senses and that thinking and reasoning was simply a process of connecting and relating ideas and thoughts that ultimately came from sensory experience. Supporting the development of science was the conception that new knowledge could be obtained by deliberate manipulation and experimentation on the external world. Empiricists, in contrast to the Rationalists, did not have a problem with the fact that the world of sensory experience was uncertain. They actively supported the idea that knowledge was tentative and provisional and encouraged an attitude of scepticism.

On the other hand Rationalist philosophers such as Descartes, Leibniz and Spinoza reasserted the Platonic idea that the human mind was an intrinsic source of reason that could generate knowledge by thought alone, without the need for any sensory input. They were supported in this view by their belief that knowledge could be acquired through the application of reason, logic and mathematics. They assumed that as the world was God's creation then God's laws would be embedded in our minds and hence reason alone should be able to understand God's world. Reflecting Plato's legacy rational knowledge was considered to have a higher status than knowledge derived from the senses since it was certain knowledge of purity and truth.

It was the philosopher Immanuel Kant, in the eighteenth century, who synthesised these two epistemological positions (Kant 1983). Kant argued that knowledge could be created by combining these two processes and that our knowledge of the world is constructed from sensory experience filtered through and structured by the rational processes of the mind. Although the Empiricists had stressed that human knowledge was constructed from sensations, because Kant asserted that there is an interaction between reason and sensory experience to build up knowledge of the world he can be seen as the father of modern constructivism. He further asserted that because knowledge of the world is mediated by innate rational processes, or 'intuitions' plus certain mental frameworks or 'categories' we see the world through space-, time- and causality-tinted spectacles and we can never actually know the real world or 'things-in-themselves'. As will be seen, this view underpins 'radical' constructivism.

Educational implications of Rationalism and Empiricism

It is worth looking at how the Rationalist and Empiricist traditions have developed, as they have a bearing on a number of educational theories. They have essentially evolved into the two poles of the 'Nature' and 'Nurture' debate in contemporary thinking. Rationalism asserts an innate human nature that all human beings possess and that in today's understanding is a product of genetics. The Empiricist tradition is dominated by the idea that human beings are fundamentally a product of their environment or nurture.

The Empiricist tradition can be most clearly traced to Marxism and to twentieth-century sociological theories. The underlying connection here is that these philosophies share the concept that the individual is born into the world as a 'blank slate'. This implies that all human beings are products of their environment, of their nurture, and hence that changing their experiences and their environment will change the person.

> It is not the consciousness of men that determines their being, but, on the contrary, their social being that determines their consciousness.
>
> (Karl Marx 1859: 1)

The political implications of this philosophy are well known: Stalin, Mao Tse-tung and Pol Pot all believed that a communist society could be created by doing away with capitalist and bourgeois economic systems and the people who supported them. The proletariat, no longer influenced by capitalism, would then create the pure communist society. The consequences of this viewpoint have led to some of the worst genocides of the twentieth century. Sociologists have adopted a similar but less draconian approach arguing that human behaviour, attitudes and thought are a direct creation of the economic and ideological structure of society. To many sociologists and postmodernists the idea of a human nature is anathema and human beings are considered to be mere puppets manipulated by external forces.

The Empiricist perspective in education rejects the notion that some knowledge comes *a priori* from the rational mind, independently of the experience of the senses. It sees knowledge as uncertain and hypothetical and asserts that values are relative and human-made or 'socially constructed'. Its view of education and learning, therefore, is a tentative one. It sees the *development* of the individual as the central concern of education and the selection of knowledge content as subsidiary and subordinate to that. Its approach lends itself to adaptation and development.

The educational implications of empiricism influenced Dewey's educational theorising, as will be discussed later.

The higher status of Rationalism over empirical experience is reflected in the history of education. The study of ancient history and the rote learning of the grammar of ancient languages dominated the 'grammar school' curriculum into the late nineteenth century, when more experiential and practical scientific subjects began to be taught. Its resultant approach to education is one that is largely knowledge-based, in which academic or intellectual pursuits are intrinsically superior to others. In our society there was until quite recently a problem concerning the lower status of practical subjects such as engineering and science in comparison with the arts and humanities.

The Rationalist theme has been influenced in the twentieth century by genetics, by theories of language acquisition and more recently by ideas coming from neuropsychology and evolutionary biology. In principle the idea of a human 'nature' might lead to a universal respect for an individual's human rights. Unfortunately the history of the twentieth century demonstrated that almost the opposite occurred, with Fascist dictators and nationalists persuading populations that one particular human nature or 'race' was superior to others. The development of 'eugenics' and other racist theories in the nineteenth century was the forerunner to the rise of Nazi ideology, the Holocaust, apartheid in South Africa and more recently 'ethnic cleansing'.

Despite these dreadful aberrations in the interpretation of genetic ideas, modern socio-biology and evolutionary psychology has continued to explore the influence of genetics on individual psychology and learning behaviour and there is now a rich scientific literature in this area: Carruthers and Chamberlain (2000), Mithen (1996), Pinker (2002) and Plotkin (1994, 2004). The Rationalist approach is also found in 'innatist' views of cognitive development such as the work of Chomsky (1988) and Fodor (1975, 1983), who assert that certain mental processes are built into the brain from birth and provide, for example, the deep structure of language and a range of innate mental concepts.

Constructivist education

In the nineteenth and early twentieth centuries the American thinkers Charles Peirce, William James and John Dewey all made significant contributions to constructivist thought (Buchler 1955; James 1901; Dewey 1938). Dewey, for example, derived a view from his pragmatist philosophical theory, which stressed that the individual learner should be an 'actor' rather than a 'spectator'. Thus learners should not be seen as simply vessels to be passively filled with received and unchallenged knowledge but should be actively engaged in constructing knowledge for themselves. However, by far the largest contribution came from the child psychologists Piaget and Vygotsky, who built up a large body of empirical and theoretical work supporting the constructivist position (Flavell 1963; Chapman 1988; Wertsch 1985), some of which is still being actively built on and interpreted today (Wood 1998; Karmilloff-Smith 1996).

Piaget's main conception was that the human mind constructed and internalised a model of how the world works, through experience, and that this was an inherent, biological, adaptive process. From birth to adulthood the brain sought to identify the rules under which external reality functioned as a means of survival. The developing cognitive system attempted to maintain 'equilibrium' with the external world by using two contrasting cognitive processes: assimilation and accommodation. Assimilation involves taking in the evidence of sensory experience and extracting meaning from it; it is the incorporation of the external world into cognitive structures. However, in order for this assimilation process to take place the cognitive structures sometimes have to change, adjust or accommodate themselves. Accommodation thus means changing the developing conceptual framework or model to cope with new or anomalous experiences. Cognitive adaptations are thus seen as a constant dialectical interaction between these two processes. For Piaget, cognitive development is an iterative process moving from lower to higher levels of sophistication and integration. The developing individual is seen as a hypothesis-testing machine trying to make sense of the world and build up an internal mental representation of the world by discovering the rules of reality. In simple terms intelligent activity involves 'assimilating the new to the old and accommodating the old to the new' (Flavell 1963). We will later see that David Kolb uses these concepts in his theory of experiential learning.

Piaget's theory is often referred to as a structuralist theory since it assumes that there are underlying mental systems of wholeness, self-regulation and transformation involved in the developmental process (Piaget 1970a). In addition, Piaget's theory is also described as a 'genetic epistemology' because it asserts that the epistemological framework of the individual is actually changing during development and that there is the spontaneous emergence and construction of cognitive complexity (Piaget 1970b).

The stages of cognitive development described and explained by Piaget have been well described and critically evaluated in the literature and will not be discussed further here (Flavell 1963; Donaldson 1978; Richardson 1998). The final 'logical operational' stage, which occurs from 11 to adulthood, is characterised by fully mature thinking and the ability to manipulate abstract concepts. Problems are now solved by deliberate investigation involving an awareness of all factors that might influence the result. The ability to think in the abstract, logically, and to be able to manipulate variables and all possible causes characterises scientific thinking; an underlying theme that connects some of the major theories of learning described here.

The work of Vygotsky in many ways complements that of Piaget although they worked in different countries and traditions. Vygotsky's work largely supports much of Piaget's thinking although there are some key differences. Vygotsky's important contribution to constructivist learning theory was to stress that learning is not just an individual event – it is also a social and cultural process mediated through a culture's symbols and language – and that social interaction and the role of teachers and facilitators are of vital importance. He argued that the social 'collective memory' is internalised in the individual. Piaget also stressed social and cultural influences on cognition in his later works (Richardson 1998). Social cognitive theory (Bandura 1977) and theories of situated cognition (Lave and Wenger 1991) can be traced directly to the work of Vygotsky and his stress on the social, contextual and constructivist nature of learning.

Vygotsky's concept of the zone of proximal development (ZPD) emphasised that the learner could be actively helped to construct knowledge and understanding by means of 'scaffolding' mediated by appropriate educational experiences and teaching interventions. The ZPD was defined as the gap between the child's level of unaided cognition or problem-solving ability and what could be achieved under teacher guidance. This scaffolding process, according to Vygotsky, is fundamentally helped by the learners' social interactions and by their immersion in the shared cultural tools of their society (Wertsch 1985). Thus for Vygotsky, and for social cognitive theory and situated cognition theory, understanding is not just constructed by the individual; it is constructed by the group, the society and the culture.

In the latter half of the twentieth century, the work of Ros Driver and others (Driver 1983; Driver and Oldham 1986; Fensham et al. 1994; White 1988) in constructivist educational theory contributed towards the development of science education. Driver's work led to the development of frameworks for understanding how children's constructions can often get in the way of learning scientific ideas, and for classroom techniques to deal with these problems. Piaget's theory had identified that the child passed through stages at which they had inappropriate conceptions of physical reality, exemplified by their inability to deal with and conserve a variety of spatial, numerical, class and causal concepts (Flavell 1963; Richardson 1998). However Driver and other constructivists showed that even older children, who have passed through Piaget's stages and are nominally logical operators, create and retain their own conceptions, which often contradict reality. These conceptions have been termed 'student's conceptions', 'alternative frameworks', 'children's science', 'children's mini-theories' and 'misconceptions' (Driver et al. 1994; Duit and Treagust 1995). They do not always resolve themselves naturally and children can persist with incorrect concepts, which, if undiagnosed and unchallenged by good teaching practice, can interfere and inhibit further learning.[3]

---

[3] Nevertheless, some radical constructivists, such as Glasersfeld, acknowledge student's own constructions as valid views of reality and challenge the use of the word 'misconception' (von Glasersfeld 1993).

Driver emphasised the view that children can be seen as 'scientists' who have created their own theories explaining reality by generating and testing hypotheses (Driver 1983). They have done this by trying to extract meaning from their experiential world, a view of the child frequently alluded to by Piaget. The theory explains why children are full of hypotheses and explanations for why the world is the way it is, even if these hypotheses can often be wrong and based on erroneous views of reality. The good science teacher finds out what the misconceptions are and devises experiential or logical challenges to help build correct conceptions.

The process of challenging mental conceptions, models and frameworks had been famously studied by Festinger, who coined the term 'cognitive dissonance' to describe the feeling that a person might have when confronted with experiential evidence that contradicted or challenged an assumption about their world (Festinger 1957). This process became a fundamental constructivist teaching technique in the science classroom and was extensively studied by Driver and colleagues (Driver and Oldham 1986).

With respect to the 'child as scientist' concept, reference should also be made to the work of Kelly on personal construct theory in adults. Kelly conceived that individuals develop a set of personal constructs based on their life experience, which they use to anticipate events. Kelly importantly theorised that individuals were like scientists:

Every man is, in his own particular way, a scientist.

(Kelly 1955: 5)

Kelly's theory of 'man-the-scientist' was developed into a method of understanding how individuals construct meanings in their life, how they gain control over their personal environment and how they can maintain mental health (Kelly 1955). Further extensions of constructivism into adult learning can be seen in work on 'lay theories'. All of us have constructed a world view that enables us to more or less survive in the physical, biological and social world. We have all constructed our own theoretical frameworks or mental models which help us make sense of the world. In some cases our own theories are alternatives to the 'standard' theories of science, sociology, economics or politics (Furnham 1998).

Finally one of the most important concepts that underpin constructivism is that articulated by Ausubel in his famous quotation:

The most important factor influencing learning is what the learner already knows. Ascertain this and teach accordingly.

(Ausubel 1968: vi)

This statement not only emphasises that learning is a building or a constructive process, rather than a simple didactic, transmission process, but also places the learner rather than the teacher at the heart of the learning process. Hence the constructivist approach is essentially a learner-centred approach beginning with the needs of the learners rather than the prescriptions of teachers.

Ausubel also acknowledged the importance of misunderstanding to learning:

> the unlearning of preconceptions might well prove to be the most determinative single factor in the acquisition and retention of subject matter knowledge.
>
> (Ausubel 1968: 336)

The idea of understanding where the learner is coming from, finding out what their existing knowledge, lack of knowledge or misunderstanding is and then designing an appropriate learning experience is fundamental to good teaching. The practice of beginning from the learner and acknowledging their individual constructs derives its rationale directly from constructivist theory and makes a direct connection to Humanistic theories of learning to be discussed later.

Constructivism and science

> Science is not just a collection of laws, a catalogue of facts, it is a creation of the human mind with its freely invented ideas and concepts. Physical theories try to form a picture of reality and to establish its connections with the wide world of sense impressions.
>
> (Einstein and Infeld 1938: 46)

That the constructivist theory of learning has parallels with the scientific method has already been mentioned. In science, experiences, observations and 'facts' are incorporated into existing or new theoretical frameworks by the process of induction. Deductions derived from new or existing theory become hypotheses, which are tested by empirical methods, creating new experiences that can be used to test the fit of the theoretical framework. Individual learning is analogous to the historical and social development of scientific knowledge in which theories are conjectured and either supported or refuted by experience and experiment (Popper 1972). The individual literally behaves like a scientist seeking the best theoretical framework to help make sense of their world. Experience is assimilated into cognitive frameworks; cognitive frameworks are accommodated to make sense of experience.

The effect of 'cognitive dissonance', when experience does not fit with an individual's conceptual framework, is seen as extremely important in this process. This is the moment when the individual is forced to reflect on and re-evaluate their understanding of the world. It may act as a powerful motivating factor for self-directed learning as in Problem-Based Learning. It may involve 'digging up' and discarding erroneous conceptions. This process also underpins the accommodative process described by Piaget. There is a strong analogy here

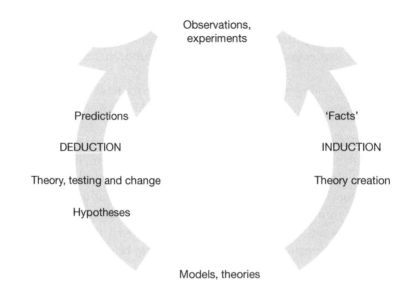

FIGURE 3.1 The hypothetico-deductive scientific method.

with Thomas Kuhn's description of 'paradigm shifts' within the history of science (Kuhn 1970); the individual may literally undergo a 'scientific revolution'. A model of the hypothetico-deductive method is shown in Figure 3.1.

An important issue is where science 'begins' in the cycle depicted in Figure 3.1. One of the earliest views of science was that of Roger Bacon, who in the thirteenth century suggested that an accumulation of observations led to the construction of theories. There is no doubt that this collection of 'facts', termed 'naïve inductivism' (Chalmers 1999), is a feature of the scientific method, but it is a rather simplistic view of science. Most science actually begins with problems and with the testing of theories by deliberate experimentation and the creation of observations. This view of scientific method has implications for constructivist pedagogy in science education and beyond (Millar and Driver 1987). For example, in Problem Based Learning learners are confronted with problems that generate learning hypotheses to be tested by group discussion and investigation in the literature (Savin-Baden and Major 2004).

We will return to the relationship between scientific method and educational theory when we look at Experiential Learning.

The range of constructivist theories

The epistemology underlying constructivism has influenced many areas of contemporary thought. The fundamental idea that our knowledge is not the simple internalisation of some outside stimulus but is a mental model constructed from within, which corresponds more or less to reality, has been interpreted in a variety of ways that have led to a spectrum of constructivist positions. For example in Berger and Luckman's work *The Social Construction of Reality* (1991) it is implied that reality itself is very much a social construction and that there is no single, coherent, real world. This postmodern viewpoint asserts that individuals experience reality as multifaceted and contradictory and rejects scientific 'objectivity'. Thus there is philosophical, educational and sociological constructivism (Matthews 1997) and there is personal, radical and social constructivism (Steffe and Gale 1995). Two ways in which these varieties of constructivism differ are in the status they ascribe to reality and the degree to which knowledge is an individual or social construct (Geelan 1997). For example the personal constructivism of Piaget, Driver and Kelly accepts that the individual learner actively constructs a mental model and works out the rules of an objective world. However, the radical constructivism of Glasersfeld suggests that the individual constructs knowledge as an adaptation to enhance survival and that the constructed model is entirely subjective and relative (von Glasersfeld 1984). He argues that its constructions do not have to necessarily map onto an 'objective' representation of the real world. However, it can be argued that a mental model that does not in some sense map onto 'reality' will not have high survival value.

Social constructivists (Solomon 1994, Gergen 1995) and Vygotsky (Wertsch 1985) assert that individual construction is fundamentally influenced by social and linguistic factors. Gergen goes so far as to suggest that knowledge not only resides in the individual but is located in societies, language and interpersonal 'dialogue'.[4]

Philips in his analysis of constructivist positions also sees an individual–social dimension but in addition identifies a dimension moving from an Empiricist to a Rationalist standpoint (Philips 1995). The key question here is whether knowledge is constructed by the human mind or it is created by 'instructions' from nature; is knowledge made or discovered?

This widening of the boundaries of constructivist thought enables it to encompass a range of educational theories that might be thought to be unrelated. For example the social and interpersonal influences and learning from the modelling of others seen as important factors in Bandura's social cognitive theory can also be seen as inherent features of constructivist models of learning (Bandura 1977). Mezirow's theory of transformative learning (Mezirow 1991) also emphasises radical personal change as a result of cognitive dissonance, a constructivist process. As Merriam points out (Merriam *et al.* 2007), Vygotsky's social constructivist concepts can also be seen as the foundation for situated cognition (Lave and Wenger 1991). Here the importance of culture, context and the constructivist principle of active learning

---

[4] The extreme edge of the constructivist spectrum is of course held by the concept of solipsism, the idea that there is no external reality (and thus no externally generated experience) and that individual experience is technically a delusion.

are seen as important influences. In adult education, situated learning, reflective practice and communities of practice are seen as related to constructivist models particularly in relation to frameworks for continuing professional development (Wenger 1998).

Constructivist implications for teaching

A feature of a good theoretical framework is that it predicts what will happen in particular situations and it enables judgments to be made concerning the choice of actions. A good educational theory should therefore suggest pedagogical interventions and techniques. The constructivist theory of learning provides a coherent set of teaching methods, which are outlined below.

1 Ascertain prior knowledge

If learning is about building on existing knowledge then an effective teacher needs to be aware of the background knowledge of their students. This may be found out from an overall familiarity with the curriculum and from knowledge of prerequisite qualifications for a course. It also readily uncovered by good questioning technique at the beginning of a teaching session.

2 Activate prior knowledge

Students may have prior knowledge but could be unaware of it or have forgotten it. An effective teacher activates students' prior knowledge at the beginning of a teaching session by reviewing previous work or by asking pertinent questions. This process brings relevant knowledge to the surface and places it on the 'mental desktop'. It is an important implication of the constructivist approach to recognise that activating prior knowledge may bring *incorrect* conceptual understanding to the surface, which will have to be dealt with and maybe challenged later.

3 Build on existing knowledge

The acquisition of new knowledge can be mediated only by existing knowledge; the unknown can be made sense of only in terms of the known. Therefore it is essential that teachers introduce and explain new concepts using knowledge that students already possess and by using analogy and metaphor to help build scaffolding and bridges to new understanding. In this respect the context and 'situation' of learning is extremely important. Not only should teachers make cognitive connections to new learning but the importance and relevance of the learning should be emphasised to ensure that personal and affective connections are made.

4 Challenge existing knowledge and misconceptions

Some of the most powerful learning occurs when students are in a state of uncertainty. This leads to 'cognitive dissonance' and a desire to resolve conflict and achieve a sense of mental equilibrium (Festinger 1957). Challenge should lead to curiosity and investigation. Teachers should structure learning situations in such a way that erroneous or outmoded conceptions are challenged and confronted by empirical evidence, demonstrations or alternative frameworks with greater explanatory power. Students should be given specifically designed problems or scenarios, as in Problem-Based Learning, that force them to question, abandon, elaborate or refine their existing understanding.

5 Facilitate the social construction of meanings; use group work

The work of Vygotsky and the later Piaget stressed the importance of the interpersonal and social nature of learning. By means of social interaction and the use of language, learners develop and elaborate their cognitive skills. Vygotsky argued that the 'collective memory' becomes a feature of the individual's psychology. This implies that individual understanding, making sense of the world and searching for meaning, is facilitated by interpersonal communication and learning together in groups. Students should therefore be given oral tasks that encourage them to use new terminology and concepts in group situations, elaborating and refining their conceptual understanding by critically exploring the views of others.

6 Stress the context and the 'situation'

The social context of learning is of paramount importance. Learning is a function of the interaction between the individual, other people and the environment (Bandura 1977). The relevance of the learning needs to be brought out and teachers and mentors need to model appropriate behaviour.

7 Encourage 'metacognition'

The construction of understanding is facilitated by reflecting on the process of learning itself, a task known as 'metacognition'. Different disciplines have their own ways of thinking, their own 'rules of the game' or 'ways of seeing'. Scientific, historical and critical thinking all involve particular ways of looking at the world and constructing meanings within their respective contexts. It is important that students be given opportunities to be inducted into these epistemological frameworks.

8 Use active learning techniques

The activation of prior learning by means of questioning, the generation of cognitive dissonance and its resolution by investigation, the importance of group work, social interaction and discussion all point in the direction of active learning techniques. Constructivist theory implies that effective learning should be learning by doing, applying knowledge and problem-solving.

9 Give learners responsibility for their learning

If, as Ausubel stated, the most important factor in learning is what the learner already knows, then the learner is at the heart of learning, not the teacher. If effective learning involves personal construction then learners must take responsibility for this fundamental process. This is essentially the most important 'metacognitive' concept that learners need to accept and it should lead to an attitude of personal responsibility towards learning. This idea needs to be discussed with and assimilated by learners, who should abandon a passive, 'spoon-feeding' attitude and adopt a more collaborative, active approach to learning with their teachers.

Experiential Learning theory (ELT)

Learning is the process whereby knowledge is created through the transformation of experience.

(Kolb 1984: 38)

Ignoring the extremes of Rationalist epistemology, in principle all learning is ultimately derived from sensory experience. Experiential Learning theory (ELT), developed by Kolb (1984), attempts to provide a mechanism for how experience can be transformed into knowledge, skills and attitudes. If constructivism is a general theory of learning then ELT provides a mechanism for how learning takes place. ELT has a theory of cognitive development and contains elements of Piagetian theory but it usually focuses on mature adult learning. It is frequently but not exclusively used to explain how learning takes place and can be optimised in environments where deliberate teaching and instruction are not taking place. For example, ELT is very useful in making sense of how learning occurs in professional working environments where learners are working or shadowing and engaged in an educational programme at the same time. The theory will be described in more detail below but briefly one interpretation of Kolb is that learning is initiated with 'concrete experience', which is transformed into 'abstract conceptualisation' by a process of 'reflective observation' and 'active experimentation'. As will be shown, there are parallels with the constructivist theory of learning as well as the process of scientific thinking.

Origins of ELT and influences on it

Kolb traces the origins of ELT to the ideas of Dewey, Lewin and Piaget, but it is also influenced by Carl Jung and Carl Rogers. Dewey put forward a theory of learning that emphasised the fundamental role of 'inner experience' and activity. Traditional (nineteenth- and early twentieth-century) education in his view was inspired by Rationalism and dominated by imposition from above, external discipline, learning from texts and teachers, the repetition of isolated skills and drills, preparation for a remote future, and static aims. The more dynamic learning that Dewey espoused, on the other hand, was concerned with the expression and cultivation of individuality, free activity, learning through experience in relevant contexts, and learning for a changing world. For Dewey, learning was also meant to be a democratic process and knowledge itself was seen as tentative and capable of change and revision. Dewey also stressed the importance of the acknowledgement of prior experience in vocational and adult education and the importance of recognising learners' personal histories and their learning styles.

Lewin's work on group dynamics, action research and organizational behaviour was based on his pioneering involvement with 'T-groups' (training groups) in the 1940s, which developed many of the small group teaching techniques we use today (e.g. structured group exercises, simulations, case studies, games and role plays). He used these methods to confront and challenge groups of learners, to make them experience conflict and the tension between theory and practice that leads to deep learning.

> Learning is best facilitated in an environment where there is dialectic tension and conflict between immediate concrete experience and analytical detachment.
>
> (Kolb 1984: 9)

His work also emphasised the importance of subjective experience and existential humanistic values as opposed to the dominant behaviourist model, which was prevalent during the time these theories were developed. He suggested that individuals should engage with a humanistic scientific process and a spirit of personal enquiry that should allow the expansion of consciousness within authentic relationships. This led to the idea that learning from experience was essential for individual and organisational effectiveness and that experiential learning could occur only in situations where personal values and organisational structures supported actions based on valid information and open and informed choices. These practices have had a profound influence on educational and organisational methods.

Whereas the influences from Dewey and Lewin fit with the Empiricist tradition of epistemology the other major influence on Kolb's ELT theory was the constructivism of Piaget, some of whose ideas have been mentioned previously. From Piaget Kolb incorporated the idea that intelligence itself is shaped by experience; it is not innate but arises from the interaction between individuals and their environment. It starts with action but abstract reasoning and symbol manipulation arise later and ultimately derive from interactions with the immediate concrete environment. Piaget asserted that experience, conceptualisation, reflection and action are the basis for the development of adult thought. Thinking develops from concrete to abstract and from active egocentrism to internalized reflection. The process is an interactive cycle between the individual and the environment. There is mutual interaction between accommodation of concepts or mental schemas to experience and the process of assimilation of experiences into existing concepts and schemas. Learning, or 'intelligent adaptation', is the balance between these two processes to maintain cognitive equilibrium.

A number of other psychologists, psychotherapists and educationalists influenced Kolb's ELT, a fact which is often ignored in general descriptions. The work of Carl Rogers in client-centred therapy and Abraham Maslow in self-actualisation psychology was used to emphasise the importance of adaptation to the affective or emotional aspects of experience. Kolb stressed that healthy adaptation required the integration of cognitive *and* affective processes and that the recognition of the socio-emotional forces influencing development throughout the life cycle of the individual provides a holistic framework for describing adult development. Kolb also saw particular relevance in Jung's theory of psychological types (Jung 1977) to his own development of 'Learning Styles', as will be described shortly.

Finally, for Kolb, ELT was also about the possibility of social action and change; hence he made specific references to Illich's assertion that education is a system of social control in an oppressive capitalist society (Illich 1972) and Paulo Freire's conception that 'knowledge is a process, not a product' and that education should be about developing 'critical consciousness' (Freire 1973).

The structure of the theory

Kolb's theory of Experiential Learning is introduced as a cyclic process, mirroring its origins in the work of both Lewin and Dewey. Indeed the terms used by Kolb to describe the phases or learning modes of the cycle in Figure 3.2 are taken directly from Lewin's work on action research. However, these modes are interrelated and transformed by the cognitive transactions described originally by Piaget.

Many interpreters of the Kolb cycle concentrate on the four phases of the cycle, seeing them as the components of a continuous process, as did Lewin. Thus 'concrete experience' is often described as the origin of the cycle, where immediate experiences are obtained. This is followed by 'reflective observation', in which experiences are transformed by reflection into 'abstract conceptualisations', theoretical knowledge or mental models. Finally 'active experimentation' is seen as goal-directed activity, testing out the consequences of new learning and planning for new experiences. This interpretation of the cycle is a useful heuristic for understanding experiential learning and underpins vocational and professional

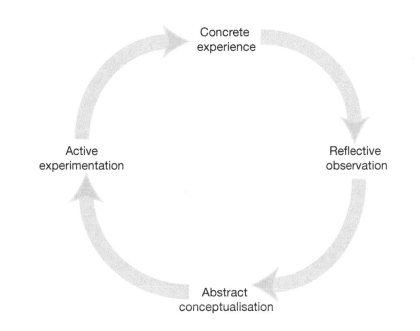

FIGURE 3.2　Kolb's Experiential Learning cycle.

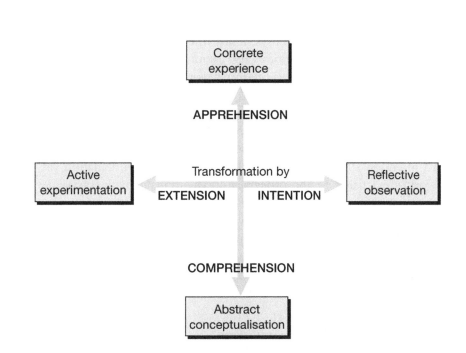

FIGURE 3.3　Prehension and transformation in the Kolb cycle.

'reflective practice' and action planning mediated by the use of portfolios and appraisal.

However, this is a simplified view that ignores much of the richness of Kolb's theory. A deeper approach focuses on the meaning of the two orthogonal axes and the relationships between the dialectically opposed learning modes as shown in Figure 3.3.

The 'Prehension' axis represents two opposed processes of how experience is grasped, either through the felt qualities of immediate experience (concrete apprehension) or via conceptual interpretation and symbolic representation (abstract comprehension). Many others have identified these opposed ways of apprehending and comprehending the world, and their interpretations may help to make this distinction more understandable. William James distinguished between 'knowledge of acquaintance'[5] and 'knowledge about'[6] (James 1901), Polanyi between 'tacit knowledge' and 'articulate knowledge' (Polanyi 1958), and Plotkin describes 'knowing by the senses' and 'knowing by the mind' (Plotkin 1994).

For Piaget this opposition between what he described as the 'figurative' aspect of thought can be described by the difference between the 'phenomenalism' of raw experience and the 'constructivism' of mental models and frameworks. In summary, at any moment individuals can focus on either the raw external world of felt perceptions and feelings or the internal world of mental constructions, models and thoughts. Simplistic descriptions of the cycle seem to acknowledge only concrete experience as the source of experience whereas Kolb clearly explains that the world of abstract conceptualisation is also a source of *inner* experience. We live in the outer world of experience and the inner world of thought simultaneously and can move between them at will.

Both the inner and outer worlds provide the raw material for cognitive processing by the second axis, of 'Transformation'. This axis is polarised between action and reflection and represents the transformation of experience by internal reflection ('intention') or by active manipulation and experimentation on the external world ('extension'). The processes on this transformative axis attempt to develop learning and create meaning. Sometimes this involves reflection and analysis, sometimes it involves action and deliberative manipulation of the external world by experimentation.[7] This process of transformation corresponds to Piaget's concept of 'operative' thought according to which logical, intellectual and sensori-motor processes construct rules to make sense of the world.

Although the relationship of Kolb's theory to some of Piaget's ideas has been

---

[5] '[T]hrough feelings we become acquainted with things'.

[6] '[O]nly by our thoughts do we know about them'.

[7] Jarvis (2006) notes that learning need not occur by non-reflection and by acceptance of the status quo.

presented in this description, it is important to recognise that Kolb's position differs in some important ways from Piaget. Whereas Piaget saw cognitive development as a gradual switch from domination by sensory experience to abstract thought and from egocentric action to internal reflection, in other words from lower to higher forms of knowing, Kolb sees all four learning modes as equipotent poles in dialectical opposition and transformation.

> The process of learning requires the resolution of conflict between dialectically opposed modes of adaptation to the world.
>
> (Kolb 1984: 29)

Certainly in the adult all these modes are more or less equally present to the individual; variations might be due to learning styles, as will be discussed later.

This description of the Kolb cycle reveals that it is more than a cycle! Although the dynamic cycle is the one most frequently described, it is important to acknowledge its deeper structure and its relationship to constructivist models of learning and to the scientific process. This more detailed explanation of the cycle reveals that all four learning modes are present to the individual *simultaneously*. The learner can choose to focus on the outer world of raw experience or their inner world of mental representations; they can choose to reflect or act on either of these sources of experience. Thus, according to Kolb, effective learning requires the integration of these four abilities; the learner must constantly move between the concrete and the abstract and between activity and reflection.

Thus Kolb sees learning as an iterative, ever-changing process rather than content acquisition and storage. Each act of understanding is a process of continual construction and invention. Nevertheless during this process experience throws up problems and mis-expectations. According to Dewey it is such problem areas that are the key sources of learning:

> The most powerful learning occurs when the student is dealing with uncertainty.
>
> (Dewey 1963: 69)

It is precisely when experiences do not fit with inner constructions that the individual has to use their intelligence, their reflections and their actions to find a resolution to the problem. This can take the form of analytical thought, information-gathering, active questioning or experimentation. As outlined earlier, this was termed 'cognitive dissonance' by Festinger and goes to the heart of the constructivist process.

Importantly for the aims of this chapter, Kolb asserted that all forms of human adaptation (learning) approximate to scientific enquiry and that the scientific method is the highest philosophical and technological refinement of the basic process of human adaptation. It provides a means for describing the holistic integration of all human functions. Thus there are conceptual analogies between the scientific method and the process of experiential learning, a relationship previously emphasised by Driver for constructivism.

> All learning is relearning. How easy and tempting it is in designing a course to think of the learner's mind as being as blank as the paper on which we scratch our outline. . . . Everyone enters every learning situation with more or less articulate ideas about the topic at hand. We are all psychologists, historians, and atomic physicists. It is just that some of our theories are more crude and incorrect than others. One's job as an educator is not only to implant new ideas but also to dispose of or modify old ones.
>
> (Kolb 1984: 28)

The process of experiential learning can be seen as a mechanism for constructivist cognition and both can be seen to have an underlying connection to the scientific method.

Finally it should be emphasised that Kolb also stressed the importance of subjective and personal felt experience in addition to objective experience. Learning can be a tension- and conflict-filled process that creates anxiety. In addition he also acknowledged that experience is contextualised and takes place in both an objective and a subjective *situation*. Furthermore there is the recognition that knowledge is mediated by interpersonal and social knowledge (previous human cultural experience) and personal knowledge (individual's subjective life experience). It is important to recognise that much of Kolb's theory is derived from work with groups and that it has exerted a significant influence on group organisational theories in business and management. Thus it can be seen that experiential learning leads to connections with theories of situated cognition (Lave and Wenger 1991) and social constructivism (Wertsch 1985). In so far as experiential learning frequently involves observing other people performing specific activities, this framework can easily be related to Bandura's social cognitive theory, in which learning from the modelling of others becomes extremely important (Bandura 1977).

Learning styles

From Jung Kolb took the idea that learning involves holistic integration of thinking, feeling, perceiving and behaving. But the psychotherapeutic work of Jung demonstrated that individuals do not all possess an equal distribution of these learning modalities, a concept developed by Kolb into his own learning styles framework. Some individuals spend their mental energies in active involvement in the outside world (extraverts) whereas others are more introspective and reflective (introverts). Jung developed a theory of psychological types, which has been turned into a commonly used psychometric testing framework by Myers-Briggs (Myers-Briggs 1962). Jung's categorisation is more associated with personality types, whereas Kolb has used his framework to develop his Learning Styles Inventory (LSI). Briefly, the LSI uses psychometric analysis to identify four learning styles designated as 'assimilative', 'divergent', 'accommodative' and 'convergent'. A further modification of this framework led Honey and Mumford to develop their own widely used system in which learners are characterised as Activists, Reflectors, Theorists or Pragmatists (see www.peterhoney.com/). There is not space to go into the advantages and disadvantages of learning styles and types; the reader is referred to a recent critical study (Coffield *et al.* 2004). Kolb, however, did recognise that they had to be used with caution:

> Psychological categorizations of people such as those depicted by psychological 'types' can too easily become stereotypes that tend to trivialize human complexity and thus end up denying human individuality rather than characterizing it. In addition, type theories often have a static and fixed connotation to their descriptions of individuals, lending a fatalistic view of human change and development.
>
> (Kolb 1984: 63)

Educational implications of Experiential Learning theory

In principle all learning (ignoring any putative 'innate' concepts) is derived from either outer or inner experience transformed by reflection or action, even learning in a classroom. Consequently experiential learning theory underpins many areas associated with other theoretical frameworks, such as adult learning, social cognitive theory, transformative learning, situated learning and learning in communities of practice. Nevertheless the practical use of experiential learning theory has been mainly orientated towards individuals in working environments or engaging in vocational work attachments and rotations, field work, work experience, simulations, apprenticeships, internships, projects, and self-directed study and research. Learning from experience 'out there' in the world has a primacy that cannot be matched by formal teaching. A number of practical suggestions, orientated towards experiential learners, arise from this framework.

1 Have experiences

Individuals need to ensure they get the experiences they need either individually or as part of communities of practice. There may be educational structures that enable this process or the individual might need to exercise autonomy and assertiveness in ensuring that appropriate experiences are obtained. Useful experiences should be challenging and should generate problems, questions and cognitive dissonance. Experiences could be enhanced by social interaction, activity and discussion. Some experiences are entirely cognitive but they can also involve practical skills, feelings and emotions. Some experiential learning is collaborative and participative and hence takes place through social interaction, a feature of 'situated' learning.

2 Reflect

Possibly one of the most important aspects of experiential learning theory is its emphasis on reflection. Experience is transformed into learning by reflection, in which the individual may engage either unconsciously or consciously. This process can be enhanced by interacting with another individual such as a facilitator, teacher, mentor, master or expert. Reflection can also be enhanced by writing, leading to the development of diaries and portfolios. The importance of reflection is further explored in Moon (1999), Kember *et al.* (2001) and Hillier (2002). Encouraging reflection leads to the development of reflective practice, which is an important component of professionalism (Schön 1983). Formal mechanisms, such as regular appraisal or supervisory meetings with a mentor or trainer, when a portfolio or reflective logbook can be discussed and future actions discussed and planned, is a major component of professional development programmes.

3 Feedback

Reflection is fundamentally enhanced by feedback, which can be seen as a type of formative assessment. Ensuring that learners have opportunities to receive constructive feedback from a trained mentor or supervisor is an important feature of experiential learning environments. Feedback can enable the learner to analyse their actions and their understanding and to plan for future learning.

4 Mental models, practical skills and attitudes

It is important to recognise that not only are mental models constructed by reflection on experience but so are practical skills and attitudes. There should be adequate opportunities for learners to map their experiences onto the experiences of others recorded in textbooks and the 'literature'. Learners should acknowledge that their own mental frameworks are socially connected to the external world of recorded knowledge that they are attempting to internalise.

5 Hypothesis testing and action planning

Learners need opportunities to test out and question their growing body of knowledge, skills and attitudes. They need to talk and debate with facilitators and other learners. They may need to be able to test out their ideas and hypotheses in practical environments. They may need to create action plans for future experiences and may require advice and support from facilitators and mentors.

6 Logbooks and portfolios

Learners can often be 'lost' in experiential learning environments if left to their own devices without supervision. However, they can be supported by having a logbook that defines a core set of experiences or procedures that should be engaged in. Portfolios can be used to record evidence of experience and reflections on those experiences. The contents of a portfolio can be used as trigger for further discussion and feedback from a mentor or appraiser.

Humanistic theory

The theories described above suggest in broad terms how individuals learn but do not contain a theory or model of the individual. However, at the heart of learning is a person with a personality, a personal history and hopes and fears. Our understanding of who this person is, where they are coming from and what makes them tick provides the final piece in our theoretical jigsaw. There are many theories of 'human nature' and the more we discover about ourselves through research in the sciences and humanities the wider these theories grow. In the early part of the twentieth century, psychoanalysis and the 'discovery' of the unconscious, through the work of Freud and Jung, was a major development in human understanding, which proposed an inner world of motives, desires, repressions, feelings and anxieties.

However, in the Unites States during the early twentieth century the behaviourist tradition in psychology largely rejected the relevance of these inner states in favour of an empirical exploration of the relationship between stimuli and responses. Into this environment came a number of important psychologists and psychiatrists who adopted a different approach. Eschewing both the psychodynamic theorising of the psychoanalysts and the 'mindless' empiricism of the behaviourists, Abraham Maslow and Carl Rogers developed a 'humanistic' or 'person-centred' approach to the individual, which has been found to provide a useful framework for dealing with individual learners and the educational environment in which they find themselves.

In general terms this psychological approach is characterised by recognising our individuality and our individual needs and by acknowledging that we wish to achieve our full potential. As a theory of the individual it is relatively structureless and value-free: our 'nature' is whoever we are and however we have constructed ourselves with our own personal knowledge and values. As such it provides a useful model of the individual, which is compatible with a constructivist theory of learning.

Maslow emphasised the concept of 'self-actualisation', the idea that we wish to become the best that we can possibly be (Maslow 1968). In this respect, one of his key ideas, which has much practical value in teaching, was to suggest that in order to achieve our full potential various basic needs must be fulfilled. This is often illustrated using the pyramid shown in Figure 3.4. At the base of the pyramid are various physiological needs such as thirst, hunger and warmth, which must be satisfied before the levels above can be achieved. The second level includes safety

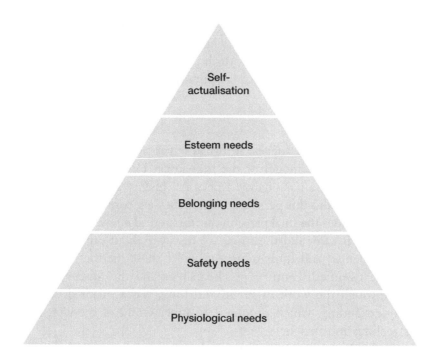

FIGURE 3.4 Maslow's 'hierarchy of needs'.

needs such as physical and psychological shelter and security. The following level is concerned with social or interpersonal needs such as 'belonging' and being part of the group.

The next level is concerned with self-esteem and prestige and the top of the pyramid is self-fulfilment and self-actualisation. The implications of this hierarchy are that to achieve the highest levels the levels below must be attained. The practical consequences of this theoretical framework can be seen in daily teaching practice. Students will not learn if their physiological and psychological needs have not been satisfactorily dealt with, if they are cold, hungry or anxious, for example. Similarly if students feel isolated and not part of the group this may inhibit their learning. If they are not given positive feedback, reinforcement and praise they may not learn optimally.

Carl Rogers was a psychologist whose psychotherapeutic work eventually led him in the direction of theories of learning and educational principles. His post-Freudian psychotherapeutic approach was to acknowledge and empathise with patients' own view of themselves in a 'client-centred' way. Understanding where the patient was coming from in their own terms was a key feature of his method. This therapeutic approach eventually transformed into an educational framework that was very much person- or student-centred (Rogers 1983). Like Maslow, Rogers acknowledged that individuals have a self-actualising tendency towards the achievement of their own potential. In addition he suggested they have a unique self-concept, need positive self-regard and should be trusted to self-actualise. He stressed the organismic and holistic nature of individuals and emphasised that they had a natural predisposition to learn. Rogers was extremely critical of conventional educational systems:

> Somehow we have managed . . . to transform one of the most rewarding of all human activities into a painful, boring, dull, fragmenting, mind-shrinking, soul-shrivelling experience.
>
> (Rogers 1983: 15)

He advocated self-initiated Experiential Learning, which allowed learners to explore their own ideas and follow their own natural interests. Building on his psychotherapeutic experience he stressed the importance of the teacher–student relationship, arguing that teachers should become 'facilitators' of learning rather than didactic transmitters of information. Facilitators should demonstrate empathy, trust and respect towards their students and be personally genuine. His student-centred theories suggested a number of principles for learning environments. For example, educational organisations should create a climate of trust to allow curiosity and the desire to learn to develop naturally. They should encourage students to take responsibility for their own learning and they should boost students' self-esteem and confidence by providing plenty of positive feedback. Learning environments should be democratic places where learners and facilitators collaborate to promote individual growth and development.

It should be apparent that the humanistic theories of Maslow and Rogers are the foundations for what we now call student- or learner-centred approaches to education. Their fundamental starting point is the individual's own place in the world, their own personal frameworks and their own mental models. They stress individual autonomy and encourage learners to take responsibility for their own learning. Hence there is a direct theoretical connection to the constructivist model of learning and to ELT. The constructivist model emphasises that what the student knows is at the heart of learning, it is their starting point for further construction: student-centredness is a fundamental principle of constructivist teaching practice. The dynamic of this building process is Experiential Learning.

Educational implications of humanistic learning theory

1   Respect learners and acknowledge who they are and where they are coming from.
2   Use their knowledge and understanding as a starting point for learning.
3   Ensure physical and psychological conditions for learning are satisfied by paying attention to the learning environment, introductions and group practices.

4   See teaching and learning as a relationship between the learner and the teacher/facilitator.

5   Give plenty of praise, support and constructive feedback.

6   Allow learners to explore and follow their own interests as much as possible.

7   Encourage and give time and space for self-directed learning.

8   Trust learners as much as possible to attain their own learning goals.

9   Conduct teaching in a collaborative and democratic way.

Synthesis: constructive experience (with a human touch)

Constructivism, the scientific method, Experiential Learning theory and humanistic learning theory have now been outlined with hints that there may be underlying connections between them as well as to other learning theories. It is now time to attempt a synthesis to see if a more all-encompassing theoretical framework can be discerned.

Parallels can be drawn between some of the processes identified within experiential and constructivist learning theory and scientific method. For example the transformation of concrete experience into abstract concepts and mental models by reflective observation is analogous to the process of assimilation in constructivism and to induction in the scientific method. The building up of mental schemas and models by incorporating sensory information provided by experience (assimilation) is equivalent to the process of inductive reasoning in science whereby the accumulation of observed facts leads to the building of theories.

Mental models and theories, however, may not fit or map onto reality, causing cognitive dissonance in the individual and hypothesis-testing in the scientific community. By acts of imagination and conceptualisation, deductions from the theoretical framework lead to hypotheses that can be tested by active experimentation, resulting in theory modification and hence accommodation via further concrete experiences, which feed into the inductive side of the cycle. Thus Experiential Learning Theory and constructivist theory are analogous to the hypothetico-deductive scientific method. In constructivist teaching practice existing mental models may be created or overthrown by appropriate experiential challenge. Learning in the individual can therefore be seen as an iterative process of theory creation and theory change, of induction followed by deduction, of assimilation followed by accommodation. These parallels are shown in Figure 3.5.

A further analogy between experiential learning and the scientific method is in the nature of the knowledge constructed. In science, theories are tentative; they are models of reality that are capable of being falsified by empirical evidence. In the individual, knowledge is constructed by an iterative process; ideas and concepts are

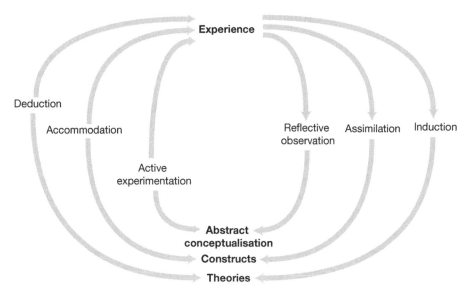

FIGURE 3.5 The parallels between concepts from constructivism, the scientific method and Kolb's Experiential Learning theory.

not fixed but are formed and reformed to create provisional knowledge through the cycle of experiential learning. This suggests that an appropriate attitude towards learning and knowledge is one of scepticism and open-mindedness. Dogmatism is not a foundation for learning; as Einstein said:

> Blind belief in authority is the greatest enemy of truth.
>
> (Einstein 1901: doc. 115)

Thomas Kuhn described how major historical changes in science produce paradigm shifts or 'scientific revolutions' when old frameworks and theories are discarded on the grounds of overwhelming negative empirical evidence and new theories are developed (Kuhn 1970). Similar changes can occur to the mental models of individuals and are explained by Kolb's theory of experiential learning and constructivist theory. Mezirow's transformative learning theory (Mezirow 1991) also emphasises changes to personal paradigms via critical reflection and cognitive dissonance and is clearly related to Kolb's framework and constructivist models of learning.

Some may argue that the hypothetico-deductive method of reasoning, which characterises a large proportion of scientific thinking, is not necessarily a model for reasoning and the creation of new knowledge in the arts, humanities and social sciences. It can also be argued that most individuals do not run their lives as if they were 'scientists', despite the claim made here that their knowledge-constructing processes are analogous to the scientific method. Here we must differentiate between content and process. Although the process may be universal, individuals and academic and artistic communities construct their own content in terms of their own mental models and their own theories of reality or aesthetics. Children construct a wide variety of theories to explain their experiences, which science teachers confront and challenge on a daily basis. Adults construct 'lay theories' by which they make sense of illness, other people's minds, their children's behaviour, money, in fact anything which helps to make sense of life. The content may be wildly different but the process is the same.

On the other hand the humanistic framework provides a relatively value-free theory of the individual that fits inside either the constructive or the experiential learning model. However, the element in the humanistic theory that makes the strongest connection to these last two theories and makes it the most useful theory for our purposes is the idea that one must begin from where the learner is; one must respect, understand and work with the learner's own constructions.

In conclusion constructive experience encompasses constructivist theory, experiential learning theory and humanistic theory which together provide a coherent and related framework for understanding the process of learning in children and adults as well as providing recommendations for educational environments. The hypothetico-deductive process of science provides connectivity between constructivist theory and experiential learning theory. Humanistic theory provides a relatively value-free theory of the individual learner. A variety of other learning theories can be seen to be derived from or strongly related to these three basic theories.

Constructive experience: implications for teaching

1   Acknowledge and respect the learner and start from where they are.
2   Ascertain, activate and build on their prior knowledge.
3   Provide appropriate learning experiences of an individual and social nature.
4   Facilitate reflection and provide feedback.
5   Recognise the tentative nature of knowledge and encourage enquiry.
6   Encourage individual responsibility for exploration, self-directed learning and action planning.
7   Develop a learning relationship, empathise and show trust.

Suggested further reading

It is difficult to find one text that adequately does justice to the constructivist model of learning. However, *Constructivism in Education* (Steffe and Gale 1995) contains a range of constructivist contributions and covers most of the main variants and interpretations. For a succinct account of the Empiricist and Rationalist debate in an educational context, read Kelly (1986). Piaget's work is monumental, with much of his later work still being analysed and interpreted. Flavell's book (Flavell 1963) is still the most comprehensive account of Piaget's early work but Richardson (1998) gives an excellent account of theories of cognitive development and the later Piaget. Kolb's *Experiential Learning* (Kolb 1984), although published over twenty years ago, is still worth reading. Not only does it outline his famous cycle, explaining its origins and its deeper meanings and ramifications, but it is beautifully and sensitively written and is a great work of synthesis and scholarship. All teachers should read *Freedom to Learn for the 80s* by Carl Rogers (1983); it can be a life-changing experience! Finally one of the best recent overall accounts of educational theory is *Learning in Adulthood, a Comprehensive Guide* by Merriam *et al.* (2007).

References

Ausubel, D. P. (1968) *Educational Psychology: A Cognitive View.* New York: Holt, Reinhart.

Bandura, A. (1977) *Social Learning Theory.* Upper Saddle River, NJ: Prentice Hall.

Benton, E. and Craib, I. (2001) *Philosophy of Social Science.* Basingstoke: Palgrave.

Berger, P. and Luckman, T. (1991) *The Social Construction of Reality.* Harmondsworth: Penguin.

Buchler, I. (ed.) (1955) *Philosophical Writings of Peirce.* New York: Dover.

Carruthers, P. and Chamberlain, A. (eds) (2000) *Evolution and the Human Mind: Modularity, Language and Meta-cognition.* Cambridge: Cambridge University Press.

Chalmers, A. F. (1999) *What is this Thing Called Science?* Maidenhead: Open University Press.

Chapman, M. (1988) *Constructive Evolution.* Cambridge: Cambridge University Press.

Chomsky, N. (1988). *Language and Problems of Knowledge.* Cambridge, MA: MIT Press.

Coffield, F., Moseley, D., Hall, E. and Ecclestone, K. (2004) *Should We be Using Learning Styles? What Research Has to Say to Practice.* London: LSDA.

Curzon, L. B. (1997) *Teaching in Further Education.* London: Continuum.

Dewey, J. (1938) *Logic: The Theory of Inquiry.* New York: Holt.

Dewey, J. (1963) *Experience and Education.* New York: Collier Books.

Donaldson, M. (1978) *Children's Minds.* London: Fontana.

Driver, R. (1983) *The Pupil as Scientist.* Milton Keynes: Open University Press.

Driver, R. and Oldham, V. (1986) 'A Constructivist Approach to Curriculum Development in Science', *Studies in Science Education.* **13**, 105–122.

Driver, R., Squires, A., Rushworth, P. and Wood-Robinson, V. (1994) *Making Sense of Secondary Science: Research into Children's Ideas.* Oxford: RoutledgeFalmer.

Duit, R. and Treagust, D. F. (1995) 'Student's Conceptions and Constructivist Teaching Approaches', in Fraser, B. J. and Walberg, H. J. (eds) *Improving Science Education.* Chicago: University of Chicago Press.

Einstein, A. (1901) *Collected Papers of Albert Einstein*, vol. 1, ed. J. Stachel. Princeton, NJ: Princeton University Press.

Einstein, A. and Infeld, L. (1938) *The Evolution of Physics.* Cambridge: Cambridge University Press.

Fensham, P., Gunstone, R. and White, R. (1994) *The Content of Science – a Constructivist Approach to its*

Teaching and Learning. London: Falmer Press.

Festinger, L. (1957) *A Theory of Cognitive Dissonance*. Stanford, CN: Stanford University Press.

Flavell, J. H. (1963) *The Developmental Psychology of Jean Piaget*. New York: Van Nostrand Reinhold.

Fodor, J. (1975) *The Language of Thought*. Cambridge, MA: MIT Press.

Fodor, J. (1983) *The Modularity of Mind: An Essay on Faculty Psychology*. Cambridge, MA: MIT Press.

Freire, P. (1973) *Education for Critical Consciousness*. New York: Continuum.

Furnham, A. F. (1988*) Lay Theories*. London: Pergamon.

Geelan, D. R. (1997) 'Epistemological Anarchy and the Many Forms of Constructivism', *Science & Education*. **6**, 15–28.

Gergen, K. J. (1995) 'Social Construction and the Education Process', in Steffe, L. P. and Gale, J. (eds) *Constructivism in Education*. Hillsdale, NJ: Lawrence Erlbaum.

von Glasersfeld, E. (1984) 'An Introduction to Radical Constructivism', in Waltzlawick, P. (ed.) *The Invented Reality*. New York: Norton.

von Glasersfeld, E. (1993) 'Questions and Answers about Radical Constructivism', in Tobin, K. (ed.) *The Practice of Constructivism in Science Education*. Hillsdale, NJ: Lawrence Erlbaum.

Hillier, Y. (2002) *Reflective Teaching in Further and Adult Education*. London: Continuum.

Illich, I. (1972) *Deschooling Society*. New York: Harrow Books.

James, W. (1901) *The Principles of Psychology*, vols 1 and 2. London: Macmillan.

Jarvis, P. (2006) *Towards a Comprehensive Theory of Learning*. London: Routledge.

Jarvis, P., Holford, J. and Griffin, C. (1998) *The Theory and Practice of Learning*. London: Kogan Page.

Jung, C. (1977) *Psychological Types: Collected Works Vol. 6*. Princeton, NJ: Princeton University Press.

Kant, I. (1983) *Critique of Pure Reason*, trans. Thomas Kingsmith Abbott. London: Longmans, Green.

Karmiloff-Smith, A. (1996) *Beyond Modularity: A Developmental Perspective on Cognitive Science*. Cambridge, MA: MIT Press.

Kelly, A. V. (1986) *Knowledge and Curriculum Planning*. London: Harper & Row.

Kelly, G. A. (1955) *The Psychology of Personal Constructs*. New York: Norton.

Kember, D. (ed.) (2001) *Reflective Teaching and Learning in the Health Professions*. London: Blackwell Science.

Knowles, M. S., Holton, E. F. and Swanson, R. A. (1998) *The Adult Learner*, 5th edn. Houston, TX: Gulf Publishing.

Kolb, D. A. (1984) *Experiential Learning*. Englewood Cliffs, NJ: Prentice Hall.

Kuhn, T. S. (1970). *The Structure of Scientific Revolutions*. Chicago, IL: University of Chicago Press.

Lave, J. and Wenger, E. (1991) *Situated Learning: Legitimate Peripheral Participation*. Cambridge: Cambridge University Press.

Lewin, K. (1951) *Field Theory in Social Science*. Washington, DC: American Psychological Association.

Marx, K. (1859) *A Contribution to the Critique of Political Economy*. Moscow: Progress Publishers.

Maslow, A. H. (1968) *Toward a Psychology of Being*. New York: Van Nostrand Reinhold.

Matthews, M. R. (1997) 'Introductory Comments on Philosophy and Constructivism in Science Education', *Science & Education*. **6**, 5–14.

Merriam, S. B., Caffarella, R. S. and Baumgartner, L. M. (2007) *Learning in Adulthood, a Comprehensive Guide*, 3rd edn. San Francisco, CA: Jossey-Bass.

Mezirow, J. (1991) *Transformative Dimensions of Adult Learning*. San Francisco, CA: Jossey-Bass.

Millar, R. H. and Driver, R. (1987) 'Beyond Processes', *Studies in Science Education*. **14**, 388–398.

Mithen, S. (1996) *The Prehistory of the Mind*. London: Thames and Hudson.

Moon, J. A. (1999) *Reflection in Learning and Professional Development*. London: Kogan Page.

Myers-Briggs, I. (1962) *The Myers-Briggs Type Indicator Manual*. Princeton, NJ: Educational Testing Service.

Philips, D. C. (1995) 'The Good, the Bad and the Ugly: The Many Faces of Constructivism', *Educational Researcher*. **24**, 5–12.

Piaget, J. (1970a) *Structuralism*. New York: Basic Books.

Piaget, J. (1970b) *Genetic Epistemology*. New York: Norton.

Pinker, S. (2002) *The Blank Slate*. London: Allen Lane.

Plotkin, H. (1994) *Darwin Machines and the Nature of Knowledge*. London: Penguin.

Plotkin, H. (2004) *Evolutionary Thought in Psychology*. Oxford: Blackwell.

Polanyi, M. (1958) *Personal Knowledge*. London: Routledge and Kegan Paul.

Popper, K. R. (1972) *Objective Knowledge*. Oxford: Oxford University Press.

Richardson, K. (1998) *Models of Cognitive Development*. Hove: Psychology Press.

Rogers, C. (1983) *Freedom to Learn for the 80s*. New York: Macmillan.

Savin-Baden, M. and Major, C. H. (2004) *Foundations of Problem-Based Learning*. Maidenhead: Open University Press.

Schön, D. (1983) *The Reflective Practitioner: How Professionals Think in Practice*. New York: Basic Books.

Solomon, J. (1994) 'The Rise and Fall of Constructivism', *Studies in Science Education*. **23**, 1–19.

Steffe, L. P. and Gale, J. (eds) (1995) *Constructivism in Education*. Hillsdale, NJ: Lawrence Erlbaum.

Tobin, K. (ed.) (1993) *The Practice of Constructivism in Science Education*. Hillsdale, NJ: Lawrence Erlbaum.

Waltzlawick, P. (ed.) (1984) *The Invented Reality*. New York: Norton.

Wenger, E. (1998) *Communities of Practice: Learning, Meaning and Identity*. New York: Cambridge University Press.

Wertsch, J. V. (1985) *Vygotsky and the Social Formation of Mind*. Cambridge, MA: Harvard University Press.

White, R. T. (1988) *Learning Science*. Oxford: Blackwell.

Wood, D. (1998) *How Children Think and Learn*. Oxford: Blackwell.

4

Psychology in education

Graham Mitchell

Can there be a psychological science that is about the best things in life? Can there be a classification of the strengths and virtues that make life worth living? Can parents and teachers use this science to raise strong, resilient children ready to take their place in a world in which more opportunities for fulfilment are available?

(Martin Seligman 2002: 29)

Introduction

THIS CHAPTER WILL EXAMINE the significant contribution psychology makes to education. There are six sections, which address different themes and topics about psychology in education. The first section introduces the principal perspectives in psychology, and these are then referred to throughout the rest of the chapter. In the following three sections we see psychology's role in measuring traits and abilities, in learning, and in motivation. The fifth section looks at developmental disorders, and how psychology can help with diagnosis and remediation. The final section examines more recent work in positive psychology.

Psychological perspectives

Psychology contributes to the study of education through different perspectives or approaches. The behaviourist approach emphasises the role of conditioning in human behaviour. Pavlov's research on salivation in dogs is well known (Bentham 2002). By association of a neutral stimulus, such as a light, with food, the light alone eventually became sufficient to elicit salivation. This is called classical conditioning. We can see immediate application for this in education. Neutral stimuli such as classrooms, books and teachers are commonly associated with pleasurable or unpleasant experiences. Although the story has become distorted with time (Cornwell *et al.* 1980), Watson and Raynor demonstrated how fear could be learnt through classical conditioning with a small boy named Albert (Thorne and Henley 1997). Positive and negative associations in classroom settings may then be responsible for some of our educational likes and dislikes.

Skinner investigated operant conditioning with a box in which rats and pigeons learnt to press a lever repeatedly to receive a food reward (Bentham 2002). The reward reinforced the lever-pressing behaviour. Skinner also showed how complex behaviours could be taught by reinforcing the behaviour's sub-components separately. This is called *shaping* and could be applied to more complex skills such as writing. The use of praise and correction in educational settings can be thought about in terms of operant conditioning. Schools' behaviour management systems tend to follow behavioural principles. We do need to question, however, whether simple stimulus–response animal models can be used to explain the complexities of classroom behaviour.

Social learning and social cognitive theories propose that we learn by modelling the behaviour of others and noting the consequences of observed behaviour (Woolfolk 2004). Bandura advanced this theory to explain why some behaviours are developed without any apparent reinforcement (Durkin 1995). Social learning is not limited to childhood and can provide a lifelong source of learning experiences.

The cognitive approach is concerned with mental processing (Bruning *et al.* 2004). The cognitive state of the student is studied, rather than thinking simply in terms of stimulus–response units of behaviour. Laboratory experiments, computer modelling and the study of deficits following brain damage are all methods used to examine processes such as attention, perception, learning, memory and language.

The psychodynamic approach places an emphasis on unconscious motives and early childhood experiences. Bowlby examined the attachment of young children to their mothers. Although we may not subscribe to Bowlby's original views today, the presence of significant others in a child's life is seen to be important for facilitating future social interactions and for providing resources for coping with stressful situations (Durkin 1995). Catch-up effects can occur for children with impoverished attachments, but these will depend on the quality of subsequent relationships with others. The study of vulnerable children on the Hawaiian island of Kauai reveals that resilience was associated with the receiving of positive attention from a close attachment figure (Prior 1999; Werner and Smith 1998).

The biological approach seeks to explain human behaviour by referring to genetic and physiological mechanisms. Brain functioning and chemical activities are seen to be relevant to an understanding of learning processes (Toates 2007). Brain imaging can be useful when looking at the neural correlates of conditions like dyslexia.

The humanistic perspective became popular in the mid-1950s. Whereas other approaches seem to emphasise determinism by examining environmental, cognitive, psychic and physiological influences on human behaviour, the humanistic approach places an emphasis on free will. Maslow and Rogers helped to introduce this far more optimistic psychological perspective, in which individuals could gain a sense of ownership of processes of growth and development. Maslow proposed a hierarchy of needs (Franken 2002). Only when basic physiological needs were satisfied would it be possible to meet higher needs including the experience of self-actualisation. Self-actualisation is related to peak experiences, reaching our potential, and gaining self-fulfilment. Student motivation and classroom procedures can be thought about in terms of a hierarchy of needs. It is also worth considering to what extent the pupil or student should experience ownership of the educational process. More recently Csikszentmihalyi (2002) has extended such ideas with the notion of flow. This is about the enhancement of our current experiences. It is better to travel hopefully than to arrive. Flow is experienced when we are so engrossed in an activity that we lose sense of time, something relevant to student motivation. Do we always have to coerce learners into activity when some ownership of the learning process could lead to better-motivated behaviour?

The social constructionist approach invites us to see that the way we interact with our social world will affect our development and current feelings (Woolfolk 2004). We are embedded in a particular culture, and our sense of self is socially constructed as we engage in social relations and patterns of language. Rather than taking traditional modes of thinking and behaviour for granted, we can adopt a critical stance when viewing educational institutions and society's educational values.

Traits, abilities and attainments

Why is it that some people seem more capable of learning than others, or are more predisposed to study a particular subject? Where do traits and abilities come from? We can frame these questions within a nature–nurture study, and recognise that we result from the dynamic developing interaction between inherited and environmental influences. Monozygotic twins, reared together and reared apart, have been used to examine the role of biological factors in determining intelligence. This is a controversial area in which some criticise a general willingness to prioritise inheritance (Rose 1997; Rose *et al.* 1984), and others criticise an overemphasis on environmental influences (Pinker 2002). Genetic and environmental determinism can limit our expectations of others in an educational setting. Early theories of development placed an emphasis on child development and viewed the adult as a stable fixed consequence of what had occurred in childhood. In lifespan development, we view development as proceeding throughout life. With this view we may be more optimistic about anyone's future progress because development is never finished, and future growth and positive change are always possible.

This does not mean that we should never look at a person's past. Recognising developmental correlates of current traits and abilities can be valuable. An awareness of the psychological and social factors that influence development can inform intervention decisions and help to promote optimal development. The child's social, emotional and intellectual worlds will all contain factors that influence development.

Can we, however, measure the consequences of a person's genetic background and past experiences? Psychometric attempts to objectively measure constructs such as intelligence and personality are commonplace. Individuals are scored using questionnaires, inventories and test sheets; but these need to be fit for purpose. A measure is declared trustworthy only when we can demonstrate that it is reliable, valid and standardised (Rust and Golombok 1999).

Reliability refers to the extent to which a measure is capable of delivering consistent findings. There are several different ways to measure reliability. Test–retest reliability involves repeating the test with the same participants and establishing the extent to which there is a correlation between the two sets of test scores.

Validity refers to the extent to which a test measures what it is claimed to. Reliable findings are insufficient if they fail to inform us about the measure we are interested in. A test claiming to measure creativity should be measuring exactly that and not something else. There are several types of validity.

A test needs to be standardised so that the performance of any particular sample of students can be compared to other students of similar age or educational level in the general population. We would therefore be able to judge, for instance, a pupil's intelligence relative to others in their own age group.

We are particularly interested in measuring traits, abilities and attainments, and it is important that we can distinguish between these three categories of measurement.

Traits are the characteristic patterns of behaviour and thinking in which we engage. These are our signature attributes. Personality measurement has received much attention over the past few decades, but perhaps the classification that has received most attention is the five-factor model associated with two researchers, Costa and McCrae (Larsen and Buss 2002). The five factors can be summed up with the acronym OCEAN: Openness to experience, Conscientiousness, Extraversion, Agreeableness and Neuroticism.

Abilities can be thought of as measures of cognitive performance that may facilitate future attainment levels (Cooper 2002). We might be interested, for example, in measuring different facets of intelligence, such as verbal or spatial intelligence. The measurement of intelligence is problematic (Richardson 1999), even though the statistical basis is sound. Intelligence tests may be culturally, racially and gender biased. We are nevertheless able to administer recognised tests in classrooms, record children's scores and then establish where that child is positioned relative to the population of children from which the child is drawn. An Intelligence Quotient (IQ) is a quantitative judgment based on comparisons with a larger population, and can be the ratio of mental age to chronological age. Popular intelligence tests for assessing ability in schoolchildren have included the Stanford–Binet and the Wechsler Intelligence Scale for Children (WISC). A general intelligence factor or thinking ability factor called g can be measured with psychometric tests, and intelligence differences do remain relatively stable over a lifetime (Deary 2003). Such differences are associated with later attainment in education and work, even health and longevity. Whalley and Deary (2001) provide data showing that high childhood IQ scores are associated with reduced mortality through to age 76. Intelligence testing has nevertheless been criticised (Gould 1981). Problems with intelligence testing become apparent when we examine the effects of positive and negative labelling. Rosenthal and Jacobson's (1966) work has sensitised us to the limiting and empowering influence of different contexts of expectation. Eighteen schoolteachers were told that particular children in their class had been identified with an unusual potential to make intellectual gains. Even though these children were randomly selected, IQ gains made during the year by the 'bright pupils' were higher than those in the control group. Findings from this study have been used to argue that positive expectations can influence intelligence test results. Chaikin, Sigler and Derlega's (1974) work also indicates that positively labelled children receive preferential treatment from teachers. Intelligence tests can also be used to determine who is entitled to educational resources. We may decide to assess ability at key stages in a person's life, and allocate educational resources in accordance with test results. This occurred with the 11+ examination system, used in parts of the United Kingdom, whereby successful children were allocated to better-resourced grammar schools, and the unsuccessful to secondary modern schools with poorer resources.

Gardner popularised the view that intelligence was much broader than previously defined. He proposed eight intelligences, namely verbal/linguistic, logical/mathematical, visual/spatial, bodily/kinaesthetic, musical, interpersonal, intrapersonal, and naturalist (Gardner 1998). Gardner's multiple intelligence approach has proved popular and today provides the basis for many classroom learning style initiatives (Gilbert 2002; Bowkett *et al.* 2007). Gardner's work nevertheless has received criticism for the marketing of well-established ideas about abilities in the guise of something new (Cooper 2002).

Goleman (1995) questioned whether IQ scores are always associated with later earning power, career advancement or interpersonal aspects of life. Sensitivity to other people's emotions and being in control of one's own emotions were claimed to be far more important qualities. Goleman's work has proved popular, with some academic researchers embracing his notion of emotional intelligence. Cooper (2002) argues, however, that additional work should be carried out before we can determine whether emotional intelligence has real value. These more recent concepts of intelligence have served to challenge views that academic success is the only real expression of intellectual worth (Rust and Golombok 1999). Different intelligence measures may nevertheless be useful for monitoring progress and for diagnosing educational problems.

The beliefs that we hold about intelligence may be important in determining motivation levels and achievement. Dweck (2000, 2006) conducted some research into two mindsets that we adopt. The fixed mindset holds that intelligence is stable, lifelong and difficult to change; whereas the growth mindset sees intelligence as dynamic and subject to change. Within a challenging educational setting, those students holding the growth mindset performed better. Dweck has also demonstrated that students' mindsets can be changed. We will return to student self-belief later.

Attainment can be measured through assignments, tests and examinations. Both coursework and end-of-course examinations provide information on individuals' academic attainment. Attainment figures are commonly used to assess individual student progress, identify learning difficulties and evaluate the work of individual teachers and schools. Concern has recently been expressed at the frequent testing of school students, within a culture dominated by performance measures.

Ability–achievement discrepancy analyses are conducted to establish whether someone's expected attainment, as measured by an IQ test, is matched by actual attainment. Such tests can be of use when diagnosing conditions such as dyslexia, but inherent in such procedures is the assumption that IQ scores are capable of predicting attainment levels.

Learning

In identifying ways to encourage learning, it is helpful to consider three areas: the processes, the learner and the teacher. There are different approaches to the study of learning processes (Pear 2001). We might be interested in the neuronal and chemical changes that occur when we learn something new. This biological approach can help to establish how a poor diet can limit learning, by investigating the rate, nature and stability of such brain changes.

The information-processing approach of the cognitive perspective permits us to examine learning and memory. Craik and Lockhart (1972) argued that material could be recalled more easily when the original encoding of information took place at a deeper level of processing. A deeper level might involve a more enriching learning experience in which additional mental processing of the learnt material takes place. Since memory is so important to processes of learning, full advantage can be taken of this idea in the classroom. It has immediate application because it causes us to think about the nature of the encoding process and the experiences of the student.

If we turn our attention to the student, we can think of learning in terms of units of stimulus–response conditioning, but this may reduce children's learning to a too mechanistic level. Bruner has argued against this approach, maintaining that attention must also be focused on the cognition of the student (Fontana 1995). The student can subjectively interpret stimuli in order to construct internal models and hypotheses, which in turn lead to expectations and predictions about the world.

In the 1960s and into the 1970s Piaget's theory of cognitive development was highly influential in educational studies and in developmental psychology (Byrnes 2001). Piaget proposed that cognitive development in children proceeds by passing through four qualitatively distinct stages, becoming more abstract and logical as the child develops (Slavin 2006). This theory suggests that children need to interact with their world to advance through the stages and to eventually experience higher-order thinking. Although Piaget is sometimes criticised for providing too rigid a structure of cognitive development, and for not taking sufficient account of environmental and cultural effects, his work has made a huge contribution to an understanding of child development. Classroom arrangements can provide children with the opportunity to actively interact with their surroundings, discovering and reflecting on their findings. The Piagetian account causes us to recognise that thinking skills develop gradually in children, and that teaching approaches should reflect the stage of development of the child.

Vygotsky provided another account of cognitive development, which placed an emphasis on language and discourse as mediators of the development of cognitive functioning. This is a social constructionist approach, viewing knowledge as socially constructed by and distributed among people in society (Woolfolk 2004). Learning therefore involves an interaction with others in social groups. The role of the teacher is important in helping the child to learn new tasks that are within their capabilities. This range of attainable but, as yet, unlearned tasks is called the zone of proximal development (ZPD). The zone for each teacher–child interaction shifts, covering different and increasingly demanding tasks and activities. The help that teachers provide in giving cues, prompting action or generally offering support is known as scaffolding. Higher-order thinking, for Vygotsky, is when there is a transfer of control from the environment to the child (Byrnes 2001). Vygotsky argued that to focus on the ZPD is preferable to the assessment of current IQ scores.

Finally we will look at the teacher. What is it that makes a teacher effective? Lepper and Woolverton (2002) identified a number of common traits that were effective in bringing about stable positive changes in students' motivation, learning and progress across a variety of situations. The acronym INSPIRE has been used to capture seven common characteristics of effective teachers.

Intelligent	Effective teachers were intelligent and knowledgeable about their subject and teaching approaches.
Nurturant	They were nurturant, warm and supportive; attentive to their students' needs and expressing confidence that they would succeed.
Socratic	A more Socratic and questioning approach was used as opposed to a didactic approach.
Progressive	A progressive approach was used in the way that students were exposed to challenges and problems. Lessons were well structured with regard being paid to student learning pathways.
Indirect	Errors were identified, but teacher interventions involved cues and tips, permitting students to recognise and correct their own errors. Recognition of student achievement was made and positive behaviour was reinforced without using effusive praise.
Reflective	Some priority was given to student understanding rather than just the accumulation of factual knowledge, by encouraging students to reflect on the issues they were studying.
Encouraging	Effective teachers helped to maintain high motivation levels by encouraging students to feel confident and sense mastery of their developing skills.

Teaching approaches cannot be based on simple formulas, but such findings may help teachers to reflect on their own practices and to consider the adoption of additional strategies, styles and approaches.

Motivation

What are the causes for varying levels of motivation and what can be done to improve pupils' motivation and enjoyment of learning?

Students have their own views about themselves. Some self-beliefs are liberating and empowering, whereas others serve to constrain and limit progress (Ormrod 2006). So often in education we keep our eye on external factors, but there is also the need to focus on internal, cognitive resources. Pajares and Schunk (2002) consider that teachers should pay regard to pupils' self-belief as much as their achievement record, on the grounds that self-belief will influence motivation and, in turn, future academic attainment. Many of the self-belief variables that we measure are reasonably stable and behave like traits. Tests are available for a number of constructs including self-esteem, self-efficacy, optimism and explanatory style.

Self-esteem refers to our sense of worth and sense of competence (Mruk 1999). We can distinguish between global self-esteem – the way people generally view themselves – and specific self-esteem – the way people view themselves in a particular domain of life, such as academic self-esteem. Whereas global self-esteem seems more important when considering overall psychological well-being, academic self-esteem correlates better with academic achievement (Rosenberg *et al*. 1995). Although some significant correlations have been found between self-esteem and academic performance (Skaalvik 1983), this in no way proves that high self-esteem improves achievement or that achievement can be improved by boosting the self-esteem of students (Baumeister *et al*. 2003). It is just as likely that self-esteem is derived from academic performance.

Praise given with the intention of boosting self-esteem can sometimes be counterproductive (McLean 2003). A mastery approach to learning, in which students value effort and personal improvement, seems preferable to a performance approach, in which students wish to gain favourable judgments for their work (Anderman *et al*. 2001). Praising ability rather than effort can encourage students to emphasise performance over mastery. Also, when failure occurs, students may attribute their failure to lack of ability and become less confident as a result. Praise can also be toxic when it is given indiscriminately and for accomplishments requiring little effort. Under such circumstances the teacher's low expectations may well lead to reduced motivation.

Another related self-belief measure is self-efficacy. This refers to a sense of capability in a specific domain of life (Gaskill and Hoy 2002). In an academic setting, self-efficacy may provide a precursor for self-concept development (Bong and Skaalvik 2003). Self-efficacy can be derived from a sense of competence based on past experience (mastery experiences), seeing how other people perform their tasks (vicarious experiences), noting one's state of anxiety or enthusiasm (emotional and physiological arousal) and the validation of one's own efforts by significant others (verbal persuasion) (Bandura 1997). Evidence suggests that self-efficacy is associated with task performance (Bandura 1997). Students with high self-efficacy scores are more likely to engage with more demanding tasks, and expend more effort and persist longer with tasks. Such student qualities are welcome in any classroom. Bandura also argues that self-efficacy plays a significant mediation role in academic achievement for factors such as gender, attitudes to school, prior attainment and cognitive ability. He implicates self-efficacy in the development of motivation, intrinsic interest and the resilience needed to buffer the negative effects of academic anxiety. This last point is relevant since school students face demands to perform well in examinations. Failure can elicit disapproval from those around and block intended career progression routes.

Confidence and higher levels of motivation can seem to grow with the experience of success, but the opposite effect is also at work. Maier and Seligman (1967) conducted behavioural research in which dogs were conditioned to avoid electric shocks. This might represent the way we adopt strategies to avoid unpleasant experiences in life. In a second stage to this work, some of the conditioned dogs were harnessed to prevent them avoiding the shock. The dogs could still put out effort, but it was wasted. The shock avoidance was now no longer contingent on the effort expended. Most dogs gave up and developed a state called *learned helplessness,* an effect we are familiar with in educational practice. It affects our confidence, our moods and emotions. It involves the loss of hope and motivation, even in bright, gifted pupils.

Explanatory style has emerged from learned helplessness research and refers to the characteristic way that we explain our failures and successes. The reformulation of the attributional style concept by Abrahamson, Seligman, and Teasdale (1978) resulted in three self-belief dimensions (internality/externality, stability/instability and globality/specificity).

With a pessimistic explanatory style, setbacks are explained in terms of internal, stable and global causes. A student attributing an examination failure to lack of intelligence is providing such an explanation. There is something wrong with me (internal), the problem will persist (stable) and it will affect other aspects of life (global). Blaming a hard examiner for failure is an example of an optimistic explanatory style. There is something wrong with the examiner (external), it is unlikely to happen again (unstable) and it will only affect this examination (specific). Peterson and Barrett (1987) looked at the explanatory style of first-year university students and found that an optimistic explanatory style was associated with higher grades. The measure has been refined more recently, but explanatory style remains a useful additional self-belief measure in motivation research.

· Self-handicapping strategies are more likely when self-belief resources are limited. Lack of effort can be used as a protective strategy. Trying to succeed may be too risky when failure is attributed to lack of ability. It may be preferable to preserve the belief that 'I could have succeeded had I tried.' Under these circumstances we may feel the safest approach is not to try (Dweck 2000). Self-belief, then, is an important study area when considering motivation in the classroom.

The humanistic approach points to the satisfaction of needs as the basis for motivation. This may provide a helpful perspective for the encouragement and maintenance of motivation in the classroom. Behavioural models suggest that current motivation levels are derived from our past conditioning. Effort is more likely when the association between effort and reward has been learned. We may be concerned though that emphasising external rewards will foster an extrinsic performance-oriented educational culture rather than an intrinsic mastery-oriented culture (Alexander 2006).

We can also investigate motivation by examining the social world of the child. The social constructions of gender identities are worth considering with the much-publicised 'under-achievement of boys', particularly at GCSE level. If boys perceive schoolwork to be a feminised activity, they may be less likely to work or to report they are working (Francis 1999).

When things 'go wrong'

The area of developmental psychopathology examines psychological problems that affect educational progress (Santrock 2008). Development-related disorders include intellectual deficits, social behaviour deficits, learning deficits and attention deficits.

Prompt identification of intellectual deficits with intelligence tests help remediation procedures to be initiated. There are, however, some disadvantages as well. Negative labelling can be most unhelpful to children identified as mentally retarded. Intelligence test results may not reflect innate learning potential as much as adjustment to the challenges of formal schooling (Peterson 1996). Halgin and Whitbourne (2003) catalogue a number of brilliant and well-known individuals who were labelled as being dull while at school. There are likely to be genetic and environmental contributions to mental retardation. Phenylketonuria is a metabolic disorder that can lead to intellectual impairment. Treatments have to be determined by a consideration of the causes of the condition, and will range from enrichment of the child's environment through to drug treatment and behavioural interventions.

With social behaviour deficits, children may display challenging behaviour that may have arisen through operant conditioning. Such behaviour may permit the child to exercise some control over the environment, by attention-seeking and influencing classroom procedures (Bennett 2003). Behavioural and cognitive–behavioural interventions can be effectively employed to reshape some dysfunctional behaviour.

Autism involves not only social behaviour deficits but other problems such as those related to communication. Whereas most children will quickly develop non-verbal communication skills, this is not the case with autism, and so social interactions suffer. There are several different types of autism, but it is common for the child to possess a limited understanding of what others might be thinking or feeling. Autism is associated with biological factors such as a higher incidence of seizure disorders by adolescence, and increases in brain cerebral cortex size (Nolen-Hoeksema 2001). Drugs and behavioural therapy are used to reduce the intensity of the symptoms.

Dyslexia is a learning disorder, affecting both reading and writing. It is, however, a disorder with very wide-ranging symptoms, including spatial ability problems. Other spatial skills and aspects of creativity may, however, be enhanced by dyslexia. In common with autism, there appears to be a diagnosis bias in the direction of boys. This may be because boys are more active and disruptive in the classroom, and therefore are more likely to be noticed. Dyslexia manifests itself at a behavioural level in the classroom, but cognitive and biological processing are both implicated in its cause. Brain scanning can be helpful in determining whether characteristic brain structure features are present. Remediation strategies include behaviour therapy, drugs, and reading strategies.

Attention-deficit/hyperactivity disorder (ADHD) is perhaps the most well-known of the attention disorders. Children with ADHD are unable to pay attention to instructions and they are also hyperactive. Poor school performance and some degree of social isolation are common consequences. Some children with ADHD grow into normal adults and become symptom-free, whereas others are affected into adulthood (Peterson 1996). Environmental factors, such as family disruption, and biological factors, such as poor frontal lobe development, are linked to this condition. Both drugs and behaviour therapy are used to treat ADHD.

Psychology can make two distinct contributions to developmental psychopathology. The first is concerned with identifying the specific nature of the problem, which makes effective remediation more likely. The second relates to the treatment and monitoring of the condition. Both clinical and educational psychologists may be involved in managing these disorders.

Positive psychology and education

Seligman and Csikszentmihalyi (2000) have argued that psychology has focused on repairing the damage caused by disease, and has neglected the process of building fulfilled individuals. Positive psychology focuses on positive cognitions about the future, such as optimism and hope. It has similar notions to those of the humanistic thinkers of several decades ago, when self-actualisation and peak experiences were being debated.

Having examined the problems caused by learned helplessness, we see that more constructive cognitions are likely to pave the way to improved motivation and success in school. Can we help children to develop beliefs that are protective and which increase resilience in the face of the many challenges life provides?

Hope will affect motivation levels and the extent to which educational experiences can be enjoyed. The Children's Hope Scale (CHS) has been developed to measure levels of hope in children (Snyder *et al.* 1997). Hope is associated with higher self-esteem, higher self-efficacy and lower levels of depression (Roberts *et al.* 2002). Interventions to build hope have involved activities, ranging from the reading of hopeful stories and subsequent discussions, to the use of a summer day camp for children with psychosocial problems. It has been demonstrated that children's hope scores will tend to rise following these interventions (Roberts *et al.* 2002).

Because positive expectations can be self-fulfilling, there is reason to treat optimism as an asset. Peterson (2000) reviews a number of benefits of optimism including positive mood, good morale, perseverance, effective problem-solving, and academic success. The Life Orientation Test is one measure of optimism for adolescents and adults (Scheier and Carver 1985). This measure provides a score reflecting the overall global optimism of the person. Attributional style questionnaires can be used to establish optimism by measuring the explanatory style of the person. The Children's Attributional Style Questionnaire (CASQ) is one example of this (Seligman 1998).

Based on the notion that pessimism is a predisposing factor for depression, intervention projects have been devised to influence a child's cognitions, particularly with regard to explanatory style, and social problem-solving skills. Roberts, Brown, Johnson and Reinke (2002) point out that such interventions are beneficial, and this supports the notion that optimism can be taught.

Although positive psychology has not escaped criticism (Held 2004), it seems that positive interventions can be made in a child's early life to help develop resilience and coping skills, in preparation for future challenges. Psychology has much to offer education. The reader is now encouraged to select additional study material from the extensive amount of psychological research work related to educational processes.

Suggested further reading

Comprehensive reviews of psychological issues relevant to education are provided by Fox (2005) and Santrock (2008). Very useful accounts of helplessness and optimism research are found in Seligman's work.

References

Abrahamson, L. Y., Seligman, M. E. P. and Teasdale, J. D. (1978) 'Learned Helplessness in Humans: Critique and Reformulation', *Journal of Abnormal Psychology*. **87**, 49–74.

Alexander, P. A. (2006) *Psychology in Learning and Instruction*. Upper Saddle River, NJ: Pearson.

Anderman, E. M., Austin, C. C. and Johnson, D. M. (2001) 'The Development of Goal Orientation', in Wigfield, A. and Eccles, J. S. (eds) *Development of Achievement Motivation*. London: Academic Press.

Bandura, A. (1997) *Self-efficacy: The Exercise of Control*. New York: W. H. Freeman and Company.

Baumeister, R. F., Campbell, J. D., Krueger, J. I. and Vohs, K. D. (2003) 'Does High Self-Esteem Cause Better Performance, Interpersonal Success, Happiness, or Healthier Lifestyles?', *Psychological Science in the Public Interest*. **4** (1), 1–44.

Bennett, P. (2003) *Abnormal and Clinical Psychology*. Maidenhead: Open University Press.

Bentham, S. (2002) *Psychology and Education*. London: Routledge.

Bong, M. and Skaalvik, E. M. (2003) 'Academic Self-concept and Self-efficacy: How Different are they Really?', *Educational Psychology Review*. **15** (1), 1–40.

Bowkett, S., Harding, T., Lee, T. and Leighton, R. (2007) *Success in the Creative Classroom*. London: Network Continuum Education.

Bruning, R. H., Schraw, G. J., Norby, M. M. and Ronning, R. R. (2004) *Cognitive Psychology and Instruction*. Upper Saddle River, NJ: Pearson.

Byrnes, J. P. (2001) *Cognitive Development and Learning*. London: Allyn and Bacon.

Chaikin, A., Sigler, E. and Derlega, V. (1974) 'Non-verbal Mediators of Teacher Expectancy Effects', *Journal of Personality and Social Psychology*. **30**, 144–149.

Cooper, C. (2002) *Individual Differences.* London: Arnold.

Cornwell, D., Hobbs, S. and Prytula, R. (1980) 'Little Albert Rides Again', *American Psychologist.* **35** (2), 216–217.

Craik, F. I. M. and Lockhart, R. S. (1972) 'Levels of Processing: A Framework for Memory Research', *Journal of Verbal Learning and Verbal Behavior.* **11**, 671–684.

Csikszentmihalyi, M. (2002) *Flow: The Classic Work on How to Achieve Happiness.* London: Rider.

Deary, I. J. (2003) 'Ten Things I Hated about Intelligence Research', *The Psychologist.* **16**, 534–537.

Durkin, K. (1995) *Developmental Social Psychology: From Infancy to Old Age.* Oxford: Blackwell.

Dweck, C. S. (2000) *Self-theories: Their Role in Motivation, Personality, and Development.* Hove: Psychology Press.

Dweck, C. S. (2006) *Mindset.* New York: Random House.

Fontana, D. (1995) *Psychology for Teachers.* London: Palgrave/BPS.

Fox, R. (2005) *Teaching and Learning: Lessons from Psychology.* Oxford: Blackwell.

Francis, B. (1999) 'Lads, Lasses and (New) Labour: 14–16-year-old Students' Responses to the "Laddish Behaviour and Boys' Underachievement" Debate', *British Journal of Sociology of Education.* **20**, 355–371.

Franken, R. E. (2002) *Human Motivation.* Belmont, CA: Wadsworth.

Gardner, H. (1998) 'A Multiplicity of Intelligences', *Scientific American Presents.* **9** (4), 18–23.

Gaskill, P. J., and Hoy, A. W. (2002) 'Self-efficacy and Self-regulated Learning: The Dynamic Duo in School Performance', in Aronson, J. (ed.) *Improving Academic Achievement: Impact of Psychological Factors on Education.* London: Academic Press.

Gilbert, I. (2002) *Essential Motivation in the Classroom.* London: RoutledgeFalmer.

Goleman, D. (1995) *Emotional Intelligence: Why it can Matter More than IQ.* London: Bantam Books.

Gould, S. J. (1981) *The Mismeasure of Man.* Harmondsworth: Penguin Books.

Halgin, R. P. and Whitbourne, S. K. (2003) *Abnormal Psychology: Clinical Perspectives on Psychological Disorders.* London: McGraw-Hill.

Held, B. S. (2004) 'The Negative Side of Positive Psychology', *Journal of Humanistic Psychology.* **44** (1), 9–46.

Larsen, R. J. and Buss, D. M. (2002) *Personality Psychology.* London: McGraw Hill.

Lepper, M. R. and Woolverton, M. (2002) 'The Wisdom of Practice: Lessons Learned from the Study of Highly Effective Tutors', in Aronson, J. (ed.) *Improving Academic Achievement: Impact of Psychological Factors on Education.* London: Academic Press.

McLean, A. (2003) *The Motivated School.* London: Paul Chapman Publishing.

Maier, S. F., and Seligman, M. E. P. (1967) 'Learned Helplessness: Theory and Evidence', *Journal of Experimental Psychology: General.* **105**, 3–46.

Mruk, C. (1999) *Self-esteem: Research, Theory and Practice.* London: Free Association Books.

Nolen-Hoeksema, S. (2001) *Abnormal Psychology.* London: McGraw-Hill.

Ormrod, J. E. (2006) *Essentials of Educational Psychology.* Upper Saddle River, NJ: Pearson.

Pajares, F. and Schunk, D. H. (2002) 'Self and Self-belief in Psychology and Education: A Historical Perspective', in Aronson, J. (ed.) *Improving Academic Achievement: Impact of Psychological Factors on Education.* London: Academic Press.

Pear, J. J. (2001) *The Science of Learning.* Hove: Psychology Press.

Peterson, C. (1996) *The Psychology of Abnormality*. London: Harcourt Brace & Company.

Peterson, C. (2000) 'The Future of Optimism', American Psychologist. **55**, 44–55.

Peterson, C. and Barrett, L. C. (1987) 'Explanatory Style and Academic Performance among University Freshmen', *Journal of Personality and Social Psychology*. **53**, 603–607.

Pinker, S. (2002) *The Blank Slate*. Harmondsworth: Penguin Books.

Prior, M. (1999) 'Resilience and Coping: The Role of Individual Temperament', in Frydenberg, E. (ed.) *Learning to Cope: Developing as a Person in Complex Societies*. Oxford: Oxford University Press.

Richardson, K. (1999) *The Making of Intelligence*. London: Phoenix.

Roberts, M. C., Brown, K. J., Johnson, R. J. and Reinke, J. (2002) 'Positive Psychology for Children', in Snyder, C. R. and Lopez, S. J. (eds) *Handbook of Positive Psychology*. New York: Oxford University Press.

Rose, S. (1997) *Lifelines: Biology, Freedom, Determinism*. London: The Penguin Press.

Rose, S., Lewontin, R. C. and Kamin, L. J. (1984) *Not in our Genes: Biology, Ideology and Human Nature*. London: Penguin.

Rosenberg, M., Schoenbach, C., Schooler, C. and Rosenberg, F. (1995) 'Global Self-esteem and Specific Self-esteem: Different Concepts, Different Outcomes', *American Sociological Review*. **60**, 141–156.

Rosenthal, R. and Jacobson, L. (1966) 'Teachers' Expectancies: Determinants of Pupils' I.Q. Gains', *Psychological Reports*. **19**, 115–118.

Rust, J. and Golombok, S. (1999) *Modern Psychometrics*. London: Routledge.

Santrock, J. W. (2008). *Educational Psychology*. London: McGraw-Hill.

Scheier, M. F., and Carver, C. S. (1985) 'The Self-Consciousness Scale: A Revised Version for Use with General Populations', *Journal of Applied Social Psychology*. **15**, 687–699.

Seligman, M. E. P. (1998) *Learned Optimism*. London: Pocket Books.

Seligman, M. E. P. (2002) *Authentic Happiness*. London: Free Press.

Seligman, M. E. P. and Csikszentmihalyi, M. (2000) 'Positive Psychology: An Introduction', *American Psychologist*. **55**, 5–14.

Skaalvik, E. M. (1983) 'Academic Achievement, Self-esteem and Valuing of the School – Some Sex Differences', British Journal of Educational Psychology. **53**, 299–306.

Slavin, R. E. (2006) *Educational Psychology: Theory and Practice*. London: Pearson.

Snyder, C. R., Hoza, B., Pelham, W. E., Rapoff, M., Ware, L., Danovsky, M., Highberger, L., Rubinstein, H. and Stahl, K.J. (1997) 'The Development and Validation of an Individual-Differences Measure of Hope', *Journal of Pediatric Psychology*. **22**, 399–421.

Thorne, B. M. and Henley, T. B. (1997) *Connections in the History and Systems of Psychology*. New York: Houghton Mifflin.

Toates, F. (2007) *Biological Psychology*. London: Pearson.

Werner, E. E. and Smith, R. S. (1998) *Vulnerable but Invincible: A Longitudinal Study of Resilient Children and Youth*. New York: Adams, Bannister, Cox.

Whalley, L. J. and Deary, I. J. (2001) 'Longitudinal Cohort Study of Childhood IQ and Survival up to Age 76', *British Medical Journal*. **322**, 819–822.

Woolfolk, A. (2004) *Educational Psychology*. London: Pearson.

5

e-Learning

Heather Rai

Students today can't prepare bark to calculate their problems. They depend on their slates, which are more expensive. What will they do when the slate is dropped and it breaks? They will not be able to write.

(Teachers Conference 1703, cited in Shoffner *et al.* 2000)

Introduction

[Students today] absorb information quickly, in images and video as well as text, from multiple sources simultaneously. They operate at 'twitch speed', expecting instant responses and feedback. They prefer random 'on-demand' access to media, expect to be in constant communication with their friends (who may be next door or around the world), and they are as likely to create their own media (or download someone else's) as to purchase a book or a CD.

(Stephen Downes 2005: n.p.)

TODAY'S STUDENTS ARE RARELY disconnected from technology. They expect to find the information they need, for an assignment or for their own interests, quickly and visually. They are permanently connected with their peers via mobile phones, MSN and e-mail, and they expect this technology to be invisible (the instructions that come with mobile phones are not written for the under-25s). Table 5.1 shows some of the contrasts between learners and teachers with respect to their differing attitudes to work. More mature students will also be familiar with writing assignments on computer and conducting literature searches online. So what impact does this have on education?

In this chapter I hope to give an introduction and an overview to current trends and techniques in e-learning including some of the more common examples of technology that are currently available in the classroom or could easily be obtained, should the reader wish. This list is by no means complete, as there are

TABLE 5.1 Digital native learners versus digital immigrant teachers

Digital native learners	Digital immigrant teachers
Prefer receiving information quickly from multiple multimedia sources	Prefer slow and controlled release of information from limited sources
Prefer parallel processing and multitasking	Prefer singular processing and single or limited tasking
Prefer processing pictures, sounds and video before text	Prefer to provide text before pictures, sounds and video
Prefer random access to hyperlinked multimedia information	Prefer to provide information linearly, logically and sequentially
Prefer to interact/network simultaneously with many others	Prefer students to work independently rather than network and interact
Prefer to learn 'just-in-time'	Prefer to teach 'just-in-case' (it's on the exam)
Prefer instant gratification and instant rewards	Prefer deferred gratification and deferred rewards
Prefer learning that is relevant, instantly useful and fun	Prefer to teach to the curriculum guide and standardised tests

Source: Jukes and Dosaj (2003).

many possibilities that are changing all the time as new products are developed; but hopefully the reader will gain enough of an overview to assess the gains to be made by trying a new technology and be more informed if they are asked by somebody else to use one for their teaching.

But, firstly, what is 'e-learning'? The term 'e-learning' has become more common in the twenty-first century but computers have been used as intelligent tutoring systems for decades. The Higher Education Funding Council for England (HEFCE) defines it as 'any learning that uses ICT' (HEFCE 2005: 5) where ICT is information and communication technology. This is a very broad definition and as applications such as Microsoft Word and PowerPoint become ubiquitous it is probably not helpful to class their everyday use as 'e-learning'. Moreover to further confuse matters, they cannot actually be totally ruled out as this is not their only use. It is possible to create interactive resources for students with PowerPoint and Word that may allow students to work collaboratively and interact with the software in ways that are not possible on paper.

In the clamour for all this new technology, there is a danger that it could become viewed as a panacea for any problems in schools, such as larger class sizes. We must also bear in mind that, as this technology is pushed into schools, the push may come from the vendors of the technology, rather than a pull from teaching staff themselves. Therefore, what is commonly seen is a few enthusiastic 'early adopters' trying the latest ideas reluctantly followed by many other teaching staff, who may feel rushed and disenfranchised by the new technology. Any changes to teaching practices need to be embraced by all staff and reassurance given that this technology is never going to replace the expert face-to-face teaching that a qualified educator can give.

Despite each one of us being surrounded by technology in the workplace and at home, educational technology is still in its infancy. A lot of technology tries to recreate what is current practice within the classroom. In the same way that the first mechanical tractor was severely restricted by being given reins for steering in an attempt to recreate the horse it replaced, this use of new technology in old ways and simply recreating on the computer what can be achieved in lecture theatres can limit the possibilities of what is available. Using technology in new ways will also ensure that the technology being employed will complement the teacher, not attempt to replace the expert in the classroom; if technology is to be successful in the classroom, it needs to add something pedagogically to existing teaching methods.

One of the reasons cited for the demise of the UK eUniversity in 2004, aside from its unfortunately launch timing (as the dot-com bubble burst) was that it tried to represent itself as an alternative to conventional university teaching, rather than as a supplement (Garrett 2004). It seems that in this case some of the positive aspects of a real campus may have been lost and these were not sufficiently compensated for with new techniques. This resulted in a failure to recruit students who still wanted to attend face-to-face teaching. Most universities in the United Kingdom will now offer a blended approach, meaning that they support face-to-face teaching with the use of online materials.

It is tempting for the technology enthusiast to try any approach that they have come across in their teaching just because it is available. Although it is invaluable to try new ideas and explore the possibilities that new technologies can offer, it is important that the technology be fitted around the educational needs of the students rather than vice versa. This may seem an obvious point but many new technologies can involve a steep learning curve in their early stages of use. Only later versions tend to become easier to use seamlessly and become invisible as tools. This is an issue for younger students who are used to using mature online tools in their own time and for older students who may be less familiar with any kind of technology.

Consideration also needs to be given to the involvement of teaching staff in the adoption of new technologies. Simply rolling out a new technology without consultation can lead to a great deal of resistance and can result in that technology not being used fully. This issue can be illustrated by the UK government's strategy to give every primary and secondary school within the United Kingdom an Interactive Whiteboard. These whiteboards look similar to a normal whiteboard but can be connected to a computer and used to interact in various ways, depending on the version used. The contents of the computer screen may be projected on to the board and marks made on the board with the pens can act as an input to the computer. The boards originated in the commercial sector, designed for group discussions, but have since been rolled out in secondary and primary schools.

Unfortunately, many of these boards have remained in the boxes they arrived in. This is in part because of the time constraints of teachers but it has not been aided by a 'push' of the technology from higher-level strategies, rather than a pull by teachers. In two papers, Miller and Glover (Glover and Miller 2001; Miller and Glover 2002) looked at what made these new tools successful in schools and concluded that primary schools had to show three key attributes:

- schools had to display a will to develop and use the technology;

- teachers had to be willing to become mutually interdependent in the development of materials;

- there had to be some change of thinking about the way in which classroom activities were resourced.

In secondary schools, they concluded that there needed to be an appreciation that a new approach to pedagogy in the school was needed alongside suitable training and reflection on the activities that were part of the changes.

Types of e-Learning

This section describes some of the more common forms of educational technologies currently in use. Many of these systems will be familiar to today's students, especially those in higher education, although not necessarily in an educational context (such as blogs). Again it should be highlighted that there is not enough space to create an exhaustive list here and this should be seen as a starting point.

Virtual learning environments

Virtual learning environments (VLEs) are portals that provide tools and facilitate the presentation of learning materials to be used by students and staff, usually over the World Wide Web. Users log on to the system and are then presented with learning materials, links, discussion boards, portfolios of marks, assessments and other online resources. The view offered to students will usually be different from that offered to staff. Students will see a list of courses that they are enrolled on and within each of these the facilities that their lecturer has chosen to use within the VLE. In contrast the lecturer will see the 'back end' of the system and will be able to upload resources for the students and select and control what means the students can have to interact with themselves and each other, such as discussion boards.

Currently the largest commercial systems on the market are *WebCT* and *Blackboard*. However, in 2005 WebCT was bought by Blackboard so it is probable that these two systems will merge in some way. An alternative, open source, system is *Moodle*. Open source software is written by a community of programmers and all the code is freely available. This means that the software is free to use and new modules are continually being created. There is, however, a cost in installing and customising the software for use.

VLEs are arguably the most common form of 'e-learning' in higher education but whether these truly offer e-learning is debatable. It depends on their use. Although these systems offer the ability to teach and interact with students in new ways, for the most part they are not used in this way. Blin and Munro (2007) identified a difference between the use of VLEs for 'resources' and 'activities'. Resources are the files that are distributed by the VLE, including items such as Word, PowerPoint and PDF files. In contrast activities are the tasks that students can participate in within the VLE, this includes such things as forums, assignments and assessments. They found that 93 per cent of the use of their VLE was in the form of resources and suggest that not until VLEs are seen as a tool to be *used* rather than a repository to store files will their full potential be reached and teaching practices really be changed. It is this untapped potential that needs to be highlighted here. There is value in providing files online and the use of these by students to support their learning; however, this is normally seen as a more administrative role of VLEs and it ignores the more interactive possibilities of the medium.

In an evaluation of the Blackboard VLE at the University of Teesside, Bingham and Yanaske (2006) found a split between the expectations of students and of staff. Staff expected Blackboard to enhance the learning experience just through its implementation, possibly because it was sold to the institution as a solution in itself. In contrast, the students saw the VLE as a tool and were focused on its content, rather than on the VLE itself. Reassuringly, the students still wanted to have face-to-face lectures. Even though the lecture notes were posted on the VLE, they saw the VLE more as a supplement to traditional learning. This was more important to the mature students, who showed the strongest preference for traditional teaching, although interestingly they also felt that the lectures did not add much to the material available online, possibly indicating a view that lectures were a passive experience. However, these students did state that question-and-answer sessions at the end of lectures and during tutorials were useful; this is probably the source of their preference for face-to-face teaching. The authors go on to stress the importance of ensuring that all users of a VLE, both staff and student, should be prepared thoroughly for its introduction. This helps to ensure that it is used effectively.

Iredale (2006) also highlights the fact that VLEs can support a knowledge transfer model, rather than radically change the way that students are taught. However, she found that the students like the way that the VLE afforded their learning 'anytime, anyplace, anywhere' (Iredale 2006). Although students may prefer face-to-face contact with their instructors, they do seem to appreciate the facility to log in at any time that they choose and participate in discussions and read notes. Again, Iredale highlights that it is the content of the VLE that is the most important factor in whether it is used by the students.

If a VLE is successfully integrated with a course it has been found that students enjoy sharing information amongst themselves and horizontal learning will occur. This kind of learning between students can easily be supported by setting up the VLE in such a way that students are free to share resources, for example through their own discussion boards. If this takes place then a community of practice may form which will then aid the students in their studies.

As a new generation of the World Wide Web evolves (the section on e-Learning 2.0, later in this chapter, has more details on this) so it is predicted that VLEs will also evolve. As a result of this, personalised learning environments (PLEs) have started to appear. In a PLE the user controls the information that they are presented with. This means that they can join any groups that they find interesting or useful, communicate with their peers and tutors in a way which suits them and learn both formally and informally through their use of the PLE. This approach to a learning environment appears to sit well with the research reported above and therefore these may well be features that we will see appear in the current VLEs in the future.

'Traditional' computer-aided learning

Computer-aided learning (CAL) is a term used to cover a huge range of teaching materials delivered by a computer. It was first used in the 1980s, usually to describe a single piece of computer software that was used to convey information to a student. However, it now seems to be used to cover all manner of computer-based teaching and therefore has sometimes fallen slightly out of favour on account of its indistinct meaning and has started to be replaced by more specific terms.

This section attempts to give an overview of the uses of computers in education that may come under this 'CAL' description. This covers a huge range of applications and therefore the list is by no means exhaustive; nonetheless, it should hopefully provide some examples of what can be achieved with a variety of resources. Before we cover these it is important to cover a theoretical approach to the design of CAL. It is very easy, and common, to get carried away with the technical aspects of the use of computers in education but, whatever technology is used, it needs to be based on sound pedagogical principles for it to be viable and useful.

Richard Overbaugh (1994) developed a practical set of guidelines that may be used in the development of courseware, or CAL, based on Gagné's nine events of learning (1975) in order to provide a structure for educators designing CAL packages. He suggested that these guidelines will provide a sound framework for the design of courseware and, although many of the points are not exclusively applicable to CAL, the emphasis is on their application on computer-based teaching. The first section, instructional design, is described in Table 5.2.

TABLE 5.2 The steps in instructional design as outlined by Overbaugh

Domain (Overbaugh)	Gagné's event	
Instructional set	Gaining attention	Title screen Highlights the purpose of the lesson and its importance Instructions
	Orientating activities	Objectives Overview Motivating Relevant pre-questions to activate prior learning
	Stimulating recall of prior learning and supplying missing prerequisites	Try to bring all users to same level before they begin Use of assessment to activate prior learning
Teaching strategies	Presenting stimuli with distinctive features	New material presented Designed to be understandable and simple Concrete Relevant Use of graphics and text to keep students' attention Effective use of colour
	Providing learning guidance	Presenting user with a sequence of information to guide them through the initial concept Elaboration Inquiry learning Discovery learning
	Enhancing retention and learning transfer	Opportunity to practise Application of learning Varied practise Review Synthesis
Student performance	Eliciting performance and assessing performance	Practice of learnt tasks Conditions close to real world application Demands within students' reach Reliable and valid assessment
	Providing feedback	Information to students about their learning Correct/incorrect Explanations Correction of errors Timely
Other design issues	Learner control	Students can sequence learning according to their learning priorities Choice over sequence also results in more positive attitudes to the software More able students can work through the content more quickly
	Teaching tools	Cueing: use of colour, highlighting, arrows etc. draws attention to important points Software can be personalised with names, background information and students' interests to engage user (novelty can wear off)
(Further stages)		**Software needs to be designed in detail (flowcharts) and programmed**

Source: Overbaugh (1994).

After following the guidelines in this table, the creator of the software needs to work through pre-programming development and the actual programming. Pre-programming development consists of the creation of flowcharts for the software structure, storyboards and supporting materials. Finally, the programming stage is completed by the designer and programmer working closely together on a draft program and subsequent revisions.

The creative use of available software

It can be very easy to create complicated solutions in e-learning when it would be possible to use more common tools more effectively and efficiently. Software that can be used in the creation and implementation of e-learning can be very expensive and also costly in the time it takes to set up, write and test a system. Therefore, in order to make the best use of the resources that are available, it is important to weigh up the pros and cons of different approaches, taking this time into account.

Tools such as Microsoft Office that are readily available to most teaching staff can be put to very good use. The software available within the Office suite can be both used to create effective learning resources for students and used by students in their learning, and these options should not be overlooked when exploring ways for students to work with computers. Excel or Access may be used to create computer models for students to work with and this may give them the opportunity to work with real data while simultaneously gaining important transferable skills with these packages.

Mind mapping software is another example of software than can be cheaply, or even freely, acquired and used creatively in the classroom. This software enables student to work on their own ideas by drawing flowcharts and diagrams of their ideas and then let them evolve clearly without the mess that can be created by continually changing ideas on paper. Groups of students can also work on the same maps or combine maps to produce group work.

Authorware

If we are to move on to professional CAL production software then *Authorware* is the classic CAL production tool. This software became the first industry standard in CAL production in the late 1980s and is still in use, although it has been largely superseded by Adobe *Flash* and *Director*. Originally it was designed so that anybody could start creating resources but as it evolved it became more complicated and the creation of packages became more of a specialised task. Teaching resources are created by assembling a flow diagram of possible routes that the user may take through the package; each node can represent a screen, piece of music, graphic and so on. Interactions with the user are also built in along this route. One major advantage of this system is that the package can easily and naturally be designed around decisions and branching so that a non-linear package is created. In fact, this was a core aspect of the software when it was created by Dr Michael Allen, as he said that he hated passive page-turning.

Aside from its complexity, a major downside to the Authorware creation software is its cost. A copy in 2007 cost just under £2,500 (although this could be considered a bargain compared with the £8,000 that version 1 cost in 1992). It is also quite limited in its flexibility compared with similar products such as Flash and Director, as very little scripting is possible. Scripting enables a programmer to control the finer details of a package and, if the expertise is there, means there is a lot more control of the final result available.

Flash

Although both are now supplied by the American software company Adobe, *Flash* offers an alternative to Authorware. Based on a product called *SmartSketch* created in 1993, it became Flash in 1996. It was written as a means to create animations for the web that would be fast to download and it seems to have fulfilled that role as it has gone from strength to strength ever since. Although it doesn't offer the 'easy' flowchart interface of Authorware it has a huge amount of flexibility for the creation of CAL packages. The software is built around a 'stage' onto which the programmer can place images, sound and video. Computer script can then be added to the items so that the user can interact with them in many ways, from a simple button to move to a new screen to a computer model of a heart beating.

This ability to model real world scenarios in a multimedia format is an excellent learning tool for the user. A computer model reacting realistically to the user's actions can provide them with intrinsic feedback that is the natural consequences of an action, such as seeing a heart beat faster as a drug is administered. This is superior to extrinsic feedback; for example, an external comment such as a text description of what will happen (Laurillard 2002).

Constructivist approaches and 'serious games'

In an attempt to move away from a didactic approach to teaching and learning, many constructivist approaches are emerging within the field of e-learning. Software packages that allow the user to explore a scenario or experiment with parameters and come to their own conclusions fit well within Diane Laurillard's intrinsic feedback paradigm as they provide the user with a realistic scenario that reacts in a similar way to the real world, which it is recreating, but in a safer, more guided manner.

A clear example of this is in medical education. Dummies and computer-based simulations allow the student to perform various investigations, try treatment options and see the effect of their choices but the 'patient' feels no discomfort and is still there for their next attempt. The amount of feedback to the student can be varied in any simulation to suit the learning needs: a beginner may be taken through a complex scenario with step-by-step help or a competent user may be left to make their own decisions entirely.

An example of this type of approach is the *Alice 2.0* software[1] produced by Carnegie–Mellon University in Pittsburgh, USA. This free software is designed to help students who are new to computer programming. It removes the need for students to type precise, syntactically correct commands to produce a functional piece of software that performs an often abstract task. Instead students select commands from a list of options on the lower part of the screen to move cartoon characters in a virtual world that they can see at the top of their screen. This approach enables them to play with the various parts and structure of a computer program and immediately see the effects. While experimenting with building blocks that are common to many programming languages, the user is hopefully building an awareness of how they work, without getting held back by mistyped commands and missing brackets in the code. Students who have started a programming course with Alice still have a steep learning curve when they do their first 'real' programming but at least they have by that point acquired the concepts and language to discuss the problems they are having and an awareness of the part of the program that may not be working correctly.

Serious games provide a similar structured yet flexible approach to learning. Games such as *Peacemaker* challenge the student to bring peace to the Middle East. This is a tall order, but the game guides the user through the various issues and viewpoints from each side in the conflict as they take the part of either the Israeli prime minister or the Palestinian president. Whether the student solves the problem or not is not the aim, rather that they grasp some key aspects of the scenario along the way. Supporters of these games argue that they allow learners to immerse themselves in an engaging environment and to develop higher-order skills, especially in games that allow the user to interact with other players in a virtual world.

There is only space here to give this very brief, and by no means exhaustive, overview of CAL. Hopefully it gives the reader an insight into what may be possible and how this technology may be implemented. One thing that may be clear is that computer-aided learning covers a wide range of possible uses for computers in education. However, one thing that all the above examples (with the possible exception of Alice 2.0) have in common is that they all contain content that is created by the designers and programmers of the software and systems.

One direction that e-learning is taking recently is in parallel to changes on the Internet in general, where the user creates the content. This is what we will cover in the next section of this chapter.

[1] Available from www.alice.org.

e-Learning 2.0

'Web 2.0' has become a controversial buzzword over the past couple of years regarding the Internet, and even those people who agree that it represents something new on the Internet can't necessarily agree what exactly Web 2.0 means. The term was coined in 2004 to cover the new applications and sites appearing on the Internet after the dot-com bubble burst in late 2001 (O'Reilly 2005).[2] A group of web pioneers noticed that even after many sites crashed and burned in 2001 a lot of sites were still standing very strong and they seemed to have things in common. Whether Web 2.0 does represent a change in web architecture or not, or in fact whether it does exist or not, there is certainly an evolution under way in the way the World Wide Web is being used, even if there is no revolution.

In the past, the contents of websites were controlled by the creators of those sites, and similarly the contents of teaching packages, such as those above, were created by the teacher or lecturer. Now students have the opportunities to discuss their work and create material collaboratively. Many sites that have been successful over the past few years have content that is created by the users of the sites, rather than by the designers. The designers of these sites set up the architecture and mechanisms that enable users to contribute and then let the users step in. Once the sites reach a critical mass of users the content can become very rich. Examples sites include *Wikipedia*, an encyclopaedia that anybody can edit, *MySpace*, *Facebook* and *Livejournal*, where, rather than creating individual home pages, users can network and create groups based on shared interests, *del.icio.us* for creating, sharing and searching web bookmarks, and *Google Docs* and *Spreadsheets*, where users can collaboratively produce documents over the web and, the more people that work on a site or project, the better it becomes.

Wikis

A wiki is a website that allows anybody visiting the site to add content, remove content or edit the content that is already on the page. Some wiki sites track who is making the changes and require people to log in and identify themselves, but others allow anonymous editing. The most famous wiki is probably Wikipedia, the online encyclopaedia that anybody can edit, should they disagree with or wish to add to an entry. There are mechanisms in place (such as the monitoring for large edits) to prevent the site falling apart through abuse but there is still the possibility that small changes can be made and these may slip through the net for some time. There have been reports in the media that its accuracy is not as high as it could be but other research has shown the accuracy to be not very different from the *Encyclopaedia Britannica* (Giles 2005). Its breadth of information and the speed at which information is updated are where Wikipedia really has its strengths,

---

[2] The dot-com crash refers to the sudden and nearly simultaneous demise in 2001 of a large number of web-based companies.

but if Wikipedia is going to be used by students they need to be made aware of its strengths and weaknesses.

Wikis may be used by students for collaborative work, and working online may enable less confident students to be involved. All users may contribute to a single piece of work by sharing contributions and peer reviewing. The peer reviews may be printed and kept as a finished piece of work. The audit trail left by the software can be useful in identifying which students are having difficulties and to confirm that all the users have contributed.

Blogs

A blog (originally called a web log) is a commentary on the writer's interests, activities and viewpoints, usually displayed with the most recent entry first. Many blogging communities, such as Livejournal and Eduspaces, provide mechanisms for bloggers to read other bloggers' entries and to comment on them, creating a community of users. Google reports over 790 million blogs in existence worldwide in May 2007, though how many of these are active is unknown.

Blogs may be used by students to keep a diary of their learning and to share problems with their peers, creating a social portfolio of their work and developing a community of practice (Wenger 1998). Seeing other students struggle with the same concepts can also help learning. It is a less formal medium than an essay and usually offers a very personal viewpoint. A number of tools are also available for students to access others' blogs on topics of interest. Also, similarly to wikis, the subjective nature of this medium needs to be emphasised to students.

Despite their popularity, resistance by students to use blogs in education has been reported. This may because they are seen as education encroaching on their personal lives rather than the experience of their personal lives being brought to their education. They may also blog in their own time and may not want the 'split personality' of two personas online.

Podcasts

Podcasts are digital media files that are distributed over the Internet. Users can subscribe to the cast using syndication feeds (see the RSS section below). The video or audio files can contain teaching materials such as lectures, interviews with experts or any other useful learning content. Once the student has subscribed to the feed they will be made aware of any new content automatically.

RSS

Really Simple Syndication (RSS) allows users to subscribe to a page, blog or podcast. Only one source address needs to be saved for each subscription and then the content is then pushed out to the subscriber. This contrasts to the pull approach as a user finds their content on a website of their own volition. This feed of information allows blogs to pull in information from other blogs and news from a number of sources to be aggregated. This aggregation of small pieces of information is analogous to the collection of small edits in Wikipedia forming an informed encyclopaedic resource. The idea that most of the web is made up of many small contributions and that a robust resource can be created by many minds working on a project is known as the *Long Tail* of the web.

As well as offering content created by their users, these sites share a number of other features and many of these are a means to exploit this collective work. *Folksonomy* is a term used to describe the 'tagging' of material by its users. Tagging involves attaching keywords to web content, rather than categorising it. It allows groups of content to be formed in an overlapping manner, in a similar manner to the way in which the brain has been shown to associate concepts and it allows users to create their own categories of web bookmarks (del.icio.us), photographs (Flickr) or blog entries (Livejournal). The use of these resources reflects a constructivist approach, as the users create their own dialogue with themselves and others as they learn, mark up and categorise material using their own taxonomies. By collaboration, these different experiences and approaches can be shared to produce a collective experience and body of learning.

But what can this offer education? This approach, in which the user creates the content, contrasts with the previous section and 'traditional' CAL, in which it is assumed that the creator of any resource is the expert and the content is static. An alternative approach to this method is one in which only the infrastructure is created by a technologist and then the students are left relatively free to explore the problem space and develop solutions. This approach does not free up any developer time, as creating a flexible yet robust system that has all the features that the users will need will take time to develop, but it allows a flexibility that is not possible with 'fixed' CAL and creates a system that may be used in a variety of ways.

> To absorb facts is only of slight value in the present and usually of less value in the future. Learning how to learn is the element that is always of value, now and in the future.
>
> (Rogers 1983: 18)

With such an approach the users become the experts and the experts become the facilitators. These learner-generated contexts shift the control of the learning to the user and are certainly not new in the fields of education. They are, however, relatively new in the field of e-learning and represent a shift from the application of pedagogy to andragogy and possibly heutagogy. Andragogy is defined as the art of allowing students to direct their own learning by motivating them to explore a topic in a way that is relevant to themselves. In addition, heutagogy is where this topic itself is also determined by the students. This content can then be pushed out and shared with others for collaborate work and communicated with others using services such as instant messaging.

It should be noted that, although Web 2.0 has influenced this shift in e-learning, this is not a totally new approach to the use of technology in education. In the 1960s Joseph Licklider saw the potential of networked computers connecting people to enable them to exchange knowledge and information and increase their ability to learn.

Pre-dating the Web 2.0 revolution, Terry Mayes and colleagues at Glasgow Caledonian University described using computers to enable students to learn from one another (Mayes *et al*. 2001). New tools that are emerging onto the World Wide Web would apply nicely to the 'dissemination' system that Mayes and his colleagues created. This project was based on Bandura's 'vicarious learning' (Mayes *et al*. 2001), in which students learn by observing the others undergoing the process of learning themselves. A computer-based system stored the previous work of students so that future students could observe the previous learning experience of others and learn from it themselves. Students could see others struggling with the same concepts as they and learn from this. Mayes and colleagues did not want to replace traditional face-to-face tutorials but thought this approach could be a useful way of dealing with large student numbers or distance learning.

Mayes *et al*.'s technique was to record previous dialogues, in video, audio and text, and then to present these to subsequent students in a static form. They saw the original group, which was being recorded, develop a strong social bond and deep levels of learning, which were passed on to the following students. Students who reviewed the previous learning experiences showed more understanding, made more use of critical evaluations and justification for their views, and derived more of their own conclusions. However, in this context it would be difficult to facilitate the online discussions year after year for the students and to archive this in a non-labour-intensive manner. Maybe this is something new blogging and wiki-based technology could aid, with the archiving of older material more automatically.

A move away from a CAL approach to a more constructivist one is also supported by research by Michelene Chi (Chi *et al*. 2001). In a comparison of a didactic style of tutoring, in which tutors explained concepts to students, and a more interactive, Socratic, approach, in which they were kept from giving any explanations or feedback, the students learnt just as much with the interactive approach but their understanding seemed to be deeper and the result of them taking more control of their own learning. They suggest that active learning, when students interpret new material in the context of prior knowledge, can be accomplished by making inferences, elaborating the material by adding details, and integrating materials. More complex or deeper forms of construction might be forming hypotheses and justifications; reflecting, summarizing, and predicting; justifying, criticizing, and exploring; or revising one's existing knowledge.

(Chi *et al.* 2001: 477).

These are just the processes that blogs and wikis can support as they enable students to reflect on their own learning, read the reflection of others and collaborate, with the facilitation of a tutor, on a joint piece of work. In their conclusion the authors go on to suggest that, since construction from interaction is so important in learning, computer-based tutoring systems should implement ways to elicit students' constructivist responses, possibly by scaffolding their learning. They say this may be difficult because a tutoring system will not be able to understand the students' remarks; however, using the computer system only as an infrastructure, with the scaffolding provided by other students or a tutor, may be a solution.

We have focused so far on web-based constructivist approaches to learning but we need not restrict ourselves in this way. Kimber, Pillay and Richards (2007) reported that students collaborating by creating their own concept maps learnt a great deal from this process. They state that students can be 'learning with technology', focusing on the cognitive and social aspects of using technology in the classroom and through this developing a deeper understanding of their subjects, and had become 'creators of knowledge and not mere consumers of information.'

A change in e-learning may have been seen since the emergence of Web 2.0 but that does not restrict us to using only the World Wide Web to benefit from these concepts. Even though we have divided this chapter into two clear headings this dichotomy is not as strong as this would suggest and there is always the possibility of using older tools in new ways.

The importance of an implementation strategy

Whatever type of e-learning is employed, it is vital that a suitable strategy for its introduction and development is employed. Leading with the technology and fitting the teaching around it is not the way to develop a successful system. The learning needs of the students should always come first but it is all too common to speak to somebody who has seen a new 'gadget' that they wish to use, without any firm consideration being paid to the pedagogy.

All of these systems have the potential to be very costly to produce or implement; therefore, as a piece of software is designed, it is important to bear in mind what costs are involved and to weigh these up against the usefulness of the software.

If there is a simple, pedagogically sound, solution then this is the best outcome. This may be something as simple as a free wiki or a cleverly designed PowerPoint file. It is the affordances[3] that a particular system can offer that are the crucial part. Once a shortlist of systems that can support the pedagogy has been made, then the simplest, fastest and cheapest on the list is probably the best choice.

Of course there will be times when a new piece of technology may inspire new ideas for teaching online, but this must always be kept in perspective and assessed against the alternatives to ensure that it really is of benefit and not just a novelty. Many commercial companies will spend large amounts of money marketing their software to academic institutions, to convince them that their money will buy a new opportunity for their students. However, the teaching staff may be more than happy with the systems they have currently and the technology will be resisted. This same teaching staff may have needs that need supporting, if the right technology can be found. Success will be found when these two strategies can be matched.

Alongside analysis of how a particular type of e-learning may help a cohort of students it is also unavoidably necessary to consider the costs that will be involved. It is very easy to underestimate the necessary development costs for a project. Things inevitably take far longer to produce than predicted; however, once some software has been produced there is usually negligible further cost in its use, so it may be used repeatedly. This needs to be considered, along with a strategy to keep the resource up to date, to keep its shelf life as long as possible.

Besides the financial efficiency of a choice, the cognitive efficiency may also be considered. There may be alternative methods for presenting information and teaching a subject, yet some may convey information much more efficiently for the students (Cobb 1997). For example, a video showing how to set up some equipment may take 2 minutes, yet a text description of this same process may take 15 minutes to read even if the teaching effect is the same.

Any technology that is used needs to be embedded in a curriculum and the learning context if it is to succeed. Laurillard claims that the reason so many technologies come and go can be attributed to a lack of organisational context, rather than the inferior qualities of teaching they offer, as many other poor-quality teaching methods remain, purely because they fit the context well and are thoroughly embedded into the teaching systems (Laurillard 2002). It may also be found that once students know of a resource's existence they will return to it in their own time, for revision or clarification, and tell others if they find it useful. In fact, students who are given the option to work through more examples of their own volition will often do far more work than when it is prescribed (Laurillard 2002).

---

[3] According to Wikipedia, an *affordance* is an action that an individual can potentially perform in their environment. See http://en.wikipedia.org/wiki/Affordance.

Furthermore, Keller and Cernerud (2002) found when they researched students' perceptions of e-learning that the strategy used to implement the system was more important than any of the background factors with respect to the students, such as age, gender, experience with computers, attitudes towards computers and learning style. Of two schools, the one with a more consistent, stable and familiar web platform and clear goals for the implementation of e-learning involving both students and teachers had much more favourable feedback from students than the one with a less consistent approach and no overall goals.

A further framework for the successful implementation of an online teaching and learning system is Gilly Salmon's 'E-tivities' (Salmon 2004). E-tivities are described as 'frameworks for online active and interactive learning.' The framework applies most closely to online discussion groups, as it was the use of these in the Open University that prompted the original research, but the five steps described in the book can equally applied to any other social, online learning activity. The stages are as follows:

1   Access and Motivation: this stage consists of helping users overcome technical difficulties and overcoming their apprehension with new technology and new people.
2   Socialisation: an online community is created through 'active and interactive e-tivities'. Users start to share thoughts and work and the moderators help people to build connections between the users.
3   Information Exchange: co-operative tasks are achieved and people interact with each other and the moderator(s) to perform these tasks.
4   Knowledge Construction: participants start to construct knowledge in their own ways. At this stage moderators help to build and keep groups going by controlling the group dynamics.
5   Development: participants take control of the group and are responsible for their own learning. Users no longer need to think about how they are going to work online and they become creative.

Salmon creates a very structured set of guidelines for moderators at each stage of the model in order for them to get the best results in their online teaching; this is a very useful guide for anyone wanting to use a discussion board. Much of the advice will also apply equally well to any group activity using blogs and wikis, and failure to support students through their experience online may create a scenario in which the technology is getting in the way of, and even preventing, the learning. Students cannot choose to understand; they can only choose to concentrate hard and try to understand (Laurillard 2002). It is up to the moderators and designers of these systems to enable learning.

Conclusion

The use of e-learning is not going to revolutionise education on its own. Even if these new technologies are absorbed into current teaching methods and become everyday practice they are not going to change the experiences of the average student beyond recognition, no matter what the vendors and creators of software may tell us. What we will see is a change in education that mirrors the changes that are happening in the way people communicate and think about information when they are not studying. Many tools are becoming available that can augment and supplement teaching and education in very valuable ways. These can enhance the experiences of students and teachers and offer new choices for teaching in the same ways that new methods of communications via the Internet have offered new ways for us to keep in touch with our family and friends even though these relationships have not essentially changed.

In the early 1990s, 'multimedia' become the buzzword for new technologies and this was also used in the context of education. Now that this buzz has decreased, the use of video, DVD and CD-ROMs is no longer seen as a separate and 'special' part of teaching. In the same way 'e-learning' will eventually become 'learning' and we will no longer differentiate what material is learned using a computer in the same way that we don't differentiate what is learned using books. For the foreseeable future, at least, technology will continue to develop and educationalists will carry on trying out and applying this new technology to the teaching of students in new ways. However, we are yet to see a huge paradigm shift in education as a whole. Changes in the World Wide Web towards Web 2.0 and, in parallel, the new technologies of e-Learning 2.0 probably currently offer the closest we have to this large change as they move away from an expert–student classroom model but they still make up a small part of the e-learning seen in schools and universities. A change may still come but there is yet to be any convincing evidence that old methods are to be replaced by new, apart from in small areas of curricula.

In an enthusiasm to embrace these new technologies it can be easy to exploit these new technologies for their own sake and novelty value. Although the use of something new can be motivating, caution needs to be exercised to make sure that these new tools are not used for their own sake. That said, there are gains to be made in the use of e-learning and, as the introduction to this chapter illustrates, if the teaching methods we use do not keep pace with our learners then we risk losing some along the way and missing out on the opportunities that new technologies may offer us. It is important that new ideas are explored and evaluated and allowed to grow into more mature ideas, as they no doubt will.

There is plenty of scope for innovation that is grounded in sound pedagogy, such as the Alice project and the work of *Futurelab*,[4] and the application of technology to pedagogic principles rather than vice versa can produce very interesting results.

[4] See www.futurelab.org.uk.

Furthermore, this often also results in more innovative projects as course materials are not simply plugged into existing software.

Hopefully, after studying this chapter, the reader will have a clearer view of some of the current issues in e-learning and feel more confident in assessing and trying out some of these ideas in their own studies or teaching. It can be a very interesting and dynamic field of study.

Suggested further reading

For background, Clark (1994) is a useful place to start. Clark and Mayer (2003) is an effective guide for those thinking about the best ways to create teaching packages and is an excellent practical resource, as are Salmon (2004) and Laurillard (2002).

In order to keep pace with the changes in this field two journals are a very useful resource for current trends and practice. These are:

ALT-J: The journal for the Association for Learning Technology. This is available in print, and online at www.alt.ac.uk/alt_j.html.

Computers and Education: Again, available in print, or online via Elsevier at www.elsevier.com.

References

Bingham, A. and Yanaske, E. (2006) 'Mismatched Expectations of Staff and Students towards Blackboard', in *Proceedings of ALT-C,* Association of Learning Technology Conference, Edinburgh, UK.

Blin, F. and Munro, M. (2007) 'Why hasn't Technology Disrupted Academics' Teaching Practices? Understanding Resistance to Change through the Lens of Activity Theory', Presentation at CAL'07 Conference, Dublin.

Chi, M. T. H., Siler, S. A., Jeong, H., Yamauchi, T. and Hausman, R. G. (2001) 'Learning from Human Tutoring', *Cognitive Science.* **25** (1), 471–533.

Clark, R. (1994) 'Media will Never Influence Learning', *Educational Technology Research and Development.* **42** (2), 21–29.

Clark, R. C. and Mayer, R. E. (2003) *e-Learning and the Science of Instruction*. San Francisco, CA: Pfeiffer.

Cobb, T. (1997) 'Cognitive Efficiency: Toward a Revised Theory of Media', *Educational Technology Research and Development.* **45** (4), 21–35.

Downes, S. (2005) *E-learning 2.0*. Available from www.elearnmag.org/subpage.cfm?section=articles &article=29-1 (retrieved 22 May 2007).

Gagné, R. M. (1975) *Essentials of Learning for Instruction*. New York: Holt, Rinehart and Winston.

Garrett, R. (2004) 'The Real Story behind the Failure of the U.K. eUniversity', *Educause Quarterly*. **27** (4), 4–6.

Giles, J. (2005) 'Internet Encyclopaedias Go Head to Head', *Nature*. **438**, 900–901.

Glover, D. and Miller, D. (2001) 'Running with Technology: The Pedagogic Impact of the Large-Scale Introduction of Interactive Whiteboards in One Secondary School', *Technology, Pedagogy and Education*. **10** (3), 257–278.

HEFCE (2005) *HEFCE Strategy for E-Learning 2005/12*. Bristol: Higher Education Funding Council for England (HEFCE). Available from www.hefce.ac.uk/pubs/hefce/2005/05_12/ (retrieved 24 January 2008).

Iredale, A. (2006) 'Successful Learning or Failing Premise? A Situated Evaluation of a Virtual Learning Environment', in *Proceedings of ALT-C*, Association of Learning Technology Conference, Edinburgh, UK.

Jukes, I. and Dosaj, A. (2003) *What causes this disconnect?* Available from www.apple.com/au/education/digitalkids/disconnect/landscape.html (retrieved 22 May 2007).

Keller, C. and Cernerud, L. (2002) 'Students' Perceptions of e-Learning in University Education', *Journal of Educational Media*. **27** (1–2), 55–67.

Kimber, K., Pillay, H. and Richards, C. (2007) 'Technoliteracy and Learning: An Analysis of the Quality of Knowledge in Electronic Representations of Understanding', *Computers and Education*. **48**, 59–79.

Laurillard, D. (2002) *Rethinking University Teaching: A Framework for the Effective Use of Learning Technology*, 2nd edn. London: RoutledgeFalmer.

Mayes, J. T., Dineen, F., McKendree, J. and Lee, J. (2001) 'Learning from Watching Others Learn', in Steeples, C. and Jones, C. (eds) *Networked Learning: Perspectives and Issues*. London: Springer.

Miller, D. and Glover, D. (2002) 'The Interactive Whiteboard as a Force for Pedagogic Change: The Experience of Five Elementary Schools in an English Education Authority', *Information Technology in Childhood Education Annual*. **2002**, 5–19.

O'Reilly, T. (2005) *What is Web 2.0: Design Patterns and Business Models for the Next Generation of Software*. Available from http://oreillynet.com/pub/a/oreilly/news/2005/09/30/what-is-web-20.html (retrieved 16 May 2007).

Overbaugh, R. C. (1994) 'Research Based Guidelines for Computer-Based Instruction Development', *Journal of Research on Computing in Education*. **27** (1), 29–48.

Rogers, C. (1983) *Freedom to Learn for the 80s*. New York: Macmillan.

Salmon, G. (2004) *E-tivities: The Key to Active Online Learning*. London: RoutledgeFalmer.

Shoffner, M. B., Jones, M. and Harmon, S. W. (2000) 'Implications of New and Emerging Technologies for Learning and Cognition', *Journal of Electronic Publishing*. **6** (1). Available from www.press.umich.edu/jep/06-01/shoffner.html (retrieved 26 November 2007).

Wenger, E. (1998) *Communities of Practice: Learning, Meaning, and Identity*. Cambridge: Cambridge University Press.

6

'Race' and education

John Stanley

'Please. Do me this one, great favour, Jones. If ever you hear anyone, when you are back home . . . speak of the East,' and here his voice plummeted a register, and the tone was full and sad, '*hold your* judgment. If you are told "they are all this" or "they do this" or "their opinions are these", withhold your judgment until all the facts are upon you. Because that land they call "India" goes by a thousand names and is populated by millions, and if you think you have found two men the same among that multitude, then you are mistaken. It is merely a trick of the moonlight.'

(Zadie Smith 2000)

Introduction

SINCE THE EDUCATION ACT of 1944, a major concern for education has been with pursuing social justice, improving life chances for all children and enriching their lives. Studies on inequalities in education have revealed forms of discrimination at all levels of the education system, indicating that the desired improvement and enrichment of children's lives has not been fairly distributed. Social class and 'race' are factors that, in combination, influence educational outcomes for all children. The chapter on 'Social Class and School', which follows, shows the prevailing influence children's social class origins tend to have on their educational achievement. 'Race' is another category used to explain educational inequality, though education is only one of a number sectors where 'race' is seen to be influential; it is, of course, an important social and political issue across the modern, globalised world. To start with, one might see 'race' as a broad social phenomenon, which carries an overbearing presence in all modern societies, like the UK, that are structured along racial lines. To understand the phenomenon of 'race' in the context of education requires an appreciation of its meaning in the discourse of social relations. It is also important to be clear what is meant by the related concept of ethnicity. Aiming for a working definition of 'race' in a field where there is still considerable debate and disagreement has its pitfalls, as Cornell and Hartmann point out:

we have to wrestle with the definition of race . . . it is common in contemporary society to talk about races, race relations and racial conflict as if we had a clear idea of what constitutes a race and where the boundary falls between one race and another. Race, however, is as slippery a concept as ethnic group.

(Cornell and Hartmann 1998: 21)

'Race' generally refers to physical characteristics of people so that skin, hair colour and physique are supposed to confirm the 'race' to which people belong. Further genetic differences between people are also used to confirm racial origins. The concept of 'race' is thus used to identify a group of people having a common ancestry. Scientific evidence does, however, make the case for there being no such thing as 'race' in the sense that humans come from different species. Social scientists have argued that 'race' is used to promote cultural stereotypes that are simplistic, malevolent and inaccurate.

The concept of the ethnic group has a slightly less pernicious impact where it is used to relate to cultural practices and identity. However, it is used to focus on people's values, traditions and practices, and the danger of indiscriminate grouping, together with a state of stasis, can misrepresent the values and practices of those people consigned to an ethnic group.

'Race' – origins and definitions

Although ideas about race can be traced back through ancient history, the categorisation of people based on the modern idea of 'race' became common in the late eighteenth and early nineteenth centuries. The acts which supported the doctrine of race were seen in the enslavement of millions of African peoples and their transportation as slave labour to the Americas. Equally, the European exploration, colonisation and imperial domination of much of the world stimulated and reaffirmed racial ideas about the inferiority of black Africans and the association of certain forms of behaviour with particular racial groups. The idea that different groups of people have different natures and that there is a clear line of distinction between them became generally accepted.

What are often called scare quotes are generally used with the word 'race'. As was shown in the previous section, this action indicates that there are some fundamental conceptual problems connected with the use of this word. The term has been used to categorise different groups of people across the globe using physical/genetic features, e.g. skin, hair, physique, facial features, and subsequently to make assumptions about their characteristics and behaviour. Such a connection is false, although a case has been made by some commentators who claim that intelligence is determined by genetics and that the low educational achievement of black pupils is due to lower, inherited intelligence. The assertions of Jensen (1969, 1973) in the USA, and Eysenck (1971) in the UK, were subjected to intense criticism, and the myth was exploded when the unreliability of the data was established.

Kamin (1977) and Mabey (1981) have convincingly repudiated the work on genetic influence. A more recently argued case supporting Eysenck and Jensen is found in Herrnstein and Murray's (1994) book, *The Bell Curve*, which claims that black people are genetically inferior to white people because of lower IQs. Once more the weakness of the research procedures and processes, to say nothing of the inadequacy of the conceptualisation of the research problem, meant the case fell apart. Science suggests that there is not a species-type difference between peoples. 'Race' is not a social category that can identify groups of people, relying on their physical appearance to predict characteristics, behaviour and educational achievement (see Nei and Roychoudhury 1983). Indeed, there are strong and reliable claims that genetic variability is found between individuals generally, and not between the so-called different 'races'. Classifying people into 'races' is a social product rather than a biological reality. The continuing development of the science of genetics seems likely further to confirm the unreliability of the concept of 'race'.

> Here we have a concept which refers to a false perception: that the only legitimate use of the term 'race' is as a device for recognising that people categorise and behave differently towards one another on the basis of and significance attached to physiological differences, not the physiological differences themselves.
>
> (Foster *et al.* 1996: 51–52)

However, even after establishing that the category of 'race' is invalid, that it has no scientific basis, the problem that it engenders does not disappear. The designation of inferiority that goes with the term 'race' serves to rationalise people's social position, achievements and treatment. Denying its validity will not remove it from the discourse of people and institutions. Even where it is denied, it has tended to be replaced by an equally difficult concept, namely ethnicity. The contemporary tendency has been to refer to a person's ethnicity rather than 'race'. This can result in the production of cultural stereotypes which mislead, over-simplify, categorise and, again, result in injustice. Reference to the ethnic origins of people from minority groups leads to a reification of ethnic categories, and promotes an ethnic absolutism that often refers to extended kinship groups residing in another part of the world, or else to static cultures. The emphasis is still on difference between groups of people and the danger is that the connotations about the specificity of human groups carried in the notion of 'race' are reconfigured under the label of ethnicity.

> We should never forget that 'race' is not a spontaneously given product of perception and experience. It is an idea built up (and slowly at that) from elements which equally well might be physical traits as social customs, linguistic peculiarities as legal institutions, lumped together and homogenised according to the precepts that they must ultimately all be biological phenomena.
>
> (Guillaumin 1995)

107

So far the discussion has focussed on 'race' at a mainly abstract level. The intention now is to begin to examine some important aspects of 'race' in the context of education.

National statistics – minority ethnic population

A useful means of understanding what is meant by the term 'ethnic minority group' is to know which are the principal ethnic minority groups in the UK. The Office of National Statistics (1996) has as principal ethnic minority groups in the UK: Black Caribbean, Black African, Black other, Indian, Pakistani, Bangladeshi. These groups make up 80 per cent of the minority ethnic population of the United Kingdom.

Pathak (2000) provides useful information to fill 'a range of gaps' on information about 'race'/ethnicity. The paper uses evidence from research, statistics and evaluation studies to define the place of different ethnic groups in education, training and the labour market.

- Ethnic minorities make up 6.6 per cent of the working age population in the UK, i.e. 2.3 million. Some 6.5 per cent of the UK population comes from a minority ethnic group.

- Indian is the largest minority ethnic group, followed by Pakistani and Black Caribbean.

- The minority ethnic population has a much younger age structure than the white population. In state schools 11 per cent of pupils are ethnic minority.

- Minority group people live mainly in the major cities of the UK, e.g. half live in Greater London.

- Over 40 per cent of Bangladeshi people live in Inner London. Overall, Bangladeshis live in the most deprived wards, followed by a smaller proportion of Pakistanis and Black Caribbeans.

- Indians live in areas of greater deprivation than African Asians.

- On entry into pre-school, children of white UK heritage have the highest mean score in cognitive skills (verbal and non-verbal), with the lowest scores being recorded for Pakistani children. Differences in scores between ethnic groups are reduced when factors such as parents' educational and occupational status is taken account of.

- Bangladeshi, Black and Pakistani pupils perform less well than other pupils in the early key stages. Pupils from these three ethnic groups also tend to achieve significantly less well by the end of compulsory education.

- Staying on in full-time education after compulsory schooling is more common among ethnic minority people (over 85 per cent) than white people (67 per cent). However, a higher proportion of young white people are in full-time employment (10 per cent) and government supported training (12 per cent) than their ethnic minority peers (3 per cent in full-time; 4 per cent government funded training).

- Ethnic minorities as a whole are over-represented in higher education; they make up 13 per cent of undergraduate students.

- Ethnic minority students are disproportionately studying at the new (post-1992) universities. White working-class students have a similar experience.

- Thirty-seven per cent of ethnic minority students get a first or upper second class degree compared with 53 per cent white graduates.

(derived from Pathak 2000)

The Pathak study presents a wide range of information on minority ethnic group educational achievements at varying levels. A study that gives a more focused picture of educational achievements is the ongoing research coming from the Centre for Longitudinal Studies at the University of London Institute of Education. The programme, called *The Millennium Cohort Study*, is tracking the progress of 15,500 boys and girls born between 2000 and 2002. The focus is on the child's early life, which is being strongly influenced by the social class, education and ethnic background of parents. The reform of pre-school opportunities in the UK by means of the *Sure Start* programme is not countering the effect of ethnic background on educational attainment. For example, the Bangladeshi children in the cohort are approximately one year behind white children in the tests on school readiness. Pakistani children are performing only marginally better. Turning to children of African and Caribbean backgrounds, a quarter are showing delayed development compared with 4 per cent of white children. A connection between social class and ethnic grouping is seen in results showing that two thirds of Bangladeshi and Pakistani 3-year-olds are from families living below the poverty line compared with 42 per cent of black children and fewer than 25 per cent of white and Indian children.

Operationalising the concepts of 'race' and education

One of the major difficulties in interpreting any kind of research is in understanding how the researcher is operationalising the concepts s/he is using. Two regular features of research into 'race' and education have been (1) the allocation of individuals into groups and (2) the issue of inequality in education. Research that investigates 'race'/ethnicity and education with this operationalisation of concepts will come up with evidence relating to achievement amongst different ethnic groups. A weakness of this work is that it has used simplistic categories, e.g. African-Caribbean, Asian, white British, other. An attempt to overcome the difficulty of operationalising 'race'/ethnicity by using a range of indicators, or by reference to self-categorisation, has been one way of trying to overcome the tendency to label whole groups of people who sometimes have little in common. A comparison of the achievements of black children with those of white children, for example, can provide misleading information. Similarly misleading is an investigation of the educational performance of pupils that does not take account of gender and social class. The indicators used to operationalise key concepts will determine in large measure what information is uncovered.

Ethnicity and difference

From the late 1980s, educators have tended to prefer to work with the notion of ethnic differences, and the Swann Report of 1985 gave support to and confirmation of teachers' choice of the concept of ethnicity. The social construct of 'race' leads to much disadvantage for some groups in society. The notion of 'race' is generally used in deprecating analyses of people's behaviour and potential, and where seemingly positive judgments are made they convey a mixed blessing – the association of black people with athletics and steel bands is dubious praise, since it carries with it the implication that academic achievement will not be very good.

By using the term *ethnicity*, instead of 'race', teachers feel that they are focusing on matters which directly affect education, namely identity and culture. The notion of 'new identities' (Hall 1988) and that of 'multiple identities' (Rex 1991) by focusing on the changing identities of people counters the stereotype of the homogenous ethnic group, but the idea of the changing identity should not take attention away from the need to challenge and get rid of racist behaviour and attitudes. There is the danger, however, that in ignoring 'race' teachers may be unaware of negative, unjust educational experiences that stem from prejudiced responses to skin or other physical features. Those negative educational experiences can involve violent behaviour and bullying as well as attitudes and practices based on racial differences.

Studies of 'race' discrimination in education have uncovered institutionalised racism as well as other processes responsible for producing or reproducing disadvantage. The term *ethnicity* then, though used by people with good intentions, and promoted enthusiastically in schools, can lead to a stereotyping of people by both anti-racists and racists. The danger lies in the assumption that tolerance will naturally be generated by knowledge of other cultures; this ignores the possibility that complex societies can be caricatured into neat, homogenous communities that defy reality. Second, it ignores the malignant nature of racism. Professed racists have been able to describe alien ways of life, by making reference to food, dress, family values and religion, as a threat to the long-established 'British way of life'. Barker (1981) claimed that racism had changed to an emphasis on cultural differences rather than inherited superiority. Racists now have two demons: the cultural and the biological. There is no doubt that focusing on differences between people can, even with the best of intentions, lead to a dangerous stereotyping of those whose lifestyles are being defined, and also to a potential misuse of information.

Difference can be used, particularly in political agendas, to promote exclusion and incite racist behaviour. Where there is, for instance, a shrinking labour market reducing job stability, extreme right-wing groups can exaggerate ethnic difference by claiming that the presence of ethnic minorities creates a threat to jobs and a social burden on the public budget. The activities of the British National Party and the support for the extreme right in France, Austria, Belgium and Holland in recent times are examples of the way that cultural difference is used to promote racist campaigns of hate and exclusion. Racism is thus developed with reference to ethnic difference. There is considerable intellectual support for this relativist position. It is seen first in the work of Nietzsche, and later the postmodernist/post-structuralist work of Lyotard, Foucault and Derrida. The problem with a relativist position is that it can deconstruct the principle of equality. Flecha (1999) provides a good example of this where the retention of the traditional identity and culture of the Gypsies is regarded as more important than that they should experience equality of opportunity in their lives.

> Gypsy cultures have frequently prevented female teenagers from attending school because their tradition includes a key family role for women that begins in adolescence. From the relativist position, one could argue that Gypsies should not be expected to adhere to the European concept of equal educational rights for men and women . . . Gender equality is presented as a European imposition rather than a basic human right . . . Such analyses focus on the negative aspects of schooling and ignore the positive ones . . . Gypsy women (can now) . . . use schooling to exercise a professional option formerly unobtainable . . . for relativists these educational opportunities are evidence of the destruction of Gypsy culture rather than of their evolution through change.
>
> (Flecha 1999: 161)

As educators seek to combat racism in their work, under whatever label it figures, it is worth recalling Guillaumin's (1995: 107) caution that, though scientists have shown that 'race' does not exist, 'millions of human beings have died as a result of their race, and millions of others are now dominated, excluded and repressed for the same reason'.

Research on 'race' and education

The race relations legislation of the 1970s made some impact at the institutional level in that it called for some official response, but it made little impact on the educational experiences of children, and so the 1980s produced numerous interpretive studies on schooling and 'race'/ethnicity, which studied a range of responses by pupils and teachers in multiracial and all-white schools.

Early research on educational achievement and minority ethnic group pupils is summarised in a review by Tomlinson (1980) of thirty-three studies of educational attainment of ethnic groups in schools. Twenty-six of these studies revealed African-Caribbean pupils were getting lower scores than white pupils on tests of performance. Moreover, the same defined group was over-represented in the category of 'Educationally Sub-Normal' and under-represented in the higher school classes. Among the findings of the Swann Report (DES 1985), looking at the educational attainments of most minority ethnic groups, was that racism, mainly unintentional, influenced under-achievement. The incidence of under-achievement was not so prevalent for some Asian groups, who were thought to experience the negative effects of stereotyping to a lesser degree than other groups. In the continuing search for explanations of minority group under-achievement, Smith and Tomlinson (1989) showed that investigations revealed school differences in educational achievements by minority group children. The various research teams argued that the differences stemmed not from differing abilities so much as different qualities of teaching and learning. Schools could make a difference to the educational achievement of pupils, whatever their ethnic origin.

As a result of research on pupil–pupil and pupil–teacher interactions (Wright 1986, 1992; Mac an Ghaill 1988; Gillborn 1990; Mirza 1992; Green 1985), the operationalization of the concept of 'race'/ethnicity changed its focus. Wright's (1986) classroom study found black boys and girls constructing an anti-school sub-culture as they reached the fourth and fifth years of schooling. Similarly, Mac an Ghaill (1988) and Fuller (1980, 1983) found that girls from ethnic minority groups, though they disliked school, used it to acquire much needed educational qualifications that would enable them to escape the double disadvantage of both 'race' and gender. Gillborn and Gipps (1996) examining research conducted in the 1970s, 1980s and 1990s found that teachers who expressed a commitment to equality were still likely to work with negative representations of African-Caribbean pupils.

What is evident in the foregoing studies is what is called institutional racism. Gillborn's (1990) study uses this notion and spells out the process clearly. He uses the idea of the 'ideal client', which teachers apply to their pupils. This concept carries a picture of 'appropriate pupil behaviour'; it has dimensions of class, 'race' and gender. The behaviour of African-Caribbean pupils confirmed for teachers the myth about the way the pupils' behaviour and attitudes represented a challenge to authority. The school then became a site of contestation as institutional disciplinary practices were applied by the school. 'Almost any display of African-Caribbean ethnicity was deemed inappropriate' (Gillborn 1990: 29). Gillborn (1995), although suggesting that teachers are not practising institutional racism deliberately, sees them contributing, generally unintentionally, to 'the processes that structure the educational opportunities of minority students' (Gillborn 1995: 42). Gillborn and Youdell (2000) further examine the issue of institutional racism looking at African-Caribbean pupils' experiences and achievements. Their conclusion is that there existed an institutional discourse of 'race' and ability that denied African-Caribbean students any chance of success in school. Youdell (2003) sets out further to investigate how 'the minutiae of everyday life in schools constitutes African-Caribbean students as undesirable learners'. Her conclusion is that in the ordinary conversation of school life the identities of African-Caribbean pupils are 'constituted as undesirable, intolerable, far from "ideal", within the hegemonic discourses of the school organisation'. The 'discursive constitution' of African-Caribbean identities that takes place in 'the apparently trivial moments of everyday life' is the seemingly innocuous way identities are constituted. Guillaumin similarly draws attention to the unconscious confirmation of racism when she claims that

> Negations are not recognised as such by our unconscious mental processes. From this point of view, a fact affirmed and a fact denied exist to exactly the same degree and remain equally present in our affective and intellectual associative networks. Just talking about race means that it will always be there in residue. 'Race' is about the least conceptional, cold and abstract of notions, so it appeals from the start to the unconscious side of the mechanisms we have for acquiring knowledge and relating to other human beings.
>
> (Guillaumin 1995: 105–106)

All can achieve

The idea that minority ethnic group experience of schooling is all bad news is misleading. There are numerous examples that contradict the view that the educational experience of all minority ethnic group children is of failure. The more recent studies of 'race' and ethnicity and educational achievement do show some educational success for certain minority ethnic group children. Gillborn and Mirza (2000) in their synthesis of research evidence on 'race', class and gender have used a broader range of ethnic group categories than earlier commentators. These categories may still hide much valuable evidence, but there has to be some sort of classification if monitoring of educational achievement is to take place, and the year 2000 amendment to the 1976 Race Relations Act insists that it must. Gillborn and Mirza use the categories white, black, Indian, Pakistani, Bangladeshi.

This study also attempts to establish,

> on the basis of the best available evidence, the relative significance of 'race' and ethnicity alongside other factors, especially gender and social class background, so as to clarify an agenda for racial equality in education.
>
> (Gillborn and Mirza 2000: 5)

The study quoted above is called *Educational Inequality*, and it acknowledges that minority communities should not be regarded as homogenous, but seen as they truly are: stratified by class and gender. The idea of a single, definitive cultural or ethnic experience is unacceptable. The reality is that educational experience and achievement can only be reliably judged at the conjunction of racial, social and gendered experience. Unfortunately, there are few other studies which take these three variables together. Gillborn and Gipps' (1996) earlier study, which was undertaken on behalf of Ofsted, was one that attempted to take account of 'race'/ethnicity, class and gender. Looking at GCSE grades A–C in England and Wales in 1995, the highest averages went to pupils from advantaged backgrounds, and girls fared better than boys when socio-economic background was the same (Gillborn and Gipps 1996: 17). The Youth Cohort Study (DfEE 1999) referred to by Gillborn and Mirza (2000) addresses the variables of 'race', class and gender together; this is another rare example. Some interesting, though 'tentative' conclusions are available:

- no group has been completely excluded from the improvement in GCSE attainments during the late 1980s and 1990s;

- by 1995 the gender gap was present within each ethnic group regardless of social class background;

- ethnic inequalities persist even when simultaneously controlling for gender and class;

- when comparing like with like, in terms of gender, class and ethnic origin consistent and significant ethnic inequalities of attainment remain clear.

The performance of African-Caribbean pupils has tended to lag behind that of white pupils, though there was an instance when, in the years 1992 and 1994, at Key Stage 1, African-Caribbean pupils in Birmingham were ahead of white pupils as recorded on national assessment tests (Gillborn and Gipps 1996). The general conclusion, however, ran true to form with the attainments of ethnic minority pupils generally lagging behind those of white pupils. As pupils moved through the junior years, that is Key Stage 2, the gap tended to widen. There are cases of African-Caribbean boys doing better at Key Stage 1 than their white counterparts, but this advantage is soon lost as school careers develop. The declining achievement of African-Caribbean pupils is explained by Gillborn and Gipps as the product of a situation of conflict created between teachers and schooling and African-Caribbean pupils. As a consequence of this seemingly unintentional outcome, levels of achievement of African-Caribbean pupils suffer. As pupils' educational careers proceed through secondary school, to the point when they take GCSE examinations, their achievements are in comparative decline, the average difference being that African-Caribbean pupils are five points lower than white peers. Nonetheless, Gillborn and Gipps reject the idea of total black under-achievement since black African pupils invariably get better results than African-Caribbean pupils.

Turning to GCSE grades A–C, which was the benchmark for a pass comparable with the old GCE O-level examination, African-Caribbean pupils are gaining less than half the national average. The results for pupils of Bangladeshi and Pakistani origin are more encouraging since they make up some of the leeway on national averages at 11 to perform in some local education authorities at or above the national average (Commission on the Future of Multi-ethnic Britain 2000).

A snapshot of variations in achievement

Notwithstanding the foregoing reservations, the consistency of much of the data from research projects suggests that the educational under-achievement of many minority ethnic group pupils is an outcome of the way the schools deal with these pupils. Gillborn and Mirza's study provides a complex picture of ethnic minority educational performance. In the first place, by claiming that 'all can achieve' – that is 'of the six ethnic minority categories analysed, each one is in the highest attaining category in at least one LEA' (Gillborn and Mirza 2000: 9). Hence the writers' claim that their study is looking at new evidence 'on how different groups share in the rising levels of attainment at the end compulsory schooling' (p. 5).

There is still some improvement to be made in the monitoring of the educational achievement of minority ethnic groups, and the writers express concern that a number of local education authorities (LEAs) applying for the Ethnic Minority Achievement Grant (EMAG) could not give a figure for minority attainment in year 11. This criticism of the monitoring of ethnic minority achievement has further support in Osler and Morrison's (2000) report for the Commission for Racial Equality (CRE), which claims that Ofsted informed neither schools nor contracted inspectors of Ofsted's responsibility for monitoring schools' procedures for preventing racism. Such strategies were recommended in the report of the Stephen Lawrence Inquiry (Macpherson 1999). A further weakness that Gillborn and Mirza (2000) point out is that only six LEAs provided baseline to GCSE performance by ethnic origin; another was that LEAs had never produced data on performance by ethnic group before and therefore some of their returns were less than adequate. This finding sits well with the Ofsted (1999) report on LEA programmes for raising the levels of minority ethnic group attainments. Fewer than one quarter of LEAs involved in that survey could provide a clear plan for improving the attainment of minority ethnic groups.

The Gillborn and Mirza study (2000) is mapping attainment at local level in a number of select LEAs. This leads to local variability and cannot provide a national picture. However, it does give 'a unique glimpse of variation between localities' (p. 8). The data relate to attainments in the summer of 1998. The report concentrates first on 'local variability' and shows that, 'of the six minority ethnic categories . . . analysed, every one is the highest attaining of all in at least one LEA' (p. 9). And 'Black pupils are capable of high achievement. In one in ten authorities that monitor GCSE results by ethnicity, pupils in all recorded Black groups are more likely to attain the benchmark than their white peers' (p. 10). Pakistani pupils have been recorded as a low attaining group, but, 'in four out of ten LEAs that monitor for ethnic origin, Pakistani pupils are more likely to attain this benchmark than white pupils locally' (p. 10). Again Bangladeshis, who at national level lag behind white averages, do at local level in many cases reverse this pattern. However, this 'snapshot of variations' (p. 11) notwithstanding, 'significant and consistent inequalities of attainment emerge for many of the principal minority groups' (p. 11). Although members of each of the principal minority groups are more likely to gain five higher GCSE grades than ever before, it must be borne in mind that African-Caribbean, Pakistani and Bangladeshi pupils are 'markedly less likely to attain five higher graded GCSEs than their white and Indian peers nationally' (p. 12). Gillborn and Mirza (2000) conclude that ethnic inequalities are 'consistently visible' and that social class and gender differences though 'associated with differences in attainment . . . (cannot) . . . account for persistent underlying ethnic inequalities: comparing like with like, African-Caribbean, Pakistani and Bangladeshi pupils do not enjoy equal opportunities'. The writers draw attention to the fact that the situation is not static and that for African-Caribbean and Pakistani pupils inequalities have increased particularly in GCSE attainments.

The changing nature of educational achievement of minority ethnic pupils, whilst showing improvements for some groups, persistently leaves other groups disappointed. Berliner (2003), reporting in the *Education Guardian* on a report by Simon Warren of the University of Birmingham and Professor David Gillborn of the Institute of Education, London, says that Birmingham LEA, 'a leader in the field of race equality in education,' is still employing a strategy that is not resulting in equality of opportunity in all schools, this in particular for African-Caribbean children. Gillborn and Warren suggest that setting, and booster groups, to help children reach targets in tests, could be working against black pupils. Typically, girls of all ethnic groups do better than boys.

The *Aiming High* national strategy, reported in the *Guardian* (11 October 2003), was the Government's new national strategy to raise achievement levels of minority ethnic pupils and specifically black pupils, whom they saw as one of the main under-performing groups in the country. Central to the strategy was focused work in thirty secondary schools. Each school received a support package including support and advice from an experienced consultant. The National College of School Leadership also contributed, and lessons learned were spread throughout England. The strategy involved bringing greater accountability and visibility to the issue. Inspections were to deliberately focus on minority group experience and the school and LEA were to publish achievement data by ethnic group and LEA. There was to be training for primary school teachers to help them support bilingual pupils as well as monitoring of bilingual pupils from foundation stage to secondary school. The result was a series of guidance documents for LEAs and teachers under the banner of *Aiming High*, which included *Aiming High: Raising the Achievement of Gypsy Traveller Pupils* (DfES 2003a), *Aiming High: Understanding the Needs of Ethnic Minority Pupils in Mainly White Schools – A Guide to Good Practice* (DfES 2004a), *Aiming High: Guidance on Supporting the Education of Asylum Seeking and Refugee Children* (DfES 2004b); and *Aiming High: Guidance on the Assessment of Pupils Learning English as an Additional Language* (DfES 2005).

School exclusions

School exclusions have a long history. Bernard Coard's (1971) short book with the long title, *How the West Indian Child is Made Educationally Sub-normal in the British School System*, drew attention to the disproportionate numbers of African-Caribbean children who were being diverted from mainstream schooling into schools for the educationally sub-normal. Another early report by the Commission for Racial Equality (CRE) (see Bourne *et al.* 1994), looking into pupil suspensions in Birmingham schools, discovered that from 1974 to 1980 it was recorded that black pupils were four times more likely to be excluded than white pupils. This problematic experience of schooling was further confirmed by Ofsted in a report in 1993, which discovered that the number of African-Caribbean pupils excluded from schools was disproportionately high, and that similar numbers attended the referral units that LEAs have to provide for permanently excluded pupils. Osler (1997) claims that the relatively excessive exclusions of African-Caribbean pupils produce an 'educational crisis' since, following exclusion, there is only a 15 per cent chance that a child will be reinstated in mainstream education. Exclusion is not the same problem for girls as it is for boys, except in the case of African-Caribbean girls, who constitute 9 per cent of female exclusions, and yet only just over 1 per cent of all girls in schools.

Although permanent exclusions from school are much lower than they were six years ago, the numbers of pupils thus excluded has risen for the second year running, according to figures provided by the Department for Education and Skills (DfES 2003b) (Table 6.1).

The total number of exclusions has risen for the second year running, though it

TABLE 6.1 Percentage of permanent exclusions

Ethnic group	1997/1998	1998/1999	1999/2000	2000/2001	2001/2002*
White	83.8	84.4	82.9	83.0	82.0
Black	10.2	9.7	9.8	8.5	8.1
Black Caribbean	6.2	5.7	5.5	4.2	4.2
Black African	1.7	1.5	1.7	1.7	1.7
Black other	2.3	2.6	2.6	2.6	2.2
Asian	3.2	2.7	2.8	2.2	3.2
Indian	0.9	0.7	0.6	0.5	0.6
Pakistani	1.8	1.6	1.6	1.2	1.8
Bangladeshi	0.5	0.4	0.6	0.5	0.8
Chinese	0.1	0.1	0.0	0.0	0.1
Other group	2.7	3.1	3.5	2.8	3.3
Group not known	0.0	0.0	1.0	3.2	3.3
Total	100	100	100	100	100

*Estimate.

is considerably lower than it was in 1997/1998. Black Caribbean pupils continue to have the highest exclusion rate among the minority ethnic groups. Chinese pupils have the smallest percentage. This exclusion from full-time mainstream education of a disproportionate percentage of black young people, and African-Caribbean in particular, shows that little has changed for this group of young people. The Commission for Racial Equality has expressed concern on many occasions about what appears to be unfair treatment. There are concerns that the needs-oriented approach recommended in the Warnock Report (1978) is still being overlooked. A further strong criticism is that the Conservative government's Education Reform Act of 1988 did nothing for the educational interests of young black pupils on a number of counts. The neo-liberal act created the 'market' for school places, giving parents the opportunity to choose schools; white parents were thus able to avoid schools with appreciable numbers of black pupils. The competition between schools for potentially able pupils to enhance league table positions has taken priority in state education over the aims of equal opportunities for all pupils. An equally important concern is the content of the National Curriculum. Gundara claims that the

> National Curriculum, and the Anglo-centric values under-pinning it, diminishes the right to knowledge for all Britons in a multicultural society.
>
> (Gundara 2000: 39)

Adjustments to the National Curriculum subsequent to the 1988 Education Reform Act have done little to address the criticism that schooling is in the main 'white, English, Christian'. The formal curriculum of schools, together with the hidden curriculum of schooling, is seen by many writers as creating an environment where black pupils are likely to fail (Mac an Ghaill 1988; Gillborn 1990; Osler 1997; Hatcher 1997). As Gillborn and Mirza (2000) and Youdell (2003) among others claim, institutional racism is still a significant influence on the educational achievement of African-Caribbean pupils.

Race relations law

Discrimination against people on the grounds of race, colour or ethnic origin was made unlawful in the 1976 Race Relations Act. The action was unlawful whether it was direct or indirect. The Commission for Racial Equality produced a code of practice, which included the elimination from all schools of racial discrimination in education (CRE 1989). The code of practice sets out to protect people who have drawn attention to unlawful practices, to identify segregation on racial grounds and to protect those who have alleged that racial discrimination has taken place. A range of practices are identified as unlawful; these include racially discriminatory assessment, admissions, allocation to teaching groups, exclusions, careers advice, grants (pp. 12–13). This legislation has to some degree combated racism in schools, but there is still considerable evidence of violence, bullying and institutionalised racism, perpetuating both educational disadvantage and racial harassment.

The Race Relations Act of 1976 has been amended by the Race Relations (Amendment) Act 2000, which makes it unlawful to discriminate against anyone on grounds of race, colour, nationality (including citizenship), or ethnic or national origin. Public bodies must also take distinct steps to promote racial equality and good race relations. Schools must now publish a race equality policy, and monitor and assess how their policies affect minority ethnic pupils, staff and parents. Of particular importance is the monitoring of pupils' achievements. The amended act requires public authorities to publish the results of their consultations, monitoring and assessments.

Consequences of the neglect of 'race'

Developments in 'race' and education from the Education Reform Act of 1988 were strongly influenced by the neo-liberal ideals of the Thatcher government; this meant letting economic growth and the market provide racial equality rather than deeming that to be the responsibility of civil rights legislation and state intervention. In this way of thinking, it is the individual rather than the rights of groups that predominate and are legitimate (Ben Tovim 1997: 210). This move towards the freedom of the individual has pervaded all educational policy since the 1988 Education Reform Act. Particularly in relation to 'race'/ethnicity and education, the pressure of state influence on schools to develop and pursue 'positive action' strategies to undermine racism in education has declined. In their place has been substituted a reassertion of 'English' and 'Christian' values in the National Curriculum (Troyna 1992). As the Berliner report stressed, the emphasis on individual achievement, competition and league tables has directed attention away from principles of fairness, justice and equality.

It is remarkable that the vital issue of 'race' should be neglected in this way, especially since numerous disturbing incidents were taking place in the late 1980s. The influence of the racism in the world outside school was felt inside schools too. There was the occasion when parents of children at Headfield Primary School in Dewsbury kept their children at home because the majority of pupils in the school came from Asian families. Burnage High School in Manchester, a boys' school in a largely working-class catchment area, had a number of difficult racist incidents despite its anti-racist policies. In September 1986, a 13-year-old pupil of Asian origin (Ahmed Iqbal Ullah) was stabbed to death in the playground by a white pupil of similar age. The subsequent Burnage Report (see Runnymede Trust 1989) was critical of certain types of 'doctrinal anti-racism' that failed to take account of other problems, which result from social inequality. Anti-racist education was taken to be a form of left-wing extremism. The tabloid press interpreted this criticism as pointing the finger of blame at the school's anti-racist policies. Instead what the committee was criticising was policies that appeared to ignore white working-class pupils. The Burnage Committee saw this as a seedbed of division and polarisation in a context of anti-racist policies.

The hostility towards strategies to combat racism, seen in the tabloid press reporting of the Burnage stabbing, is still about. Nick Seaton, of the Campaign for Real Education, claims that a Qualifications and Curriculum Authority (QCA) call for a national curriculum that values cultural diversity and the prevention of racism is addressing an issue that is nothing more than political correctness (Campaign for Real Education 2003). The aim of the QCA report, called *Respect for All*, is to respond to the recommendations of a report made by the committee that looked into another racist murder, that of Stephen Lawrence.

The Stephen Lawrence Inquiry report (Macpherson 1999) was first concerned with the poor response of police officers to the murder of Stephen Lawrence, a black London teenager. However, the Macpherson Report went on to claim that racism was present in all institutions. The need for some radical thinking and a determined response to tackle institutionalised racism in all public services, especially in areas of family life and education, was stressed. Clearly the treatment of racism in schools is a persistent issue, and ridding schools of racism, either institutional or personal, is still some way from being achieved. Indeed the role of education in transmitting racism is well documented. Among the many recommendations made by the Stephen Lawrence Inquiry to counter racism, some were specifically directed at education. The first of these recommendations is that the National Curriculum should incorporate the prevention of racism and the promotion of cultural diversity among its objectives. Second, that LEAs and School Governors should be obliged to implement strategies to combat racism, including recording racist incidents, reporting such incidents (which must involve the pupils' parents, governors and LEAs), publications of racist incidents each year, school by school, publication of pupil exclusions on an annual and school-by-school basis. Finally, Ofsted inspections should be required to check the implementation of the anti-racist strategy of each school inspected.

The revised National Curriculum in 2000 included Citizenship, which involves introducing pupils to the diversity in 'national, regional, religious and ethnic identities . . . and the need for mutual respect and understanding'. Sivanandan (2000) in *Macpherson and After* is very critical of the commitment seen in remarks like 'respecting cultural differences'. Other direct action stemming from the Macpherson Report was the setting up of the Advisory Group on Raising Ethnic Minority Pupil Achievement and the Race, Education and Employment Forum, both coming from the DfEE. The CRE (2000) issued a paper intended to focus on action in schools to promote equality and cultural diversity. The focus here is on distinct aspects of school life such as leadership and management, curriculum, admissions, exclusions, parent and community involvement. There is an attached audit sheet to enable schools to monitor their standards.

Conclusion

The concept of 'race' has no scientific basis. However, even when the validity of 'race' is denied and the word *ethnicity* is substituted, it does not remove the association of difference and inferiority where social position, achievement and treatment are concerned. Careful clarification of a working definition of 'race' and ethnicity is an important starting point for study and research in 'race' and education. In research studies, the way in which concepts are operationalised will significantly influence what is found out about 'race'/ethnicity and education. A searching study and analysis of issues may well uncover apparently good intentions, or misguided ones. An instance of the latter is seen in Flecha's (1999) case of the education of Gypsies, or Youdell's (2003) investigation of the 'minutiae' of life in school that make African-Caribbean students 'undesirable, . . . intolerable within the hegemonic discourses of the school organisation'.

The need to monitor educational achievement by ethnic group is stressed in the work of many commentators, and the reluctance of some local education authorities to carry out routine monitoring has been addressed by the Race Relations Amendment Act, 2000. The picture of minority ethnic group achievement is changing in some cases, but in others an endemic record of failure persists; this may be better addressed when consistent, reliable records are kept.

Despite the passing of almost thirty years since the 1976 Race Relations Act, education's mission to enrich children's lives is still not fairly distributed and the barrier to success created by 'race'/ethnicity is still a serious problem. Moreover, the harassment and victimisation of children on racial grounds, both inside and outside school, shows that expelling the evil of racism from schools and society is still a long way from being realised.

Suggested further reading

The Oxford Readers volume on *Racism* (Bulmer and Solomos 1999) provides a wide-ranging critical overview of both the historical development and the contemporary focus on ideas about racism. These papers introduce the reader to the broad parameters of 'race' as a field of study. The way in which 'race' affects children's life chances is shown by Gillborn and Gipps (1996) when they draw attention to the mounting incidence of racial harassment and violence together with an increased number of school exclusions. Gillborn and Gipps (1996) and Connolly and Troyna (1998) provide a comprehensive overview of research into 'race' and education. The virulent nature of racism is shown in Connolly (1998) when racism is seen in children at a very early age. Troyna and Hatcher (1992) sound a similar warning when they reveal institutionalised racism and individual racism interwoven in the lives of children in three 'mainly all-white primary schools'. The importance of taking account of gender and social class in conjunction with 'race' is seen in Gillborn and Gipps (1996). Gaine and George (1999) also address the interaction of 'race', class and gender. Mirza (1992) provides a good example of an interpretative study in which young African-Caribbean women show that their aspirations are different from black boys and white girls. Gillborn and Mirza (2000) provide a synthesis of recent research evidence on educational experience and achievement, which again emphasises the interaction of racial, social and gendered experience. Useful journals include *Multicultural Teaching, Race and Class* and *Race, Ethnicity and Education*.

References

Barker, M. (1981) *The New Racism*. London: Junction Books.

Ben-Tovim, G. (1997) 'Why "Positive Action" is "Politically Correct"', in Modood, T. and Werbner, P. (eds) *The Politics of Multiculturalism in the New Europe*. London: Zed Books.

Berliner, W. (2003) 'Gifted, but Black', *Education Guardian*, 14 October, p. 2.

Bourne, J., Bridges, L. and Searle, C. (1994) *Outcast England: How Schools Exclude Black Children*. London: Institute of Race Relations.

Bridges, L. (1994) 'Tory Education: Exclusion and the Black Child', *Race and Class*. **36** (1), 33–48.

Bulmer, M. (1986) 'Race and Ethnicity', in Burgess, R. G. (ed.) *Key Variables in Social Investigation*. London: Routledge and Kegan Paul.

Bulmer, M. and Solomos, J. (1999) *Racism*. Oxford: Oxford University Press.

Campaign for Real Education (2003) *Campaign for Real Education Newsletter*, No. 49, Spring.

Cashmore, E. and Troyna, B. (1990) *Introduction to Race Relations.* London: Routledge.

Coard, B. (1971) *How the West Indian Child is Made Educationally Sub-Normal in the British Education System.* London: New Beacon Books.

Commission for Racial Equality (CRE) (1989) *Code of Practice for the Elimination of Racial Discrimination in Education.* London: CRE.

Commission for Racial Equality (CRE) (1997) *Racial Attacks and Harassment.* London: CRE.

Commission for Racial Equality (CRE) (2000) *Learning for All: Standards for Racial Equality in Schools.* London: CRE.

Commission on the Future of Multi-ethnic Britain (2000) *Report on the Future of Multi-ethnic Britain* (Parekh Report). London: Profile Books.

Connolly, P. (1992) 'Playing it by the Rules: The Politics of Research in "Race" and Education', *British Educational Research Journal.* **18** (2), 133–148.

Connolly, P. (1995) 'Racism, Masculine Peer-Group Relations and the Schooling of African-Caribbean Infant Boys', *British Journal of the Sociology of Education.* **16** (1), 75–92.

Connolly, P. (1998) *Racism, Gender Identities and Young Children.* London: Routledge.

Connolly, P. and Troyna, B. (eds) (1998) *Researching Racism in Education.* Buckingham: Open University Press.

Cornell, S., and Hartmann, D. (1998), *Ethnicity and Race: Making Identities in a Changing World.* Thousand Oaks, CA: Pine Forge Press.

Department for Education and Employment (DfEE) (1999) *The Youth Cohort Study.* London: HMSO.

Department for Education and Skills (DfES) (2003a) *Aiming High: Raising the Achievement of Gypsy Traveller Pupils.* London: DfES.

Department for Education and Skills (DfES) (2003b) *Exclusions 1997–2002.* London: DfES.

Department for Education and Skills (DfES) (2004a) *Aiming High: Understanding the Needs of Ethnic Minority Pupils in Mainly White Schools – A Guide to Good Practice.* London: DfES.

Department for Education and Skills (DfES) (2004b) *Aiming High: Guidance on Supporting the Education of Asylum Seeking and Refugee Children.* London: DfES.

Department for Education and Skills (DfES) (2005) *Aiming High: Guidance on the Assessment of Pupils Learning English as an Additional Language.* London: DfES.

Department of Education and Science (DES) (1985) *Education for All* (Swann Report). London: HMSO.

Donald, J. and Rattansi, A. (1992) *Race, Culture and Difference.* London: Sage.

Edwards, J. (1995) *When Race Counts: The Morality of Racial Preference in Britain and America.* London: Routledge.

Eysenck, H. (1971) *Race, Intelligence and Education.* London: Temple-Smith.

Flecha, R. (1999) 'Modern and Post-Modern Racism in Europe', *Harvard Educational Revue.* **69** (2), 150–171.

Foster, P. (1993) 'Some Problems Identifying Racial/Ethnic Equality or Inequality in Schools', *British Journal of Sociology.* **44** (3), 519–535.

Foster, P., Gomm, R. and Hammersley, M. (1996) *Constructing Educational Inequality.* London: Falmer Press.

Fuller, M. (1980) 'Black Girls in a London Comprehensive School', in Deem, R. (ed.) *Schooling for Women's Work.* London: Routledge and Kegan Paul.

Fuller, M. (1983) 'Qualified Criticism, Critical Qualifications', in Barton, L. and Walker, S. (eds) *Race, Class and Education.* London: Croom Helm.

Gaine, C. and George, R. (1999) *Gender, 'Race' and Class in Schooling: A New Introduction.* London: Falmer Press.

Gillborn, D. (1990) *'Race', Ethnicity and Education.* London: Unwin Hyman.

Gillborn, D. (1995) *Racism and Antiracism in Real Schools.* Buckingham: Open University Press.

Gillborn, D. and Gipps, C.(1996) *Recent Research on the Achievement of Ethnic Minority Pupils.* London: HMSO.

Gillborn, D and Mirza, H. (2000) *Educational Inequality: Mapping, 'Race', Class and Gender – A Synthesis of Research Evidence.* London: Ofsted.

Gillborn, D. and Youdell, D. (2000) *Rationing Education: Policy, Practice, Reform and Equity.* Buckingham: Open University Press.

Green, P. (1985) 'Multi-ethnic Teaching and the Pupils' Self-concepts', in Department of Education and Science, *Education for All.* London: HMSO, Annex B.

Guillaumin, C. (1995) 'The Changing Face of "Race"', in Bulmer, M. and Solomos, J. (eds) *Racism.* Oxford: Oxford University Press.

Gundara, J. (2000) *Interculturalism, Education and Inclusion.* London: Paul Chapman.

Hall, S. (1988) 'The Toad in the Garden: Thatcherism among the Theorists', in Nelson, C. and Grossberg, L. (eds) *Marxism and the Interpretation of Culture.* Champaign, IL: University of Illinois Press.

Hatcher, R. (1997) 'New Labour, School Improvement and Racial Equality', *Multicultural Teaching.* **15** (3), 8–13.

Herrnstein, R. J. and Murray, C. (1994) *The Bell Curve: Intelligence and Class Structure in American Life.* New York: Free Press.

Jensen, A. (1969) *Environment, Heredity and Intelligence.* Cambridge, MA: Harvard Educational Review.

Jensen, A. (1973) *Educability and Group Differences,* London: Methuen.

Kamin, L. (1977) *The Science and Politics of IQ.* Harmondsworth: Penguin.

Mabey, C. (1981) 'Black British Literacy', *Educational Research.* **23** (2), 83–95.

Mac an Ghaill, M. (1988) *Young, Gifted and Black.* Milton Keynes: Open University Press.

Macpherson, W (1999) *The Stephen Lawrence Inquiry: Report of an Inquiry.* London: HMSO.

Mirza, H. S. (1992) *Young, Female and Black.* London: Routledge.

Nei, M. and Roychoudhury, A. K. (1983) 'Genetic Relationship and Evolution of Human Races', *Evolutionary Biology,* **14**, 1–59.

Office for Standards in Education (Ofsted) (1999) *Raising the Attainment of Minority Ethnic Pupils: School and LEA Responses.* London: Ofsted.

Office of National Statistics (1996) *Social Trends,* 30. London: HMSO.

Osler, A. (1997) 'Exclusion Drama Turns into a Crisis for Blacks', *Times Educational Supplement,* 10 October.

Osler, A. and Morrison, M. (2000) *Inspecting Schools for Racial Equality: Ofsted's Strengths and Weaknesses.* Stoke on Trent: Trentham Books.

Pathak, S. (2000) *Race Research for the Future: Ethnicity in Education, Training and the Labour Market.* Department for Education and Employment.

Rex, J. (1991) *Ethnic Identity and Political Mobilisation in Britain.* University of Warwick: Centre for Research into Ethnic Relations.

Rollock, N. (2006) 'Beyond the Status Quo? Challenging Normative Assumptions about Race', *British Journal of the Sociology of Education.* **27** (5), 673–677.

Runnymede Trust (1989) *Racism, Anti-racism and Schools: A Summary of The Burnage Report.* London: Runnymede Trust.

Sivanandan, A. (2000) *Macpherson and After.* London: Institute of Race Relations.

Smith, D. and Tomlinson, S. (1989) *The School Effect: A Study of Multiracial Comprehensives.* London: Policy Studies Institute.

Smith, Z. (2000) *White Teeth.* London: Penguin Books.

Tomlinson, S. (1980) 'The Educational Performance of Ethnic Minority Children', *New Community.* **8** (3), 78–85.

Troyna, B (1992) 'Can You See the Join? An Historical Analysis of Multicultural and Anti-racist Education Policies', in Gill, D. *et al* (eds) *Racism and Education.* London: Sage.

Troyna, B. and Hatcher, R. (1992) *Racism in Children's Lives.* London: Routledge.

Warnock, M. (1978) *Report of the Committee of Inquiry into the Education of Handicapped Children and Young People.* London: HMSO.

Wright, C. (1986) 'School Processes: An Ethnographic Study', in Egglestone, J., Dunn, D., and Anjali, M. (eds) *Education for Some: The Educational and Vocational Experiences of 15–18 Year Old Members of Minority Ethnic Groups.* Stoke on Trent: Trentham Books.

Wright, C. (1992) *Race Relations in the Primary School.* London: David Fulton.

Youdell, D. (2003) 'Identity Traps or How Black Students Fail: The Interactions between Biographical, Sub-cultural, and Learner Identities', *British Journal of Sociology of Education.* **24** (1), 2–20.

7

Gender in education

Jane Martin

The education system is not primarily an agent for the promotion of greater choice among students. It can only be said to provide equality of opportunity for people to fulfil the expectations which the dominant group in society has already laid down. It is when students conform to these expectations that inequality is perpetuated. While the prevailing belief is that women are inferior, and while this is taught within education with all the 'massaging' of the evidence that such teaching requires, women will continue to find themselves devalued, in the lowest paid, least skilled jobs, with least power to change those conditions.

(Spender 1980: 31)

THE FIELD OF GENDER and education has shifted dramatically since Dale Spender wrote these words for the collection of essays entitled Learning to Lose. Now, what is considered to be of concern with regard to gender equity (and inequality) in the British education system is the apparent 'under-achievement' of boys. To understand this shift of emphasis demands that we place it in perspective. My purpose in this chapter is to adopt a longer time frame, to tease out the way in which debates about gender in education have been framed historically. To map this terrain I shall outline briefly the history of postwar education policy in England and the influence of social and cultural changes, particularly as they have affected gender distinctions.

The chapter is divided into three parts. It begins with a discussion of historical perspectives on gender and education, before moving on to more recent concerns, considered in their policy context. Overall, in the post-Second World War period, traditional expectations and roles meant the great majority of girls were trained for domesticity, even at the expense of academic ability. Nonetheless, gendered inequality did not come under scrutiny as an educational issue until the early 1970s. Thus, feminist practitioners began to play a role in the gender policy-making process, acquiring a wide range of knowledges, strategies and understandings that helped them mount forceful challenges to schooling (Weiner 1994). However, the 1990s saw a redefinition of established debates about the relationship between gender and schooling triggered by the annual publication of national statistics charting the performance of boys and girls in taking and passing public examinations. Still widely discussed in the English media, the insinuation is that girls' success has been at the expense of boys' failure. Against this landscape, popular and policy discussions about the issues have been couched in such a way as to obscure the fact that not all boys are under-achieving and not all girls are succeeding in education. And yet, it is most important that we see gender as relational: on the one hand, to critique the overly simplified and populist focus on gender binaries, and on the other, to direct attention to the intersections of gender, 'race', sexuality, special needs and social class. A critical exploration of the relationships between identity, education and biography may help to facilitate this (Coffey 2001).

1944 to the early 1970s: the myth of meritocracy?

Under the influence of wartime radicalism, the passing of the Education Act (1944) provided free secondary education for all. But this did not mean 'that all children now received what had before the Act been described as secondary education' (Thom 1987: 131). The Labour governments of 1945–51 ratified selection procedures on the lines of 'age, ability and aptitude', as recommended in the Norwood Report and the White Paper *Educational Reconstruction* (both published in 1943). Ellen Wilkinson and George Tomlinson, her successor as Minister for Education, were both committed to the idea of three types of school, which were intended to cater for three different 'types' of child. In their view, the process of selection, resting upon children's performance in the 11+ examination, provided the basis for opening up educational opportunities to the working classes. Discussion on equality did not deal with gender, however. State policy endorsed the view that women are different from men, not only biologically but also intellectually, psychologically and socially. Thus, for example, while Norwood interspersed the word 'child' with 'boy', criteria particular to girls' schooling featured in a lengthy chapter on domestic subjects. Idealized notions of 'the nation' and family culture were used as a rationale for welfare state development in the post-Second World War period, sustaining the belief in a woman's place being in the home (Deem 1981).

Whereas many in power saw the domestic role of women as crucial for the construction and rehabilitation of social harmony and cohesiveness, the development of employment policies during the postwar labour shortage increasingly made other roles possible. Rhetoric and reality had not always cohered, as was shown by the introduction of government recruitment programmes aimed specifically at attracting experienced women workers into a number of occupations, including domestic service, nursing, teaching and textiles. At the same time, large numbers of women workers who had done men's jobs during the war were made redundant and working mothers had to return to the home on account of the reduction in state day nursery provision. Many others responded to the influential writings of John Bowlby on the dangers of 'maternal deprivation' for normal child development (Riley 1983). This was consistent with the notion of companionate marriage popularized in the 1940s and after. Men were still intended to be the main breadwinners and women the main carers, using their equal-but-different talents to promote the common good of family members. When mediated by government policies, the invoking of official ideologies about maternity and motherhood was never benign for women, for it structured much of the thinking that went into the development of policies, sustaining the belief that a woman's place was in the home. Part-time employment for married women was one way to reinforce gender divisions in paid work, and the need to accommodate men who had served in the military services was applied to limit the entry of girls into higher education. In 1946, for instance, the Minister of Labour, George Isaacs, persuaded the vice-chancellors of British universities not to admit female school-leavers 'except where they are of exceptional promise' (cited in Briar 1997: 97). This was an example of overt discrimination. Other gendered inequalities were more covert and largely overlooked during this period.

Throughout the 1940s and 1950s girls had to do much better than boys to obtain a place at a selective grammar school (Thom 1987). At the time, policy and theory around educational practice suggested that boys mature later than girls and it would be unfair to exclude them from grammar schools on the basis of test results at the age of 11 (Epstein *et al.* 1998). The presumption was that the boys would catch up by the age of 14. Because the achievement of girls was seen as a problem for boys, local authorities either adjusted boys' scores upwards or added new tests to skew the results. Ironically, in many areas it was the girls who were disadvantaged as the single sex grammar schools had more places for boys. In another bequest from the past, conjectures about male potential were reinforced by the messages contained in the discourse of overstrain and the figure of the 'healthily' unconcerned boy. Cohen (1998) points out that in nineteenth-century English culture the élite male was supposedly distinguished by his 'natural' mental superiority. Such a view of scholarly achievement meant that hard work was a sign of *lack* of ability and this 'contributed to producing the underperformance of boys as an index of their mental health' (Cohen 1998: 27). In contrast, too much intellectual work was construed as detrimental for typically 'diligent' and 'industrious' girls, who were seen as susceptible to overstrain. Medical practitioners warned girls of the risks evoked by too much intellectual work and as late as the 1930s it was claimed that a girl who worked hard might get brain fever (Rendel 1997). So, when it came to male–female 11+ result patterns, common sense and social observation suggested the difference 'is not real because it does not last, it is not a phenomenon produced by the test, it is a phenomenon produced by "Nature"' (Thom 1987: 141). Adjustments to ensure that boys were not disadvantaged continued into the 1970s and beyond, with many local authorities still using the test results not as a qualification for entry to grammar school but as a selective filter to fill the places available (Miller 1996).

It is against this background that we need to make visible the role schools play in the process of gender identity construction, offering interpretations of what it means to be 'male' or 'female'. Messages about gender values may be revealed in various ways, across a diversity of areas, including the formal and hidden curriculum, the ethos of the school and the educational objectives defined as important. It is very obvious, however, when the purposes and content of education are discussed.

In a book entitled *The Education of Girls*, published in 1948, John Newsom, then Chief Education Officer for Hertfordshire, attacked the academic grammar schools for ignoring domestic skills and placing too much emphasis on public examinations and obtaining professional careers. Yet even here the cult of motherhood and domesticity was still prevalent. When the girls' grammar school attended by Mary Evans debated the issue that 'A Woman's Place is in the Home', she remembered:

> The school decided this was certainly the case. Women should be at home, waiting for us to come home and ready to ferry us about to dancing class or whatever else. If women did not do this, and accept this way of life, then their only alternative fate was to be an unmarried schoolmistress. In the late 1950s this career did not look attractive and the dichotomy between employed woman and wife and mother remained absolute.
>
> (Evans 1995: 64)

Newsom insisted that it was wholly inappropriate for 99 per cent of girls to share either the curriculum or the ethos of boys' schools because 'The fundamental common experience is the fact that the vast majority of them will become the makers of homes' (1948: 110). The overwhelming significance of this has been graphically described by many. In the modern schools, catering for about 70 to 75 per cent of secondary pupils, housecraft and mothercraft were championed as an integral part of the curriculum for the 'less able', predominantly working-class girls (McCulloch 1998: 120–126). But there were some who deplored this view. In *Marriage Past and Present*, published in 1938, Margaret Cole, politician, historian, journalist and author, foresaw the ever-increasing numbers of women engaging in paid work (even after marriage). She tried to challenge the assumption that domestic subjects were especially suited for less academic girls, wanting them to become status subjects and win parity with subjects like geometry. She saw no contradiction in the dual aim of preparing girls for both home and work, but ultimately it was the perceived incompatibility between the two that was visited upon the schools (Hunt 1987).

Educationally the result was a school curriculum sharply divided into 'masculine' and 'feminine' areas contributing to differentiation of treatment and opportunity. For the young female population leaving school at 15, the Ministry of Education continued to point to that special curriculum for girls, organized around familial concerns. Hence the Crowther Report, *15 to 18*, produced by the Central Advisory Committee for Education in 1959, repeated the common refrain that in the modern schools:

> The prospect of courtship and marriage should rightly influence the education of the adolescent girl . . . her direct interests in dress and personal appearance and the problems of human relations should be given a central part in her education.
>
> (quoted in Riley 1994: 37)

The 1959 *Report on Early Leaving* indicated that grammar school girls were much more likely to leave school before taking national exams (Deem 1981), and Jackson and Marsden's (1962) in-depth study of eighty-eight working-class children in Huddersfield who passed for grammar school and stayed on into the sixth form showed that working-class girls were even less likely than working-class boys to go from grammar school to university, especially a prestigious one. Cultural attitudes and material provision all worked towards encouraging girls to train as teachers, which cost £255 at that time, compared with £660 a year for undergraduates – mainly white, middle-class men. That being the case, teaching was the favoured career goal of many female grammar school pupils and nearly half of the girls Jackson and Marsden researched went to colleges of education: by 1958 there were 100 teacher training colleges for women, eighteen for men and eighteen co-educational institutions (Heward 1993: 23–24). Ultimately, when universal student grants became available in the early 1960s,

> women represented on average 25% of the university population in Britain: in Oxford they were 15% and only 10% in Cambridge.
>
> (figures from the Robbins Report quoted in Dyhouse 2003: 173)

Gendered attitudes also meant that relatively little use was made of women's skills and qualifications, despite there being economic concerns about a shortage of skilled workers. Consequently, women graduates were much more likely to have to accept non-graduate employment than male graduates and 'the proportion of women workers in jobs classed as skilled continued to decline in this period, having fallen from 15.5% in 1951 to 13.9% in 1961' (Mackie and Patullo 1977: 99).

By the 1960s a radical restructuring of English state education opened up new possibilities for change. In 1964, when the Labour Party was returned to office, it took the opportunity to promote a national policy of comprehensive education in place of the class-divided grammar/secondary modern system. It did so by means of a circular, known as 10/65, requesting local authorities to choose a development scheme and start the planning process. Granted that gendered equality was not much discussed in this wider campaign, the gradual implementation of comprehensive schooling increased the number of children educated in mixed-sex state secondary schools. This meant a changing balance of power among women and men staff in senior and managerial positions; however, the accepted norm was that co-education was preferable to single-sex education on both academic and social grounds (Deem 1981). Simply put, it was hoped that the presence of female pupils would provide incentive and inspire emulation for boys to work harder. As Arnot (1984: 50) noted, 'never it would seem has the argument been reversed.'

In theory, Deem (1981) maintains that the expansion of the secondary school curriculum should have been 'helpful' to girls. Overall, the removal of barriers to female success in the 11+ examinations inevitably benefited some, predominantly middle-class girls, but in general terms that advantage did not extend to all girls. Continuity from earlier tripartite patterns of provision was especially striking in relation to gendered curriculum assumptions. In practice, Benn and Simon (1972) found that very few schools offered a common curriculum to all their pupils in the early days of the comprehensive reform. Home economics, metalwork, needlework and woodwork were still explicitly, or by default, separate subjects for girls and boys and the 1975 report on curricular differentiation noted a resilient pattern of students making stereotyped subject choices. Selection and streaming on the basis of academic ability echoed the former grammar/secondary modern divide, and a tendency for girls to be channelled into arts subjects exacerbated differences in life outcomes. For the first time since the Second World War there were uncertainties in the jobs market, which had major implications for the school–work transition. Young people were particularly affected by the decline of vocational apprenticeships and industrial jobs with release for college training, cutbacks in teacher training and fierce competition for university places in arts courses. In this context, oppositional gender constructions continued to impact on lives, despite the feminist challenge and the increasing numbers of women participating in paid work.

1975 to the mid 1990s, equal opportunities?

At a policy level the Sex Discrimination Act of 1975 made direct and indirect discrimination on the grounds of sex and marital status illegal in a number of spheres of public life, including education. Demands for reform of the law were first expressed formally in 1967, by two women MPs, the Conservative Joan Vickers and the Labour Lena Jeger. Unsuccessful on this occasion, pressure gradually produced results. When Labour regained power in 1974 the support of the elected minister, Roy Jenkins, helped to overcome the opposition of some Home Office officials, although the then Department of Education and Science was unenthusiastic (Rendel 1997). In the field of education the legislation applied only to maintained and not to independent schools. It covered admissions, curricular and non-curricular facilities, extra-curricular activities, rules regarding pupils' dress and appearance, school discipline, and standards of discipline careers guidance, and set up the Equal Opportunities Commission (EOC).

In the sociology of education literature a wide range of feminist perspectives began to highlight the gendered nature of schooling. There was criticism of gender differentiation across a diversity of areas as studies began to show the ways in which patriarchal relations are deployed and used in schools. Teaching styles were challenged to avoid a tendency to encourage competition between the sexes in sports, academic learning and examinations. Attention also turned to management hierarchies within schools. Most were dominated by male teachers and the proportion of women holding senior posts in secondary schools was highest in such female 'spaces' as home economics and girls' games. Further, although the 'female' atmosphere of primary schooling was seen to undermine the performance of boys, it seems that even here sexual divisions were constantly reinforced. For instance, Clarricoates (1980) found that many primary school teachers readily clustered behaviour and attitudes into two categories, one for boys and another for girls, drawing on exaggerated notions of masculinity and femininity. Such findings were backed up by research undertaken by Stanworth (1986) and Riddell (1989) in a mixed further education college and two rural comprehensive schools in the south-west of England respectively. In both studies teachers' typifications of male and female pupils were found to accommodate traditional gender codes, as did pupil resistance to schooling. In one maths lesson observed by Riddell, for example, a girl produced a large make-up kit, 'spread out the cosmetics on the desk top as if it were a dressing table' and proceeded to apply the make-up. 'Amazingly, the male teacher completely ignored what was going on' (1989: 193). Writing about her single-sex grammar school, Irene Payne (1980: 15) has similarly shown how some girls used a feminine preoccupation with appearance in order to position themselves

> in opposition to the 'masculinity' of school rules about appearance. I can remember bouffant hairstyles, fish-net stockings, make-up and 'sticky-out' underskirts being the hallmarks of rebellious girls.

Feminist studies of mixed comprehensive schools undertaken in the 1980s were particularly concerned with ways in which girls were steered away from traditionally 'masculine' subjects. Hence, Griffin (1985: 78–79) found that girls who pursued such subjects 'were either presumed to be interested solely in flirting with the boys or discounted as unique exceptions.' Riley (1994: 60) illustrated how gender differences can be perpetuated by teachers with particular reference to subjects traditionally perceived as male. Hence the male head of design and technology tried to ensure that the limited places in technical drawing were filled by boys.

Finally, Riddell (1989) found some teachers drew on a laddish construction of masculinity to appeal to certain pupils with history lessons dedicated to gory details of trench warfare during the First World War and English lessons privileging texts with male characters and often dealing with the problems of the male adolescent. One teacher even explained Queen Mary's (1516–58) persecution of Protestants in terms of her 'unfulfilled life' since she had to sacrifice her social role as wife and mother 'for political reasons' (1989: 188). Another asked the girls to imagine her situation: 'you may have a career and you may want to return to it afterwards, but still at the heart of your lives will be getting married and having children. It's the most natural thing in the world' (ibid.).

Alongside all this feminist educators worked hard to introduce classroom practice with which to challenge patterns of gender-segregated achievement. In Manchester, one of the best-known projects of this kind was initiated to encourage female interest in the sciences. Working within the action research framework, the Girls into Science and Technology Project (GIST, 1980–4) 'worked directly with teachers, attempting to reduce gender-stereotyping on the part of pupils and teachers, and promoting "gender-fair" interaction in classrooms' (Weiner 1994: 86). Other groups such as Girls into Mathematics (GAMMA) extended the focus on contact and communication networks both for support and for knowledge dissemination, producing films, exhibitions, teaching and in-service packs to encourage innovation and reform. Discussion of strategies to actively challenge gender inequalities in education demands attention to the meaning of equality explored by Hughes (2002), who asks: does equality mean 'the same' and, if so, what measures of sameness should be used? Do you argue for women's rights on equal terms with men or should feminists be arguing that women's difference is at the root of their equality? The implications are evident in debate over the introduction of national curricula in England and Wales, following the 1988 Education Reform Act (broadly the same in Wales, but with the Welsh language incorporated).

The National Curriculum logic is that all students are entitled to develop the same learning skills and experience the same areas of knowledge. Initially mathematics, science and English were defined as core up to 16 years, together with seven foundation subjects – art, geography, history, music, physical education, technology and a modern foreign language (after age 11). Since 1998, however, the compulsory elements have been reduced and more choice has been reintroduced at 14-plus. Yet feminist research has verified the ways in which the assumed knowledge base of the new curriculum structures embody gendered understandings, besides a need to consider the modes of curriculum delivery that shape the teaching and learning of school subjects (Paechter 1998). Based on a far more sophisticated reading of the political, social and cultural climate, this position is very different from equal opportunities approaches that fail to address power differences embedded within the teaching and learning of school subjects. As Raphael Reed (1998: 62) suggests, one consequence of increasing demands to make the curriculum more relevant in content to boys' interests (e.g. greater use of computers and interactive learning, using football scores to teach mathematics) is a 'further masculinization of teaching styles and classroom environments.' Stereotypically male subjects are being privileged over other ideas or sets of knowledges and old differential subject choice patterns have re-emerged with the trend toward increased flexibility at Key Stage 4 and the disapplication of the National Curriculum.

Nonetheless, contemporary schoolgirls have greater access to education and training and increasing educational success generally. Analysing school statistics for the years 1985 to 1994, Arnot *et al.* (1996) found that more girls were entered for school-leaving examinations, more girls than boys were gaining five GCSEs grades A*–C, but girls in single-sex schools seemed to be at a substantial advantage. However, boys continued to achieve higher performances in relation to their entry than girls in nearly all subjects. It is also the case that interactions based on class and/or ethnicity remain crucial for both sexes. Within the GCSE results, for example, groups such as middle-class white boys and Indian and Chinese boys continue to achieve highly whereas white working-class, African-Caribbean and Bangladeshi boys tend to underachieve in the British education systems (Gillborn and Gipps 1996).

Contexts, changes and continuities: under-achieving boys?

We turn now to a necessarily brief consideration of current policy debates to contextualize the discussion of changes and continuities in gender and achievement in the new millennium. The introduction and support of a quasi-market in education crystallized by the Thatcher Conservative administrations of the 1980s, cast pupils and students as educational clients, within a framework of parental involvement and parental power. Examination and assessment performance league tables and a more stringent school inspection process (set up in 1992) all serve as mechanisms to 'measure' educational standards and performance, with an unprecedented emphasis on the phenomenon of the failing school. These new regimes have had a dramatic impact on schools, parents and pupils with a policy of local management of schools, open enrolment and a pupil-led funding formula crucial to the strategic processes of school choice. Ball and Gewirtz (1997: 214) point to the accretive value of 'successful' girls in their study of the marketing, selection and recruitments of schools, parents and pupils in fourteen case study schools. Not only do they become 'a valuable and sought-after resource' but 'their presence in school normally conveys positive impressions to parents about ethos and discipline.' This should not surprise us, for it rests firmly on popular conjecture about the civilizing influence of girls. It now becomes necessary to review aspects of contemporary debates about gender achievement.

Girls' improved educational performance has produced a furore of concern over threats to male breadwinning, the association of men and crime, the collapse of family life and the crisis of fatherhood. Yet Gorard *et al.* (1999: 442) demonstrate that a tendency to confuse percentage points with percentages has led to a misrepresentation of the GCSE results. Their analysis of the figures for all pupils at school in Wales from 1992 to 1997 shows girls doing better at Key Stages 1 to 4 in English and Welsh, at Key Stage 4 in languages, and in some design subjects and humanities, with no achievement gaps in mathematics and science, and gaps at other levels either static or declining. On the basis of these research findings the researchers speculate that the educational phenomenon of the 'growing gender gap' does not actually exist. Acknowledging that the picture is far from simple, the problem needs to be well understood given the implications for participants and policy-makers. A number of points will be made.

Literacy has been at the centre of debates about gender and achievement, especially in the primary schools, but it is important not to forget that girls have traditionally excelled at language-based subjects. The opening statement of the 1993 Ofsted report, *Boys and English*, was unequivocal: 'Boys do not do as well as girls in English in schools.' On the other hand, classroom-based research suggests that boys' greater show of interest in the new forms of technology (video, computer, CDs and DVDs) may be a better preparation for changing world literacy than may often be the case for girls (Clark and Millard 1998; Marsh 2003). Moreover the patterns of achievement change at the post-compulsory level since the few young men who enrol on A-level courses in English literature are more likely to outperform their female counterparts. With regard to mathematics, data from the Leverhulme Numeracy Research Programme – a longitudinal study of teaching and learning in English primary schools between 1997 and 2002 – highlighted girls not doing as well as boys in mathematics overall (Lucey *et al.* 2003). At GCSE, the tendency to play safe with examination entries of girls in mathematics means more girls than boys achieve grade C from the Intermediate tier, but mathematics departments in schools encourage continuation only with a B or C grade gained from the Higher tier. It is salient that more boys got A★ grades in GCSE mathematics, biology, chemistry and physics in August 2003 and more boys took the elite single science subjects of physical and chemistry than either biology or the balanced science associated with state schools (Curtis 2003) and yet three years later it was reported that 'boys are lagging seven years behind girls in performance in GCSE examinations' (Smithers 2006) in reference to a statement by the then Schools Minister Jim Knight that girls' results were improving faster than boys'. Notably, only in physics were males still gaining more A★ passes than females but, when we look at A★ to C passes for mathematics, physics, chemistry and biology, only in biology is there any noticeable difference between boys and girls, with boys having a slight edge (Joint Council for Qualifications 2006).

In terms of further qualifications, there has been a swift acceleration both in the proportion of 18-year-olds achieving A-level over the last twenty years and the number of entries from females. But subject choice is still heavily influenced by gendered views of future adult work. Fewer young women opt for business studies, computing, economics, mathematics, physics and technology, whereas the reverse is true of biology, French, history, home economics, psychology and sociology. Yet it is the case that those who make non-traditional choices excel compared with their fellows, presumably as a result of their being exceedingly able. Unsurprisingly, vocational qualifications are even more gendered than their academic counterparts. Whereas the overall numbers of young men and women entering the Modern Apprenticeships scheme (launched in 1994) are now almost equal, young men predominate in Engineering Manufacturing (96 per cent), Motor Industry (97 per cent), Construction (99 per cent) and Information Technology (67 per cent). Young women predominate in Hairdressing (92 per cent), Health and Social Care (89 per cent), Childcare (97 per cent) and Travel Services (86 per cent). In the words of the EOC 'these vocational choices and channelling make an almost immediate impact on earning potential and are a contributing factor to the 20% pay gap which exists between men and women' (EOC 2001).

In a speech at the 11th International Conference for School Effectiveness and Improvement, the then Schools Standards Minister Stephen Byers argued that 'the laddish anti-learning culture' was impeding boys' achievement (*The Guardian*, 6 January 1998). As a result of these concerns each local authority was required to address the issue of male disadvantage in drawing up its Education Development Plan. But the preoccupation with masculinity is not new. Early sociological investigations into the educational experiences of adolescent boys in the secondary school document the ways in which boys construct their masculine identities in the classroom. Influenced by neo-Marxist ideology, Willis's (1983) study focused on a group of anti-school working-class 'lads' who rejected the legitimacy of schooling because it had no relevance for the type of unskilled manual jobs that they wanted/expected to get on leaving school. These male students linked their counter-school culture to that of the factory floor; in so doing they asserted definitions of masculinity that positioned mental work and having girls as friends as effeminate. Similarly, in *Schooling the Smash Street Kids*, Corrigan (1979) used the analogy of a 'guerrilla struggle' to represent the ability of white, working-class, heterosexual boys in the north-east of England to monopolize space in the classroom, despite the 'occupying army' of teachers. Although these studies are useful in drawing attention to the articulation of social class as a variable in the construction of gender difference, they have been criticized by feminists for their neglect of gender-power dynamics and the variety of masculine forms that exist across a spectrum of difference (Skelton 2000).

More recent work on gender identity construction in education addresses these concerns. For instance, Connell (1995) outlines four versions of masculinity, which he calls hegemonic, subordinate, complicit and marginalized. Although these categories are helpful in that they enable us to take account of gender as a lived social practice, as Francis (2000) notes, the flip side of this explanatory framework is the suggestion of a hierarchy of 'types'. This may imply something more fixed than it really is, besides the problems such categorizations pose for the very concepts of masculinity and femininity. So, Francis argues instead that 'there are different strategies of constructing oneself as masculine, or feminine, rather than different types of masculinity and femininity' (2000: 16). Boys/men negotiate and take up a variety of masculinities and some of these confer power and prestige, whereas others are stigmatised and subordinate.

Significantly, dominant constructions of masculinity have implications for the broader topic of special educational needs (SEN). This is particularly clear among young boys positioned as slow learners, poor at sport and lacking physical strength and skill, who may resort to overtly challenging behaviour that may, in turn, make them liable to being classified as having special needs. Benjamin (2003) also highlights the need to take other underlying social inequalities into account. So, for example, African-Caribbean children of both sexes are more vulnerable to exclusion from school than their white peers (Osler and Vincent 2003), working-class boys are found in greater numbers in 'less acceptable' categories of emotional and behavioural difficulties and moderate learning difficulties, and middle-class boys dominate the non-stigmatized category of specific learning difficulties.

At the other end of the spectrum, figures for the degree finals in 2001 show that more men than women gained firsts in percentage terms, but, as 54 per cent of those taking finals were women, a greater number of women got top marks (*The Guardian*, 16 January 2001; 13 April 2002). However, if you take the figures for firsts and upper seconds together they show that more women achieved one of the two top classes, 59.9 per cent compared with 51.8 per cent of men. So, how can we make sense of this educational success story? As Mahony (1998: 39) points out, in the 1970s and 1980s perceptions of the differential abilities of boys and girls triggered a very different reaction to concerns about schoolgirl attainment in maths and science. Consequently, 'it took a good deal of persuasion by (mainly) feminists before policy makers would look beyond the innate capacities of girls themselves for explanations.' In contrast, the perception of boys as innately clever continues. Conversely, so does a tendency to imply that girls' academic attainment is the result of compliant hard work, even though there was no corresponding decline in female performance after the initial reduction of coursework in GCSEs in the mid-1990s (Arnot *et al.* 1999). Moreover deep connections between knowledge and power mean that girls' good performance in a particular subject may affect its status and perceived difficulty, as well as its place in contemporary society. Despite media reports of betrayal and the idea that schools have neglected boys' learning needs (*The Independent*, 27 November 2003), men are still over-represented both in top jobs and in the most powerful positions in society. Also, it is deeply ironical that evidence once used to help explain the under-achievement of girls, such as the issue of boys' laddish attitudes, is being used across time to signify different conclusions. Female school performance *has* improved but there is plenty of evidence to support the argument that this is *despite* the continuing male dominance in the classroom, the playground, curriculum content and greater demands on teacher time and energy (Francis 2000).

Conclusion

To come full circle and return to the quote with which we started, it remains the case that gender constructions have consequences in the workplace and in society. Despite any early learning disadvantage, top jobs continue to go to men. Female graduates can expect to earn 15 per cent less than their male equivalents by the age of 24 and it is mostly men on very high salaries who comprise the new élite in the financial and multinational sectors. The counterpoint to this is that professions like law and medicine are losing much of their traditional power and status just at the time when large numbers of women are coming into them (Walkerdine *et al.* 2001).

In many ways, media talk of 'troubled masculinities' is masking another story. In this story, the script is one of rising assessment performance of boys *and* girls over the past fifty years, making the phenomenon one of relative rates of improvement for both sexes. But this is absent from the dominant discourses that Epstein *et al.* (1998) see played out in the public debates about boys and achievement. And, more worryingly, the 'poor boys' discourse, the 'failing schools failing boys' discourse and the 'boys will be boys' discourse have all achieved a common-sense status within which female success is socially constructed as pathology. Contemporary schoolgirls may have greater career ambition, they may show an awareness of the gender-discriminatory nature of the adult workplace, plus inequality of housework and childcare, all of which may have provided new motivation for educational achievement as Francis (2000) suggests, but where will the exam results get them? Will this new generation of girls have the power to change conditions, and which girls are we talking about? Working-class girls with few or no qualifications are hardly ever mentioned; middle-class girls may go on to resolve the contradiction of 'career' and 'motherhood' by employing other women. As the authors of *Growing Up Girl* conclude: 'the much hyped girl power and female future looks decidedly unsteady and, for most, extremely difficult' (Walkerdine *et al.* 2001: 216).

Suggested further reading

You may like to dip into the *Feminist Critique of Education* (Francis and Skelton 2005a), which charts the development of feminist thinking in the field of gender and education in the last fifteen years. For a text which provides an accessible overview of contemporary debate see *Reassessing Gender and Achievement* by Becky Francis and Christine Skelton (2005b). With a particular focus on the intersection of gender and class, among other things *Growing Up Girl* by Valerie Walkerdine, Helen Lucey and June Melody (2001) unravels some of the psycho-social costs of educational success for some élite girls.

References

Arnot, M. (1984) 'How shall we Educate our Sons?', in Deem, R. (ed.) *Co-education Reconsidered.* Milton Keynes: Open University Press.

Arnot, M., David, M. and Weiner, G. (1996) *Educational Reforms and Gender Equality.* Manchester: Equal Opportunities Commission.

Arnot, M., David, M. and Weiner, G. (1999) *Closing the Gender Gap: Postwar Education and Social Change.* Cambridge: Polity Press.

Ball, S. J. and Gewirtz, S. (1997) 'Girls in the Education Market: Choice, Competition and Complexity', *Gender and Education.* **9** (2), 207–222.

Benjamin, S. (2003) 'Gender and Special Educational Needs', in Skelton, C. and Francis, B. (eds) *Boys and Girls in the Primary Classroom.* Maidenhead: Open University Press.

Benn, C. and Simon, B. (1972) *Half Way There: Report on the British Comprehensive-School Reform.* Harmondsworth: Penguin.

Briar, C. (1997) *Working for Women? Gendered Work and Welfare Policies in Twentieth-Century Britain.* London: UCL Press.

Clark, A. and Millard, E. (eds) (1998) *Gender in the Secondary Curriculum.* London: Routledge.

Clarricoates, K. (1980) 'The Importance of being Ernest . . . Emma . . . Tom . . . Jane: The Perception and Categorization of Gender Conformity and Gender Deviation in Primary Schools', in Deem, R. (ed.) *Schooling for Women's Work.* London: Routledge and Kegan Paul.

Coffey, A. (2001) *Education and Social Change.* Buckingham: Open University Press.

Cohen M. (1998) 'A Habit of Healthy Idleness: Boys' Underachievement, Schooling and Gender Relations', in Epstein, D., Elwood, J., Hey, V. and Maw, J. (eds) *Failing Boys? Issues in Gender and Achievement.* Buckingham: Open University Press.

Cole, M. (1938) *Marriage Past and Present.* London: J. M. Dent and Sons.

Connell, R. W. (1995) *Masculinities.* Cambridge: Polity Press.

Corrigan, P. (1979) *Schooling the Smash Street Kids.* London: Macmillan.

Curtis, P. (2003) 'GCSE Results 2003 – Key Points;, *The Guardian* 23 August. Available at http:// education.guardian.co.uk/gcses2003/story/0,,1026494,00.html (accessed 17 September 2007).

Deem, R. (1981) 'State Policy and Ideology in the Education of Women, 1944–1980', *British Journal of Sociology of Education.* **2** (2), 131–143.

Dyhouse, C. (2003) 'Troubled Identities: Gender and Status in the History of the Mixed College in English Universities since 1945', *Women's History Review.* **12** (2), 169–193.

Epstein, D., Elwood, J., Hey, V. and Maw, J. (eds) (1998) *Failing Boys? Issues in Gender and Achievement.* Buckingham: Open University Press.

Equal Opportunities Commission (2001) *Gender Issues in Modern Apprenticeships.* Manchester: Equal

Opportunities Commission.

Evans, M. (1995) 'Culture and Class', in Blair, M. and Holland, J. with Sheldon, S. (eds) *Identity and Diversity: Gender and the Experience of Education*. Clevedon: Multilingual Matters.

Francis, B. (2000) *Boys, Girls and Achievement*. London: Routledge-Falmer.

Francis, B. and Skelton, C. (2005a) *Feminist Critique of Education*. London: Routledge.

Francis, B. and Skelton, C. (2005b) *Reassessing Gender and Achievement*. London: Routledge.

Gillborn, D. and Gipps, C. (1996) *Recent Research on the Achievements of Ethnic Minority Pupils*. London: Ofsted.

Gorard, S., Rees, G. and Salisbury, J. (1999) 'Reappraising the Apparent Under-achievement of Boys at School', *Gender and Education*. **11** (4) 441–454.

Griffin, C. (1985) *Typical Girls? Young Women from School to the Job Market*. London: Routledge and Kegan Paul.

Heward, C. (1993) 'Men and Women and the Rise of Professional Society: The Intriguing History of Teacher Education', *History of Education*. **22** (1), 11–32.

Hughes, C. (2002) *Key Concepts in Feminist Theory and Research*. London: Sage.

Hunt, F. (ed.) (1987) *Lessons for Life. The Schooling of Girls and Women 1850–1950*. Oxford: Basil Blackwell.

Jackson, B. and Marsden, D. (1962) *Education and the Working-class*. London: Routledge and Kegan Paul.

Joint Council for Qualifications (2006) *National Provisional GCSE (Full Course) Results – June 2006 (All UK Candidates)*. Available at http://image.guardian.co.uk/sys-files/Education/documents/2006/08/24/GCSEs2006.pdf (accessed 17 September 2007).

Lucey, H., Brown, M., Denvir, H. Askew, M. and Rhodes, V. (2003) 'Girls and Boys in the Primary Maths Classroom', in Skelton, C. and Francis, B. (eds) *Boys and Girls in the Primary Classroom*. Maidenhead: Open University Press.

McCulloch, G. (1998) *Failing the Ordinary Child? The Theory and Practice of Working-Class Secondary Education*. Milton Keynes: Open University Press.

Mackie, L. and Patullo, P. (1977) *Women Who Work*. London: Tavistock.

Mahony, P. (1998) 'Girls will be Girls and Boys will be First', in Epstein, D., Elwood, J., Hey, V. and Maw, J. (eds) *Failing Boys? Issues in Gender and Achievement*. Buckingham: Open University Press.

Marsh, J. (2003) 'Superhero Stories', in Skelton, C. and Francis, B. (eds.) *Boys and Girls in the Primary Classroom*. Maidenhead: Open University Press.

Miller, J. (1996) *School for Women*. London: Virago.

Newsom, J. (1948) *The Education of Girls*. London: Faber and Faber.

Ofsted (1993) *Boys and English*. London: HMSO.

Osler, A. and Vincent, K. (2003) *Girls and Exclusion: Rethinking the Agenda*. London: RoutledgeFalmer.

Payne, I. (1980) 'Sexist Ideology and Education', in Spender, D. and Sarah, E. (eds) *Learning to Lose*. London: Women's Press.

Paechter, C. (1998) *Educating the Other: Gender, Power and Schooling*. London: Falmer Press.

Raphael Reed, L. (1998) '"Zero Tolerance": Gender Performance and School Failure', in Epstein, D.,

Elwood, J., Hey, V. and Maw, J. (eds.) *Failing Boys? Issues in Gender and Achievement*. Buckingham: Open University Press.

Rendel, M. (1997) *Whose Human Rights?* Stoke-on-Trent: Trentham.

Riddell, S. (1989) 'Pupils, Resistance and Gender Codes: A Study of Classroom Encounters', *Gender and Education*. **1** (2), 183–198.

Riley, D. (1983) *War in the Nursery: Theories of the Child and Mother*. London: Virago.

Riley, K. A. (1994) *Quality and Equality. Promoting Opportunities in Schools*. London: Cassell.

Skelton, C. (2000) *Schooling the Boys*. Buckingham: Open University Press.

Smithers, R. (2006) 'Boys Seven Years behind Girls as GCSE Results Gap Remains', *The Guardian*, 20 October 2006. Available at http://education.guardian.co.uk/gcses/story/0,,1926961,00.html (accessed 17 September 2007).

Spender, D. (1980) 'Education or Indoctrination?', in Spender, D. and Sarah, E. (eds) *Learning to Lose*. London: Women's Press.

Stanworth, M. (1986) *Gender and Schooling: A Study of Sexual Divisions in the Classroom*. London: Hutchinson.

Thom, D. (1987) 'Better a Teacher Than a Hairdresser? "A Mad Passion for Equality" or, Keeping Molly and Betty Down', in Hunt, F. (ed.) *Lessons for Life: The Schooling of Girls and Women 1850–1950*. Oxford: Basil Blackwell.

Walkerdine, V., Lucey, H. and Melody, J. (2001) *Growing Up Girl*. Basingstoke: Palgrave Macmillan.

Weiner, G. (1994) *Feminisms in Education*. Buckingham: Open University Press.

Willis, P. (1983) *Learning to Labour: How Working-class Kids Get Working-class Jobs*. Aldershot, Gower.

8

Schooling and social class

Michael Wyness

> The history of all hitherto existing society is the history of class struggles.
> (Marx and Engels [1848] 1985: 79)

Introduction

MUCH HAS BEEN WRITTEN about the demise of social class and other meta-narratives such as gender and nationality. The advent of consumerism and globalization and the decline of Marxism as a political and intellectual force worldwide have at the very least complicated the view that our social positions, identities and affiliations are governed by conventional material differences. Similarly within education, the conventional view that children of different class backgrounds are mapped on to different class trajectories as they move through the school system has been challenged by an educational establishment committed to raising the standards of all children and ensuring that at least half of all young people have access to higher education.

However, despite the rise of the 'individual' and the overall economic well-being of many developed countries, material differences between groups within society are widening. In a UNICEF report on the state of the world's children it was reported

> that the proportion of children living in poverty in the developed world has risen in 17 out of the 24 OECD nations for which data are available. No matter which of the commonly used poverty measures is applied, the situation of children has deteriorated over the last decade.

> (UNICEF 2006: 235)

The UK Labour government has made the reduction of child poverty a key plank of its social policy since coming to power in 1997. However, the UK still has one of the highest rates of child poverty among developed countries and policies more generally designed to tackle social inequality have been unable to reverse the widening gap between the richest and poorest sectors of society (Wheeler *et al.* 2005). According to one commentator, 'the gap between rich and poor was greater in 2002–03, the latest year for which data is available, than it was in 1996–7, when Labour came to power' (Elliott 2004: n.p.).

This chapter examines social inequality as a continuing feature within the UK. It focuses on the role that education and schooling play in reinforcing these trends, while at the same time identifying the way that the current government has used social and educational policy to tackle child poverty and social inequality. In the first section we explore the contention that, despite generating policies that set out to equalize conditions for all children, social class differences between children are reinforced through the education system. In the second section we examine a number of factors that mediate the relationship between the children, the school and their future class identities. Among other things we discuss the relationship between the child and the curriculum, the influence of the family and the countervailing importance of the peer group as social frame of reference for particular groups of working class children. In the final section we analyse government policy and highlight the ambiguous relationship between education policy and social class.

Social class and its reproduction

One approach to researching social inequality is to look at how social class differences are reproduced from generation to generation. In the 1950s and 1960s in the UK there was an expectation that the links between children's class of origin and their social class of destination would be broken as the state invested heavily in trying to ensure that working-class children had opportunities to become socially mobile. Despite these political and economic commitments, the evidence during this period suggested that there was limited movement between the social classes (Halsey *et al.* 1980). More recently, longitudinal studies that follow large samples of children from birth into adulthood corroborate these findings, and report a generational transmission of disadvantage. The Centre for Longitudinal Studies (CLS) at the University of London draws on birth cohort studies from the 1958 National Child Development Study and the 1970 British Cohort Study in making more explicit links between the child's social class of origin and their social class of destination. Researchers referred to size of family, housing and income as indicators of social disadvantage. Drawing on these indicators, they argue that as children get older social disadvantages persist, with 16-year-olds just as likely to experience similar levels of poverty as when they were aged 11, and 'poor' teenagers remaining in poverty once they reach adulthood and well into their thirties (Blanden and Gibbons 2006).

Schooling and social class reproduction

Schooling and education tend to reinforce these class-based trends. A recent Joseph Rowntree report identified relatively poor levels of educational success associated with whether a pupil was entitled to free school meals, parents' employment status, family structure and parents' level of educational qualifications (Cassen and Kingdom 2007). According to 2003 figures, 68 per cent of children from economically affluent families gained five or more GCSEs at A*–C grade as opposed to 35 per cent of children from economically poor backgrounds. If we refer more specifically to those children receiving free school meals the figure is 25 per cent (DfES 2006).

Recent research has combined assessments of young children's development with socio-economic data in accurately predicting the level of educational attainment by the age of 26 (reported in Evans 2006). The Millennium Cohort Study also focuses on the early years with language and cognitive development markedly different for children from poorer backgrounds compared with their more affluent counterparts (CLS 2007). The researchers place particular emphasis on a child's 'school readiness', with children from families in poverty up to a year behind more affluent children by the time they reach 3 and thus less able to engage with the culture and expectations of the early years of primary school.

The relationship between social class and education is a complex one. Ethnicity, for example, is a powerful intervening variable. Social disadvantage is a complex idea with ethnicity as well as social class being a significant factor. Both factors combined suggest, for example, that a small group of middle-class African-Caribbean pupils will do better than their working-class counterparts. However African-Caribbean pupils are the lowest attaining of ethnic minority groupings if we look simply at all middle-class pupils (Gillborn and Safia Mirza 2000). Children of Pakistani and Bangladeshi origins are seen as being particularly vulnerable because English is a second language. Other research suggests that this is likely to be a short-term problem, with African and Asian children catching up white children by the time they get to secondary school (Cassen and Kingdom 2007). Nevertheless, educational failure is likely to be located in poor urban areas where there is a predominance of families of Bangladeshi, Pakistani and Caribbean origin.

Class, schooling and the relational dimension

The broader picture of social inequality and schooling tends to focus on material factors such as income, health and employment status. If we draw on social and cultural influences, what we might call relational criteria, we can build up a more subtle and multilayered understanding of how schooling contributes to the reproduction of inequality. Moreover, a closer look at the everyday lives of thousands of school children and their families reveals an intermingling of social and cultural as well as economic factors that complicate and on occasion contradict the broader picture.

The child and the curriculum

Children's relationship to knowledge through the school curriculum can have a significant effect on their ability to thrive in school. Middle-class children are better equipped to engage with the curriculum than working-class pupils. For middle-class children there is a seamless link between their own lives and interests and school-based knowledge, which is abstract and formal in nature. Knowledge here becomes an end in itself: middle-class children find it easier to enter into an intellectual world of abstract ideas that connect with their own affiliations and identities. Given this relationship between middle-class pupils and the curriculum there is a tendency to take a more negative view with respect to working-class children, with the latter alienated from the school curriculum. Hatcher (2000) argues that the curriculum does not connect with working-class children's everyday lives and relations with their families, as their experiences are more likely to be shaped by more immediate influences from the community and the street. And in some respects working-class children enter an alien environment when they go to school. However, the curriculum also offers more tangible rewards. The dominant ideas and conceptual tools that make up the curriculum can be grasped by working-class children as a means of gaining qualifications. Although this still puts working-class children at a disadvantage in the classroom, it does at very least suggest one possible route to educational achievement for children who lack the cultural means to progress throughout their school careers

Cultural and social capital

The family has been a key resource in both reinforcing and challenging the relationship between 'origins and destinations' since Douglas's (1967) classic analysis of family influences in education in the early 1960s. However, it is the persuasive, if at times opaque, force of Bourdieu's (1997; Bourdieu and Wacquant 1992) theory of social and cultural capital that locates the family as a primary force in class reproduction. There is still the recourse to material factors in trying to explain the differential education outcomes for working-class and middle-class children. But cultural and social factors are drawn on in explaining how these material differences are passed on generationally.

Social and cultural capital are in many respects the intangible resources that parents and communities pass on to their children. Middle-class parents, in particular, invest these resources by socialising their children into the dominant culture. Social capital consists of the contacts, social networks and friendships that constitute the everyday social relations people possess. The social networks inhabited by middle-class parents, such as the golf club, the private housing estate and the parent/teacher association give them social advantages in providing their children with a wider range of opportunities and a more appropriate social frame of reference as their children progress through the school system.

Bourdieu's (1997) notion of cultural capital is more diffuse in that it includes levels of educational qualification as well as a more embodied notion that includes dispositions, attitudes and speech patterns. In effect an individual's identity and personality reflects their social class position. Thus our taste in music, our dress code, even the way that we carry ourselves in public, all demonstrate in a number of ways our social class and differentiate us from others. But, again unlike more conventional Marxist analyses, in which personal attributes are either ignored or inferred from economic status, an individual has to work at displaying their cultural capital. A more nuanced analysis here focuses on the these personal habits and predispositions in terms of the notion of 'habitus'. Bourdieu argues that these cultural resources are deployed by middle-class parents in maintaining their class positions and passed on to their children through processes of socialization.

In effect what we are saying here is that educational success and failure are governed by parents' access to these social and cultural resources. Unlike more conventional Marxist analyses that emphasis the relative positions of people within the social structure, there is an important relational or interactive component to the theory. In a conventional Marxist sense parents possess their 'capital', but they also need to invest it. How they use these resources has important consequences for their children's life chances. Thus working-class children fail because their parents have limited access to the above resources, whereas middle-class children are more likely to succeed because their parents are in tune with dominant modes of thought and speech found within the school and have the right social frames of reference.

Lareau (1989) in her research on the relationship between US families and elementary or primary schools refers to the significance of cultural and social capital in terms of parents' relative 'connectedness'. Applying Bourdieu's model to a class analysis of parental involvement in their children's schooling, she refers to three key dimensions: the extent to which parents see education as a teacher's responsibility; the level of parental support at home for their children's schooling; and the extent to which both parents are reference points when the school comes into contact with the family.

Middle-class parents are said to be more connected to their children's schooling in that they see themselves as being jointly responsible for their children's education with the school; they are likely to 'speak the same language' as teachers and take a more informed and structured interest in their school work; and both parents are likely to get involved with their children's schooling. Not only do middle-class parents take a greater interest in their children's educational progress, they are more informed, more sceptical of educational issues. Relations between working-class parents and the school, on the other hand, are characterised by 'separateness'. Their children's education is seen as the school's responsibility, their interests in their children's schooling is sporadic and largely concerned with social and emotional rather than 'educational' issues, and mothers tend to take sole parental responsibility when it comes to getting in contact with school. From the school's vantage point this perceived lack of parental responsibility for their children's education is seen as an obstacle to teachers in terms of delivering the curriculum and supporting children's educational and social development (Connell *et al.* 1982).

Parents and risk management

The more recent work of Stephen Ball and his colleagues (Ball *et al.* 1995; Ball 2003) has linked Bourdieu's theory to contemporary UK educational policy. The introduction of a quasi-market in education in the late 1980s and the rise of an audit culture have placed more importance on the role of the parent as an educational consumer.

> The new culture of schooling, a culture of commodification and output indicators which articulates with the culture of choice and relative advantage into which parents are being drawn.
>
> (Ball *et al.* 1995: 65–66)

Although middle-class parents' access to the different forms of capital gives them a clear advantage in comparison with working-class parents, these market opportunities have placed particular strains on the former as they attempt to retain if not improve their social class position. Parents here become risk managers and invest their cultural and social capital in trying to minimize the chances of their children's academic failure. The key point in their children's academic careers is the last year of primary school. Middle-class parents are now more likely to regulate their children's futures by searching the Internet for information about the best state secondary schools, 'naturalizing' their children's entry into higher education, spending far more time visiting prospective schools and networking with those who are likely to have some local influence in school choice. Middle-class parents are, in general, investing far more of their economic, social and cultural capital in their children's futures. Ball (2003) refers to the emotional and psychological costs: parents report higher levels of anxiety as they commit themselves to 'doing the right thing' for their children. They also refer to the guilt sometimes felt at not being able to make the right choice for their children.

Ball and his colleagues (1995) in an earlier piece of work distinguish between different 'circuits of choice' that map on to middle-class and working-class households. Parent choice is part of a decision-making strategy undertaken by all parents in one way or another when their child is about to enter secondary school. Middle-class parents have a wider range of schools from which to choose, including in some cases schools in the private sector. They are also in a position to prioritize school choice over other family commitments. They have the time, space and material resources to make 'strategic' choices. Working-class parents, on the other hand, are constrained by time and social geography: getting their children to a more distant school is likely to be a problem if there is limited transport or the school timetable does not mesh with their own domestic or work timetables. Ball *et al.* (1995) argue that working-class parents have to make 'accommodative' choices: they are constrained by local circumstances and their own experience of schooling, which may be less sanguine than their middle-class counterparts' experiences.

Family dynamics and school readiness

Whereas educationalists have acknowledged the school as a socialising domain, social scientists have tended to emphasize the family as the primary socialising agency, with parents being the most formative influence on their children, particularly in the early years (Wyness 2006). This assumption is reinforced on a daily basis by primary school teachers, who continually refer to their pupils as the products of their parents. In an early analysis of home–school relations Sharp and Green (1975: 86) argue that primary school teachers generally expect parents to provide them with 'school trained child(ren)', children who have been socialized by their parents such that they easily take on their new roles as pupils in the first few months of their schooling. Their analysis of 'school readiness' confirmed the view that parents with limited social and cultural capital are less likely to be able to produce 'school trained children'. Consequently teachers are more likely to spend their time managing working-class children's behaviour in class than providing them with a formal education that prepares them for their later school years.

More recently, Gillian Evans in her ethnography of working-class life in South London explores the dynamics between parents and children and observes that 'formal learning plays little part in the way that caring relationships are established at home' (2006: 45). Working-class family values conflict with expectations found in school; the lack of school 'readiness' and 'connectedness' here being seen as an important factor in children's educational failure in later years. Thus working-class children are more likely to spend their non-school time on non-educational activities; they are less likely to be pushed by their parents, particularly when they claim to dislike school. Education is effectively seen as a separate sphere of activity associated with what goes on within the school.

Peer group

A final mediating factor is the peer group. The relations that children and young people have with their peers are more likely to be correlated with levels of crime and delinquency (Muncie 2004). However, poverty is often conceptualized in terms of social exclusion, which refers to a cluster of risk factors that include educational and public order criteria. There are also a number of well-known pieces of research that link school disaffection among young males to social class and the reproduction of inequality. Thus the work of Willis (1977), Corrigan (1979) and Mac an Ghaill (1988) all argue that the peer group in some way or another both underpins educational failure and provides an alternative set of values that compensates for a young working-class male's anticipated educational failure.

More recent research locates the street and the peer culture as a dominant social and moral frame of reference for many young men in inner-city areas. Evans (2006), for example, argues that charismatic rebel peers provide alternative role models for young boys in the absence of appropriate adult male role models in school and where discipline is a problem in some schools and classrooms. The street becomes the location for the development of reputation and social identity: the site where conventional rules on what is appropriate behaviour are inverted.

> Rather than making their behaviour seem pathological, my proposal is for research that might help us begin to understand how it is that young boys in certain kinds of social situations, like on the street and in failing schools, can come to structure their relations with one another in such a way that troublesome, violent and intimidating behaviour becomes a social good.
>
> (Evans 2006: 115)

Evans' research is an ethnography of family life in a local setting and there is no attempt to generalize her data to other young males brought up in similar urban working-class areas in the UK. Nevertheless, within this context we might speculate that school rules, the curriculum, examinations and the compulsory nature of schooling are unlikely to connect with everyday lives of many working-class boys. Other rules and conventions generated in the peer group become more compelling. This view is corroborated by Horgan (2007): findings from her study of primary school-aged children's experiences of poverty in Northern Ireland identify levels of 'disenchantment' from schooling at around the ages of 9 and 10 among boys from disadvantaged backgrounds. The peer group can act as a conflicting source for young boys that challenges the dominant expectations around schooling, making it more difficult for them to commit themselves to the educational project.

Tackling inequality

'Bucking the trend'

While the research emphasis has been on trying to establish the relationship between social class inequality and educational achievement, the political context in Britain since the late 1990s has been one of challenging the deterministic relationship between origins and destinations through the introduction of policies of social inclusion. Contemporary research agendas to some extent have reflected this policy approach. Thus the CLS research not only focuses on the intergenerational transmission of inequality, it also looks at factors that break this cycle of disadvantage. Key factors here in producing 'resilience in the face of adversity' are linked to the parents' positive relationship to education and their children's schooling. Thus the ability of working-class parents to provide a more educationally stimulating home environment for their children (CLS 2007: 2) reduces the risk of their falling into poverty in adulthood. Children from working-class backgrounds are also more likely to do well in school if both parents are involved in supporting their children's education, and where children's schooling is integrated into the routines of domestic life within households. For Blanden and Gibbons (2006) reading was a particularly important domestic activity, with working-class parents being in a stronger to position to 'buck the trend' if they read regularly to their children.

UK government policy: challenging inequality

Turning to recent UK education policy, attempts are being made to limit these social class inequalities in education with a view to reducing levels of poverty and social exclusion. Whereas the previous Conservative administration promoted the role of the *individual* in and against the broader society, the Labour Party on coming to power in 1997 made clear undertakings to improving the life chances of particular *groups* within society. The commitment to reducing child poverty, and the setting up of the social exclusion unit to tackle a range of social problems from racism through to teenage pregnancy, were expected to have a significant impact on the well-being of young working-class children. Education Action Zones were created in 1999 in areas where schools were under-performing. With a mixture of support from local businesses and community and parents, schools within these areas were expected to 'create a culture of expectation, achievement and opportunity in areas of significant social and economic disadvantage' (Birmingham City Council 2007: n.p.).

Pre-school children were also targeted, with children from the age of 3 onwards given free access to early years education through the childcare system. There are also a number of initiatives designed to tackle inequalities between families, giving young children from all social class backgrounds the opportunity to thrive within the formal school sector. Children's centres have been opened up in most communities across the UK through the *Sure Start* initiative (Glass 1999). The government's most recent child-related project, *Every Child Matters*, offers a more integrated institutional approach to supporting children's physical social and educational well-being. Schools are now to work alongside the health and social services in offering more holistic support for children and their families. Although evaluations of *Sure Start* have identified its failure to reach the most excluded families and communities (Ward 2007), there is undoubtedly here a commitment to equality of opportunity at pre-school level with 'school readiness' being seen as a crucial precondition of educational success for working-class children.

Government policy: reinforcing inequalities

Despite the Labour government's commitment to greater social inclusion, there are important continuities with the earlier Conservative emphasis on individual differences, which arguably reinforce existing social class differences in terms of opportunities and outcomes. The Conservatives' attempts to create a quasi-market in education emphasized the role of the individual parent as a consumer of their children's education, with parental choice being promoted against the 'collectivist' powers of the educational establishment, including Local Education Authorities (Whitty 1992). Market values imply a differentiated educational product. Thus the introduction of the City Technical Colleges and 'grant maintained' schools, the retention of grammar schools and the long-held commitment to the private sector created the impression that all parents had a choice of where to send their children when they left primary school. The Labour government has extended this approach by introducing foundation schools with subject specialisms, self-governing independent state schools, and City Academies alongside existing LEA community schools and the government's expansion of the range of faith schools. Notable in terms of social class differences are three things. First, as with the Conservative educational regime, the current government is creating not simply a market in schooling, but a new hierarchy of schools within the state sector. Specialist schools, City Academies and trust schools are being created ostensibly to bring 'more choice and higher standards' but are arguably creating distinctive choices for middle class parents committed to maintaining their class positions (BBC News 2006: 1) Second, there is the government's ambivalence towards grammar schools. The process of introducing more socially inclusive comprehensive schools in the 1960s and 1970s was never completed, with a number of LEAs retaining a hierarchical distinction between 'academic' grammars and other state schools. Chitty (1999) provides evidence that the existence of grammar schools, predominantly populated by middle-class children, has a depressing effect on exam results of other surrounding state schools. Schools in areas without grammar schools do far better than their counterparts in areas with grammar schools. Third, as was noted earlier, it is only parents living in more affluent areas that have the economic, social and cultural capital to take advantage of this choice in secondary schooling. While middle-class parents have greater social and cultural capital, they also tend to live in areas where their local schools tend to be those with the best reputations.

Individual differences within the classroom

Differentiation also takes place within schools. The Labour party rejected its long-held support of mixed ability teaching prior to the 1997 election.

> The modernisation of the comprehensive principle requires that all pupils are encouraged to progress as far and as fast as they are able. Grouping children by ability can be an important way of making that happen.
>
> (Tony Blair quoted in Carvel and Macleod 1997: 7)

For many, Blair was making a policy statement on what had already become standard practice in most UK schools. However, this did formalize the uniqueness of the English and Welsh system in bunching pupils together on the basis of perceived abilities from primary school onwards. In most developed countries the teaching of mixed ability groupings of pupils is the norm, and, as Boaler (2005) notes, ability groupings have fateful consequences for the great majority of children. As many as 88 per cent of children placed in groups or sets at the age of 4 continue in the same sets until they leave school. The emphasis on setting generates low expectations among children within lower status groupings, who work their way through the education system in terms of relatively poor levels of achievement. Moreover, Boaler's research reinforces the link between educational outcomes and social class origins; children taught within mixed ability classrooms are more likely to do well in school than children taught in single ability groupings (Boaler 2005). Boaler's work on learning strategies and social class connects with large-scale comparisons of national education systems that suggest that the UK, despite its relatively high standard of living, has one of the most unequal education systems compared with other developed countries (Green 2003).

Conclusion

Labour government policy on education seems to act in a contradictory manner when challenging the problem of social inequality within the UK. As Clyde Chitty (1999) argues,

> [T]here are obvious contradictions involved in affirming a commitment to 'social justice' and 'community' while, at the same time, pursuing competitive market policies in education.

The government has also vigorously pursued the 'school improvement' agenda, which emphasizes improving educational standards for all children. In the past few years there have been rising levels of educational performance across the board, particularly in relation to the GCSE examinations taken by 15- and 16-year-olds (BBC News 2007). However, the educational outcomes of all children tell us very little about the relative differences between groups of children. Hatcher (2000: 184) distinguishes between 'polarising improvement' and 'equalising improvement'. The emphasis on absolute standards has led to the polarizing of outcomes for pupils with middle-class pupils and schools doing proportionately better than pupils in working-class areas. Although there may be some 'equalising' outcomes in that some schools in deprived areas have been able to take advantage of educational changes, the great majority of children from poor areas have limited opportunities to improve their chances of educational success (Mortimore and Whitty 1997). In many respects many of the initiatives designed to improve the life chances of working-class children, particularly in the early years, are very likely to be monopolized by middle-class parents.

As we have seen in this chapter, material factors still shape the relationship between different groups of pupils within the English and Welsh education system. However, the relationship between social class and education is a complex one. A closer 'micro' analysis of the lives and experiences of young people and their families reveals a number of mediating factors that provide a nuanced account of how class inequality is reproduced from generation to generation. Social and cultural factors are critical, with parents playing a crucial role in acting as a conduit between the child and the education system. How parents understand, experience and relate to the education system has an important bearing on children's life chances. As we have tried to demonstrate, middle-class parents have a number of advantages over their working-class counterparts in ensuring that their children are educationally successful.

Suggested further reading

Recent research commissioned by the Joseph Rowntree Foundation (Hirsch 2007) is useful in providing up-to-date statistical data on the relationship between poverty and education. The UNICEF (2006) data gives a more global perspective. For rich empirical analyses of the significance of cultural and social factors, see Evans (2006) and Ball (2003) and Connell *et al.* (1982).

References

Ball, S. (2003) *Class Strategies and the Education Market: The Middle Classes and Social Advantage*. London: RoutledgeFalmer.

Ball, S., Bowe, R. and Gewirtz, S. (1995) 'Circuits of Schooling: A Sociological Exploration of Parental Choice of School in Social Class Contexts', *Sociological Review*. **43** (1), 52–78.

BBC News (2006) 'Blair Wants Another 200 Academies', 30 November. Available at http://news.bbc.co.uk/1/hi/education/6157435.stm.

BBC News (2007) 'GCSE Results Rise at all Grades', 25 August. Available at http://news.bbc.co.uk/1/hi/education/4182006.stm.

Birmingham City Council (2007) *Education Action Zones*. Available at www.services.bgfl.org/services/eic/eazs.

Blanden, J. and Gibbons S. (2006) *The Persistence of Poverty across Generations*. Bristol: Policy Press.

Boaler, J. (2005) 'The "Psychological Prisons" from which they Never Escaped: The Role of Ability Grouping in Reproducing Social Class Inequalities', *Forum*. **47** (2–3), 135–143.

Bourdieu, P. (1997) 'The Forms of Capital', in Halsey, A. H., Lauder, H., Brown, P. and Wells, A. (eds) *Education, Culture and Economy and Society*. Oxford: Oxford University Press.

Bourdieu, P. and Wacquant, L. (1992) *An Invitation to Reflexive Sociology*. Cambridge: Polity.

Carvel, J. and Macleod, D. (1997) 'Teachers Welcome Reform', *Guardian Weekly*, 13 July, p. 9.

Cassen, R. and Kingdom, G. (2007) 'Tackling Low Educational Achievement', *Joseph Rowntree Findings*. Available at www.jrf.org.uk/knowledge/findings.

Centre for Longitudinal Studies (CLS) (2007) 'The Intergenerational Transmission of Disadvantage and Advantage', *CLS Briefings*, February. Available at www.cls.ioe.ac.uk.

Chitty, C. (1999) 'The Comprehensive Ideal', in Chitty, C. and Dunford, J. (eds) (1999) *State Schools: New Labour and the Conservative Legacy*. London: Frank Cass.

Connell, R. W., Ashenden, D. J., Kessler, S. and Dowsett, G. W. (1982) *Making the Difference: Schools, Families and Social Division*. London: George Allen and Unwin.

Corrigan, P. (1979) *Schooling the Smash Street Kids*. London: Macmillan.

Department for Education and Science (DfES) (2006) *Social Mobility: Narrowing Social Class Educational Attainment Gaps*. Available at www.dfes.gov.uk/rsgateway.

Douglas, J. W. B. (1967) *The Home and the School*. London: Panther.

Elliott, L. (2004) 'Labour Fails to Stop Widening of Income Gap', *Guardian Unlimited*, 24 June. Available at http://society.guardian.co.uk/socialexclusion/story/0,,1246042,00.html.

Evans, G. (2006) *Educational Failure and Working Class White Children in Britain*. Basingstoke: Palgrave.

Gillborn, D. and Safia Mirza, H (2000) *Educational Inequality: Mapping Race, Class and Gender*. London: Ofsted.

Glass, N. (1999) 'Sure Start: The Development of an Early Intervention Programme for Young Children in the United Kingdom', *Children and Society*. **13**, 257–264.

Green, A. (2003) 'Is UK Education Exceptionally Unequal? Evidence from the IAALS and PISA Surveys', *Forum*. **45** (2), 67–70.

Halsey, A. H., Heath, A. and Ridge, J. (1980) *Origins and Destinations*. Oxford: Clarendon Press.

Hatcher, R. (2000) 'Social Class and School: Relationships to Knowledge', in Cole, M. (ed) *Education, Equality and Human Rights*. London: Routledge.

Hirsch, D. (2007) 'Experiences of Poverty and Educational Disadvantage', Joseph Rowntree Foundation. Available at www.jrf.org.uk/knowledge/findings/socialpolicy/pdf/2123.pdf.

Horgan, G. (2007) 'The Impact of Poverty on Young Children's Experience of School', Joseph Rowntree Foundation. Available at www.jrf.org.uk/knowledge/findings/.

Lareau, A. (1989) *Home Advantage: Social Class and Parental Intervention in Elementary Schools*. London: Falmer.

Mac an Ghaill, M. (1988) *Young, Gifted and Black: Student–Teacher Relations in the Schooling of Black Youth*. Milton Keynes: Open University Press.

Marx, K. and Engels, F. [1848](1985) *The Communist Manifesto*. Harmondsworth: Penguin.

Mortimore, P. and Whitty, G. (1997) *Can School Improvement Overcome the Effects of Disadvantage?* London: Institute of Education.

Muncie, J. (2004) *Youth and Crime*, 2nd edn. London: Sage.

Sharp, R. and Green, A. (1975) *Education and Social Control*. London: Routledge and Kegan Paul.

UNICEF (2006) 'Child Poverty in Rich Countries, 2005: Part I', *International Journal of Health Services*. **36** (2) 235–269.

Ward, J. (2007) 'Sure Start Failing Ethnic Minorities, Says Report', *Guardian Unlimited*, 10 July. Available at http://society.guardian.co.uk/children/.

Wheeler, B., Shaw, M., Mitchell, R. and Dorling D. (2005) *Life in Britain: Using Millennial Census Data to Understand Poverty, Inequality and Place*. Bristol: Policy Press.

Whitty, G. (1992) 'Education, Economy and National Culture', in Bocock, R. and Thompson, K. (eds) *Social and Cultural Forms of Modernity*. Cambridge: Polity.

Willis, P. (1977) *Learning to Labour*. Farnborough: Saxon House.

Wyness, M. (2006) *Childhood and Society: An Introduction to the Sociology of Childhood*. Basingstoke: Palgrave.

9

Special educational needs and inclusion in education

An historical overview

Mary Kellett

> I am part of an oppressed group of people who need to challenge the cultural barriers that stop them being able to reach their full potential.
> (Simone Aspis, the first person with a learning difficulty to be appointed as a national spokesperson for a British political party, Green Party Press Office, 2001)

Introduction

THE FOCUS OF THIS chapter is special educational needs and inclusion. Both terms are in common usage at the time of writing and the relationship between them is one of the issues explored, along with an examination of the principal ideological and pedagogical debates. Before that, the historical origins of special education are explained in order to assist better understanding of how special educational needs and inclusion have evolved into their present form. Attention is paid to important legislation that has shaped the course of special education over time and pedagogical approaches such as behaviourist and interactive teaching methods that were developed. The final part of the chapter looks at inclusion, beginning with the social model it is built upon, how it is developing and the impact it is having both at policy level and in the grass roots of the classroom.

The origins of special educational needs

We pick up the historical trail in the nineteenth century when discourses on education produced the 'medical' and 'charitable' models of disability. The medical (sometimes known as 'deficit') model viewed children's behaviour in terms of *internal* biological differences, categorising 'syndromes' and 'conditions' as defects within the child. This perspective disregarded any *external* factors such as poverty, health or life experience as having any bearing on the nature of the disability. The charitable model saw disabled children as tragic figures, deserving of pity. This was a disempowering perspective that categorised them as passive recipients of philanthropy. Once again, the fault was seen to lie within the child – disability was a personal defect. Because of the dominance of these discourses, when basic education for most children was established (Forster's 1870 Education Act and the 1872 Education (Scotland) Act), no provision was made in these Acts for disabled children or children with learning difficulties.

Doctors could diagnose four levels of special 'condition': *idiot, imbecile, feeble-minded* and *moral-defective.* The Departmental Committee on Defective and Epileptic Children investigated whether the education system could be adapted for any of these children. The committee concluded that *imbeciles* were best placed in an asylum, the *feeble-minded* and *moral-defectives* could attend special schools but *idiots* were deemed ineducable and excluded from the education system altogether (Report of the Departmental Committee on Defective and Epileptic Children 1898). The differentiation of these categories was not clearly defined and school boards were required to appoint a medical officer to decide a child's 'condition' and educational placement (1913 Mental Deficiency Act). In Scotland, the Education of Defective Children (Scotland) Act 1906 gave school boards the ability to cater for defective children in special schools or classes. Those incapable of learning were, as in England, assigned to institutions by their local parish councils.

The 1921 Education Act required that numbers of 'feeble-minded' and 'backward' children within each local authority were recorded so that separate education could be provided. This maintained a powerful link between the diagnosis of a category and the allocation of a particular type of education. It was this impetus that led to the development and rapid adoption of the intelligence test (Burt 1937) as a diagnostic tool to determine degrees of special educational need.

The 1944 Butler Act heralded a radical reappraisal of the education system (Stakes and Hornby 1997). The use of the terms 'subnormal', 'remedial' and 'maladjusted' became common. Educationally subnormal children were identified as those retarded by more than 20 per cent for their age but not so low grade as to be ineducable. This accounted for approximately 10 per cent of the child population, 1 per cent of whom attended special schools or hospitals, the remainder being taught in small groups within the umbrella of a school. An increasing number of special schools were opened between the 1950s and 1970s and the number of hospital special schools also grew.

Behaviourist teaching

The 1970 Education (Handicapped Children) Act and the 1974 Education (Mentally Handicapped Children) (Scotland) Act finally brought all children into the framework of education irrespective of their disability or degree of learning difficulty. The absolute right to a full education for all children without exception was established and the 'ineducable' category abolished. As a consequence of this, educators began to turn their attention to better understanding ways in which children with severe and complex learning difficulties could be taught (Rose 2001). Many of the approaches adopted were based on behaviourist methods. This model assumed that many behaviours are learned, including, for example, challenging or difficult behaviour. Rather than diagnosing a deficit the behaviourist model begins by identifying what the child needs to learn and then constructs a way of teaching this behaviour. These techniques were adapted to teach a whole range of skills in a behaviourist-based curriculum. The Skills Analysis Model (Gardner *et al.* 1983) is one such example. It advocated breaking the teaching process down into six small steps:

- identify core areas of the curriculum;

- subdivide these areas into their component parts;

- write targets for each identified component;

- prioritise the targets;

- write a programme to teach each target;

- assess and record whether the target has been achieved.

Although these methods achieved some modification in undesirable behaviour and acquisition of certain discrete skills, the approach was heavily criticised because it promoted learning without understanding and skills acquired in this way could not be transferred to other situations (McConkey 1981; Collis and Lacey 1996).

This new interest in special education was reflected in the setting up of the Warnock Committee in 1974 to review provision in the United Kingdom. The Warnock Report (1978), and the resulting 1981 Education Act that it informed, was a watershed in the history of special education. For the first time it created the concept of a special educational 'need' and appropriate *provision* rather than a 'condition' and *treatment*. The committee regarded the terms 'educationally subnormal' (England and Wales) and 'mentally handicapped' (Scotland) as causing unnecessary stigmatisation, particularly in later life. It was decided that these would be replaced by one term 'children with learning difficulties'.

What is a special educational need?

As described above, the idea of a special educational 'need' was first coined in the Warnock Report along with the term 'children with learning difficulties'. But what exactly do we mean by these terms? Pupils are deemed to have a special educational need when they are unable to reach their learning potential without either additional support or adaptations to their learning environment. This can be for a variety of global and/or specific reasons. There could be global cognitive delay when pupils may experience difficulty learning at the same level or pace as their typically developing peers. There may be a specific learning difficulty with, for example, reading or writing (sometimes known as dyslexia, although dyslexia is itself a large umbrella term for many specific difficulties) or numeracy. Equally there may be a specific difficulty related to, for example, attention span or memory. Emotional and behavioural difficulties can also interfere with the learning process and require special support. Equally, there are children who are very able (the current educational term for this is 'gifted and talented') and not able to reach their learning potential without adaptations to their learning environment and additional resources. It should be clear from these examples that provision for a special educational need is all about accommodating the individual learner through provisions and adaptations that *enable* rather then *disable*.

The Warnock recommendations

The Warnock Committee recommended that special educational need be seen as a continuum. A five-stage assessment procedure was established with progressively greater input from professionals at each stage along the continuum, culminating in a 'statement'. This *Statement of Educational Need* (*Record of Need* in Scotland) was to be produced when a child required extra educational provision. The document legally committed the Local Education Authority to meet the child's identified special educational needs. Parents were to be involved in the process and a 'named person' would act as a key contact for them.

The Warnock Report judged that one in five children would require special educational provision at some time during their school career. Therefore a more flexible approach was required where the majority of children with special educational needs could be identified and helped within the ordinary school. Adaptations to the school building, the curriculum and teaching techniques were to be considered where this would help meet a child's 'special educational need'.

Integration (not to be confused with inclusion, which is discussed later) was encouraged by the Warnock Report (1978) and was described as a way of bringing children with special educational needs into the community of mainstream schools. This could be achieved in three different ways:

- locational integration – special units or classes set up within an ordinary school;

- social integration – children attending a special class or unit but eating, playing and socialising with other children;

- functional integration – children with special needs joining a mainstream class either on a part-time or full-time basis.

Interactive approaches

A backlash from behaviourist teaching resulted in the promotion of interactive teaching approaches (Collis and Lacey 1996; Nind 2000) and an emphasis on person-to-person interaction as a basis for learning. More attention was given to creating a responsive learning environment (Ware 1996). For pupils with severe and complex learning difficulties some of these approaches, such as *Intensive Interaction* (Nind and Hewett 1994), were developed from a theoretical basis of caregiver–infant interaction with an emphasis on contingent responding and working from a child's strengths – in other words building on what a child could do rather than concentrating on what a child could not do.

The labelling culture

However laudable the abolition of inappropriate labels such as 'idiot' or 'imbecile' is, if one label is simply replaced by a different one the potential for denigration and ridicule is not necessarily removed. The substitution of these terms by categories such as 'mentally retarded', 'educationally subnormal' and 'maladjusted' led to abusive taunts of 'retards' and 'subnormals'. It has taken a long time to learn from these early blunders and even in the 1980s and 1990s we were compounding, not lessening the problem. One of the consequences of Warnock's 'continuum' of special educational need was that it reinforced categorisation. Along this continuum children could have a range of learning difficulties categorised as mild, or moderate (ESN), severe and complex (SLD), profound and multiple (PMLD), or emotional and behavioural (EBD). Inevitably this led to increased use of the abbreviated terminology and terms such as 'EBDs,' 'SLDs' and 'PMLDs' were soon in common use among professionals. The problem with this is that the word 'child' or 'pupil' does not appear anywhere, suggesting that the category relates to something less than human. Even when the odd child acknowledgement tag was thrown in for good measure (e.g. 'our EBD kids' rather than 'our EBDs') the child part always came after the label. Child activists felt that this put the spotlight on the disability rather than the child. A child is a child first and foremost, some children also happen to have learning difficulties. Hence, in the last decade it has become common practice to refer to children who have special needs as, for example, a child *with* severe and complex learning difficulties rather than an SLD child. This applies equally to adults as well as children, the value of the human individual being always prized above the learning difficulty.

Curricular initiatives

The Education Reform Act 1988 introduced the National Curriculum in England and Wales and gave an impetus to considering how the whole curriculum could be made accessible for children with special educational needs. The relevance and importance of the National Curriculum for children with special educational needs has been controversial. Some writers have argued that it brought new opportunities to previously excluded children (Carpenter *et al.* 1996). Others saw significant parts of it as inappropriate or limiting (Fletcher-Campbell 1994). There was criticism that the prescriptive nature of the National Curriculum placed too much emphasis on product, not process. National Curriculum 2000, one of a series of revisions to the original National Curriculum, went some way to redress this and offered guidance on meeting pupils' diverse learning needs.

Another concern was that the first level of attainment was so far beyond the reach of some pupils that they would have no realistic opportunity of achieving at anything (Tilstone 1991). In 1998 the Qualifications and Curriculum Association (QCA) introduced eight 'P' levels, preparatory levels of attainment leading up to level 1, but there has been criticism that even these level descriptors are too widely spaced to be meaningful for many pupils with profound learning difficulties. Assessment by level of attainment is also viewed by some as anti-inclusionary because it leads to grouping of children by ability.

Other statutory curricular initiatives including the national numeracy and literacy strategies (1998 onwards) widened the gap further when whole class, prescriptive teaching aimed at middle ability children largely replaced literacy and numeracy small group work in primary schools. Five years later, this approach was modified (*Excellence and Enjoyment* paper, DfES 2003a) giving schools greater control of the way they implemented the curriculum. It cleared the way for schools to develop more innovative and individual approaches to literacy and numeracy and encouraged the involvement of parents in learning partnerships. These were positive steps towards better provision for children with special educational needs. However, there is still widespread debate about whether any adapted 'National Curriculum' is appropriate for all pupils, particularly those with profound and complex learning difficulties. On the one hand, it is a powerful enactment of the common humanity of all children and their rightful entitlement to the same curriculum. On the other hand, a 'one-curriculum approach' may be inhibiting for some groups of children if it prevents time being spent on training for essential life skills or complementary teaching approaches and therapies that are known to be beneficial. Ultimately, the onus is on teachers to use the National Curriculum in ways they judge to be relevant. There are many fine examples of teachers successfully including pupils, even those with very profound learning difficulties, in a meaningful way. One such example was documented by Tilstone *et al.* (2000: 14).

> It is hard for her teachers and caregivers to know when Manjula is learning because she does not use speech or any kind of sign language. However, by including her in the visit to the cathedral they are providing her with important experiences, shared with other children. In fact, these experiences give Manjula the opportunity to show that she is aware of important things during the visit. Sitting in her wheelchair, beneath the cathedral's Rose Window, Manjula is left for a few minutes to look, listen, and feel where she is. As the sun shines through the window, Manjula smiles and wrings her hands with pleasure. Back in school, Manjula's teacher and learning support assistant help her to make a 'sensory' picture book as part of a topic on the cathedral. They make her a personal tape of the kind of organ music heard during the visit. This brings learning to life for Manjula, and brings other real benefits. Some of her classmates also enjoy the organ music and the class teacher organises a small 'listening group'. Manjula's mother and father when they hear about this successful activity, decide to make her a tape of Buddhist chants used in their community temple. Thereafter, whenever the family visits the temple, they play the tape in the car and Manjula gets very excited with anticipation. The curriculum experience described here has been well matched to Manjula's needs, and importantly, this has been 'negotiated' on the basis of her response to an activity. She might have been left out of the visit, but instead she was included and showed her educators, friends and family that she was developing a seemingly new awareness that could help her develop valuable choice making skills.

The government introduced a new strategy in 2004, 'Removing Barriers to Achievement' for children with special educational needs (DfES 2004), which focused on early intervention and support and placed greater emphasis on personalised learning. It advocated more children being taught in mainstream schools, with special schools becoming centres of excellence and working closely with mainstream schools to share expertise. Special schools continued to educate children with the most severe and complex needs. The Education and Skills Committee report on Special Educational Needs (2006) called for a major review of special educational needs provision and stressed the importance of local flexibility within any nationally proposed framework. The policy initiatives that emanated from the *Every Child Matters* (DfES 2003b) and Children's Act (2004) agendas broadened the face of special educational needs provision to take account of wider life skills. This is encapsulated in the five aims of *Every Child Matters* – be healthy; stay safe; enjoy and achieve; make a positive contribution; achieve economic well-being – which require a collaborative inter-agency approach to special educational needs. In particular, closer partnerships between education, health and social services and the voluntary sector are recommended. Momentum is building around through the Extended Schools and Children's Centres programme (HM Government 2007a,b) and promises to deliver better special educational need provision for all children.

Resourcing special educational needs

The Education Act 1993 placed a duty on the Secretary of State to issue a Code of Practice and the power to revise it from time to time. The first Code of Practice came into effect in 1994 (DfEE 1994) and was updated in 2001 (DfEE 2001). It provides practical advice to LEAs, maintained schools, early education settings and others on carrying out their statutory duties to identify, assess and make provision for children's special educational needs. In this respect it maintains an approach that looks for individual difficulties rather than developing a whole school approach, but the involvement of pupils themselves in this process was at least one step towards empowerment and the wider emphasis on children's rights.

In the past, special educational needs were entirely funded from LEAs. Since the introduction of the local management of schools more and more of these funds have been devolved to schools themselves. The Standards and Frameworks Act (1998) required local authorities in England and Wales to delegate at least 80 per cent of their overall education budget directly to schools. The remaining 20 per cent is used to support advisory services and fund provision for pupils with statements of special educational needs. With a large portion of direct funding coming to individual schools, head teachers have been able to appoint more Special Educational Needs Coordinators, or SENCOs (many schools now refer to these as Inclusion Coordinators, or INCOs) to oversee the organisation and management of special educational needs. However, the majority of the funds are spent on employing assistant teaching staff to support the children's learning and for ongoing staff training.

Inclusive education

The drive towards inclusion grew out of the social model of disability. This perspective views society, rather than a particular condition associated with an individual, as being disabling. In other words it is society's failure to adapt the environment to accommodate an individual's condition that is the disabling factor. In educational terms this translates as mainstream schools needing to adapt their physical environment, teaching styles and curricular provision where necessary to meet the diverse needs of all pupils.

The context for inclusion is situated within a human rights discourse predicated by the United Nations Convention on the Rights of the Child (1989) and a standpoint of equality. Segregation of children from their peers is seen as a denial of those human rights. Inclusion and participation are essential to human dignity and to the enjoyment and exercise of human rights. The UNESCO Salamanca Statement (1994) called on the international community to endorse the approach of inclusive schools by implementing practical and strategic changes. The Centre for Studies on Inclusive Education (2002) emphasised that this statement was a clear commitment to 'education for all' within the mainstream system. The concept of inclusion extends beyond special educational needs and disabilities to the wider embracement of human diversity; of gender, ethnicity, sexuality, cultural heritage and religion.

In 1997 the United Kingdom's commitment to inclusion was underlined by the Green Paper *Excellence for All Children* (DEE 1997). The paper supported the move from segregated to mainstream education for more children. Special schools were to have a more flexible role, part of which would be to provide active support for children moving to mainstream schools and act as a source of training and information for mainstream staff.

If schools are to educate a diverse range of learners in one and the same classroom then a variety of different teaching approaches need to be considered. This may involve physical changes to the learning environment, sometimes additional adult support and invariably adaptations to the curriculum. The emphasis on 'diversity' steers thinking towards the total learning environment rather than individual 'need' or 'difficulty'. Some argue that inclusion involves accessing specialist teaching skills (e.g. Hornby and Kidd 2001), whereas others claim that no special set of methods or pedagogies is needed to teach children with diverse learning experiences (e.g. Thomas and Loxley 2001). These opposing viewpoints illustrate deep-rooted tensions that exist among professionals in their different approaches to inclusion. This will now be examined further.

The inclusion debate

The road towards inclusion has not been entirely smooth. Although there have been few ideological objections to inclusion, there have been many concerns raised about its feasibility in practical terms. There has been some resistance from teachers who worry that they do not have the skills to teach children with learning difficulties or children with emotional and behavioural difficulties and are concerned about the impact inclusion will have on other typically developing pupils in their classes (Florian 1998). Some even argue that children with severe learning difficulties may actually be worse off because they will not get the specialist teaching they have received in the past or the small classes that typically populate special schools. One of the difficulties appears to be that inclusion moved too quickly, before mainstream schools and mainstream teachers had enough time to adapt. Pupils began to move out of special schools and into mainstream but the specialist teaching skills did not move with them. Specialist teachers stayed with the remainder of the pupils left in special schools and the government's aim, for this expertise to be used to support children in mainstream and provide training for mainstream staff, did not wholly materialise. However, there is evidence that this situation is changing, with initiatives such as the Barnardo's special school that successfully transformed itself into an inclusion advisory service (Bannister *et al.* 2003) and the government's commitment to retaining special schools as centres of excellence (see Government response to Education and Skills Committee report on special educational needs 2006).

A major concern for teachers is that inclusion will work only if properly resourced. Children with diverse and multiple disabilities need more staff to be able to accommodate their needs – sometimes on a one-to-one full-time basis. Despite increased recruitment of assistants to support classroom teachers, insufficient numbers and insufficient training remain major obstacles. Clough and Nutbrown (2002) in their exploration of early years educators' attitudes to inclusion found mixed responses:

> A lovely idea – inclusion – and when it's good, it's great! I have been able to have children in the nursery with Down's Syndrome and children with various emotional difficulties – abused children – but when they (the LEA) asked us to take in a child with autism, well, we had to say 'no'. Too risky – I was frightened that if we did – something terrible would happen and it would be my responsibility. So yes, lovely idea – but it really is an ideal that will never be achieved – total inclusion is impossible.
>
> (Janie, nursery teacher, 3–10 years – cited in Clough and Nutbrown 2002)

It is noteworthy that this early years teacher thinks in terms of being asked to *take in* a child with autism, as if the child is somehow 'outside' the frame. There is no apparent conception of the child's entitlement to be included as of right, or of the nursery's obligation to adapt its provision in order to accommodate all children, whether autistic or not. The other point that is evident from this quote is that many teachers are clearly receiving neither the training that would help them to know and understand autism nor the support and resources required.

The Special Education Needs and Disability Act (2001) has caused many schools to reconsider their attitude to inclusion. Schools can refuse a child only if their admission would harm the education of other pupils in the school. The Act places education within the remit of the Disability Discrimination Act and therefore it is illegal to discriminate against a student because of his or her disability. Local Education Authorities and schools are required (and post-16 education providers in due course) to develop access for disabled pupils to premises and the curriculum.

Some schools encountered difficulties in the transition towards greater inclusion and one of the initiatives that served as a self-help tool was the *Index for Inclusion* (Booth *et al.* 2000). The *Index* provided a set of materials to guide schools through the inclusion process promoting the building of supportive communities to foster high achievement for all pupils.

The *Index* involves a process of school self-review on three dimensions concerned with inclusive school cultures, policies and practices. The process entails a progression through a series of school development phases. These start with the establishing of a coordinating group. This group works with staff, governors, students and parents/carers to examine all aspects of the school, identifying barriers to learning and sustaining and reviewing progress. The investigation is supported by a detailed set of indicators and questions which require schools to engage in a deep and challenging exploration of their present position and the possibilities for moving towards greater inclusion.

(Booth *et al.* 2000: 2)

It is at the grassroots level of the classroom that much of the inclusion debate is played out. We have already considered some of the training and resourcing issues above, and we now examine some of the practical and pedagogical issues related to everyday classroom management. Most support for pupils who have learning difficulties is provided by teaching assistants and a primary pedagogical concern is whether this support should be provided 'in' or 'out' of the classroom. In the past it was common practice for pupils to be taken out of their classroom and supported on a one-to-one or small group basis. From an inclusive perspective this is seen as problematic, as an inclusive ideology adapts the learning environment to the pupil's needs rather than creating a separate 'exclusive' learning environment. Moreover, there are consequences for the social and cultural dimensions of learning if support is provided outside the classroom. Increasingly, the preferred scenario is for teaching assistants to work alongside pupils within the classroom context. There are some tensions inherent in this provision as some teachers still feel that pupils would benefit from the kind of focused one-to-one support that could be provided outside the classroom.

Inclusion has not evolved without its critics. Such criticisms (e.g. Farrell 1997; Wilson 1999) focused on the tension that exists between the philosophical principle of inclusion and a continuing level of support for specialist segregation (Croll and Moses 2000). Although critics embrace inclusion as an educational ideal, they discuss the need for a pragmatic response. They suggest that special schools still have a role to play with regard to children with severe learning difficulties and emotional and behavioural difficulties, and question the capacity of mainstream schools to meet their needs and the problem of inadequate resources and funding. Many of these issues were also raised by the Education and Skills Committee report (2006). In its response, the government affirmed its commitment to retaining special schools both as centres of excellence and as a choice provision for children with the most severe and complex needs.

Exclusion

Despite the laudable ideology of inclusion there are still a great many pupils who are excluded from schools, not because they are deemed 'ineducable' in the historical sense but because they are judged to be 'too difficult'. Most of these pupils fall into the special need category known as emotional and behavioural difficulties. In such cases, pupils are passed out to special schools or Pupil Referral Units (PRUs), some of which are residential. In principle these 'referrals' are for an agreed fixed term with the aim being to reintegrate pupils back into mainstream schools. In practice this does not always happen as often as the ideology suggests and placement becomes all but permanent. Visser *et al.*'s research (2002) on pupils with emotional and behavioural difficulties concluded that not enough was being done to encourage schools to become more open, positive, diverse communities that are 'barrier-free' to pupils with emotional and behavioural difficulties. Again, this was something that was picked up on by the Education and Skills Committee report (2006), which succeeded in pressing the government into action over children with special educational needs in PRUs, noting the need to plan and act much earlier if children with emotional and behavioural difficulties are to avoid long stays in PRUs.

Conclusion

As you will have gathered from reading this chapter, special educational needs and inclusion are complex and hotly debated issues. When we see inclusive education in the context of history, we see how the thinking behind it is evolving. One of the aims of this chapter has been to explore where different arguments about inclusive education are mutually supportive and where there is tension and conceptual confusion. There tends to be agreement at the moral stage of defining inclusive education, but when we move on to enact inclusion in practice the ideological unity becomes more fragmented (Clough 2000). This is partly because it is relatively early in the inclusion time line and we are still working hard to get it right. Valuing diversity is at the centre of these efforts. Any attempt to define the difference between 'special education' and 'inclusive education' centres on this crucially important aspect of diversity. 'Special education' might be defined in terms of 'separate but equal' whereas 'different but equal' more aptly describes 'inclusive education'. Looking back over the historical origins of special education that have been charted in this chapter, readers may be tempted to think that inclusive education is going to be just another phase that will pass. What persuades me otherwise is the ideology of human rights that underpins it. Given this, I see the task ahead as not so much mapping the dots but joining them up.

Suggested further reading

Those interested to find out more about the practical aspects of inclusion at ground level should look at Westwood's (2007) *Commonsense Methods for Children with Special*

Educational Needs. Now in its fifth edition, this volume scythes through shifting theoretical debates to focus on the practicalities of special educational provision at the chalk face of the classroom. It focuses on teaching and learning issues that teachers commonly face in their practice.

If you are interested in very severe and complex special needs, read *People with Profound and Multiple Learning Disabilities: Collaborative Approach to Meeting Complex Need* by Lacey and Ouvry (2006). Their book offers chapters on personal and social aspects of complex needs, ways in which learning and development can be encouraged, and the practicalities of including people with profound disabilities in the community. The book is set in a context of interdisciplinary and inter-agency collaboration and shows how complexity of need does not need to lead to a fragmented life.

If you want to find a good 'dip-in' text with short, readable chapters on a wide range of issues relating to inclusion then Nind *et al.* (2003) have edited two excellent companion books. The first volume looks at learners and learning contexts and explores examples of good practice. The second volume compares and evaluates different approaches to inclusion within the education sphere. The chapters in both volumes draw on a particularly diverse group of authors and provide multiple perspectives on inclusive education.

For readers who relish an in-depth theoretical discussion of inclusion, a seminal text is Thomas and Loxley (2001) *Deconstructing Special Education and Constructing Inclusion*. If you want more on the personal pupil perspective, turn to Allan (1999), for an inspiring and accessible book that charts the personal experiences of 11 pupils with special educational needs. A good article that explores the challenges of educational inclusion for pupils who are perceived as the most difficult to include is Visser *et al.* (2002). Readers who are particularly interested in early years would find Jones' (2004) *Supporting Inclusion in the Early Years* helpful and Rose (2001) focuses on special education in the primary age range. Nick Peacey has written a good chapter on special education need and inclusion in the secondary sector in Capel *et al.*'s (2005) *Learning to Teach in the Secondary School: A Companion to School Experience*.

References

Allan, J. (1999) *Actively Seeking Inclusion: Pupils with Special Needs in Mainstream Schools*. London: Falmer.

Bannister, C., Sharland, V., Thomas, G., Upton, V. and Walker, D. (2003) 'Changing from a Special School to an Inclusion Service', in Nind, M., Sheehy, K., and Simmons, K. (eds) *Inclusive Education: Learners and Learning Contexts*. London: David Fulton.

Booth, T., Ainscow, M., Black-Hawkins, K., Vaughan, M. and Shaw, L. (2000) *Index for Inclusion: Developing Learning and Participation in Schools*. Bristol: CSIE.

Burt, C. (1937) *The Backward Child*. London: University of London Press.

Capel, S., Leask, M. and Turner, T. (2005) *Learning to Teach in the Secondary School: A Companion to School Experience.* London: Routledge.

Carpenter, B., Ashdown, R. and Bovair, K. (1996) *Enabling Access.* London: David Fulton.

Centre for Studies on Inclusive Education (2002) *The Salamanca Statement (1994).* Available from http://inclusion.uwe.ac.uk/csie/slmca.htm (accessed 4 December 2007).

Children's Act (2004) London: HMSO.

Clough, P. (2000) 'Routes to Inclusion', in Clough, P. and Corbett, J. (eds) *Theories of Inclusive Education: A Students' Guide.* London: Paul Chapman.

Clough, P. and Nutbrown, C. (2002) 'The Index for Inclusion: Personal Perspectives from Early Years Educators', *Early Education.* **36**, 7–11.

Collis, M. and Lacey, P. (1996) *Interactive Approaches to Teaching.* London: David Fulton.

Croll, P. and Moses, D. (2000) 'Ideologies and Utopias: Education Professionals' Views of Inclusion', *European Journal of Special Needs Education.* **15** (1), 1–12.

Department for Education and Employment (1997) *Excellence for All Children: Meeting Special Educational Needs.* London: DfEE.

Department for Education and Employment (1994) *The Code of Practice on the Identification and Assessment of Children and Special Educational Needs.* London: DfEE.

Department for Education and Skills (2001) *Code of Practice on the Identification and Assessment of Children and Special Educational Needs.* London: DfES.

Department for Education and Skills (2003a) *Excellence and Enjoyment – A Strategy for Primary Schools.* London: DfES.

Department for Education and Skills (2003b) *Every Child Matters.* London: HMSO.

Department for Education and Skills (2004) *Removing Barriers to Achievement: The Government's Strategy for SEN.* London: DfES

Education Act (1870) London: HMSO.

Education Act (1921) London: HMSO.

Education Act (1944) London: HMSO.

Education Act (Handicapped Children) (1970) London: HMSO.

Education Act (1981) London: HMSO.

Education Act (1993) London: HMSO.

Education and Skills Committee (2006) *Special Educational Needs.* London: The Stationery Office.

Education Reform Act (1988) London: HMSO.

Education (Scotland) Act (1872) London: HMSO.

Education (Scotland) Act (1906) London: HMSO.

Education (Scotland) Act (1974) London: HMSO.

Farrell, P. (1997) 'The Integration of Children with Severe Learning Difficulties: A Review of the Recent Literature', *Journal of Applied Research in Intellectual Disabilities.* **10** (1), 1–14.

Fletcher-Campbell, F. (1994) *Still Joining Forces? A Follow Up Study of Links between Ordinary and Special Schools.* Slough: NFER.

Florian, L. (1998) 'An Examination of the Practical Problems Associated with the Implementation of Inclusive Education Policies', *Support for Learning.* **13** (3), 105–108.

Gardner, J., Murphy, J. and Crawford, N. (1983) *The Skills Analysis Model.* Kidderminster: BIMH Publications.

Government response to Education and Skills Committee report on special educational needs (2006) London: HMSO.

HM Government (2007a) *Extended Schools: Building on Experience.* London: The Stationery Office.

HM Government (2007b) *SureStart.* Available at www.surestart.gov.uk/ (accessed 4 December 2007).

Hornby, G. and Kidd, R. (2001) 'Transfer from Special to Mainstream – Ten Years Later', *British Journal of Special Education.* **28** (1), 10–17.

Jones, C. (2004) *Supporting Inclusion in the Early Years.* Buckingham: Open University Press.

Lacey, P. and Ouvry, C. (2006) *Profound and Multiple Learning Disabilities: Collaborative Approach to Meeting Complex Need.* London: David Fulton.

McConkey, R. (1981) 'Education without Understanding', *Special Education: Forward Trends.* **8** (3), 8–11.

Mental Deficiency Act (1913). London: HMSO.

National Curriculum (2000) Available at http://curriculum2000.co.uk/new_curriculum.htm.

Nind, M. (2000) 'Teachers' Understanding of Interactive Approaches in Special Education', *International Journal of Disability and Education.* **47** (2), 183–199.

Nind, M. and Hewett, D. (1994) *Access to Communication: Developing the Basics of Communication in People with Severe Learning Difficulties Through Intensive Interaction.* London: David Fulton.

Nind, M., Rix, J., Sheehy, K. and Simmons, K. (eds) (2003) *Inclusive Education: Diverse Perspectives.* London: David Fulton Publishers.

Nind, M., Sheehy, K., and Simmons, K. (eds) (2003) *Inclusive Education: Learners and Learning Contexts.* London: David Fulton Publishers.

Report of the Departmental Committee on Defective & Epileptic Children. Vol. II. Minutes of Evidence, Appendices etc. (1898) London: HMSO.

Rose, L. (2001) 'Primary School Teacher Perceptions of the Conditions Required to Include Pupils with Special Educational Needs', *Educational Review.* **53** (2), 147–156.

Special Education Needs and Disability Act (2001) London: The Stationery Office.

Standards and Frameworks Act (1998) London: The Stationery Office.

Stakes, R. and Hornby, G. (1997) *Change in Special Education Provision: What Brings It About?* London: Continuum.

Thomas, G. and Loxley, A. (2001) *Deconstructing Special Education and Constructing Inclusion.* Buckingham: OUP.

Tilstone, C. (1991) (ed.) *Teaching Pupils with Severe Learning Difficulties.* London: David Fulton.

Tilstone, C., Lacey, P., Porter, J. and Robertson, C. (2000) *Pupils with Learning Difficulties in Mainstream Schools.* London: David Fulton.

UNESCO (1994) *World Conference on Special Educational Needs: Access and Quality* (Salamanca Statement). Paris: UNESCO.

United Nations (1989) *Convention on the Rights of the Child.* New York: United Nations.

Visser, J. Cole, T. and Daniels, H. (2002) 'Inclusion for the Difficult to Include', *Support for Learning.* **17** (1), 23–26.

Ware, J. (1996) *Creating a Responsive Environment.* London: David Fulton.

Warnock, M. (1978) *Special Educational Needs. Report of the Committee of Enquiry into the Education of Handicapped Children and Young People.* London: HMSO.

Westwood, P. (2007) *Commonsense Methods for Children with Special Educational Needs*, 5th edn. London: Routledge.

Wilson, J. (1999) 'Some Conceptual Difficulties about Inclusion', *Support for Learning.* **14** (3), 110–112.

10

Comparing educational systems

Trevor Corner and Nigel Grant

> The nature of things is more securely and naturally deduced from their operations out upon another than upon our senses. And when by the former experiments we have found the nature of bodys, by the latter we may more clearly find the nature of our senses.
>
> (Isaac Newton, *Questiones.* 1664)

Introduction

THE FIRST PROBLEM THAT needs to be dealt with in comparative education is in deciding what it is for, both generally and in terms of the individual considering making use of it. It is an inherent part of the work of government bodies, national and international agencies and senior managers in education to take evidence of the relevant experience of others to illuminate their own problems.

Comparative studies in education are based on a body of methodological research work which has enabled it to evolve over the past 100 years (Holmes 1981; King 1979; Watson 2001). Most students who study comparative or international education (or both) are not specialists in the field themselves. Quite properly, they are looking to the study to give them comparative insights into some other field, whether it be a teaching subject, the curriculum, educational policy or management. This is just as well, for the capacity to provide this perspective is one of the strengths of the subject's appeal, namely its value to the non-specialist.

This raises fundamental questions about approaches to the subject. Methodological discussions are concerned with finding the most effective ways of explaining the behaviour of educational systems, and it is in this light that the relative merits of the various approaches – national case-studies, cross-cultural thematic studies, the construction of models and typologies, and the search for valid generalisations – have to be considered. For the purposes of research, there is general agreement that the study of comparative education has to progress from accurate *description* to *analysis,* and from that to the forming of *generalisations* about the working of educational systems. There are strong disagreements about the best ways of achieving this (Crossley 2001), but little dispute about the broad aims themselves. But when one considers the position of the non-specialist student other criteria must be thought of as well; and these will influence the way in which the subject is presented.

Comparative perspectives

What, then, can non-specialist students gain from the study of comparative education? To say that they can develop a 'comparative perspective' on their own special fields, albeit true enough, needs further elaboration. Leaving aside particular interests, one might suggest that a comparative perspective can offer the following elements at least:

1 Awareness of the differences between systems and their policies and practices in various countries

Whether these are more important than the similarities is arguable; but the point needs to be made that educational problems, and the ways of tackling them, can differ considerably from those with which we are familiar.

2 Similarities between systems also have to be made clear

If only the differences are dealt with, the impression may be conveyed that the experience of other countries is irrelevant to one's own, and the main point of pursuing such study at all is lost.

3 The importance of the context within which the educational process functions has to be stressed

It is crucial to realise that education does not work in a vacuum, but is profoundly influenced by the geographical, demographic, historical, economic, cultural and political aspects of the society which it serves. At the same time, lest the impression be conveyed that the relationship between education and society – any society – purely reflects the context, the influence of the system *on* its context also has to be examined. It has to be understood that no educational system operates in isolation, but has a complex and dynamic relationship with its natural and social environment.

4 The relevance of other countries' experiences to one's own follows logically from this

Otherwise, it may be felt that comparative study, fascinating though it may be for the specialist, has little to offer anyone else. Not that one would argue for the direct *application* of other systems' practices to one's own country; this may be feasible sometimes, but involves serious dangers. The experience of other systems can contribute to an understanding of one's own; indeed, it can be argued that this is the most valuable contribution of comparative education to the non-specialist.

Strategies in comparative education

If, then, these are acceptable as learning objectives, we can go on to consider various approaches as *strategies of* study. One popular method is the 'themes' approach, which starts by taking particular topics such as the curriculum, primary schools, vocational training, educational planning and so forth, and comparing them across a number of selected systems, with the aim of formulating valid generalisations about the behaviour of educational systems in particular circumstances. An important alternative, the 'systems' approach, examines complete educational systems as functioning units in their particular societies. These are not really disagreements about where the study should be going, but about the most effective starting-point.

The *themes approach* has the advantage of coming to grips with the real stuff of comparative education – comparison and analysis – right from the start. But it presents great difficulties for those without much knowledge of other educational systems, for there are many temptations to make comparisons out of context and thus fall into some serious errors. The possibility of such error is large, but a few examples will serve.

1 Education does not necessarily mean the same thing in all societies

It may have quite different aims, operate under different conditions, and be assessed by different criteria. The differences are not absolute, or comparative study would lose much of its point. But there is much to be said for emphasising the differences, as these are likely to be overlooked or misunderstood if we go directly into cross-cultural comparison. For example: politicians and even senior managers in education are fond of reinforcing their arguments with assorted pieces of evidence from the experience of other countries. Many advocates of comprehensive schooling in the United Kingdom seek comfort in vague statements about European reforms and higher financial investment in schools; their opponents were equally fond of dire warnings of what they thought had been happening in the Soviet Union or, perversely, what continues to happen in the United States. Such arguments often ignore the constant American debates on school choice, charter schools, private religious schools and the merits or otherwise of restructuring one or other of the state systems (Good and Braden 2000). That much of this 'evidence' may be wrong is not really the point; even when the information was accurate, it could easily be used with little appreciation of the differences between the other systems and one's own (Grant 1968).

Advocates of greater emphasis on lifelong learning in the UK make use of the Scandinavian countries, the United States or France as models or as inspiration; supporters of bilingualism in Scottish, Welsh, Irish or English schools point to Canada, Catalonia, Israel, Finland and the Faeroes (Haugen *et al.* 1980; Baker 2001). Again, this is not to say that the comparisons are invalid, let alone the causes. The situation in the Faeroes or Catalonia, where there is a strong numerical base for the language and vigorous institutional support, does not easily transfer to the circumstances of the Gaels of the Western Isles or the Punjabi speakers of Glasgow, Birmingham or London, where the languages are penetrated to some degree by the use of English. The purpose, expectations and effectiveness of using the language may not be only through education:

> The ownership of two languages has increasingly become seen as an asset as the 'communication world' gets smaller. As swift communication has become possible in recent decades . . . so the importance of bilingualism has been highlighted.
>
> (Baker 2001: 417)

This applies to some extent to all the countries that now have to deal with the implications of the Internet and its role in promoting or demoting the use of languages (Naughton 1999). In this postcolonial age the sense of *loss* of language is widespread, extending from nationalist sensitivities in the older colonies of England – Scotland, Wales, Ireland – to ethnic minority migrants such as Sikhs, Kurds or Berbers, as it is a danger that faces them when they are confronted with the daily imperative of mastering the host language, English, French or Arabic (Davies 2003).

The differences between systems can be quite profound. The very word 'education' can have different connotations in different societies. Indeed, some languages are unable to make the distinctions that others find essential. In English, for example, the single word 'education', although constantly doing battle with 'training', 'pedagogy' or 'lifelong education', normally has to fulfil all the functions of *Bildung, Ausbildung* and *Erziehung* in German, *éducation, instruction* and *enseignement* in French, while Russian has a whole battery of words. But, even when the same word is used, the associations that go with it may be different. A good example of this may be seen in comparisons between the United States and the United Kingdom; these were particularly common during discussions in the 1960s on the comprehensive reorganisation of schools in the UK, and especially in England, where the issue can still arouse more controversy than in

Scotland or Wales. Ten years of devolution to the Scottish Parliament and Welsh Assembly (the Northern Ireland Assembly having regularly been in abeyance) has further enlivened the debate on the extent of the British systems growing apart. Interestingly, little serious evidence has yet come about to indicate different standards of achievement developing across the kingdom when all relevant social factors have been taken into account (Phillips 2000).

It is more difficult to generalise about school standards (or anything else) in the United States than in England. American education is more decentralised, and its financing is much more dependent on the resources of the particular areas where the schools are located. Standards in American schools therefore vary greatly from state to state, and within each state, and *any* generalisation thus has to be hedged about with qualifications.

But just suppose, for the sake of argument, that even broadly equivalent groups – those following academic courses to proceed to higher education – do show a marked disparity in standards (as many American educationists would readily concede). What exactly are we comparing? Debates on the range of scholastic attainment as measured by examinations are common on both sides of the Atlantic, though few American teachers, parents or students would accept this as the only criterion of what the school is trying to do. American schools devote a great deal of time to socialisation, to the preparation of the student for life in American society, stressing the development of social and communication skills. It may be that the outward manifestations of this – the patriotic rituals, the varied social events, the morale-boosting sessions for the school football team and so on – would strike English teachers as faintly comical. But the same could be said of a German *Gymnasium* teacher's impression of the games and character-building by which some remaining grammar schools still set such store. The German final school certificate, the *Abitur* or *Reifeprüfung* (test of maturity), the Danish *Studenterexamen* and *Højere Forberedelsereksamen* and many of the European final school certificates taken mostly between 18 and 20 years of age are both broader and academically ahead of the English A-level. Interest in a broader and deeper version of the A-level has actually been helped by comparisons with the American Students Aptitude Tests (SAT) and the International Baccalaureate, which is now offered in an increasing number of English schools and FE colleges.

These are examples of how even the meaning of 'education' can be affected by different sets of priorities. But many other factors determine what education is, what it can do, and how its aims are defined; these have to be considered if any useful comparisons are to be made. In countries such as America, France, Spain or Britain, for example, it is at least *possible* to consider leaving the choice of textbooks to the schools and the open market; the *actual* decision can be taken on a variety of grounds. But in the Baltic States, the Faeroes or Iceland, decisions are severely constrained by the small numbers speaking the national languages, whatever policy the authorities might prefer.

Again, the existence of substantial linguistic minorities in Russia, India, Belgium, Spain and a host of other countries raises problems that now have to be considered by the relatively homogeneous countries like England or Denmark where the settlement of immigrants and their descendants has confirmed their development into multicultural societies too. As for matters like distance and difficulties in communication, these are not *major* factors in Denmark, Ireland, the Netherlands or most of the United Kingdom, but they are in a huge country such as Russia and they were in the United States when the pattern of educational organisation was taking shape, and are in India and China. The increased power of international agencies over education policy and practice worldwide has increased cross-cultural transfers, shown by the impact on the post-Soviet Union countries in Europe or Asia where curricula, policies and the very purpose of education have been through considerable transformation (Crossley and Watson 2003).

Climate, demographic patterns and economic circumstances raise needs or impose severe constraints that do not occur in the developed world. UNESCO highlights those situations in developing countries where there are insufficient means to guarantee even universal primary education and where population growth or war can nullify every hard-won advance. These background conditions are so important for the functioning of education – and even for defining it – that they must be taken into account if we are to make any sense of the systems themselves.

2 The parts of any educational system are interdependent, and have to be examined in relation to the whole

Many attempts to make international comparisons across several countries fall into the trap of assuming that things with the same name must have the same function. They may, but there can also be substantial differences. 'Primary school', for example, means in England and Wales a school for children between the ages of 5 and 11 (although it is now common for there to be an optional Reception Class, which takes children aged 4); but in Scotland it is from 5 to 12, and in the Republic of Ireland usually from 4 to 12. This is within an area, the British Isles, with close past or present political links; elsewhere, the difference can be greater. What is usually translated as 'primary school' or *école primaire* or *Grundschule* can cover the ages of 7 to 16 in Denmark and in Sweden. Rapid change in developed countries in pre-school education has, in practice, led to most children having some form of schooling experience from 3 years of age and often earlier. Various systems organise their structures differently, preferring in some cases to make the main division of primary/secondary at mid-adolescence, the end of compulsory schooling, and in others at the point of transition from undifferentiated to subject specialised teaching.

Similarly, the term 'secondary school' may mean the entire stage from pre-adolescence onwards (as in the systems of the British Isles or the United States), or it may be only the stage entered *after* compulsory school, as in Scandinavia. But this does not apply everywhere; in some countries, only *certain* post-compulsory schools – generally those leading to higher education – are designated as 'secondary', thus distinguishing them from vocational or trade schools (Bell and Grant 1977).

Many common schools in Central and Eastern Europe provide the whole course from 6 to 17; and when this happens, the term 'secondary' is applied to the *entire* school, *including its primary section.* There were, and still remain in some of these countries, 'secondary specialised schools', which can be entered after completion of the *general* secondary school. Further, changes may take place but old titles may remain in use. Even on official notices, they use the formal title together with the informal and old-fashioned title, which is what everyone says and had a different structure, in brackets, as in Germany, where unification of East and West has fundamentally affected the direction of reforms after 1990 (Wilde 2002). It is a dangerous business, especially when translation is involved, to pull institutions with similar-sounding titles out of context for separate examination.

Opportunities for misunderstanding do not end there. Schools and students in England, Wales and Scotland are often compared unfavourably with those elsewhere. School effectiveness and outcomes have been used, often in official publications, to suggest a crisis of falling standards, especially in English schools, with a perceived inability to stand up to global competition. Where evidence of widening participation and increasing pass rates of school-leaving examination is discussed this is countered by suggestions of lowering standards. The Third International Mathematics and Science Study (TIMSS) has done one of the most extensive comparisons of pupil achievements in maths and science and is regarded as providing some of the most convincing evidence for the relative failure of schools in England and Wales. However, various reasons, such as different age participation and response rates from participating schools, make even these comparisons in subjects seen as 'culture-free' somewhat flawed. A common view of education during the twentieth century has focused on its under-achievement, inequality and a perceived fall in standards, perhaps because more is expected from education by each succeeding generation.

In England (as in most European countries) the end of secondary schooling is still quite a reasonable point at which to consider what standards have been achieved. Enough of the age group stay on to make the judgment worthwhile, but with widening access to higher education there is increasing differentiation of standards for entrance. But this is even more so in the USA, where something like four fifths of the age cohort proceeds to tertiary education. Some take only short-cycle courses, some of these transfer to full higher courses, others enter longer ones from the start but drop out, and some of these drop back in again, making it difficult to keep track of any particular age group, but a reasonable estimate would be that about a half eventually complete first degrees.

Admittedly, the standard of American degrees varies considerably, and with the advent of league tables for UK universities disparity of degree standards are increasingly questioned. Some American universities and colleges (public and private) can easily stand comparison academically with any higher educational institutions in the world, whereas others award degrees too inadequate to be recognised in other countries (or in the United States itself); and in between can be found almost every imaginable variety, from the admirable to the abysmal. But, with very few exceptions, even the worst could be reckoned to come up at least to English A-level standard and, of course, most go well beyond that. It follows, therefore, that in the United States a higher proportion of the population reaches at least A-level standard than was ever admitted to grammar school in England in the heyday of selective schooling. Even by the narrowest scholastic criteria more get there in the end; and, unless we postulate some mystic law whereby certain standards must be attained by a fixed age, American education appears to perform more creditably than its detractors (on both sides of the Atlantic) would allow. To attempt an adequate assessment of a system, we have to look at all of it, not just a part. A similar point could be made about the age of starting primary school and the relevance of pre-school provision.

Nor need such considerations be confined to the formal school system, for other organisations can attend to 'curricular enrichment', as the Pioneers did in the former Soviet Union. That is all gone now, but there are some parallels in China and Cuba, and of course the *folkehøjskoler* in Denmark and the various Church organisations in some countries, particularly in Latin America, fulfil some needs for 'public enlightenment', especially for young adults. Many countries have youth and adult organisations in the cultural, linguistic, nature and athletic areas. The limitations of most of these are that they often lack adequate support and finance; they also tend to be fragmented too so that they touch few of the young people or children they are aimed at. But they are there, and sometimes function as a vital adjunct to the normal experience of formal schooling (Webber and Liikanen 2001).

There other examples, but these should make the general point – *educational systems have to be examined as wholes, and in their contexts,* before cross-cultural studies can be expected to yield much benefit. Objective data on particular institutions can seem quite precise; but unless they are seen in relation to other institutions in the same system, and unless that system is examined in the light of the factors that make it what it is, we are in danger of misunderstanding how it works. Further, since the most common use of evidence out of context is to back up educational arguments at home, there is the additional danger that such misunderstandings may simply reinforce misunderstanding of one's own system. This is not what comparative education is for.

What, then, is it for? What, particularly after all these warnings about the importance of context, is the relevance of education in other countries to our own problems? And what is its usefulness for teachers?

Part of the answer has to do with *informing educational policy*. Individual teachers rarely feel they have much of a role to play here, but they often have more influence on the success or failure of policies than they may be aware of. In some countries they have considerable discretion in the choice of subject matter, method and even organisation, and therefore have an obligation to make thoughtful and informed choices rather than fall back on precedent or hunch. They are also involved in the larger issues in their capacity as citizens. Unless teachers are to be reduced to functionaries, the uncritical executors (however efficient) of decisions taken by someone else, wider understanding of the options available in the educational process is not only desirable but, at a time of constant educational change, necessary.

This could be said for educational theory in general, or any of its contributory disciplines. What benefits, then, can be expected for the thoughtful teacher from this particular kind of educational study?

Borrowing ideas

The possibility of borrowing ideas is usually the first that comes to mind and is often held to be the main purpose of comparative education. In their view of its possibilities governments are all too often limited to seeing it (if at all) as a method of identifying practices that could be transplanted to their own country. But great care is needed here. Quite apart from the risk that the other countries' practices may be misinterpreted anyway, they may be too closely bound up with their specific contexts to be applicable anywhere else.

Certainly, the exportation of practices has often had unfortunate effects. After the Second World War, for example, the new communist governments in Eastern Europe drew heavily on Soviet models. This was hardly surprising, in view of the political hegemony of the USSR; the newly established régimes not only were inclined to display political loyalty, but were also trying to reform their traditional systems along Marxist–Leninist lines, and at that time the USSR was the only country with experience of this.

Unfortunately – but, given the political atmosphere of the time, unsurprisingly – the remodelling on Soviet lines was quite uncritical. History was taught from a Russocentric viewpoint, textbooks were modelled on their Soviet counterparts (and sometimes were straight translations), even degrees were often renamed to correspond to Soviet practice, and of course policy was modelled on that of the USSR, sometimes even to the wording, whether appropriate to local conditions or not (Grant 1982, 2000).

The former British and French colonial empires are clearer illustrations of the effects of uncritical borrowing. Most ex-colonial countries still retain their inheritance of British- or French-style school systems with examinations linked to assumptions about the relationship between paper qualifications and job expectations that are wildly out of keeping with these countries' needs and conditions. The damage caused is not so much by the persistence of inappropriately Europeanised curricula, which are changing anyway; it is rather caused by the expectation that going to school will provide certificates leading to white-collar jobs in the city, when the vast majority are certain to be disappointed at some stage. Large numbers of young Africans thus receive just enough schooling to make village life unacceptable, but not enough to fit them for anything else – an explosive situation due in part to an educational system devised in London or Paris that makes little allowance for conditions in Lagos or Bamako, let alone a tribal village (MacIntosh 1971).

We continue to see the adoption of European and American models over much of the developing world. These systems differ greatly, of course, but they have all been devised to meet the needs of relatively affluent and highly industrialised societies, quite different from the low-income agrarian countries to which they have been exported. We have seen something of this in postcolonial Africa, yet it is not just from former colonial powers that inappropriate models are received, but from the industrial world in general. It has become increasingly obvious that these models do not serve the needs of the 'Third World' countries, even if they could afford them; but, as long as they offer such great advantages to those lucky enough to go through the whole process successfully, they make it difficult to devise other and more suitable models.

This is not to say that importation can never be valuable. For all the uncritical borrowing from the USSR in Eastern Europe, there were *some* valuable innovations, such as the development of systems of adult education and the breaking down of some of the more rigid class barriers between different kinds of school. On a more limited scale, there is the spread of Folk High Schools across the Scandinavian countries, and even some influence on adult education in Germany and Great Britain (Korsgaard 2002).

Again, for all the unfortunate effects of over-hasty and uncritical adoption of American progressive methods, their positive contribution has to be recognised as well. 'Progressivism' may have run its course by now, but it has left its mark on practice. Whenever a primary teacher teaches capacity by getting children to pour water into cans rather than recite tables, s/he is using what at first were American 'progressive' methods. That this is rarely apparent is an indication of how far these methods have been naturalised. The adoption by the Open University and the post-1992 universities in the United Kingdom of a credit system owes much to American practice,[1] and has created a degree of flexibility hitherto lacking in British higher education. But this has not been a straight copy, but an adaptation of an American procedure to the rather different needs of part-time students in the UK, which still managed to avoid some of the problems in the USA. It could be added that the Open University in its turn has had a considerable impact on higher education in many other countries, especially the United States.

There are many other examples of effective borrowing, with one thing in common: they were taken from systems sufficiently like the importing ones to fit in, or were adapted to do so. This, possibly, is one of the most valuable contributions of comparative studies: not only can they set forth a range of alternative ideas and practices but, intelligently applied, they can help distinguish what can reasonably be imported from what can not; and by examining educational practices in context can help indicate the kind of adaptation needed to fit them into another system.

Educational policy and analysis

Comparative education can render a particularly valuable service by providing a background of contrasts against which to examine our own problems. If our horizons are bounded by our own system, many of its practices may seem natural or inevitable; yet they may have arisen in circumstances that no longer obtain, and may now be unnecessary, arbitrary or even harmful. It is not impossible to examine one's own system critically from the inside, but it is more difficult without a comparative perspective. The very existence of other assumptions and practices can provide a necessary challenge to some of our own. It does not automatically follow that we *have* to change; even if we are alone in this practice or that, it may still fit our own circumstances. But the existence of alternatives obliges us to justify rather than assume, so that if we do adhere to something there is a chance of knowing why we do it.

An example can be seen in the horizontal and vertical divisions within the school system. In most of the United Kingdom it is taken for granted that the division between primary and secondary school at 11 or 12 reflects a qualitative and necessary change in pedagogical styles, and even that it has some natural sanction. Sensible and convenient it *may* be but it is not inevitable. The break at this point is also found in the USA, Italy, France and some German states; but in

---

[1] A practice that is now widespread across the higher education sector in the UK, and this at both undergraduate and postgraduate levels.

Denmark, Sweden, Spain and some countries of Eastern Europe (and was in all of them before the Soviet system collapsed) the main division, and the main point of differentiation, is at 15 or 16.

The same variation applies to *vertical* division into parallel schools for the same age group, as was common throughout Great Britain before comprehensive reorganisation. Segregation of this kind was regarded as quite unacceptable in the former USSR but as absolutely essential in most German states, where nearly two thirds of young people receive their post-secondary education in vocational institutions covering over 350 state-regulated and recognised occupations (Idriss 2002). In the USA, the common school is taken for granted, but so is *internal* division (known as 'tracking'). In every case, the matter is open to argument; and here the existence of alternatives can be a useful corrective to the widespread habit of taking one's own practice as the norm.

Comparative studies can also clarify our ideas of what is possible, a useful step before deciding whether something is *desirable*. International practice is frequently evoked over some of the more emotive issues like school uniforms or sexual differentiation, but they are often not the best examples, as they are closely bound up with a broader complex of social expectations and pressures. It would be rash, for instance, to attribute too much of the disorder in many American schools to the schools themselves; there are too many other forces in operation. But curriculum policies, for example, can profitably be looked at with an eye to what is being done elsewhere, as in the debate in the UK on specialisation versus generalisation, or the relation between school and work.

To take one example, little is expected in the English-speaking countries of average or below-average pupils in the learning of foreign languages. In the British systems, languages were formerly largely confined to the 'academic' schools or streams and, although there are an increasing number of secondary schools that teach languages, many teachers are still convinced that trying to teach languages to any but the top third of the ability range is a waste of time. Whether it is desirable that they should do so is, of course, another argument; but international evidence does not support the idea that the average child has some inherent linguistic incapacity. Bilingual and multilingual communities are common throughout the world; and even school-based learning can be extremely effective. In Scandinavia, for instance, all children learn at least one foreign language (usually English), and many learn at least one more besides; the levels of competence vary, but are generally high. Unless we believe in some kind of inborn incapacity among the Americans and British, we have to reject the idea that 'languages for all' is *impossible*. Discussions of the *desirability* of such a policy has a chance of being considered on its own merits, then, without unnecessary presuppositions.

But an international perspective can also provoke re-examination of some of our educational concepts (or slogans): 'standards', 'discipline', 'indoctrination', 'excellence', 'leadership', 'freedom of choice', 'general culture', and so on. We are not always clear just what we mean by them; and one incentive to clarify our definitions is seeing how different they are elsewhere. For example, 'democratic education' would mean maximum curricular choice and grass-roots control to most Americans, but would suggest a centrally determined uniform curriculum to the French, on the grounds that the child must be free of the chances of local circumstance. 'Leadership' has positive connotations in England, but in Scandinavia is still regarded with suspicion outside the business schools.

Teachers and academics in most countries have a fairly clear notion about what is meant by (say) 'university standard', but usually have difficulty in defining this. 'Indoctrination', in the sense of a deliberate inculcation of values, may be more obvious to someone looking at a system from outside than to someone actually in it; 'indoctrination' may turn out to be something that *other* people do, but which we prefer to call something else – 'moral education', perhaps, or 'citizenship'. Unless we are prepared simply to dismiss other interpretations as 'wrong' just because they are different, their very existence requires us to attempt a definition of *our* terms. We may, once again, decide that they are valid and useful, but at least we should have a better idea of what we are talking about.

Conclusion

Comparative education thus has the capacity to do in space what educational history does in time; it can provide the opportunity to understand better the workings of the educational process by giving us a wider view than the here and now. At a time when everyone in contemporary educational systems is faced with unprecedented challenges, as crises of resource and direction loom ever larger, and as the need to educate for future uncertainty becomes more urgent, the importance of clear and radical thinking could hardly be more obvious. This is not to say that *everything* is on the agenda for change; tribal customs may after all have their place, but it does not help to confuse them with laws of nature.

Comparative education cannot, of course, pretend to offer any uniquely valid set of answers, but can claim to be one useful tool for the better understanding of the educational process in general and one's own system in particular. Although it uses big ideas over the global scale, it is rooted in precise observation of the particular. It will continue to have a role in informing government policy just as governments will continue to have a vital interest in their educational systems. Some new tasks are providing practical and purposeful goals for advising governmental educational reforms, investigating the role of public and private agencies in education, and analysing changing structures and forces such as private education, partnerships, e-learning and the Internet (Corner 2000).

Suggested further reading

In comparative education, publications age very rapidly and for this reason the journals are the best source for up-to-date articles. Some well-established journals in the UK are *Comparative Education, Compare* and *Oxford Studies in Comparative Education.* Internationally, the principal journals in English are *Comparative Education Review*, the *International Review of Education, The European Journal of Education* and *Harvard Education Review.* Various other international journals exist within particular domains in education and will often carry articles of a comparative nature.

References

Baker, C. (2001) *Foundations of Bilingual Education and Bilingualism*, 3rd edn. Clevedon: Multilingual Matters.

Bell, R. E. and Grant, N. (1977) *Patterns of Education in the British Isles.* London: Allen and Unwin.

Corner, T. (2000) 'Education and the Third Wave', in Matheson, C. and Matheson, D. (eds) *Educational Issues in the Learning Age.* London: Continuum

Crossley, M. (ed) (2001) 'Comparative Education for the 21st Century: An International Response', *Comparative Education.* **37** (4) (special issue).

Crossley, M. and Watson, K. (2003) *Comparative and International Research in Education: Globalisation, Context and Difference.* London: RoutledgeFalmer.

Davies, A. (2003) *The Native Speaker: Myth and Reality.* Clevedon: Multilingual Matters.

Good, T. and Braden, J. (2000) *The Great School Debate.* London: LEA Publishers.

Grant, N. (1968) 'Comparative Education and the Comprehensive Schools', *Scottish Educational Studies.* **1** (2), 16–23.

Grant, N. (1982) 'Work Experience in Soviet and East European Schools', in Eggleston, J. (ed.) *Work Experience in Secondary Schools.* London: Routledge and Kegan Paul.

Grant, N. (2000) 'Tasks for Comparative Education in the New Millennium', *Comparative Education.* **36** (3) 309–317.

Haugen, E., McClure, V., Thomson, D. S. (eds) (1980) *Minority Languages Today.* Edinburgh: Edinburgh University Press.

Holmes, B. (1981) *Comparative Education: Some Considerations of Method.* London: Allen and Unwin.

Idriss, C. (2002) 'Challenge and Change in the German Vocational System since 1990', *Oxford Review of Education.* **28** (4), 473–490.

King, E. (1979) *Other Schools and Ours*, 3rd edn. New York: Holt Rinehart and Winston.

Korsgaard, O. (2002) 'Learning and the Changing Concept of Enlightenment: Danish Adult Education', *International Review of Education.* **46** (3), 305–325.

MacIntosh, J. (1971) 'Politics and Citizenship', in Lowe, J., Grant, N. and Williams, T. D. (eds) *Education and Nation-Building in the Third World.* Edinburgh: Scottish Academic Press.

Naughton, J. (1999) *A Brief History of the Future: The Origins of the Internet.* London: Weidenfeld and Nicolson.

Phillips, D. (ed) (2000) *The Education Systems of the United Kingdom.* London: Symposium Books.

Watson, K. (ed) (2001) *Doing Comparative Education Research: Issues and Problems.* London: Symposium Books.

Webber, S. and Liikanen, I. (eds) (2001) *Education and Civic Culture in the Post-Communist Countries.* London: Palgrave.

Wilde, S. (2002) 'Secondary Education in Germany 1990–2000: One Decade of Non-reform in Unified German Education?' *Oxford Review of Education.* **28** (1) 39–51.

11

Early childhood education in the UK

J. Eric Wilkinson

> It should be noted that children at play are not playing about; their games should be seen as their more serious-minded activity.
>
> (Montaigne, 1533–92)

Introduction

THE ORIGINS OF EARLY childhood education in Britain go back nearly 200 years to the time of the social reformer Robert Owen. As part of his model village in New Lanark, Scotland, he established a nursery, reputedly the first in the world, for young children whose parents worked in the local woollen mills. The emphasis was on a stimulating child-centred curriculum based on play, exploration, singing and dancing. Unfortunately, after Owen left in 1825 to establish New Harmony in America, the nursery was discontinued, largely as a result of the greed for profit generated by the industrialisation of Britain in the nineteenth century.

In recent times, much attention has been given to education in the early years, a trend that is evident in most Western countries. There are three main reasons for this. First, research has demonstrated the all round psychological and social benefits to the child that high quality early childhood education offers. Second, it has been shown that a good early years experience has positive effects on subsequent educational achievement, and third, early childhood services contribute to meeting the objectives of a healthy and prosperous society by promoting a more effective labour force and a more supportive family environment.

Since the 1980s, the findings of seminal research (McCartney, 1984; Phillips *et al.,* 1987) on the lasting effects of early childhood education on children's psychological and social development are now well established. It has also been demonstrated that children's educational attainment is improved. A review of the relevant literature was undertaken by Sylva and Wiltshire (1994). They concluded:

> When pre-school education is of high quality it leads to lasting enhancement of educational performance and later employment. It does this through encouraging high aspirations, motivation to learn and feelings of task efficacy, especially for children from disadvantaged backgrounds.
>
> (Sylva and Wiltshire 1994: 47)

This finding was echoed by Ball (1994) in the report of the Royal Society of Arts: *Start Right: The Importance of Early Learning*.

In a later review of the literature, Melhuish (2004) also concluded that early childhood education has lasting beneficial effects on young children, a finding echoed in many countries such as the US, Scandinavia and New Zealand.

However, the most powerful study to demonstrate the positive effects of early childhood was the longitudinal study undertaken by Sylva *et al.* from 1997 to 2004. The study aimed to compare and contrast the developmental progress of over 3,000 children selected from a wide range of social and cultural backgrounds in six local authorities in England that have differing pre-school experiences (Sylva *et al.*, 2004). The Effective Provision of Pre-school Education (EPPE) project investigated the effects of pre-school education and care on children's development and attainment for children aged 3–7 years old. The EPPE team collected a wide range of information on 3,000 children who were recruited at age 3+ and studied longitudinally until the end of third year in primary school. Data were collected on children's developmental profiles (at ages 3, 4/5, 6 and 7 years), background characteristics related to their parents, the child's home learning environment, and the pre-school settings children attended. The early years settings were drawn from a wide range of providers (local authority day nurseries, integrated centres, playgroups, private day nurseries, nursery schools and nursery classes). A sample of 'home' children (who had no or minimal pre-school experience) were also recruited to the study at entry to school for comparison with the pre-school group.

Sylva *et al.* explored five questions:

- What is the impact of pre-school on children's intellectual and social/behavioural development?

- Are some pre-schools more effective than others in promoting children's development?

- What are the characteristics of an effective pre-school setting?

- What is the impact of the home and childcare history on children's development?

- Do the effects of pre-school continue through Key Stage 1 at age 6/7 years?

The key findings were:

- Pre-school experience, compared with none, enhances all-round development in children.

- Duration of attendance (in months) is important; an earlier start (under age 3 years) is related to better intellectual development.

- Full-time attendance led to no better gains for children than part-time provision.

- Disadvantaged children benefit significantly from good quality pre-school experiences, especially where they are with a mixture of children from different social backgrounds.

- Good quality can be found across all types of early years settings; however quality was higher overall in settings integrating care and education and in nursery schools.

- High-quality pre-schooling is related to better intellectual and social/behavioural development for children.

- Settings that have staff with higher qualifications have higher-quality scores and their children make more progress.

- Where settings view educational and social development as complementary and equal in importance, children make better all-round progress.

These findings demonstrate in a powerful way how good-quality early childhood education can benefit children who attend.

As far as the impact of early childhood education and care on wider social issues is concerned, it is now recognised that nursery provision counteracts poverty by facilitating parental economic activity, it provides the main caregiver (usually the mother) with temporary relief from constant vigilance and it can provide employers with continuity in valued personnel if provision for very young children is readily accessible.

Parents are now more economically active than at any time since the Second World War. But is this trend for more working parents good for children? Some would argue that the 'demand' on mothers to work puts them in a very invidious position and at times children can be neglected. In such situations early childhood education and care have a vital role to play. In countries where it is the cultural norm for parents to work (for example, Denmark) the state provides extensive early childhood services to suit the needs of the parents. There is no evidence to suggest that children are disadvantaged in such circumstances.

Not until fairly recently has it become widespread in the UK for mothers with young children to work. This has been particularly pronounced in families with children under 3 years of age. However, there is a lingering view that children under the age of 3 are better off with their mothers rather than in a nursery or with a childminder. The work of Bowlby (1952) on the psychological impairment of children as a consequence of maternal deprivation is still surprisingly influential, despite more research that demonstrates that young children are quite capable of appropriate bonding with a range of adults (Schaffer 1977). However, the issue about whether working mothers can have detrimental effects on their child's well-being still remains unresolved. The work of Belsky (2001) in the USA and more recently in the UK supports the view that, if a child is placed in childcare outside the home for more than 20 hours per week when the child is under 1 year of age, there may be some detectable negative effects when the child is slightly older if the childcare is not of the highest quality. These negative effects are associated with anti-social behaviour such as aggression and overt disobedience, though it is not clear whether, for a small minority of children who remain at home until the age of 3, non-attendance at group care contributes to the emergence of more acute anti-social behaviour such as physically assaulting other children.

However, given the convincing evidence in support of pre-school education, writers such as Moss and Penn (1996) have consistently argued that quality early childhood education should be made universally available by the state to families with young children. The government responded robustly to these arguments by introducing a policy of free pre-school places, albeit part-time, for all 4-year-olds whose parents wish it from 1999 and for all 3-year-olds whose parents wish it from 2001 (DfEE 1998a; Scottish Office 1998).[1] The publication in 1998 of the government's policy for the early years entitled *Meeting the Childcare Challenge* (subsequently referred to as the *Childcare Strategy*) represented a sea-change in the relationship between the state and the family with young children such that the state was set to take a much more proactive role in the provision of early years services.

Pre-school education and national childcare strategies

The common features of the Childcare Strategy for all parts of the UK are:

- raising the quality of care;

- making childcare more affordable;

- making childcare more accessible by increasing the number of places and improving information.

[1] From August 2006, free education places are being provided on a pilot basis in three local authority areas in Scotland for 2-year-olds living in vulnerable circumstances.

The strategy is based on five principles: quality, affordability, diversity, accessibility and partnership.

The key element of the government's approach is that early childhood services should be based on 'partnerships' between the local authorities and the different types of provider. The partnerships between the local authorities, the private sector and the voluntary sector should:

- ensure that services enhance the care, play and educational experience of young children and the care and play experience of children up to age 14, including those with special educational needs and those with disabilities;

- bring together the maintained, private and voluntary sectors in a spirit of co-operation and genuine partnership, based on existing good practice;

- be directed by the diverse needs and aspirations of children locally, and of their parents, and pay attention to the support of families;

- be further directed by the requirements of the local labour market and the needs of local employers, seeking advice from the local Training and Enterprise Council as appropriate;

- generate genuine partnership and debate between all providers and others, and seek agreement about how needs can best be met;

- recognise that the private and voluntary sectors have particular strengths;

- recognise that these sectors often give support to, and in turn are supported by, parents;

- understand the reality of the constraints on the local authority, both financial and other; and

- pay regard to value for money, taking both cost and quality into account, including recognition that the majority of childcare provision normally will be, or will become, financially viable within a short period.

(DfEE 1998b)

Partnership with parents

Although the government's policy of promoting partnerships between the different providers of pre-school education and local authorities is welcome, the partnership that individual nurseries have with parents is crucial. Attending a nursery is often the first step to independence for most children. Parents must have confidence that when they send their child to a nursery their child will be well cared for and be helped to learn. However, it must not be forgotten that the home environment in general is richly educative (Tizard and Hughes 1984).

In their relationship with parents, different nurseries operate different models of partnership. In the independent sector (where parents often have full-time employment) partnership depends on effective and efficient communication, whereas in the voluntary sector parents take an active involvement in the delivery of a caring and stimulating environment.

Most nurseries now recognise the importance of continuity between home and nursery, often interpreting their role as helping parents to provide complementary experiences at home to those in nursery: for example, reading stories, responding to questions, etc. Many nursery teachers and nursery nurses now regard it as part of their job to communicate with parents about the progress of individual children.

Early childhood services in the UK

There are three main categories of provision for children under 5 years of age in the UK: local authority services, voluntary services and private services. This arrangement, unique to the UK, is often referred to as the 'mixed-economy model' of early years services.

As far as local authority provision is concerned, until recently there have been two sub-divisions – *education*-based services and *social (work)* services. Of the specifically educational provision there are three types – nursery schools, nursery classes attached to primary schools and (with the exception of Scotland) reception classes in primary schools. These types of provision are staffed by both nursery teachers and nursery nurses. Of the social (work) services there are day nurseries, family centres and children's centres staffed largely by nursery nurses. With the exception of reception classes, the differentiation between these two types of provision is being eroded, largely as a result of the pioneering work on integration in Strathclyde Region in Scotland in the late 1980s (Penn 1992; Wilkinson 1995). Since then many local authorities have established 'integrated' (or 'combined') centres where education and care are fully integrated.

In the voluntary sector, playgroups run by local mothers, assisted by a playgroup leader, are the most common, though most of the places in these groups are for one or two short sessions each week with a small charge bring levied for each session. Less prevalent are mother and toddler groups and crèches.

In the private sector, provision varies widely from childminders (who look after children in their own homes) through private nurseries (very similar to local authority nursery schools) to nursery classes in fully independent schools. Childminders and private day nurseries are available to address the needs of working parents who are willing to meet the costs of these services. Such costs vary between £100 and £250 per week.

Moss and Penn (1996) undertook an extensive and useful comparison of the different types of provision and clearly demonstrated substantial shortcomings in the current system. Despite the implementation of the Childcare Strategy there was still wide variation in 2003 in, cost, staffing and opening times of early childhood services in the UK resulting in a complex piecemeal system (see Table 11.1). Although implementation of the Childcare Strategy has resulted in significant improvement in access to early years services, there are still major concerns about whether the services are meeting the diversity of family needs.

As far as the organisation of services is concerned the vast majority of places are part-time, attendance being for half a day, either mornings or afternoons. In 2006, although virtually all 3- and 4-year-olds attended an early years setting, 85 per cent on a part-time basis. In addition, most nursery schools and classes close for school holidays. Furthermore, there is a professional distinction between nursery nurses and nursery teachers, resulting in differentiation of status, remuneration and promotion prospects.

In ideological terms there is still a widespread view among parents and some professionals in the UK that very young children (i.e. under 3 years) could be seriously impaired unless they are reared by their mothers. This means that in the

TABLE 11.1 Differences between education and care for young children

	Daycare	Education
Main aims	Various: supporting parents, promoting equality, caring for children, providing stable and safe environment	Promoting children's learning; preparation for primary school
Curriculum	Of peripheral concern: basic play materials, rough groupings of material	Central, extremely sophisticated: eighteen basic areas, subdivided into many parts each with many ideas about practice
School	Little contact with primary school	Dovetailed with National Curriculum
Staff	Two-year vocational training in nursery training; multi-role job description	Staff formally qualified to teach in primary school sector following four-year BEd course; main task to teach, any other tasks a distraction from teaching
Children	Focused on children aged 0–5; view of child's paramount need: to feel safe and secure	Focused on children aged 3–5; view of children's paramount need: to learn and master basic linguistic and numerical tasks
Style of learning	Meaningful learning diffuse, occurs throughout day, in many situations	Meaningful learning intense, concentrated into short periods in educational setting
Staff accountability	Through staff support, supervision and managerial oversight	Through written development; planning individual or team-based
Effectiveness	Mainly measured by child/parent satisfaction	Mainly measured by children's developmental outcomes

Source: Penn and Wilkinson (1995).

UK there is very little educational provision for under-3s in the local authority sector, despite comparative evidence that many other European countries provide extensive and successful facilities for under-3s. However, this attitude is now being challenged. Provision for under-3s is being taken seriously by respective government departments. For example, in Scotland, guidelines have been issued to those professionals working with very young children (Learning and Teaching Scotland 2003) and provision for under-3s is improving, though largely in the private and voluntary sectors. In addition, the government's Sure Start programme is now impacting on those children deemed to be in disadvantaged circumstances and pilot schemes are under way in Scotland to provide free education places for 2-year-olds living in vulnerable situations.

Since 1998, the number of children experiencing early childhood education and care in the UK has increased dramatically. Table 11.2 shows the percentage of 3- and 4-year-old children in England by type of provider in 2006. The proportion of children accessing early years services in England has virtually doubled since the mid-1990s. In 1998 the estimated proportion was in the range 50–60 per cent, whereas in 2006 virtually all 3- and 4-year-olds attended some form of early years provision, albeit mostly on a part-time basis. In terms of the difference between the two age groups, the majority of 3-year-olds attend the services provided by the private and voluntary sectors, whereas most 4-year-olds attend maintained nursery schools and reception classes in primary schools.

In Scotland, the pattern of provision is somewhat different from that in England and Wales. There is no equivalent of the reception class. Where available, parents choose to send their children to a nursery school, nursery class, day nursery, family centre, playgroup or private nursery. However, the dramatic increase in the number of 3- and 4-year-olds accessing early years provision witnessed in England has also been replicated in Scotland (Scottish Executive 2006a).

Theoretical perspectives

The theoretical basis of pre-school provision is both complex and extensive. It is complex not only because it is intricately interwoven with several academic

TABLE 11.2 Percentage of 3- and 4-year-olds by type of early years education provider in England 2006

Form of early years provision	3-year-olds	4-year-olds
Private and voluntary providers	57	19
Independent schools	4	5
Maintained nursery and primary schools	38	79
All providers	99	103

Source: Department for Education and Skills (2006).
Note: some children attend more than one provider so the above figures include double counting.

disciplines but because the different types of provision give different emphasis to different theories. It is extensive because the field has received much research attention from a wide variety of domains and individuals. The design, restructuring and revision of institutional systems for the education and care of young children is inherently based on an understanding, whether implicit or explicit, of this theoretical background.

The principal theoretical strands that inform and shape provision for families with children under 5 are:

- *ideology* of childcare and child rearing;

- *psychology* of child development;

- *the nature* of education and care of children.

Childcare is inextricably bound up with the realisation of equal opportunities and the relief of disadvantage. As such it is immersed in ideology and is a matter of public responsibility. 'Childcare makes a contribution to the relief of disadvantage and the promotion of equality' (Cohen and Fraser 1991: ii). The recent Millennium longitudinal study at the London University Institute of Education (Hansen and Joshi 2007) has shown that disadvantaged children may be as much as a year behind non-disadvantaged children on many psychological measures by the age of 3.

Central to such matters is the relationship between the family, the child and the state. This relationship has been undergoing a sea-change over the past ten years partly in response to the metamorphosis occurring in family life in Britain. In response to this trend, the government, inspired by the work of Giddens in *The Third Way* (Giddens 1998), generated a range of policies, including the expansion of free early childhood education for 3-to-5-year-olds and the introduction of the means-tested childcare tax credit for working parents to support the family wishing to access services for a child under 3. This has resulted in a significantly enhanced role for the state in the rearing of young children (see Wilkinson 2003).

How childcare affects children and families is a critical feature of developmental psychology:

> Far from disrupting the family by taking over some of its childcare functions, day care services ought to be seen as providing experiences that complement those obtained at home, with corresponding advantages for child development.
>
> (Schaffer 1990: 153)

Equally, the kind of learning experiences, activities, knowledge and values children are expected to engage with as part of their upbringing and induction into the world are also critical.

The pre-school curriculum

Since the time of the first nursery in New Lanark, 'play' has been a central feature of nursery activities. It was not until after the Second World War, however, that governments began to take an interest in the activities inside the nursery. In Scotland, the 1950 Primary Memorandum published by the then Scottish Education Department defined the aim of nursery education:

> The aim of nursery school education is to provide the right conditions for growth, and so to ensure the harmonising of the whole personality of the child. Whenever reference is made to aspects of development, whether physical, mental, emotional, spiritual, or social, it must not be forgotten that these are all inter-dependent aspects of a unity.
>
> (Scottish Education Department 1950: 127).

The Memorandum went on to state:

> The value of the physical aspect is perhaps the most obvious. In general, the term covers medical care, adequate rest and sleep, balanced diet, play within doors and in the open air, suitable clothing, and training in hygienic habits.
>
> (Scottish Education Department 1950: 127).

In other words, it was the healthcare aspect of nurseries that was stressed by central government in the post-war period. This stress on health was the dominant influence in nurseries for some thirty years, many nurseries being under the direct supervision of the Ministry of Health (DES 1967). In day nurseries, healthcare was paramount; children had to be protected from disease and squalor. It was not until the 1970s that a change took place when attention was paid to children's intellectual needs. In *Before Five* (Scottish Education Department 1973), the aim of nursery education was broadened into activities aimed at child development:

> The ideal educational environment in these years will afford opportunities for the child to develop his physical, intellectual, social and emotional capacities.
>
> (Scottish Education Department 1973: 1)

For the first time, priority was to be given in early childhood education to a child's broad developmental needs. In 2000 the then Department for Education and Employment (DfEE) in England established the 'Foundation Stage' as a distinct period in the English education system (DfEE 2000).

The Foundation Stage is defined as that period in a child's life from age 3 to the end of the reception year, that is, age 5. To offer guidance on appropriate learning experiences for children at this stage, the Qualifications and Curriculum Authority (QCA) in England issued a set of curriculum guidelines referred to as *Curriculum Guidance for the Foundation Stage* for professionals working with children in the age range 3–5. The guidance specified six areas of development as the framework within which detailed learning outcomes, referred to as early learning goals, are stipulated. These areas were:

- personal, social and emotional development;

- communication, language and literacy;

- mathematical development;

- knowledge and understanding of the world;

- physical development;

- creative development.

To help practitioners in planning early years activities, the guidance issued by the QCA identified the concept of 'stepping stones' that showed the knowledge, skills, understanding and attitudes that children need to learn during the Foundation Stage in order to achieve the desired early learning goals. In each curriculum area specified alone the guidance outlined four progressive steps a child needs to take in order to reach the specified early learning goals and hence be in a position to benefit from more formal education in a primary school setting.

More recently the Department of Education and Skills has introduced a *Statutory Framework for the Foundation Stage in England* (DfES 2007). The Early Years Foundation Stage (EYFS) framework builds on the Guidance for the Foundation Stage by integrating education and care of young children into a single document, the aim of which is to achieve the five outcomes specified in *Every Child Matters* (Chief Secretary to the Treasury 2003) of staying safe, being healthy, enjoying and achieving, making a positive contribution and achieving economic well-being by:

- setting the standards for the learning, development and care young children should experience when they are attending a setting outside their family home, ensuring that every child makes progress and that no child gets left behind;

- providing for equality of opportunity and anti-discriminatory practice and ensuring that every child is included and not disadvantaged because of ethnicity, culture or religion, home language, family background, learning difficulties or disabilities, gender or ability;

- creating the framework for partnership working between parents and professionals, and between all the settings that the child attends;

- improving quality and consistency in the early years sector through a universal set of standards which apply to all settings, ending the distinction between care and learning in the existing frameworks, and providing the basis for the inspection and regulation regime;

- laying a secure foundation for future learning through learning and development that is planned around the individual needs and interests of the child, and informed by the use of ongoing observational assessment.

The EYFS has been given legal force through an Order and Regulations made under the Childcare Act 2006. From September 2008, it will be mandatory for all schools and early years providers to implement in Ofsted-registered settings attended by young children – that is, children from birth to the end of the academic year in which a child has his or her fifth birthday.

In Scotland, the then Scottish Consultative Council on the Curriculum, in its report *A Curriculum Framework for 3–5* (Scottish Office 1999) defined the aims of early childhood education as to:

- provide a safe and stimulating environment, in which children could feel happy and secure;

- encourage the emotional, social, physical, creative and intellectual development of children;

- promote the welfare of children;

- encourage positive attitudes to self and others and develop confidence and self-esteem;

- create opportunities for play;

- encourage children to explore, appreciate and respect their environment;

- provide opportunities to stimulate interest and imagination;

- extend the children's abilities to communicate ideas and feelings in a variety of ways.

To help achieve these aims, the Scottish Curriculum Framework document outlines curriculum guidelines in terms of planned learning experiences based on five aspects of children's development and learning. These are:

- emotional, personal and social development;

- communication and language;

- knowledge and understanding of the world;

- expressive and aesthetic development;

- physical development and movement.

Unlike the new English Early Years Framework, the Scottish Framework remains as guidance to service providers and is not enshrined in legislation, although the Framework plays a crucial role in the inspection of services by HMIE.

The significant difference between the Scottish Framework and the new English Early Years Framework, in terms of curriculum areas, is that in the English Framework mathematical development in the form of problem-solving, reasoning and numeracy comprises a discrete curriculum area, whereas in the Scottish guidelines mathematical development is integrated into knowledge and understanding of the world. However, the biggest difference between the Scottish Framework and the English Framework is the inclusion in the latter of the welfare requirements of all early years settings. In Scotland such requirements are contained in a separate document issued by the Scottish National Care Commission (Scottish Executive 2002).

Thus, for the first time in the 200-year history of nursery education in the UK, governments have specified the parameters of children's learning. The drivers for this policy are based on raising standards of educational achievement in the compulsory school years and facilitating parents to be more economically active. Reports such as *World's Apart* (Ofsted 1996), which compares educational achievement internationally, have had a major impact on successive government's policy despite evidence to show that performance in external examinations such as A-levels and Highers has improved (for example, Scottish Executive 2006b). Nevertheless the present government's emphasis on early childhood education, which forms a key element of its Childcare Strategy, is to be warmly welcomed.

Although definition of the curriculum by central government agencies is generally accepted amongst early childhood professionals, its delivery and impact on children's general well-being are more controversial. With the influx of young children into reception classes in England and Wales, which have inferior child–teacher ratios compared with nurseries, formalisation of the pedagogy for such children has taken place in a number of settings. Some 4-year-olds in reception classes no longer enjoy a spontaneous, play-based, caring and stimulating environment associated with good nurseries. Instead they are subject to school pressures to conform and engage with formal, highly structured learning. Although there is much to be said for stimulating children intellectually from an early age, excessive rigidity can have undesirable psychological consequences. It has been recently demonstrated by Sylva *et al.* (2007) that pedagogical practices and activities 'where staff take a more active role in children's learning, including scaffolding young children's play, especially in the communication and literacy domains of the curriculum' produce the best results.

Introduction of the Foundation Stage and its associated Framework is intended to reinforce a more child-centred pedagogy, which has its roots in the writings of Jean-Jacques Rousseau in the eighteenth century in France (see Wilkinson 2003) and was developed by Pestalozzi, Froebel, the MacMillan sisters and others.

Quality of the nursery experience

Defining quality

Of paramount importance in pre-school education is the pursuit of quality, partly motivated by 'value for money' in public sector services, but also motivated by the now well established relationship between quality and children's progress. The importance of quality in early childhood services was raised in the Rumbold Report (DfES 1990). Since then, various organisations (for example, European Childcare Network 1991, 1996) and several local authorities have recognised that quality matters. However, defining quality in early childhood services is not straightforward. The complex problems of definition have been discussed at length (Moss and Pence 1994; Abbott 1994; Dahlberg *et al*. 1999). To reach a universal definition of quality is not feasible – definitions vary according to the perspective of a particular stakeholder group.

As claimed by Dahlberg *et al*. (1999) it is more fruitful to examine the different meanings attributed to quality by the various influential stakeholders. They identify two categories of meaning – one descriptive and relative, the other evaluative and quasi-objective. In the former category of meaning, referred to by Pence and Moss as the 'inclusionary paradigm', the process of reaching a common understanding between the various immediate stakeholders is central. The primary purpose in this paradigm is to deliver a service to children and families that both professional educators/carers and parents agree is worthwhile. Clearly such an approach contributes to the development of a dynamic early years setting. Unfortunately it ignores the political realities associated with funding and accountability – features with which recent governments are concerned.

In the second category of the meaning attributable to quality, that is, the evaluative meaning, the primary purpose is to assess how well a service performs and/or meets its aims and objectives. In order to do this a benchmark of quality is usually stipulated in advance against which judgments can be made. Very often this is the paradigm used by researchers in this field (for example, Harms *et al*. 1998; Sylva *et al*. 2004). Although the strength of this approach affords some degree of comparative analysis (see, for example, Stephen and Wilkinson 1995), the weakness is that context, culture and choice are ignored.

In moving the debate forward it seems not unreasonable to explore the possibility of combining the two paradigms into a unified process of quality definition and quality assessment. Such an arrangement would initially draw on the evaluative tradition by establishing a broad quality framework through mutual agreement between a number of stakeholders. The framework would then be used in such a way as to give individual nurseries the opportunity to describe their practice and generate supportive evidence which would be available for external scrutiny. In their work with the Scottish Independent Nurseries Association (SINA) Wilkinson and Stephen (1998) specified such a framework based on defined standards in six key areas:

- the learning environment;

- the social experience;

- partnerships;

- staff;

- management;

- accommodation and resources.

This approach to quality assurance was adopted by the Centre for British Teachers in its scheme *Quality Matters* (CfBT 2000).

Assessment of quality

Two approaches to the assessment of quality can be identified in practice. The qualitative approach relies on the professional judgment of teachers, nursery nurses and others, whereas the quantitative approach is based on 'objective' measurement often using pre-specified scales. The former approach, which characterises inspections by Her Majesty's Inspectorate of Schools, has the advantage of being more comprehensive and detailed but is open to potential bias and possible dispute. It is also only feasible to undertake intensive inspections at lengthy intervals of time (in the case of Ofsted inspections, every five to six years). The latter approach to quality assessment is potentially more rigorous and quasi-objective but necessarily depends on a more rigid definition of 'quality'. Such an approach has been used in the longitudinal research study undertaken at the London Institute of Education in the Effective Provision of Pre-school Education project. Using the revised edition of ECERS (Harms *et al.* 1998) and its English Extension (ECERS-E), comparisons were made between the different types of provider – public, private and voluntary. On the vast majority of indicators, nursery schools and classes were rated highest and playgroups in the voluntary sector were rated lowest, a finding not consistent with quality of provision in Scotland for these services in partnership with a local authority.

Assessment of attainment

Traditionally, the assessment of the educational progress of young children has been overwhelmingly concerned with the teaching and learning process either to help in pedagogical planning (Wolfendale 1993) or in screening children for special educational needs (Lindsay and Pearson 1981). Blenkin and Kelly (1992) make out a strong case for the primacy of the pedagogical purpose in assessment:

We have throughout this book advocated those forms (of assessment) we consider most conducive to the promotion of educational growth in pupils – those which are formative, holistic, emphasising strengths rather than weaknesses, judgmental rather than metric.

(Blenkin and Kelly 1992: 165).

Since the introduction of national testing by the Conservative government in the 1980s, a sea-change has taken place in the purpose of assessment (Blatchford and Cline 1994; Burgess-Macey 1994). Information from assessment is now required to evaluate the effectiveness of different educational institutions, principally schools.

Lindsay (1997) identified seven purposes of assessment in two main categories: those which are child-focused and those which are focused on the establishment. In the child-focused category he includes such matters as screening, monitoring and pedagogy, and in the establishment-focused category he locates resource planning and accountability.

There is considerable debate in the literature (Drummond 1993; Lindsay 1997) whether any one scheme for assessing 4- and 5-year-old children – sometimes referred to as Baseline Assessment – can adequately address each of the purposes. Wolfendale (1993) identified a number of concerns and dilemmas that are 'an amalgam of technical educational and socio-political issues'. Despite what Wolfendale refers to as 'a long list of objections to Baseline Assessment – at every level – theoretical, ideological, practical and financial', she concluded:

Paradoxically in fact there does appear to be a consensus, based on reality principles, that a form, or forms of on-entry-to-school assessment is a viable idea.

(Wolfendale 1993: 33)

However, considerable concern has been expressed about the purpose and practice:

Early years educators need to treat the issue of assessment very carefully. We need to be clear about which purposes of assessment we are working towards, and which models of the early years curriculum and of children's learning underpin our models of assessment. We cannot uncritically adopt a model handed down from the National Curriculum and assessment procedures.

(Burgess-Macey 1994: 48)

Similarly, Lindsay concluded: 'Baseline assessment is potentially a very useful addition to the education system – but only if developed and used wisely' (Lindsay 1997: 26). Several Baseline Assessment schemes now in use throughout the UK use formative procedures in which information about a particular child's learning is generated on the basis of the professional judgment of those involved with the child (Black and Willan 1998). It is now regarded as good practice in early childhood education that assessment information can play a vital role in ensuring that all children engage with the learning process as effectively as possible (Wilkinson et al. 2001).

The new Early Years Framework in England recognises the importance of assessment:

> Ongoing assessment is an integral part of the learning and development process. Providers must ensure that practitioners are observing children and responding appropriately to help them make progress from birth towards the early learning goals.
>
> (DfES 2007: 16)

The Framework also recognises the distinction between formative and summative assessment and endorses the use of both procedures in all early childhood education settings. Whereas formative assessment is used mainly to guide how individual children can be supported in everyday planning, summative assessment is required to address each child's achievements:

> All providers must make arrangements for each child within the final year of the EYFS to be assessed throughout the year by a practitioner. Practitioners must use the 13 scales and have regard to the scale points to complete the EYFS Profile as a record of achievement.
>
> (DfES 2007: 17)

From 2008, each early years setting will be required to draw up a profile of each child's achievements based on the six areas of learning. Testing of children at this age is not encouraged. The EYFS Profile is a way of summing up each child's development and learning achievements at the end of the EYFS. It is based on practitioners' ongoing observation and assessments in all six areas of Learning and Development. Each child's level of development must be recorded against the thirteen assessment scales derived from the early learning goals.

One of the sensitive matters as far as assessment is concerned is who gets access to the assessments, particularly the summative assessment. The Framework clearly states that each child's profile should be available to the relevant local authority and a summary given to parents, though the full profile should also be available to the respective parent is requested.

Providers must permit the relevant local authority to examine and take copies of documents and other articles relating to the EYFS Profile and assessments.

- a written summary reporting the child's progress against the early learning goals and the assessment scales;

- where the parent requests it, a copy of the EYFS Profile;

- details of the arrangements under which the EYFS Profile and its results may be discussed between a practitioner and the parent, giving a reasonable opportunity for the parent to discuss the EYFS Profile and its results with that practitioner.

Such an approach to assessment and record-keeping is both sound and sensible for the wide range of professionals who work with young children and their families.

Conclusion

Early childhood education has come a long way since the days of Robert Owen. Although much of the original informality has been retained, there is a more formal definition of children's early years experience. It is now considered to be one of the most important sectors of education. Rapid expansion of provision has thrown into sharp focus the debate about the nature of experiences most beneficial to young children. It is now accepted that exposure to a formal pedagogy too soon can have detrimental effects on children's subsequent education. In many European countries – particularly in Scandinavia – formal school does not begin until children are over 7 years old. Children's experiences prior to this are firmly rooted in experiential learning – exploration, play, music and social activities. In Scotland much of this spontaneity is also in evidence. In England and Wales, however, the situation has been far from ideal. During the 1980s and early 1990s too much emphasis was placed on formal learning. Only with the introduction of the Foundation Stage is the situation beginning to change for the better.

A rounded, quality nursery experience has untold benefits for children, parents and the wider society. It is fundamental not only to the subsequent schooling process but to the promotion of a more tolerant and understanding society. The challenge now facing early years professionals is to find an appropriate mechanism in which more effective collaboration is pursued. As the 2003 Green Paper states:

> We want to put children at the heart of our policies, and to organise services around their needs. Radical reform is needed to break down organisational boundaries.
>
> (Chief Secretary to the Treasury 2003: 9)

References

Abbott, M. (1994) 'Introduction: The Search for Quality in the Early Years', in Abbott, L. and Rodger, R. (eds) *Quality Education in the Early Years*. Buckingham: Open University Press.

Ball, C. (1994) *Start Right: The Importance of Early Learning*. London: Royal Society of Arts.

Belsky, J. (2001) 'Developmental Risks (Still) Associated with Early Childcare', *Journal of Child Psychology and Psychiatry*. **42** (7), 845–859.

Black, P. and Willan, D. (1988) *Inside the Black Box*. London: School of Education, King's College.

Blatchford, P. and Cline, T. (1994) 'Baseline Assessment: Selecting a Method of Assessing Children on School Entry', *Education*. **3** (13), 10–15.

Blenkin, G. M. and Kelly, A. V. (1992) *Assessment in Early Childhood Education*. London: Paul Chapman.

Bowlby, J. (1952) *Maternal Care and Mental Health*. Geneva: World Health Organization.

Burgess-Macey, C. (1994) 'Assessing Young Children's Learning', in Keel, P. (ed.) *Assessment in the Multi-ethnic Primary Classroom*. Stoke-on-Trent: Trentham Books.

Centre for British Teachers (2000) *Quality Matters*. Reading: CfBT.

Chief Secretary to the Treasury (2003) *Every Child Matters*. Norwich: The Stationery Office.

Cohen, B. and Fraser, N. (1991) *Childcare in a Modern Welfare System*. London: IPPR.

Dahlberg, G., Moss, P. and Pence, A. (1999) *Beyond Quality in Early Childhood Education and Care*. London: Falmer Press.

Department for Education and Employment (1998a) *Meeting the Childcare Challenge*. London: HMSO.

Department for Education and Employment (1998b) *Early Years Development and Childcare Partnerships – Planning Guidance 1999–2000*. Sudbury: DfEE Publications.

Department for Education and Employment (2000) *Curriculum Guidance for the Foundation Stage*. London: QCA.

Department for Education and Science (1967) *Children and their Primary Schools* (the Plowden Report). London: HMSO.

Department for Education and Science (1990) *Starting with Quality: The Report of the Committee of Inquiry into the Quality of Educational Experience Offered to Three- and Four-Year Old Children* (the Rumbold Report). London: HMSO.

Department for Education and Skills (2006) *Provision for Children under Five Years of Age in England*. London: DfES.

Department for Education and Skills (2007) *Statutory Framework for the Early Years Foundation Stage*. London DfES.

Drummond, M. J. (1993) *Assessing Young Children's Learning*. London: David Fulton.

European Childcare Network (1991) *Quality in Services for Young Children*. Brussels: Commission of the European Communities.

European Childcare Network (1996) *Quality Targets in Services for Young Children*. Brussels: Commission of the European Communities.

Giddens, A. (1998) *The Third Way*. Cambridge: Polity Press.

Harms, T. and Clifford, R. M. and Cryer, D. (1998) *Early Childhood Environment Rating Scale*, revised edn. New York: Teachers College Press.

Hansen, K. and Joshi, H. (eds) (2007) *Millennium Cohort Study Second Survey: A User's Guide to Initial Findings*. London: Institute of Education.

Learning and Teaching Scotland (2003) *Care and Learning for Children Birth to Three*. Dundee: L&T Scotland.

Lindsay, G. A. (1997) *Baseline Assessment: A Positive or Malign Initiative?* Coventry: Institute of Education, University of Warwick.

Lindsay, G. A. and Pearson, L. (1981) *Identification and Intervention: School-Based Approaches*. Oxford: TRC.

McCartney, K. (1984) 'Effect of Quality Day Care Environment on Children's Language Development', *Developmental Psychology*. **20** (2), 244–260.

Melhuish, E. C. (2004) *A Literature Review of the Impact of Early Years Provision upon Young Children, with Emphasis Given to Children from Disadvantaged Backgrounds*. Report to the Comptroller and Auditor General. London: National Audit Office. Available at www.nao.org.uk/publications/nao_reports/03–04/268_literaturereview.pdf.

Moss, P. and Pence, A. (1994) *Valuing Quality in Early Childcare Services.* London: Paul Chapman.

Moss, P. and Penn, H. (1996) *Transforming Nursery Education.* London: Paul Chapman.

Ofsted (1996) *World's Apart: A Review of International Surveys of Educational Achievement involving England.* London: HMSO.

Penn, H. (1992) *Under Fives – the View from Strathclyde.* Edinburgh: Scottish Academic Press.

Penn, H. and Wilkinson, J. E. (1995) 'The Future of Pre-five Services in the United Kingdom', *Early Child Development and Care.* **108**, 147–160.

Phillips, D., McCartney, K. and Scarr, S. (1987) 'Child Care Quality and Children's Social Development', *Developmental Psychology.* **23** (4), 537–543.

Schaffer, H. R. (1977) *Mothering.* Glasgow: Fontana.

Schaffer, H. R. (1990) *Making Decisions about Children.* Oxford: Basil Blackwell.

Scottish Education Department (1950) *The Primary School in Scotland.* Edinburgh: HMSO.

Scottish Education Department (1973) *Before Five.* Edinburgh: HMSO.

Scottish Executive (2002) *National Care Standards – Early Education and Childcare up to the Age of 16.* Edinburgh: Scottish Executive.

Scottish Executive (2006a) *Statistics Publication Notice: Pre-school and Childcare Statistics.* Edinburgh: Scottish Executive.

Scottish Executive (2006b) *Statistics Publication Notice: SQA Examination Results in Scottish Schools: 2005/06.* Edinburgh: Scottish Executive.

Scottish Office (1998) *Meeting the Childcare Challenge – A Childcare Strategy for Scotland.* Edinburgh: The Stationery Office.

Scottish Office (1999) *A Curriculum Framework for Children 3–5.* Dundee: Scottish Consultative Council on the Curriculum.

Stephen, C. and Wilkinson, J. E. (1995) 'Assessing the Quality of Provision in Community Nurseries', *Early Child Development and Care.* **108**, 99–114.

Sylva, K. and Wiltshire, J. (1994) 'The Impact of Early Learning on Children's Later Development', *Education Section Review.* **18** (2), 47.

Sylva, K., Melhuish, E., Sammons, P., Siraj-Blatchford, I. and Taggart, B. (2004) *The Effective Provision of Pre-School Education (EPPE) Project: Final Report.* London: University of London, Institute of Education.

Sylva, S. Taggart, B., Siraj-Blatchford, I., Totsika, V., Ereky-Stevens, K., Gilden, R. and Bell, D. (2007) 'Curricular Quality and Day-to-Day Learning in Pre-school', *International Journal of Early Years Education.* **15** (1), 49–65.

Tizard, B. and Hughes, M. (1984) *Young Children Learning.* London: Fontana.

Wilkinson, J. E. (1995) 'Community Nurseries: Integrated Provision for Pre-Fives', *Early Child Development and Care.* **108**, 1–106.

Wilkinson, J. E. (2003) *Early Childhood Education – the New Agenda.* Edinburgh: Dunedin Academic Press.

Wilkinson, J. E. and Stephen, C. (1998) 'Collaboration in Pre-School Provision', *Early Years.* **19** (1), 29–38.

Wilkinson, J. E., Johnson, S., Watt, J., Napuk, A. and Normand, B. (2001) 'Baseline Assessment in Scotland: An Analysis of Pilot Data', *Assessment in Education.* **8** (2), 171–192.

Wolfendale, S. (1993) *Baseline Assessment: A Review of Current Practice, Issues and Strategies for Effective Implementation.* Stoke-on-Trent: Trentham Books.

12

A brief history of state intervention in British schooling

Graham A. Martin

Study the past if you would divine the future.
(Confucius (551–479 BC)

A beginning

England and Wales

BEFORE 1870 ELEMENTARY SCHOOLS provision was funded by charitable donation, they worked in isolation of one another and elementary schooling was largely free of any regulatory legislation.[1] The majority of these charity or voluntary schools had the aim of turning the children of the poor into good Christians who would thereby make a disciplined and productive contribution to society. Even with such high ideals and with some continuing fear that revolution might spread from the continent, there was extensive scepticism over the desirability of educating the poor (Ball 1983). Some influential people saw little purpose in, or good coming from, educating these children lest it cause them to be discontented with their allotted lowly place in life. This viewpoint is well illustrated in the now generally removed verse of the children's hymn:

> The rich man in his castle,
> The poor man at his gate,

[1] See Stephens (1998) for a detailed account of eighteenth-century developments in England, Wales and Scotland.

He made them, high or lowly,
And ordered their estate.[2]

Carr and Hartnett have suggested that according to some influential people of the time educating the poor was both unnecessary and undesirable: 'It was unnecessary because they did not need to be educated in order to take their predetermined place in the social order. It was undesirable because it had the potential to be socially disruptive' (Carr and Hartnett 1996: 78).

Others in positions of power may well have believed in the divine ordering of society but took the view that it was necessary to provide some basic education to improve public order and control. In this way the 'lower orders' would gain some spiritual and moral uplift. An MP named Mr W. Williams addressing the anniversary meeting of the Educational Clothing Society[3] in 1820 offered the view that 'To enter into the question of the expediency of educating the poor was now totally unnecessary, because, though doubts had been expressed on that topic some years ago, no person could be found at present, who would not subscribe to the necessity of educating them, if by so doing they could be rendered moral in their habits and religious in their conduct' (*The Times* 1820).

Two societies were prominent in establishing charity schools but it should be remembered that their involvement was to support and advise individual schools and not to establish any kind of network or organised system of schooling. The Church of England (Anglican) was served by the splendidly named *National Society for the Education of the Poor in the Principles of the Established Church* (known as the National Society) created in 1811, which was itself affiliated to the *Society for the Promotion of Christian Knowledge* (SPCK), which had been in existence since 1699. The educational aspirations of the non-conformist churches were served by the *British and Foreign School Society* (known as the British Society), established in 1808 as the *Royal Lancastrian Society*.

The aim of these societies was to bring religious observance and morality to the masses and so began the strong connection between church and schooling. Dennis and Skilton have suggested that these religious groups 'preferred to see children not educated at all than educated by their rivals' (1987: 165). The evangelical imperative to deliver education to the largest possible numbers for the least possible cost concentrated the curriculum on the 3 Rs (Reading, wRiting and aRithmetic) and fashioned methods of delivery confined to rote learning and drill enforced by rigid discipline and frequent harsh punishment. Its effects are most vividly conveyed by a description of 1809, which stated that 'a single master

---

[2] From *Hymns for Little Children* by Mrs Cecil Frances Humphreys Alexander, 1848.

[3] This society was supported by some powerful people including His Royal Highness the Duke of Sussex and William Wilberforce. They prided themselves that they supported not just the poor but those who were in 'absolute nakedness and distress'. They sought out 'misery in its most wretched haunts and administered relief to those who seemed to be not only cut off from the comforts of humanity, but also from humanity itself' (*The Times* 1820).

could conduct a school of 1000 children; that one book would serve for the whole school; and that 500 boys [sic] could spell and write the same word at the same moment' (Gordon and Lawton 1978: 130).

Despite financial difficulties and the lack of suitable teachers (not a situation suffered by Sunday schools, for which the day meant that educated people not only were available but would dutifully give their services) these charity schools began to be seen as making a valuable contribution. In 1833 the government awarded its first grant for education, allotting the sum of £20,000 (in the region of £1.5 million in 2007 terms) between the two religious societies to match charitable donations for the purpose of building schools. This was the first time that the state had involved itself in the provision of elementary education but it was accompanied by the clear assertion that there was no intention to move towards a state-run system of schooling. The Lord Chancellor, Lord Brougham, reported in 1834 to the Parliamentary Committee on the State of Education, that with regards to the promoting of general education he thought 'legislative interference is in many respects to be altogether avoided or very cautiously employed because it may produce mischievous effects'[4] and that 'it is wholly inapplicable to the present condition of the country, and the actual state of education' (Maclure 1973: 39). His reservations applied to both the funding of schools, where he perceptively anticipated state funding would cause the withdrawal of charitable donations leaving the government with the full cost, and legislation requiring compulsory attendance.

Nevertheless, the provision of funding was, almost inevitably, followed in 1839 by the requirement that schools submit to government inspection and thereby official influence (Stephens 1998). The involvement of the government with its largely secular intentions created a tension with the church groups that has characterised almost two centuries of educational development in all parts of Britain. Increasingly, government funding came with an ever more specific stipulation (known as a Code) on what would be taught in elementary schools. This culminated in 1862 with the *Revised Code* for England and Wales. Through this directive, funding was unequivocally linked to the results of inspections, a process known as *payment by results*. In introducing this measure Robert Lowe stated that 'if it is not cheap it shall be efficient; if it is not efficient it shall be cheap' (McBride 1994: 10). This did much to standardise the experience of the children in the elementary schools as it required that careful attention be paid to the basics of education (the 3 Rs) in order to obtain the grant. Any excesses in the time spent away from these basics, e.g. on religious instruction, were eradicated and pupils' attendance began to be a matter of greater concern to the teachers.

Throughout this period the move towards the universal education of the poor was inextricably linked to the question of child labour. It was the norm for even

---

[4] Many commentators would observe that politicised educational changes in the 1980s and 1990s would prove just what a perceptive prediction this was!

very young children to work and some employers regarded the family as the unit of employment.[5] In 1818 Robert Peel in a parliamentary debate on the manufacture of cotton asserted that children could work in cotton spinning for as much as 15 hours a day. The result of this, he suggested, was that 'every natural instinct was counteracted, every feeling and inclination natural to a child was thwarted and suppressed'. He declared himself 'not romantic enough to maintain that persons, even of their tender age, were not to work; he did not deny the necessity of young children earning their bread by the sweat of their brows; but was it therefore to be inferred that no limitation or measure should be set to their weary toil?' (*The Times* 1818a). A measure of how important the earnings of children were to the family income is evident from the willingness of some parents to obtain false certification of age and to dress their children in a manner associated with greater age.

Despite the financial difficulties and the reservations of the country's governors, there was massive growth in the provision of schooling throughout the first half of the nineteenth century due to the charitable support of the established church and the non-conformists. This was worthy in intent but it was patchy and poorly resourced. It was becoming increasingly clear that, 'as an educational provision for a rapidly increasing population growing up in a society whose traditional structure had been shattered by economic change, they were clearly inadequate' (Ball 1983: 14).

The degree of civil unrest and lawlessness predicted by some had not really materialised[6] although some large conurbations created to provide a readily available labour force for the rapidly expanding manufacturing industries were already showing signs of social decay. Often these were the areas least well served by schools owing to the poor economic plight of the inhabitants and their consequent inability to contribute to the upkeep of a school, compounded by the absence of rich benefactors living in such deprived areas. Some notable philanthropic employers provided elementary education for the children of their employees, with the children spending half their time at school and half at work, but generally the provision of schooling in these areas was poor.

Although the increase in the number of charitable elementary schools levelled off as the century moved through its second half,[7] the interest of the established church and the non-conformists in the education of the children of the poor had

---

[5] A colliery manager in writing to the mine owner in 1854 reported that 'When a child first goes into the pits he is taken down by the father . . . parents . . . lured by the wages, are never backward in sending their children to the pits as soon as they can get them into employ' (Jones 1984: 331–332). This obvious transfer of responsibility for the children being in this employment is perhaps explained as he goes on to report 168 deaths in the mines over a four-year period and that 46 per cent of these were children under 5 years of age!

[6] Nonetheless, 'ragged' or 'industrial' schools were created in the 1830s with the specific intention of providing the 3 Rs and industrial training for those perceived to be 'potentially delinquent'.

[7] This was particularly true in the case of the non-conformist British Society as they increasingly looked to extend their flock through charitable activities in the Empire.

been well established. By the mid-nineteenth century there were as many dissenters as were in the Anglican congregation but by 1860 schools in England supported by the National Society accounted for three quarters of the school population with some 10 per cent supported by the British Society (Stephens 1998). The moral and social benefits of a populace with at least a basic level of education was beginning to be more widely appreciated and the economic imperative was growing. Conditions were now such that some decision-makers, but by no means all, saw a more planned system of elementary education as a necessity and that the state would have to take a lead role.

Scotland and Wales

In Scotland a similar function to that of the Royal Society and the British Society was served by the Church of Scotland. Here there had been a form of elementary education from the mid-sixteenth century and there was already a rudimentary form of inter-school organisation, which pre-dates what was available in other parts of Britain. Not only were educational ethos and Presbyterian religious faith strongly connected, but the schooling system had been effectively proposed by John Knox and his fellow reformers in the *Book of Discipline* in 1560. From the end of the seventeenth century a small amount of local taxes had been used to help the establishment and funding of elementary schools. This meant that the Church of Scotland and from the middle of the nineteenth century the Free Church were running schools with more state backing than in England. A consequence of this was that for Scots in the nineteenth century education was more than a basic instruction and/or scholarship; 'it had become a badge of identity, a potent symbol of Scottishness and one of the way in which a sense of nationhood was preserved without in any way threatening the basic structure of the union with England' (Devine 1999: 389). This point was amplified by the Earl of Rosslyn in a House of Commons debate in 1818 when he stated: 'Into whatever country Scotsmen emigrate, they have always succeeded in improving and humanizing that country, as well as in deriving emolument from the exercise of their own talents and acquirements' (*The Times* 1818b).

In Wales the fear of social unrest was fuelled in the second quarter of the century by the activities of the Chartists and the Daughters of Rebecca. Here, as in England, education was seen as a way to ameliorate these ills, although the extent of the perceived ignorance of the populous was compounded by language difference. The government decided to instigate an enquiry and three commissioners visiting all parts of the principality collecting evidence. The three-volume report (1847) bound in blue leather from these non-Welsh-speaking Anglican commissioners stated that they had found education in a parlous state, but perhaps of more impact were their scandalous comments on the Welsh language, non-conformist religion and the morality of Welsh people. So strong was the reaction that the reports became known as 'Brad y Llyfrau Gleision' or the 'Treachery of the Blue

Books' and its effects left an indelible scar on the Welsh psyche. Real learning, advancement and authority became synonymous with the English language, which became the language of the school. From this point onwards and for a century and more to come, legislation would be enacted for 'England and Wales' (Roberts 1998).

The foundations of a structure

England and Wales

By the second half of the nineteenth century the distribution of schools in England and Wales was largely a reflection of the relative activity of the various religious groups and the presence in specific localities of wealthy benefactors, rather than the result of demographic need. This resulted in the poorest urban areas and the sparsely populated rural regions being served least well. It was estimated by William Forster, Vice-President of the Board of Trade and in charge of the Education Department, that although three quarters of a million children between the ages of 2 and 12 were receiving some education, at least 1.5 million children were not. To solve this problem the Elementary Education Act of 1870 (known as the Forster Act) aimed to 'fill in the gaps' by creating elementary schools in these neglected areas. The importance of this initiative to Gladstone's Liberal government was emphasised by Forster, who completed his speech introducing the Bill to parliament by saying that for Britain to hold her place 'among the nations of the world we must make up the smallness of our numbers by increasing the intellectual force of the individual' (Maclure 1973: 105).

The new schools created by the 1870 Act were funded by local rates and controlled by an elected School Board independent of existing structures. Through the enactment of a local by-law the Boards could make attendance at school compulsory for enrolled children between the ages of 5 and 13 and by 1873 some 40 per cent of the population were subjected to such compulsion (Stephens 1998). This expectation increased and by 1880 all pupils up to the age of 10 years old were required to attend school. This legislation was also significant in controlling the amount of religious instruction taught in the elementary school curriculum[8] and it established the right of parents in all public elementary schools, including those run by the churches, to withdraw children from religious instruction on grounds of conscience. Further, schools established from this point forward and funded by the local rates would not be permitted to teach any religious observance (e.g. catechism) that was distinctive to a particular denomination.

The 1870 Act was the first step towards establishing a state system of education but its critics saw it as being much more concerned with quantity than quality.

---

[8] This matter engaged the Prime Minister, Gladstone, in much debate and correspondence. See Matthew (1982).

The elementary education it made more widely available was seen by some contemporary observers as of very little benefit.[9] There was also considerable reluctance on the part of influential politicians, including Forster, towards the full involvement of the state in the control of education. This was in sharp contrast to the centralised systems already established on the continent of Europe (notably Prussia and France) and is an ideological stance that persists amongst the New Right to this day (Chitty 1996). Similar legislation was enacted for Scotland in 1872 and this resulted in the majority of elementary schools being transferred to School Boards (largely to alleviate the financial difficulties of the church) to the point that by 1891 only 10 per cent of elementary schools were still in the control of a religious charity, notably the Catholic church (Stephens 1998), thus bringing in a more co-ordinated strategy for schooling some years ahead of the situation in England and Wales.

Although the 1870 Act made elementary education more widely available it was still subject to fees. By 1890 there was strong pressure, led by the trades unions and Gladstonian Liberals, for elementary education to be free of charge. To resist this desire was seen by the Tory government as a sure way of losing the recently given working-class vote so in 1891 a Free Education Act was passed (Simon 1965). The progress of this Bill was not without opposition, as the Anglicans, and some supporters of the voluntary schools, saw this as reducing their revenue thereby making them more dependent on the government and they were concerned that it would lead to a greater secularisation of schooling.

An Act of parliament in 1899 created the Board of Education with the remit to oversee everything related to education in England and Wales, which it did, in part, by the issuing of regulations or codes. The Elementary Code of 1900 provided voluntary schools (those established by religious charities) with a block grant to replace the previous subject-based system of *payment by results*.[10] The code specified, for the first time, the particular subjects that an elementary school was normally expected to teach. These were English, arithmetic, geography, history, singing and physical training together with drawing for boys and needlework for girls. If circumstances made it possible then provision could be made to teach science, French and algebra.

Scotland

If the 1870 Elementary Education Act was a compromise, the comparable 1872 Elementary Education (Scotland) Act was more a continuation of the more interventionist Scottish approach. From 1872 onwards, elementary schools were

---

[9] Silver (1983) draws on contemporary accounts to explore the opposition to aspects of education we now take for granted, e.g. state control, compulsory attendance, equal access for all etc.

[10] In 1900 it was still schools established by the religious charities that educated the majority of children but the best School Boards were beginning to show what could be achieved with greater resources and legal powers (Ball 1983).

no longer operated by the Protestant churches. All elementary schools in Scotland, except those belonging to the Catholic and Episcopalian churches, became the responsibility of about 900 School Boards created by the 1872 Act. The Act made attendance compulsory for children aged 5 to 13. Boards had the responsibility of enforcing compulsory attendance and parents had the duty of making sure that their children were educated (Scotland 1969; Stephens 1998). The Act unfortunately required that 'all religious education given in public schools was according to the reformed faith' (Devine 2000: 101). A direct consequence of this was that the Catholic Church and the Episcopalian Church kept their schools out of the public system and, at great sacrifice to themselves because of the considerable expense, continued to run their own network of schools.

Local co-ordination and control

England and Wales

The Education Act of 1902 (Balfour Act) abolished School Boards[11] and created Local Education Authorities (LEAs) in England and Wales. County and County Borough Councils were given responsibility for elementary and post-elementary schools whereas the larger non-county borough councils and urban districts had an oversight of elementary schools only (under Part III of the Act). It also permitted, but did not require, LEAs (but not Part III Authorities) to create secondary schools if they so desired. Secondary schools were not at this time conceived of as a staged phase of education to which pupils naturally progressed on completion of elementary education; they were few in number and the age range of their pupils overlapped with the senior section of the elementary school. Elementary schools provided education which was seen as complete in itself and most children would spend their entire school career in the elementary school with only the exceptional few being able to transfer and gain the benefits of secondary education.

The creation of secondary schools became a popular aspiration that could be funded from the rates so the number of children attending secondary schools increased threefold between 1902 and 1939 (Sharp and Dunford 1990). A succession of regulatory codes served to widen further the curriculum gap between the elementary and the secondary school, the latter becoming increasingly modelled on the academic curriculum of the public school. A 1913 memorandum from the Board of Education (Circular 826) indicated that the secondary school had the two main functions of providing a general education for those who would go on to the professions or to university and catering for those who would complete their formal education at 16 years old. Reconciling the needs of these two groups, particularly with respect to preparing the second group for the world of work, was

---

[11] The Scottish Act of 1918 abolished boards in Scotland and responsibility was placed with larger bodies, which could have a strategic perspective.

identified as a specific challenge for the secondary school so the Board indicated that it would permit some vocational courses in the final year of schooling.

Throughout the first quarter of the twentieth century there was a tension between those who wanted to retain a strong separation between the parallel systems of elementary and secondary education and those who wished for a system that provided primary and secondary education for all.[12] The Education Act of 1918 (Fisher Act) required that older pupils (11 years and above) in elementary schools should be accommodated in separate schools or classes and it raised the school leaving age to 14. The Hadow Report of 1926 furthered this desire for a distinct secondary phase of schooling and suggested that the separation should be at age 11 and that all children should be allocated to secondary grammar or secondary modern schools according to the results of examination. The modern school would have the more practical curriculum of the two and pupils could leave at a younger age although the committee wished to have the minimum school leaving age raised to 15 years old.[13]

The notion that at secondary level different types of children should receive different types of education gained credence throughout this period. In 1938, by which time more than half of elementary school pupils over the age of 11 years were being taught in separate accommodation (Sharp and Dunford 1990), the Spens Report recommended that there should be three kinds of secondary education: the grammar and modern as previously suggested, and a technical school. It suggested that pupil transfer should be possible between the schools and that all three should be accorded parity of esteem.[14] These views were reinforced five years later in the Norwood Report (1943), which had a strong formative effect on what was arguably the most significant piece of education legislation of the twentieth century with regards to creating a truly national system of education or, as it was often described, a national system locally administered.

Scotland

After 1902 a board system was still favoured in Scotland, so the change into a more centralised education system did not happen until 1918. School Boards in Scotland were parochially constituted and wholly elected and so for good or ill exercised some independence from local government. These *ad hoc* bodies survived until the Education (Scotland) Act of 1918, which replaced them with larger education

---

[12] A 'secondary education for all' was an election slogan of the first ever Labour government, which took office in December 1923.

[13] Raising the school leaving age to 15 years old was not actually achieved until 1947 and it was 1972 before the school leaving age was raised to 16.

[14] The view that all types of secondary school should be seen as of equal worth (parity of esteem) was often expressed from this point on. The view held by the majority of the population that this patently was not the case has fuelled much heated debate in the pre- and post-comprehensive periods.

authorities, which were themselves separately elected, for a further ten years. This Act also gave the Catholics and the Episcopalians the reassurances they needed to bring the few remaining church-funded schools into the public system. These *ad hoc* authorities operated from 1918 to 1929 and were replaced by county and city councils in 1929 (Matheson 2003).

The phased and segregated provision

England and Wales

The 1944 Education Act created a Ministry of Education and thereby gave much more power and influence over educational matters to the government. The LEAs had specific duties but it was the Minister who had the ultimate responsibility to ensure that these were carried out. The beneficial result of this was 'more unity and standardisation in the national education service, and perhaps even a small reduction in the grosser disparities in educational opportunities between different parts of the country' (Sharp and Dunford 1990: 18).

This Act required that education in maintained schools in England and Wales should be free to everyone of school age, that the concept of elementary education be discarded[15] and that LEAs reorganise educational provision into 'a continuous process conducted in three successive stages' (Part II.7), namely primary, secondary and further education, with the responsibility of contributing towards the 'spiritual, moral, mental and physical development of the community' (Maclure 1973: 224). Children of school age were to be housed in separate schools with transfer between the two at age 11. It was to be the duty of the parents of school age children to ensure that they were educated according to their 'age, ability and aptitude' (Section 36). However, the Act is not at all clear what this actually meant.[16] For example, it had replaced elementary schools with primary schools without any real guidance on how they were different. The way that secondary education should be structured is not specified in the Act but this legislation is widely credited with ushering in the 'tripartite system' of secondary modern, secondary technical and secondary grammar schools as recommended in the earlier reports. To clarify their desires the new Ministry promptly issued the pamphlet 'The Nation's Schools' in which it set out the very clear intention that secondary schools should be organised on the tripartite principle (Hyndman 1978). Similarly the 1945 Scottish legislation ushered in a bipartite system of senior secondary and junior secondary schools.

In return for financial support voluntary schools could give up some of their autonomy and become 'Aided' schools, which retained much of their denominational character, or they could surrender the larger proportion of their

---

[15] As were the old Part III authorities, whose remit extended only as far as elementary schools.

[16] Gordon and Lawton (1978) observe that the word 'curriculum' is not used in the 1944 Act and the only subject considered is religious education/instruction (p. 32).

self-governance and become 'Controlled' schools. The day should begin in all schools with a corporate act of worship[17] and every school established by an LEA would teach religious instruction according to a syllabus agreed by local representatives of denominational groups (Bell 2004). The Act stated the general principle that parents have the right to expect their children to be educated according to their wishes (Part IV.76) and confirmed the right of parents to withdraw children from these activities on grounds of conscience (Part II.25).

The Education Act of 1944 was a hugely significant piece of legislation in establishing much greater coherence of provision and a system of education more centrally controlled by the state. In itself it contained little that was innovative; it can be seen from the above how heavily it drew on the wisdom of the preceding years. Its immense impact is due, as much as anything else, to its optimistically looking forward to the end of the war, to a future in which the desire was not just to replace what had been destroyed but to reconstruct for a better future. At the core of the Act is a desire to achieve a compromise between all interested parties and one notable way of achieving this was to say very little about what actually went on inside the schools – the curriculum. The decades that followed can be characterised by the craving of successive governments to specify the purpose of education and to delve ever deeper into the details of the day-to-day experience of children and their teachers.

In 1963 the Ministry of Education publish an influential report called *Half our Future* (the Newsome Report) that specifically focused on the school experience of children of average and below average ability and between the ages of 13 and 16.[18] In it the view was expressed that the secondary curriculum should make clear acknowledgment of the world of work and it tried to set out a curriculum that stood somewhere between the rigidity of a 3 Rs strategy and the seemingly laissez-faire approach of progressive education. The report draws on an impressive array of data which indicated, *inter alia*, that this group of pupils received less than their fair share of resources from their LEAs and that there was wide difference in reading test scores between schools and between areas, although they did identify a general rise in attainment particularly over the previous twenty-five years. Some two fifths of secondary modern schools were identified as having serious deficiencies. The Newsome Report added to the growing voice of opinion that, although genetically endowed ability undoubtedly exists it was, however, significantly affected by the social and physical environment and so selection at 11 could be leading to a considerable waste of individual talent and national potential.

---

[17] The only exception was where the physical accommodation of the school made this impossible (Part II.25).

[18] This report was something of a counterbalance to the Crowther Report (1959), which had concentrated on the more able in the school population.

Differences between Scotland and England

The 1945 Education Act (Scotland) was broadly similar to that of 1944 Education Act. These acts made secondary education accessible to all. The English Act created the tripartite system (grammar, secondary modern and technical schools) whereas the Scottish Act introduced a bipartite system in Scotland (junior secondary and senior secondary schools sometimes labelled grammar schools). These remained dominant until the 1960s. The British education systems that had emerged in the first half of the twentieth century had embodied the view that transfer of children from primary to secondary schools was best made at 11 years old (12 in Scotland) and that tests at that age would establish intellectual qualities that were fairly well fixed. Much of this was due to ideas emanating from the new field of Educational Psychology and particularly the work on intelligence by the English psychologist Cyril Burt. The development of IQ (Intelligence Quotient) tests which claimed to measure a generalised intellectual ability led to the 11+ examination (the Qualifier in Scotland) that selected children for the secondary school to which they were best suited.[19] The secondary grammar (or senior secondary) school would cater for the most able children by providing an 'academic' curriculum suited for those who might progress to university and a career in the professions, secondary technical schools would cater for those with moderate ability through a curriculum focused on their practical aptitude and a future career as a skilled worker, and the secondary modern schools took those children who did not fit into either of these categories and would earn their way through unskilled occupations, while in Scotland the junior secondary would take all those who failed to gain entry to senior secondary.

Comprehensivisation

Although some LEAs quickly became ardent proponents of the tripartite system[20] many others were seeing the benefits of one single secondary school serving a community – the comprehensive school. In rural areas this was often a matter of simple expediency. For example in 1949 Anglesey established its first comprehensive school so that there were enough pupils to fill the building (also to create the potential to generate a viable sixth form) and so that children would not have to travel large distances to gain the education to which they had been allotted. In other areas school planning was based on more educational and socio-cultural

---

[19] Sir Cyril Burt has been seen as the founder of Educational Psychology in England and his work had an immense formative effect on the structure of the British educational systems. However re-examination of his findings has raised a considerable degree of scepticism about the reliability, validity and even honesty of significant amounts of the data. This is taken by some reviewers to indicate that at least part of his findings were fabricated (Palmer 2001).

[20] The reality in most LEAs was a bipartite system of secondary schooling, as the secondary technical schools proved to be more expensive to establish than either of the others.

reasoning. By the 1950s doubt was being cast on the reliability of the 11+ selection methodology and, perhaps more importantly, on the fundamental view that children could be so neatly categorised (Hyndman 1978). Additionally, sociologists and politicians were beginning to see separate schools as unrepresentative of the society they served and as being in themselves socially divisive. Parents were increasingly concerned that the promised 'parity of esteem' was just not there in reality or perception. For these reasons some London boroughs were quick to follow the example of Anglesey. Secondary education became increasingly politicised as the Conservative governments hardened their support for grammar schools and the Labour party adopted as policy what had been their principle for some time before, namely the abolition of selection at 11 (Tomlinson 2005). By 1963 the combination of these factors meant that most LEAs were developing schemes for at least partial comprehensivisation and this was encouraged by the Education Act of 1964. This enabled greater freedom regarding the age of transfer to secondary education and made it possible to create 'middle schools' catering for the needs of the 8 to 13 age range (Sharp and Dunford 1990).

Within months of the election of a Labour government in 1964 the Secretary of State for Education and Science issued an 'invitation' to LEAs (DES 1965) to reorganise their secondary provision on comprehensive principles in order to eliminate selection at 11. The circular offered six possible patterns of provision and expected plans to be submitted within twelve months. However it was 1977 before all but one (Tameside) of the LEAs had presented schemes.[21] Nevertheless by 1979 well over 90 per cent of children in England were being educated in comprehensive schools (Barber 1996).

In Scotland, 95 per cent of children are educated in the state sector and of these nearly 100 per cent of children are educated in comprehensive schools, a tiny number being educated in specialist schools where selection is on the basis of artistic talent, not academic achievement or potential. As early as 1947 the Scottish Advisory Council on Education had recommended a comprehensive system with a common curriculum core and a common examination. This had been ignored by the Scottish Education Department, but it was only a matter of time before this more egalitarian approach would be adopted. By 1965 already one fifth of Scottish secondary schools were comprehensive (Bryce and Humes 1999: 39).

From the 1950s through to the early 1970s schools had enjoyed considerable freedom to decide for themselves (with very few checks) what they would teach and how they would teach it. It had become the practice of the government of the day to issue guidance and advice through 'pamphlets' and 'circulars' rather than directives through legislation. Similarly LEAs would provide advice but often had little evidence on what was actually going on inside schools and classrooms. There

---

[21] A more subtle response was employed by some LEAs, who employed the tactic of submitting a scheme that would take up to fifteen years to effect. Ample time for at least one change of government!

was a particular sense of emancipation in the primary schools that had been freed from having to prepare pupils for selection at 11 as they were increasingly adopting a methodology that had been gaining prominence since the 1920s (Simon 1994). This 'progressive' approach to teaching and learning was generally taken to be synonymous with *child-centred* or *discovery learning* and emphasised the importance of the child's experience within a stimulating environment. Barber (1996) has observed that 'This was the time when primary classrooms shifted from the serried ranks of uniformed children learning their tables into the informal, cheerful, buzzing places they tended to be in the 1980s' (Barber 1996: 41).

The importance of nurturing environments and stimulating experience was further highlighted in the report from the committee chaired by Lady Plowden and entitled *Children and their Primary Schools* (Central Advisory Council for Education 1967). This inquiry was the first to look into primary education since the Hadow Reports of 1931 and 1933[22] and it was tasked to look at all aspects of primary education as well as transfer to secondary school. It recommended positive measures to redress the effects of social deprivation, and a shift in the age of transfer to secondary education by the restructuring of the primary phase into First Schools for 5- to 8-year-olds and Middle Schools for 8- to 12-year-olds. The tone of this report is boldly progressive (child-centred) with much concern expressed on imposing rigid subject divisions on the learning of young children (Part 5). It drew on the educationalist's arguments against selective schooling from age 11[23] to make a strong case against the practice of streaming (selection by attainment within year groups) in primary schools, placed great stress on the importance of the relationship between schools and parents, and wished to encourage the steady expansion of nursery education. Schools in Wales were given a similar consideration by a committee chaired by Professor Gittins (1967), who had been a member of the Plowden inquiry. Their strongest recommendations were for the benefits of increased bilingual education and the interesting notion that the quality of religious assembly and instruction would be improved if freed from legislative necessity.

The major debates of this period, then, were to do with the particulars of the learning experience gained in primary schools and progression to, and the organisation of, secondary schools. But it should be noted at this point that the comprehensivisation of the secondary sector was not simply a debate about structural issues. It encompassed views on what children should be taught in secondary schools, the ways they should learn, the learning groups they should

[22] Sir William Hadow led inquiries into *The Primary School* (1931) and *Infant and Nursery Schools* (1933).

[23] As stated earlier in this chapter the confidence in the 11+ was beginning to erode. In particular the Plowden Report (chapter 20) cited doubts on the accuracy of the selection process, the contrasting provision resulting from this judgment and the effects of segregation by achievement. See Maclure (1973: 319–323).

experience and the relationships between teacher and pupil and between teachers and parents. This debate was further energised in 1976 by the then Prime Minister, James Callaghan, in a speech at Ruskin College, Oxford. His central point was that schools were failing pupils, parents and the country because not all were providing the standard of education they should have been and they were not sufficiently locked into the economic needs of the nation (Brooks 1991). He saw the goal of education as being 'to equip children to the best of their ability for a lively, constructive place in society and also to fit them to do a job of work. Not one or the other, but both' (Callaghan 1976: 202). This prompted the so-called *Great Debate* on education, the agenda of which was largely dominated by industrialists (e.g. the Confederation of British Industry) and caused many teachers to feel that they were being marginalised and gave them a glimpse of how the balance of control over the curriculum would change in the forthcoming years. Callaghan's speech was clearly an attack on what had been described elsewhere as the 'secret garden' of education.[24] He emphasised that when matters of education are being considered 'parents, teachers, learned and professional bodies, representatives of higher education and both sides of industry, together with the Government, all have an important part to play in formulating and expressing the purpose of education and the standards that we need' (Callaghan 1976: 201).

The Ruskin Speech and the public debate that followed was not a 'back to basics' campaign like the one advocated by the John Major government in the 1990s, but a clear statement that standards must improve and that work in schools must be better matched to a modern technological society (Riley 1998). Callaghan was careful not to subscribe to the reactionary voices (e.g. the Black Papers – see Chapter 2 above), even though he expressed reservations about progressive methods, or become enmeshed in the details of a curriculum debate, but he did state his belief in a 'basic curriculum with universal standards' (Callaghan 1976: 202) and 'the strong case for the so-called core curriculum of basic knowledge' (Callaghan 1976: 203). This significant event in the evolution of British education (Phillips 2001) was commemorated at Ruskin College twenty years on by a speech from Tony Blair, soon to be elected Labour Prime Minister. In this rather more detailed presentation of the party's policy he too emphasised the need to raise standards for all and especially in the core skills of literacy and numeracy. He saw their task as 'a change of culture – from a commitment to the excellence of the few, to support for the talents of the many' (Blair 1996: n.p.). There are further echoes of Callaghan in the often quoted phrase 'education is the best economic policy there is' used by Blair in many campaigning speeches. This core idea expressed by Callaghan, of the connection between educational achievement of all individuals

[24] It had been argued from the 1960s that education, and particularly matters to do with the curriculum, was a 'secret garden' that could be entered only by those who had the key. Access was seen by some to be by the use of obscure technical language and reference to spurious research.

and the economic prosperity and international competitiveness of the nation, has underpinned education debate and strategies for the past thirty years and remains a burning topic today.

The commodification of education

Callaghan was not the only moderniser; similar themes were developed by the succeeding Conservative government but from a quite different ideological perspective: that of the New Right (Chitty 1996; Tomlinson 2005). They believed that progressive views of education had gained too much prominence (in primary and secondary education) and education should be seen as a discipline for life in which children were introduced to knowledge in a controlled and structured manner and they advocated a return to core values – back to basics (Thatcher 1993). The White Paper *Better Schools* (DES/Welsh Office 1985) is a good example of this as it set out the two aims of the government as being to raise standards everywhere and to reduce expenditure. The extent to which they were intending to become involved in the detail of schooling was evident in the view that broad agreement on the objectives and content of the curriculum was a necessary step towards the raising of standards.

The debate on what the curriculum should contain continued throughout the 1970s and early 1980s with the clear implication that there should be a 'core' or 'entitlement' curriculum of which only the essential irreducible features would be prescribed by the government. This was, however, insufficiently robust for the Conservative government of Margaret Thatcher. Their intention was to sweep away the powers of the LEAs and the influence of educational pressure groups (e.g. the NUT) and replace them with strong central direction but local accountability. Chitty observes that:

> Thatcherism, and its revised version for the 1990s, can be seen as an uneasy attempt to link the principles of the free-market economy with an atavistic emphasis on the family, traditional moral values and the strong state. It involved rolling back the frontiers of the state in some areas, while pursuing policies of repression and coercion in others.
>
> (Chitty 1996: 260)

This ideological belief was embedded in the view that standards in education (and in other social institutions, e.g. the National Health Service) would be driven up by the introduction of a market economy and this led to the commodification of education. The viewpoint was notably articulated by the MP Sir Keith Joseph (later Secretary of State for Education) from about the same time as James Callaghan's Ruskin College speech. It too is concerned with improving the economy but this time by evoking traditional values. Its central ideas are that market forces will drive up standards without state intervention. The education marketplace would be self-regulating as consumer choice would lead to provider competition and therefore self-improvement. For individual enterprise to flourish the consumers (largely seen as the parents) must be provided with the information needed to make informed choices. Lawton argues that as a direct consequence of this the 1988 Education Reform Act (ERA) is ideologically facing in two directions as the national curriculum it created was 'centralizing in the control it exerted, but was also a market device – providing data for parental choice' (Lawton 1994: 92). This is supported by Barber, who suggests that:

> The basic premise behind the [1987 Thatcher] government's programme . . . was that market forces would solve problems in the public sector just as they solved them in the private sector.
>
> (Barber 1996: 36)

At the 1988 North of England Conference the then Secretary of State for Education, Kenneth Baker, defined the new Act as being 'about enhancing the life chances of young people. It is about the devolution of authority and responsibility. It is about competition, choice and freedom . . . it is about quality and standards . . . it is not about enhancing central control' (Batho 1989: 88). Despite this last assertion, when the legislation came along to implement these ideas it gave over 400 additional powers to the Secretary of State for Education!

Moves to diminish the powers of the LEAs and to promote the ideology of the marketplace are evident throughout the 1980s. The 1980 Education Act gave teachers and parents a right to be represented on school governing bodies and required LEAs to justify their decisions and create an appeals mechanism for when parents had exercised their preference of school for their child but been turned down (Sharp and Dunford 1990). Parents with limited financial means who wished their children to be educated at independent schools were given the right under this legislation to make application to the Assisted Places Scheme for fee remission and have this administered directly from the DES.

The 1986 Education (No. 2) Act reduced the influence of the LEA on school governing bodies by giving parents parity of representation and so created a much stronger connection between the school and the community it served. Other sections were concerned with how the school should function and a miscellaneous section dealt with issues that had received recent public attention such as the abolition of corporal punishment, the appraisal of teachers' performance and freedom of speech within the confines of a school. These examples serve to show how schools have become increasingly more accountable to parents and the general public and how the view that market forces would drive up standards was being operationalised. In reality what had been created was a quasi-market (Power 2002) as much control and therefore distortion was introduced to the market by government measures such as the creation of new and preferentially treated schools and the *Assisted Places Scheme*. A review of research on the marketisation of education in three countries leads Power to suggest that what is needed is to

> ask how we can use the positive aspects of choice and autonomy to facilitate development of new forms of community empowerment rather than exacerbating social differentiation.
>
> (Power 2002: 62)

A national curriculum enshrined in law

The 1988 Education Reform Act (ERA) turned out to be prescribing much more than a basic entitlement curriculum, as every school had to teach to all pupils between the ages of 5 and 16 the *core subjects* of English, Maths and Science together with the *foundation subjects* of History, Geography, PE, Art, Modern Foreign Language (for pupils 11 and over), Technology and Music. All schools had to teach RE and there were 'themes', e.g. Personal Social and Health Education (PSHE), which ran across the subject strands. Welsh was made compulsory for schools in the principality. With the exception of RE the Act contained very little detail on the curriculum, as it was an enabling device for the Secretary of State to be empowered to create legally binding Orders clarifying the expectations in each subject. These details were worked out by subject groups who worked more or less in isolation and in an apparently random sequence. Unsurprisingly the National Curriculum that subsequently began to take shape[25] was somewhat over-inflated and lacking in cohesion. Commentators have suggested that it 'has suffered from the lack of an over-riding philosophy or vision, being based on the assumption that the best way forward was to impose on a school a specified set of subjects, based on the grammar school tradition' (Docking 2000: 81–82). Docking goes on to state how detailed attainment targets, programmes of study and assessment arrangements were expected for each subject even though a rationale for the choice of these particular subjects was never made clear. Others are even less complimentary, seeing this curriculum as a reinstatement of the 1903 grammar school curriculum (Brighouse 1999). Even the Prime Minister of the day observed that 'I never envisaged that we would end up with the bureaucracy and the thicket of prescriptive measures which eventually emerged' (Thatcher 1993: 593), although the blame was placed firmly on the technocrats and not politicians.

The National Curriculum was and remains much more than some value-neutral statement of what all children should enjoy as their educational entitlement. It holds together because of the glue that is the market ideology of the New Right

---

[25] The early curriculum proposals for many subjects created enormous controversy and heated debate between those who had opposing views on the essence and methodology of the discipline field. The battlegrounds for English and History were probably some of the bloodiest.

government. West and Pennell have suggested that the 'emphasis on consumer choice was anchored in an overarching belief in the superiority of market forces as a means of organising education and society generally' (2002: 207). The evidence is all around, not least on the DfES website, which proclaimed that in the view of the government, a New Labour government that is, the National Curriculum has four main purposes: to establish an entitlement, to establish standards, to promote continuity and coherence and to promote public understanding.[26]

According to the politicians the attainment targets, programmes of study and externally moderated tests that were to be introduced at 7, 11, 14 and 16 would enable pupil to be compared with pupil, class with class, school with school and LEA with LEA. Educationalists were far less convinced that the data from such straightforward tests could have such universal application. The resulting 'league tables' were as notable for what they ignored, e.g. the social circumstances of the school's catchment area, the ethos of the school, school/home links, the history of funding, the profile of the teachers, as for what they included. The role of parents in the management of schools was increased further through changes to the rules on electing school governors, and schools were given greater control of their own budgets through a process known as local management of schools (LMS). The result of LMS was to give school governing bodies massively enhanced control over the day-to-day arrangements of the school and to impose a corresponding reduction in the power of the LEA. This was the marketplace at its sharpest as the money that LEAs had to devolve to schools was according to a formula based on that school's ability to attract pupils.

Furthermore, schools were enabled by the ERA to opt out of LEA control entirely and become grant maintained (GM) schools, receiving their funding directly from the government. As an inducement, schools that chose to follow this course invariably enjoyed an enhanced income when compared with other schools in the locality. Despite this incentive the desire to break the ties with the LEA was not as strong as the government had wished and expected (Barber 1996). A similar 'opt-out' opportunity was created for Scottish schools by the Self-Governing Schools etc. (Scotland) Act 1989 but had almost no impact, as is evident from the legislation to repeal this option, which in reality applied to only one school. St Mary's Episcopal Primary School, Dunblane, was named in the Standards in Scotland's Schools etc. Act 2000, a law enacted in part to bring that school back under local authority control.

A new type of school was created by the ERA, to be known as a City Technology College (CTC). These were to be sponsored by private donations and were to be free from the influence of the LEA.[27] They were to have innovative work practices

---

[26] For the latest incarnation of the aims of the National Curriculum, see http://curriculum.qca.org. uk/aims/index.aspx.

[27] In most respects the 'technology' can be defined as information and communications technology (ICT) and these schools were to be characterised by an enterprise culture.

for both teachers and pupils and would generate examples of best practice. Despite being once described by Margaret Thatcher as the flagship of Conservative education policy they never attained the numbers or innovative prominence to make them major players in the marketplace. Nevertheless, as Gregory observes:

> The Education Reform Act builds upon the changes already in place and gives the final and fullest expression to the government ambition of putting into place a version of a market-driven national education service.
>
> (Gregory 2002: 93)

The ERA, like all English legislation of the time, applied to both England and Wales and it has been recognised by a number of observers that the introduction of a national curriculum had the unexpected effect of starting to differentiate the curricula of these countries. Phillips and Harper-Jones describe this as a 'curious contradiction' and identify the contributory factors of devolution as including bilingualism, the National Curriculum in Wales and the particular approach to inspection (Phillips and Harper-Jones 2002).

The determination that educational provision had to improve was further reinforced in the 1992 White Paper *Choice and Diversity* (DFE/Welsh Office 1992). The improvement was deemed necessary largely because of the perceived failings of the comprehensive system of secondary schooling. What was seen to be necessary was a greater concern for individual needs and local circumstances, both of which could be better served by diversity in the secondary sector. There was no overt intention to reintroduce selection at 11 but to create specialist schools built on the ideas of the existing CTCs that would cater for particular talent. Specific mention is made of technology schools and, where business sponsorship was acquired, these would be known as technology colleges. Later developments enabled the appearance of schools with specialisms such as Languages (1995), Sports and Arts (1997) and Business and Enterprise, Engineering, Science, and Mathematics and Computing (2002), Music, and Humanities (2003).

In order for parents to exercise their choice, thereby driving up standards, and for schools to be held accountable for their performance, the public were to be provided with regular school inspection reports compiled by the Office for Standards in Education (Ofsted), which was brought into being by the 1992 Education (Schools) Act to replace the infrequent inspection of schools by HMI.[28] Ofsted was to recruit and train its own inspectors and each inspection team had to include a 'lay inspector' who was to have no previous professional involvement with education. The Act brought in parallel provision for Wales, while Scotland

---

[28] In Scotland schools are inspected by Her Majesty's Inspectorate of Education (HMIE); in Wales the Office of Her Majesty's Chief Inspector (OHMCI) has been replaced by Estyn – Her Majesty's Inspectorate for Education and Training in Wales. These bodies have sought to establish a productive relationship with schools and teachers and neither has the perceived confrontational stance associated with Ofsted.

was not included and so continued with a process that involves external scrutiny from HMI together with school self-review (Dunford 1999). The introduction and development of the Ofsted inspection regime has generated, in England at least, much passionate debate and has been portrayed as yet another example of the reduction of the teachers' professionalism and the involvement of government in the day-to-day matters of the school (Millet *et al.* 2001).

The Education Act 1993, the longest education legislation of the twentieth century, affirms and extends the regulatory powers of the Secretary of State with particular mention of improving standards, encouraging diversity and increasing opportunities for choice. A notable example of these new powers was for the Secretary of State to intervene directly where Ofsted judged a school to be under-performing. The process by which schools attained grant-maintained status was simplified and new ways to establish GM schools were introduced. Also these schools were to be funded by either the Funding Agency for Schools (in England) or the Schools Funding Council for Wales. Where more than 75 per cent of the schools in an area chose to 'opt out' these bodies would replace the LEA.

The pace of legislation was building and would not slacken. Lawton (1994) reflects on the flood of education legislation between 1979 and 1994 and suggests that it can be summarised as six ideological concepts:

1   A desire for more selection;
2   A wish to return to traditional curricula and teaching methods;
3   A desire to reduce the influence of experts and educational theory by encouraging common-sense traditional practices (where market choice prevails, experts are unnecessary);
4   An appeal to parental choice as a means of encouraging market forces;
5   A wish to reduce educational expenditure (a very high priority from 1979 onwards);
6   A process of increased centralization which had the additional purpose of reducing the power and autonomy of LEAs.

(Lawton 1994: 95)

All of these have been exemplified already and, with the possible exception of 1 and 3, their presence will be evident up to the present day despite the electorate's rejection of the politics that spawned them.

More central driving and some signs of rationality

The three stages of education identified in the 1944 Act are restated in the Education Act 1996 together with a statement on compulsory school age and the duty of parents to ensure their children are educated. Most importantly the Act gave legal status to the views of parents by specifying that those involved in the provision of education were, within reasonable considerations, to 'have regard to the general principle that pupils are to be educated in accordance with the wishes of their parents'. The Education (Scotland) Act 1996 created the Scottish Qualifications Authority, merging the Scottish Examinations Board (for academic qualifications at school level) with the Scottish Vocational Education Council (for vocational qualifications at all levels), and specified its general, accreditation, quality, advisory and incidental functions.

As stated earlier the substance of the National Curriculum was put together in something of a chaotic manner with disparate subject groups working to tight deadlines. It quickly became evident to educational professionals that its bureaucracy needed simplifying, its intentions needed clarifying and the whole thing needed reducing in scale in order to make it manageable. The task of doing this was given to Sir Ron Dearing, who argued in his final report (Dearing 1994) that its excessive prescription should be removed and the professionalism of teachers restored within a clear framework of accountability. In Barbers' view:

> The perspective of the serious, practically minded teacher who had to put it into practice was applied to it at last. Suddenly it all began to make sense. More importantly, Dearing reasserted the importance of professional discretion. He had listened carefully to representatives of teacher unions saying to him that the reason the National Curriculum had driven teachers out of the zone of indifference was that it had undermined their professionalism. He took this seriously.
>
> (Barber 1996: 64)

In 1995 a more streamlined National Curriculum was introduced, which gave teachers more flexibility but retained the same number of subjects. Sir Ron was called on again in 1996 to report on the confusing array of external examinations available to the 14- to 19-year-olds (Dearing 1996).

The 1990s had seen an avalanche of regulations and legislation on education culminating in 1997 with heavily market-driven legislation from the outgoing (not that they knew it at the time) government, parts of which would be repealed in the same year by their successors. The Education Act 1997 extended the assisted places scheme to include fee-paying primary schools and it was made permissible for schools to create admission arrangements that included a home–school partnership agreement to be signed by the parents. Primary schools were to adopt a 'baseline assessment scheme' that would inform the teacher's planning and provide a starting point for the measurement of future educational achievements. For secondary schools governing bodies were required to set school performance targets relating to the achievement of pupils in public examinations and pupils must be provided with a programme of careers education. Policies designed to promote high standards of behaviour were to be put in place and disciplinary detention outside school hours was made lawful even where there was no parental consent. There were changes to the rules governing the exclusion of pupils from school and the appeals procedure. The powers of Ofsted were extended to include the inspection of LEAs,[29] and the Qualifications and Curriculum Authority and the Qualifications, Curriculum and Assessment Authority for Wales were created to replace both the National Council for Vocational Qualifications and the School Curriculum and Assessment Authority.

Before very much progress was made on these measures the Conservative administration found themselves out of office for the first time in 18 years. The first contribution of the New Labour government was the very brief Education (Schools) Act 1997, which was enacted within months of the election. It abolished the provision of funds to assist with the fees of pupils attending private schools (Assisted Places Scheme) in England and phased out the scheme in Scotland. Soon afterwards the new government published its first White Paper, titled *Excellence in Schools* (DfEE 1997), in which, much to the surprise of many and albeit given a new spin, New Labour endorsed the Conservative idea of specialist schools. The party that had long championed the cause of comprehensive schooling on grounds of equality were now adopting the stance that 'standards matter more than structures' and the post-comprehensive era had begun (Chitty and Dunford 1999). Education was to be put at the heart of government and this would benefit the many and not just the few. The government would work in partnership to raise standards, under-performance would not be tolerated and intervention would be in inverse proportion to success (Docking 2000). The new Education Secretary also announced a further review of the National Curriculum and the Conservative government's idea of introducing into the daily activities of primary schools a dedicated hour for literacy and one for numeracy. The National Literacy Strategy introduced in 1998 and the National Numeracy Strategy introduced the year after were not just a welcome boost to the importance of core skills but were also notable because their level of prescription meant that in this aspect of their work most primary school teachers were for the first time told not only what to teach (which had been the case since the introduction of the National Curriculum) but also how to teach. In the view of Ofsted: 'Since their inception, the two national strategies have had a significant positive effect on teaching practice and on pupils' achievement' (Ofsted 2005: 1). In contrast, however, Oliver observes:

> The history of the implementation of the NLS demonstrates very clearly the conflict between centrally generated policies that are seen as prescriptive and the primary teacher's own professional judgement.
>
> (Oliver 2004: 10)

The White Paper led to the School Standards and Framework Act 1998, which was the first major piece of education legislation enacted by the new government and boldly stated that the raising of standards was every school's main priority.

---

[29] Ofsted's powers were further extended by the Teaching and Higher Education Act 1998 to include the inspection of initial teacher training.

Local Education Authorities were required to produce an Education Development Plan for the approval of the Secretary of State, who was given further powers to intervene where standards were not acceptable. The structure of the school system was altered yet again by redesignating maintained schools (including GM schools) as community, voluntary (aided and controlled) or foundation schools, with specialist schools being allowed to select 10 per cent of their entrants according to their ability in the favoured field. A clear sign of the relaxation of the strictures of the National Curriculum was that secondary schools were allowed to make arrangements so that some of their pupils could receive part of their education in a further education college. Local Education Authorities were tasked with limiting the size of infant classes and setting up Early Years Development Partnerships, and provision was made for the creation of Education Action Zones (EAZs). EAZs were to bring together schools and other interested partners with the purpose of collectively raising the quality of their provision in socially disadvantaged areas.

A new century of choice and change

It was clear from the White Paper and this legislation that there would be no about-turn in education policy despite the electoral change. The desire for a more equal and meritocratic society is evident but there was no wholesale dumping of New Right policy. Reflecting on the period since the election of a New Labour government, West and Pennell suggest that 'policy changes have been at the margins and the market-orientated philosophy continues largely unabated' (2002: 218). Perhaps the most surprising part of this, given earlier Labour Party rhetoric, has been the continuation of the diversity of provision in the secondary stage (Phillips and Furlong 2001; Whitty 2002). What had become the traditional left-of-centre arguments in support of the comprehensive school had been replaced by a call for specialist schools. By September 2003 some 38 per cent of secondary schools were designated 'specialist' schools but the efficacy of these changes has yet to be established (Levačić and Jenkins 2006). The controversial nature of the policy was given added zest by an unfortunate slip when the Prime Minister's official spokesman declared that 'The day of the bog-standard comprehensive school is over' (O'Leary and Owen 2001: 2). This saddled the government with the apparent view that the majority of comprehensives were mediocre at best – an interpretation vigorously denied. However, Labour politicians soon turned this around to the view that no longer was the 'one size fits all' view of secondary schooling acceptable. It is evident that similar thinking is being applied to primary schools as they are encouraged to develop a 'distinctive character' by 'developing strengths in sport or music or special needs or working very closely with the local community' as urged in the booklet *Excellence and Enjoyment: A Strategy for Primary Schools* (DfES 2003a).

The revisions to the National Curriculum announced in 2000 included for the first time a clear set of goals. The three core subjects of English, Maths and

Science remained but the eight foundation subjects were increased to ten by the addition of Information and Communication Technology (ICT) and Citizenship. Of these ten only ICT, PE, Citizenship and RE are compulsory at key stage 4.

The Standards in Scotland's Schools etc. Act 2000 aimed to raise the standards in Scotland's schools by giving new powers to Scottish Ministers and new duties to education authorities and schools. Education authorities were to extend their duty, established under the Education (Scotland) Act 1980, to provide adequate and efficient provision, such that they were to have regard for the development of the individual child. The Scottish Ministers were to set 'national priorities' and to define and publish 'measures of performance'. Education authorities and schools were to create development plans that should be formulated in consultation with parents and pupils respectively. The inspection of schools in Scotland had remained with HMIE, there being no Scottish equivalent of Ofsted, and this legislation extended their inspection powers to include the school education functions of education authorities and pre-school education centres resourced from public funds.

The Education Act 2002 implemented the proposals set out in the White Paper *Schools – Achieving Success*, published in 2001. In the foreword of this paper Estelle Morris, the then Secretary of State for Education and Skills, sets out the ambitious intentions of the government with more than a nod towards Callaghan's vision: 'An education that teaches us the joy of learning and gives us the qualifications for employment, that builds confidence and self-esteem and gives us the skills and values to meet the demands of a fast changing world: that is the education we are seeking for all of our children' (DfES 2001: 3). The legislation increased further the powers of the Secretary of State to intervene in schools and LEAs that have serious weakness but it is also a bold attempt to enable innovation in the education sector. It gives the Secretary of State and the National Assembly of Wales (NAW) the power to modify legislation, suspend legislative requirements or confer new powers if this will facilitate experimental pilot projects that will make the curriculum more suitable to particular needs. Such projects will have to ensure that children still receive a broad and balanced curriculum and that pupils with special educational needs are not disadvantaged. They are to be time-limited and subjected to rigorous evaluation, and what has been learnt and achieved by the project is to be widely disseminated. Similarly, a school that satisfies prescribed criteria can apply for exemption from certain aspects of the National Curriculum. Details of why and how this might be done were later circulated in the booklet *Disapplication of the National Curriculum (Revised)* (DfES 2003b).

The Act enabled the creation of a new kind of school to be known as an Academy. Provided that the same safeguards were in place as above, the Academy is permitted to have an emphasis on a particular subject area or areas, and this new type of school was specifically to address the persistent problem of inner-city under-achievement. This legislation also extended to the range of schools that could be involved in EAZs and the inspection powers of Ofsted were further increased to include a duty to report on the management and leadership of schools.

Significantly the legislation separates key stage 4 of the National Curriculum from the preceding three stages. This gives the Secretary of State the powers to amend the subjects studied in this stage or to abolish this stage altogether. This is consistent with the desire expressed in the White Paper to 'create space for the 14–16 curriculum to allow students to pursue their talents and aspirations', to have 'high quality, widely recognised vocational options available to students of all abilities' and to remove 'structural barriers to a coherent 14–19 phase' (DfES 2001: 34).

Further radical reform to the secondary system was announced by the government in early 2003 when the Secretary of State set out the four key principles that would underpin further changes to the sector. All schools would be encouraged to innovate in the way they teach and organise themselves and this would be built on strong leadership. Teachers would be relieved of some of the more routine tasks which could be undertaken by trained classroom assistants and new partnerships would be created beyond the classroom (DfES 2003e). Each of these can have massive impact on the system of schooling, with the introduction of Higher Level Teaching Assistants (HLTA) creating a step-change in the definition of a teacher's role (TTA 2003).

The observations of Docking in relation to the first administration of the current government seem just as apposite today in that, 'while continuing to rely on the dual strategies of competitive forces and central intervention, the Government has shifted the balance more towards the latter with an explicitly evangelical flavour and sense of mission to its drive to improve levels of achievement in schools' (Docking 2000: 35).

The Green Paper *Every Child Matters* (DfES 2003c) and the resulting *Children Act* of 2004 heralded the era of wrap-around multi-agency care and development of children. In launching the Green Paper the Education Secretary, Charles Clarke, asserted:

> Today marks a turning point in the way we protect, nurture and support children. In the past there has been a piecemeal approach to reform that has papered over the cracks but left children at risk. The tragic death of Victoria Climbié made us realise that we simply can't go on like this anymore.
>
> (DfES 2003d: n.p.)

The intention enshrined in the Act is to assure the well-being of all children through a multi-agency strategy for supporting children in achieving five outcomes: be healthy; stay safe; enjoy and achieve; make a positive contribution; and achieve economic well-being. This legislation is having a major effect on how professionals working with children are trained, practise and interact with each other.

A complementary strand of recent debate has been to do with secondary schooling and in particular the end of phase examinations and the extension of choice in secondary schooling. Mike Tomlinson, the former Chief Inspector of Schools, was set the task of making sense of the myriad of external examinations available to 16- to 19-year-olds. The essence of the challenge was 'to bind every pupil into a seamless system of vocational and academic exams' (Ashley 2005) and thus end the academic/vocational divide that has traditionally characterised British education. The recommendations in his final report were aimed at addressing the weaknesses in the current system by raising participation rates and achievement; establishing a clear core of literacy, numeracy and key skills; strengthening vocational routes; providing greater stretch and challenge for all pupils; and reducing the assessment burden. These measures would make the system clearer and easier to understand for everyone involved including employers. His proposal would create, within a unified diploma framework, a 'common format for all 14–19 learning programmes which combine the knowledge and skills everybody needs for participation in a full adult life with disciplines chosen by the learner to meet her/his own interests, aptitudes and ambitions' (DfES 2004). The proposals were welcomed by the Chief Inspector of Schools of the time

> because they specify an appropriate 'core' curriculum, pay careful attention to the parity of esteem between academic and vocational routes, accredit the achievements of a wide range of learners, and recommend that the rate of pupils' journeys through the accreditation system should be dictated by their achievement rather than their age.
>
> (Bell 2004: 2–3)

The report immediately met with major resistance from all parts of the political divide as it was seen as an unacceptable threat to the 'gold standard' represented by A-levels. On the day of its publication the Prime Minister, Tony Blair, assured the CBI that 'The purpose of reform will be to improve upon the existing system, not replace it . . . GCSEs and A-levels will stay' (Wintour 2005). Unsurprisingly then, the White Paper detailing the government's response to Tomlinson's report rejected the central proposal for one Diploma to replace 14–19 examinations (DfES 2005a). The paper announced that specialised vocational diplomas were to be created in fourteen broad subject areas which could be studied from the age of 14. Students must achieve at least a grade C in Maths and English to pass the diploma; four of these would be available from 2008 and a further four by 2010, with the rest coming on stream by 2015. Also there was to be a new diploma to recognise the achievement of students gaining five GCSEs (including Maths and English) at grades A* to C or equivalent. The initiative would be supported by the creation of 200 vocationally led schools by 2008 together with a further twelve skills academies (DfES 2005a). In introducing these measures to parliament the then Secretary of State for Education, Ruth Kelly, agreed with Tomlinson that there were 'historical weaknesses' in the educational system but disagreed with his remedies. She promised that 'in my reforms there will be a relentless focus on the basics' and that 'We cannot afford to let intellectual snobbery leave us with a second class, second best vocational education system.' To others an important opportunity had been lost.

Later in the same year the government published a White Paper entitled *Higher Standards, Better Schools For All – More Choice for Parents and Pupils*, setting out its 'next vital steps' in reforming the school system. Much emphasis was placed on the importance of catering for the individual needs of the child and of creating a system that provides choice with a meaningful role for parents in effecting that choice. In the Foreword the Prime Minister states that 'We must put parents in the driving seat for change in all-ability schools that retain the comprehensive principle of non-selection, but operate very differently from the traditional comprehensive. And to underpin this change, the local authority must move from being a provider of education to being its local commissioner and the champion of parent choice' (DfES 2005b: 1). The proposal preventing Local Authorities (LAs) building new schools generated much heated debate and a little ground was given in the resulting legislation allowing them to be one of the bidders in competition with others.

The paper led to the Education and Inspections Act (2006), which, as indicated, required LAs to have a new strategic role, i.e. a duty to promote choice and diversity through the provision of schools in their area and to respond to parental issues regarding the schools in their area. It also gives LAs new powers to deal more quickly with under-performing or failing schools and to require them, where necessary, to enter into partnerships to bring about improvements. The Act embeds the strategies presented in the government's response to the Tomlinson Report (DfES 2005a) by creating a pupil entitlement to the new specialised Diplomas and it extends to primary or special schools the opportunities given to secondary schools through the Education Act (2005) to become a foundation, voluntary or Academy school. The banning of schools selecting by ability or through interviewing procedures is reasserted. Teachers and others working in schools are given new powers for disciplining pupils and parents are required to take responsibility for their children from the very start of exclusion from school.

Scotland and Wales

Throughout this time Scotland maintained its long established independence on matters of education while Wales moved increasingly towards an education that would recognise and celebrate national and cultural distinctiveness. This is in contrast to the recent past for, as Phillips and Daugherty observe,

Competition between educational institutions, the 'market' in educational services and nationally determined performance standards and accountability procedures dominated policy in Wales as in England.

(Phillips and Daugherty 2001: 97)

Most of the functions of the Secretary of State for Education and Skills were transferred to the Assembly for Wales by the Government of Wales Act (1998). The White Paper *Better Governance for Wales* (2005) affirmed the government's intention when drafting legislation for Wales to 'delegate to the Assembly maximum discretion in making its own provisions' (Wales Office 2005: 9) and this was evident in the Education and Inspection Act (2006), which emphasised the role of the Assembly in all matters relating to schooling (Part 10).

When introducing the influential paving document *The Learning Country: A Comprehensive Education and Lifelong Learning Programme to 2010 in Wales* (2001) the Minister for Education and Lifelong Learning identified the scale of the improvements to be made and set them within a 'distinctively rich and diverse inheritance'. She pointed out how members of the Welsh Assembly share 'key strategic goals with our colleagues in England – but we often need to take a different route to achieve them' and how future legislation from Westminster will be taken as 'enabling in character and the National Assembly will have the discretion as to the extent of their application in Wales' (National Assembly for Wales 2001: 2–3). With reference to this document it has been argued that '2001 represents the year when the duality of education policy became reality' (Phillips and Harper-Jones 2002: 302). The industry of the Welsh Assembly in working towards this vision is illustrated by the vigorous way they have brought forward orders to better fit Westminster legislation to the Welsh context. League tables for secondary schools were discontinued in 2001, KS1 tests were abolished in 2002 and all end-of-stage tests will be phased out by 2008. It is interesting to note in contrast to English developments that the achievements to date acknowledge, and future plans assume, a continuing partnership with LEAs and a continued confidence in the comprehensive school system (Welsh Assembly Government 2006).

Scottish legislation follows a similar pattern to the issues discussed earlier in this chapter. The Standards in Scotland's Schools etc. Act (2000) establishes the statutory right for every child to have school education and the duty of education authorities to provide it. The Act applies a framework for raising standards and requires Scottish Ministers to identify 'national priorities', e.g. literacy or the reduction of truancy. The Scottish Schools (Parental Involvement) Act (2006), as its title indicates, was intended to promote the involvement of parents in the schooling of their own children and in schooling in general. It required education authorities to communicate with parents on the education of their children and to establish a complaints procedure for when things go wrong.

Conclusion

The endpoint for this short history of developments in schooling is a few years into the beginning of the twenty-first century and the state systems of education are probably in as great a state of flux now as they have ever been. In its third term of office the New Labour government continues to seek the 'third way' through policies that are a mix of ideologies packaged in the wrappings of pragmatism. Power (2002) has suggested that

> the Blair government has claimed to be developing policies on the basis of 'what works' rather than being driven by any one ideological approach. Yet it remains unclear whether the current mixture of apparent discordant strategies can succeed in delivering the claimed benefits of devolution and choice while also overcoming prevailing patterns of inequality.
>
> (Power 2002: 63)

The National Curriculum applies to England and in modified form to Wales whereas Scotland has the 4–16 Guidelines, which are not compulsory but are adopted practice whenever possible. The National Curriculum is still thought of as in need of revision although it is now clearly more manageable and child/teacher-friendly. With calls for the curriculum needing to reflect economic necessity reaching back to a time before Callaghan's landmark speech it may be surprising and disappointing that an eminent educationalist should observe in the *Guardian* Education Supplement that 'Most subjects have grown out of the secondary elitist tradition and are aimed at producing specialists. So what we have is a fine academic curriculum, which is fine if you want to be a geographer, historian or scientist' (White, quoted in Crace 2003: n.p.). In 1994 Lawton suggested that 'Education policy since 1991 has seemed to be lurching from one disaster to another' (Lawton 1994: 92) and an observer in 2008 might be hard pressed to see conspicuous sure-footedness.

The pace and diversity of change over the past twenty-five years has been unprecedented at any other time in the development of state schooling in Britain. Much of its effect has been to create the paradox of increasing control being taken by the centre while simultaneously shifting responsibility and accountability to the edges. Gone are the days when a primary school teacher needed a good-sized car boot to carry home his or her National Curriculum documents, but central control remains pervasive and detailed with promise of more to come. Education will always need to be a forward-looking and dynamic aspiration for the nation but we would be wise to heed the reservations of Gregory, who suggests that:

> It cannot be good for a liberal society that the tentacles of central government reach so far into our schools as they work to provide education for the young. We need to find

ways to revitalize educational debate. Education is too important to be left to teachers. But, as importantly, it is too important to be given over to central government.

(Gregory 2002: 100)

Suggested further reading

The study of historical events is a continual fascination, as they can be approached from so many different perspectives; this is particularly so for education, as it permeates just about every aspect of human life. For a detailed socio-economic view of the formative years of state schooling there is much stimulation in Stephens (1998), who manages to cover a vast expanse in a small volume. He, together with Silver (1983), Gordon and Lawton (1978), Wardle (1974) and Simon (1965) consider some of the early controversies in education, e.g. compulsory attendance and the education of girls, that are now taken-for-granted elements of a modern educational system. The roots of unresolved debates, such as selective education or national identity in educational provision, can also be found in these works.

For access to original material, Maclure (1973) remains a rich source of early information on England and Wales in particular. For a specifically Scottish perspective readers should consult the second volume of Scotland's (1969) work, which covers the period 1872 to the late 1960s, or Clark and Munn (1997) for a more recent discussion. The full texts of Acts of Parliament for England and Wales since 1988 and for Scotland since 2000 are now readily available on the Internet (www.opsi.gov.uk/acts.htm).

The intimate involvement of the government in the details of schooling that began in the Thatcher era is well illustrated in Barber (1996) while the controversies of more recent developments are thoroughly explored in Chitty and Dunford (1999), Docking (2000), Phillips and Furlong (2001), Whitty (2002) and Tomlinson (2005).

References

Ashley, J. (2005) 'You Don't Need an A-level to Spot the Flaw in Blair's Logic', *The Guardian*, 24 February.

Ball, N. (1983) *Educating the People: A Documentary History of Elementary Schooling in England, 1840–1870*. London: Maurice Temple Smith.

Barber, M. (1996) *The Learning Game – Arguments for an Education Revolution*. London: Gollancz.

Batho, G. (1989) *Political Issues in Education*. London: Cassell.

Bell, D. (2004) *Changes and Continuity: Reflections on the Butler Act*. Speech to commemorate the sixtieth anniversary of the 1944 Education Act: House of Commons, 21 April 2004. Available at www.sociology.org.uk/as4e4b.doc (accessed 12 September 2007).

Blair, T. (1996) Speech given at Ruskin College, Oxford, 16 December. Available at www.leeds.ac.uk/educol/documents/000000084.htm (accessed 4 December 2007).

Brighouse, T. (1999) 'Home and School', in O'Hagan, B. (ed.) *Modern Educational Myths: The Future of Democratic Comprehensive Education*. London: Kogan Page.

Brooks, R. (1991) *Contemporary Debates in Education: An Historical Perspective*. London: Longman.

Bryce, T. G. K. and Humes, W. M. (1999) 'Scottish Secondary Education: Philosophy and Practice', in Bryce, T. G. K. and Humes, W. M. (eds) *Scottish Education*. Edinburgh: Edinburgh University Press.

Callaghan, J. (1976) 'The Ruskin College Speech', in Ahier, J., Cosin, B. and Hales, M. (eds) (1996) *Diversity and Change: Education, Policy and Selection*. London: Routledge/Open University.

Carr, W. and Hartnett, A. (1996) *Education and the Struggle for Democracy: The Politics of Educational Ideas*. Buckingham: Open University Press.

Central Advisory Council for Education (1967) *Children and their Primary Schools* (the Plowden Report). London: HMSO.

Chitty, C. (1996) 'The Changing Role of the State in Education Provision', in Ahier, J., Cosin, B. and Hales, M. (eds) (1996) *Diversity and Change: Education, Policy and Selection*. London: Routledge/Open University.

Chitty, C. and Dunford, J. (eds) (1999) *State Schools: New Labour and the Conservative Legacy*. London: Woburn Press.

Clark, M. and Munn, P. (eds) (1997) *Education in Scotland: Policy and Practice from Pre-school to Secondary*. London: Routledge.

Committee under the Chairmanship of Professor Gittins (1967) *Primary Education in Wales* (The Gittins Report). London: HMSO.

Crace, J. (2003) 'Revision Period', *Guardian Education*, 4 November. Available at http://education.guardian.co.uk/egweekly/story/0,5500,1076702,00.html (accessed 10 May 2007).

Dearing, R. (1994) *The National Curriculum and its Assessment: Final Report*. London: SCAA.

Dearing, R. (1996) *Review of Qualifications for 16–19 Year Olds*. London: DfES.

Dennis, B. and Skilton, D. (eds) (1987) *Reform and Intellectual Debate in Victorian England*. London: Croom Helm.

Department for Education and Employment (1997) *Excellence in Schools*. London: HMSO.

Department for Education and Science (1965) Circular 10/65: *The Organisation of Secondary Education*. London: HMSO.

Department for Education and Science/Welsh Office (1985) *Better Schools*. London: HMSO.

Department for Education and Skills (2001) *Schools – Achieving Success*. London: HMSO.

Department for Education and Skills (2003a) *Excellence and Enjoyment: A Strategy for Primary Schools*. London: DfES Publications.

Department for Education and Skills (2003b) *Disapplication of the National Curriculum (Revised)*. London: HMSO.

Department for Education and Skills (2003c) *Every Child Matters*. London: The Stationery Office.

Department for Education and Skills (2003d) *Every Child Matters*. Press Notice 2003/0175.

Department for Education and Skills (2003e) *A New Specialist System: Transforming Secondary Education*. London: DfES.

Department for Education and Skills (2004) *14–19 Curriculum and Qualifications Reform: Final Report of the Working Group on 14–19 Reform* (Tomlinson Report). London: DfES Publications.

Department for Education and Skills (2005a) *14–19 Education and Skills*. London: HMSO.

Department for Education and Skills (2005b) *Higher Standards, Better Schools For All – More Choice for Parents and Pupils*. London: HMSO.

Department for Education/Welsh Office (1992) *Choice and Diversity*. London: HMSO.

Devine, J. (2000) 'A Lanarkshire Perspective on Bigotry in Scottish Society', in Devine, T. M. (ed.) *Scotland's Shame? Bigotry and Sectarianism in Modern Scotland*. Edinburgh: Mainstream.

Devine, T. M. (1999) *The Scottish Nation 1700–2000*. Harmondsworth: Penguin.

Docking, J. (ed.) (2000) *New Labour's Policies for Schools: Raising the Standards?* London: David Fulton.

Dunford, J. (1999) 'Inspection: From HMI to OfSTED', in Chitty, C. and Dunford, J. (eds) *State Schools: New Labour and the Conservative Legacy*. London: Woburn Press.

Gordon, P. and Lawton, D. (1978) *Curriculum Change in the Nineteenth and Twentieth Centuries*. London: Hodder and Stoughton.

Gregory, I. (2002) 'Policy, Practice and Principles', in Davies, I., Gregory, I. and McGuinn, N. (eds) *Key Debates in Education*. London: Continuum.

Hyndman, M. (1978) *Schools and Schooling in England and Wales: A Documentary History*. London: Harper & Row.

Jones, E. J. (1984) *Modern Wales: A Concise History c. 1485–1979*. Cambridge: Cambridge University Press.

Lawton, D. (1994) *The Tory Mind on Education 1979–94*. London: Falmer.

Levačić, R. and Jenkins, A. (2006) 'Evaluating the Effectiveness of Specialist Schools in England', *School Effectiveness and School Improvement*. **17** (3), 229–254.

Lingen, R. R. W., Symons, Jellynger C. and Vaughan Johnson, H. R. (1847) *Reports of the Commissioners of Inquiry into the State of Education in Wales* (The Blue Books). Available at www.llgc.org.uk/index.php?id=thebluebooks (accessed 4 December 2007).

McBride, P. (1994) 'State Intervention in Technical Education in the UK', *Education + Training*. **36** (1), 10–12.

Maclure, J. S. (1973) *Educational Documents England and Wales 1816 to the Present Day*. London: Methuen.

Matheson, D. (2003) 'Education in Scotland', in Griffin, R. and Brock, C. (eds) *Education Systems of the British Isles*. Saxmundham: John Catt.

Matthew, H. C. G. (1982) (ed.) *The Gladstone Diaries*, vol. 7. Oxford: Clarendon Press.

Millet, A., Dillon, J. and Adey, J. (2001) 'Inspection', in Dillon, J. and Maguire, M. (eds) *Becoming a Teacher*, 2nd edn. Buckingham: Open University Press.

National Assembly for Wales (2001) *The Learning Country: A Comprehensive Education and Lifelong Learning Programme to 2010 in Wales*. Cardiff: National Assembly for Wales.

Norwood, Cyril (1943) *Curriculum and Examinations in Secondary Schools – Report of the Committee of the Secondary School Examinations Council appointed by the President of the Board of Education in 1941* (The Norwood Report). London: HM Stationery Office.

Ofsted (2005) *The National Numeracy and Literacy Strategies and the Primary Curriculum*. London: Ofsted.

O'Leary, J. and Owen, G. (2001) 'Blair to Axe "Bog Standard" State Schools', *The Times*, 13 February.

Oliver, A. (2004) 'Primary Education in England', in Browne, A. and Haylock, D. (eds) *Professional Issues for Primary Teachers*. London: Paul Chapman.

Palmer, J. A. (ed.) (2001) *Fifty Major Thinkers on Education*. London: Routledge.

Phillips, R. (2001) 'Education, the State and the Politics of Reform', in Phillips, R. and Furlong, J. (eds) *Education, Reform and the State: Twenty-Five Years of Politics, Policy and Practice*. London: Routledge/Falmer.

Phillips, R. and Daugherty, R. (2001) 'Educational Devolution and Nation Building in Wales', in Phillips, R. and Furlong, J. (eds) *Education, Reform and the State: Twenty-Five Years of Politics, Policy and Practice*. London: Routledge/Falmer.

Phillips, R. and Furlong, J. (eds) (2001) *Education, Reform and the State: Twenty-Five Years of Politics, Policy and Practice*. London: Routledge/Falmer.

Phillips, R. and Harper-Jones, G. (2002) 'From Ruskin to the Learning Country: Education Policy, the State and Education Politics in England and/or Wales, 1976–2001', *Educational Review*. **54** (3), 297–305.

Power, S. (2002) 'Devolution and Choice in Three Countries', in Whitty, G. (ed.) *Making Sense of Education Policy*. London: Paul Chapman.

Riley, K. A. (1998) *Whose School is it Anyway?* London: Falmer.

Roberts, G. T. (1998).*The Language of the Blue Books: The Perfect Instrument of Empire*. Cardiff: University of Wales Press.

Scotland, J. (1969) *The History of Scottish Education*. London: University of London Press.

Sharp, P. and Dunford, J. (1990) *The Education System in England and Wales*. London: Longman.

Silver, H. (1983) *Education as History*. London: Methuen.

Simon, B. (1965) *Education and the Labour Movement: 1870–1920*. London: Lawrence and Wishart.

Simon, B. (1994) *The State and Educational Change: Essays in the History of Education and Pedagogy*. London: Lawrence and Wishart.

Stephens, W. B. (1998) *Education in Britain 1750–1914*. Basingstoke: Macmillan.

Teacher Training Authority (2003) *Professional Standards for Higher Level Teaching Assistants*. London: Teacher Training Authority.

Thatcher, M. (1993) *Margaret Thatcher: The Downing Street Years*. London: Harper Collins.

The Times (1818a) 'Parliamentary Intelligence'. 28 April, p. 2.

The Times (1818b) 'Parliamentary Intelligence'. 27 May, p. 2.

The Times (1820) 'Educational Clothing Society'. 18 January, p. 3.

Tomlinson, S. (2005) *Education in a Post-Welfare Society*, 2nd edn. Maidenhead: OUP.

Wales Office (2005) *Better Governance for Wales*. HMSO.

Wardle, D. (1974) *The Rise of the Schooled Society: The History of Formal Schooling in England*. London: Routledge & Kegan Paul.

Welsh Assembly Government (2006) *The Learning Country: Vision into Action*. Cardiff: The Department for Education, Lifelong Learning and Skills.

West, A. and Pennell, H. (2002) 'How New is New Labour? The Quasi-market and English Schools 1997 to 2001', *British Journal of Educational Studies*. **50** (2), 206–224.

Whitty, G. (2002) *Making Sense of Education Policy*. London: Paul Chapman.

Wintour, P. (2005) 'Frustration at a Missed Chance for Reform', *The Guardian*, 24 February. Available at http://education.guardian.co.uk/1419education/story/0,,1423961,00.html (accessed 15 September 2007).

Compulsory education in the United Kingdom

Estelle Brisard and Ian Menter[1]

> It is time to realise that 'compulsory education' is impossible. You cannot compel children and adolescents to 'go to school.' If you use more draconian discipline than most of us would now wish to see, you may, in theory, be able to compel all of them to sit quietly at their desks. But if they do not wish to learn, they will not learn.
>
> (William Whitson, letter to *The Herald*, 5 January 2004)

Introduction

COMPULSORY EDUCATION – A SIMPLE phrase, but what does it mean? For a child born a thousand years ago, it would have meant very little. The emergence of education as a social system only started – and then only in Western Europe and for a small proportion of children – during the middle ages. Few children born in England or Scotland in 1600 would have received 'an education'. By 1800, a boy born to the landed classes or into a clerical family might well have been compelled to attend school and a girl of the same background might have received an education from a private governess. However, by the year 1900, every child born in Britain was required by law to attend school to the age of 14. Exemptions from this rule were possible only where the child possessed a certificate that they had reached the educational standard required by the local by-laws (DfES 2003).

By the 1990s, not only was attendance at school compulsory for the majority of children from the age of 5 until the age of 16 but, for much of the time spent there, the content of the curriculum had also become compulsory – at least in England, Wales and Northern Ireland. By the year 2000, the majority of children in England aged between 5 and 11 were compelled to attend school, compelled to follow a defined curriculum and compelled to be taught for part of the day

---

[1] Following the untimely death of Estelle Brisard in 2006, this chapter has been revised for the new edition by Ian Menter.

through a centrally determined method – the literacy and numeracy strategies. Those who were not compelled to attend school were nevertheless to be educated 'otherwise' (see below) and those attending private schools were not required to follow the National Curriculum or the national strategies.

In this chapter we trace the apparent steady encroachment of the state, through its education system, on the 'freedom of the child', from the nineteenth century through to the present. The first half of the chapter examines these historical developments in more detail and seeks to explore what were the intentions and motivations behind each element of compulsion. In the later part of the chapter we describe and critically examine the current situation across the four countries that constitute the UK. There is a sense in which it is helpful to judge developments in other parts of the UK as responses to English developments – sometimes accepting and adopting similar policies and sometimes reacting against and developing alternative policies.

The development of compulsory education in the UK

The emergence of state education

Green (1997) has noted that the education systems of the UK developed after the formation of the British state. Therefore, by contrast with several other European countries the education system played a less significant part in the formation of national identity. Rather, the way in which the education system developed may be seen as a reflection of the existing 'settlement' of national identity. As we shall see, the notion of national identity in the context of Great Britain or of the United Kingdom is far from settled. 'British' has often been confused with 'English' – particularly by the English and by people from outside the UK.

In tracing the emergence of state education systems we can see the strong influence of a 'voluntary' sector. Green goes so far as to suggest that:

> Both in the eighteenth and nineteenth centuries this voluntary approach was held to be morally, and educationally, superior to compulsory schooling schemes in continental Europe. These were associated with despotism and subservience, in contrast to the freedoms enjoyed by British citizens, which were seen as being essential to British character. Voluntarism . . . meant freedom for pupils from compulsory attendance, and freedom for schools from state interference.
>
> (1997: 94)

Towards the end of the nineteenth century this voluntaristic ideology started to be in considerable tension with some other strong emergent beliefs. There was a powerful belief in the rights of all children to be educated to a basic level of literacy in order to engage with the modern world. There was also a separate but often related belief in the development of society through education. But third and most powerfully of all was the belief that, in the interest of maintaining morality in society, all people should be able to read – in order to have personal access to the messages contained in the Bible.

Thus it was from the outset that the churches played a major role in the provision of schooling. Even before elementary schooling was made compulsory in 1880, a very large majority of children were attending some form of schooling for at least a year or two, with a strongly Christian dimension. The quality of provision was very variable and few stayed beyond the age of 11. In 1893 the leaving age was set at 11, but by 1900 it had been raised to 14.

Driving the development of schooling and its emergence as a state system was the motor of the industrial revolution. The nineteenth century saw both an enormous expansion of the population in Britain (almost doubling in the fifty years from 1821 to 1871, to an estimated 26 million) but also very large increases in the proportion of that population who were children and of the proportion who were living in urban settlements.

Provision of secondary education during the nineteenth century was even more varied than that of elementary schooling. Secondary schools existed largely as foundations established to provide entry into the higher professions, often via one of the universities, and the pupils were largely children from middle and upper social classes although, even at this time, it was possible for a small number of pupils from poor backgrounds to gain admission. It was not until 1902, with the creation of Local Education Authorities in England and Wales, that a national system of secondary education began to emerge. The Board of Education had been established in 1899 and by 1904 it had defined a four-year secondary programme leading to a certificate.

These developments of elementary and secondary education, together with major developments in university education, effectively established – by the end of the nineteenth century – the framework for education in Britain that still exists today.

It is possible to understand the way in which state education developed in its compulsory form as a continuing struggle between different interest groups in society. Raymond Williams (1961) offered a very interesting account along these lines in his influential book *The Long Revolution*. The revolution of Williams' title was the gradual emergence of social democracy in Britain by the second half of the twentieth century. He examines the way in which transformations in a number of social and cultural institutions, including the press, broadcasting, fiction and drama, have played a part in the creation of this society.

In his account of the development of education, Williams identifies three groups who each played a part in the way in which state education was constructed in the late nineteenth century, but who, he also argues, could still be identified at the time he was writing, in the second half of the twentieth century. The three groups he identified were:

- the public educators – who argued that 'men had a natural human right to be educated, and that any good society depended on governments accepting this principle as their duty';

- the industrial trainers – who 'promoted education in terms of training and disciplining the poor, as workers and citizens';

- the old humanists – who promoted 'a liberal education, in relation to man's health as a spiritual being' (1961: 162–163).

As we trace compulsory education through the twentieth century it is not difficult to see these three groups continuing to argue their cases, sometimes in co-operation with each other and sometimes in opposition.

The development of state education in the twentieth century

The legacy of the nineteenth century for elementary schools was a tightly defined and – in the light of subsequent developments – narrow, knowledge-based curriculum. This was broadened, at least in theory, when the Revised Code was published in 1904. The purpose of elementary schools was 'to form and strengthen the character and develop the intelligence of children, and . . . assist both girls and boys, according to their different needs, to fit themselves, practically as well as intellectually, for the work of life' (quoted by Ross 2000: 21). As secondary schools developed in the early part of the twentieth century, however, their curriculum was based very much on subjects, including English, Latin, geography, history, mathematics and science, drawing, manual work, physical exercises and housewifery (in girls' schools) (see Ross 2000).

So both in the emerging primary and in the secondary curriculum we can see the influence of Williams' industrial trainer strand and of the public educator strand. The old humanist strand is there too, in the commitment to particular forms of intellectual knowledge, but this came increasingly to the fore as the century progressed, through the development of a child-centred philosophy, which emphasised the individualism of each human being; drawing on ideas from the burgeoning discipline of psychology, as well as some traditional philosophical strands, educationists argued for an approach which was based on the individual needs of the child. This way of thinking was especially prevalent in relation to younger children and was clearly articulated in the Hadow Reports of 1926, 1931 and 1933.

The Second World War had a major impact on the development of the 'welfare state'. It was recognised that families whose young people had served the country so bravely in wartime deserved the kind of social support that should now be affordable, at least once post-war reconstruction was fully under way. So it was that the National Health Service and the social security system both emerged at this time. In education the coalition government of the day supported the development of the 1944 Education Act, under the leadership of the Secretary of the Board of Education, R. A. Butler. The significant achievement of this legislation was to establish the provision of universal secondary education for the first time. This was achieved through creating a two-stage approach to compulsory education, bringing in a transfer from primary to secondary education at the age of 11.

A further 'achievement' of the act was to introduce and legitimate differentiation in secondary schooling, a feature that was the subject of considerable contestation throughout the rest of the twentieth century and indeed continues in different ways to this day. The idea that underpinned this policy was that children could be classified by their ability to benefit from different forms of education. It was believed that some children were capable of greater intellectual development than others, according to their supposedly innate – and therefore fixed – level of intelligence. So it was that children could legitimately be channelled into a grammar school, a secondary modern school or a technical school. The channelling (actually selection) was largely achieved through the administration of a public examination, the '11+', as it became known. Sociological studies carried out during the 1950s and 1960s claimed to show how this system severely curtailed opportunity for children from working-class backgrounds, which led the Labour party to commit itself to the provision of 'comprehensive education' in 1965, a universalist approach to compulsory schooling, which aimed to see all children attending their local neighbourhood school. This goal was only partially achieved during the later part of the century and, under 'New Labour', around the last turn of the century, we witnessed the emergence of a new discourse of specialisation, through which secondary schools are encouraged to develop a profile in a particular area of the curriculum and pupils can be selected, in part through their aptitude in this field, whether it be the arts, sport, languages or whatever other field the school claims strength in.

The private schooling sector (in which some schools are confusingly described as Public Schools) has continued its parallel existence throughout the whole historical period, effectively ensuring that a sector of society, mostly those with sufficient wealth to have the choice, is removed from the state school population. Schools in the private sector are not required to offer the National Curriculum, or to administer national tests. There is a further group of students who are not educated in school at all but may be taught at home, often by one or both of their parents. For those parents who are against schooling as a form of education or who believe their children will not benefit from institutional provision, it remains possible to opt out. However, both the private sector and home schooling are subject to legal requirements, designed to ensure that the education, health and welfare needs of children are met.

The legal dimension to the compulsion in school attendance – or education otherwise – has been given added significance over recent years because of two factors. First, there has been the increased emphasis on 'parental choice' of the school that their children will attend. The discourse of choice was very much a part of the Conservative government's approach to the marketisation of education in the late 1980s and the 1990s. 'Open enrolment' was a phrase derived from their 1988 Education Reform Act, which imposed on schools the requirement to admit children who wished to attend. This requirement could not be entirely open-ended, however, for very practical reasons, including the physical size of a school and the need to organise pupils into viable class units. So what was the parent who could not secure a place for their child at their chosen school meant to do? Although there were appeal procedures and parents were often offered a range of alternatives, in the end the law required them to ensure their child was educated. As Harris says:

> The basic legal duty on a parent to ensure that his or her child receives an efficient full-time education suitable to his or her age, ability and aptitude, 'either by regular attendance at school or otherwise,' has not changed since the Education Act 1944.
>
> (1993: 43)

The second factor that has increased the significance of compulsion is the increased attention that has been paid to truancy. This has been a high priority under both Conservative and Labour governments. Truancy rates (actually more positively described as attendance rates) have been a key performance indicator for schools since the development of published profiles and performance tables during the 1980s. It was the Labour government, however, that introduced new legislation aimed at bringing the parents of frequent truants to court. In fact, few cases have reached the courts and those that have have usually resulted in some embarrassment for the LEA concerned, if not the government, as they have tended to appear as vindictive attacks on very needy, poor and often dysfunctional families.

In the development of compulsory education in the United Kingdom over the past hundred years or so, England can be seen as having been the main driving force – because of its size and the locus of power in Westminster – at least until devolution in the late 1990s. However, it is often said that education is more highly valued in each of the three smaller parts of the UK than it is England. Certainly, Scottish identity has a strong element of pride in its education provision. This stems in part from the success of the Scottish ancient universities in the stimulation of the 'invention of the modern world' (see Herman 2001). Since the creation of the uneasy union between England and Scotland in 1707, education together with the church and the legal system have been seen as the triumvirate of Scottish distinctiveness. Among those who have written about the separate development of the Scottish education system, Humes and Bryce (2003) have described its distinctiveness not only in terms of organisational differences (which are described below) but also in terms of national culture and identity, including a particular set of values (see also Paterson 2003).

The particular distinctive elements of the provision of compulsory education in Wales and Northern Ireland are discussed in the next section of this chapter.

Compulsory education in the twenty-first-century UK

Organisation

As noted in the first section of this chapter, currently all pupils aged between 5 (or 4 in Northern Ireland) and 16 must receive full-time education either at school or through alternative arrangements approved by the state. Education is free at the point of delivery in each of the 22,800 state-maintained primary schools and the 4,306 secondary schools of the UK and statutory education is organised as a continuous progression between primary and secondary education with very slight variations in the age of transfer to secondary education between the four countries (Figure 13.1).

It can be argued that, over the last fifty years, compulsory education in the UK, and in England more particularly, has been characterised by the two seemingly conflicting trends of *rationalisation* and *diversification* of its provision. Table 13.1 presents a complex system of state-maintained, selective and independent schools together with more recently introduced schemes such as Grant-Maintained schools

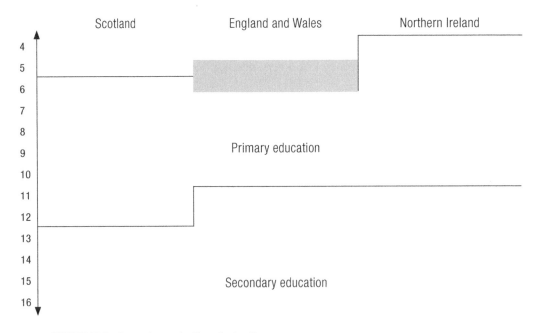

FIGURE 13.1   General organisation of schooling

TABLE 13.1 Primary and secondary schools in the UK

	WALES	ENGLAND	NORTHERN IRELAND	SCOTLAND
PRIMARY SCHOOLS	*Public sector: 1,555*	*Public sector: 17,504*	*Public sector: 879*	*Public sector: 2,184*
	• Infant (4–7) • Junior (7–11) • Combined infant and junior (5–11)	• Infant (4-7) • Junior (7-11) • Combined infant and junior (5–11)	• Infant (4–7) • Junior (7–11) • Combined infant and junior (5–11)	All 5–12
	Of which Welsh-medium: 458		Of which integrated schools: 37	Of which • Gaelic-medium schools: 58 • Denominational (Roman Catholic): 329
	In some parts: Preparatory schools (5–12/13)	In some parts: First schools (5–8) Middle schools (9–14)	In some parts: Preparatory departments of grammar schools (4–12): 17	
SECONDARY SCHOOLS	*Comprehensive and non-selective*	*Mostly comprehensive, some selection*	*Selective*	*Comprehensive and non-selective*
	Public sector: 224 Of which Welsh-medium schools: 54 Non maintained: 56	Public sector: 3,367 • State-maintained comprehensive: c. 2,800 • Grammar schools: c. 160 • Modern: c. 130 • Middle deemed secondary: c. 300 Non-maintained: 2,261	Public sector: 235 • Grammar schools: 69 • Secondary intermediate: 159 Of which • Integrated schools: 40+ Non-maintained: 25 • Irish-language schools: 5 • Integrated schools: 11	Public sector: 381 Of which schools offering • Gaelic-medium education: 61 • Denominational (Roman Catholic): 56 • Integrated community schools: 170+ • Schools of Ambition: 52 Non-maintained: 122

(now Foundation schools). There has also been a number of distinct national initiatives, such as the emergence of *Integrated Schools* in Northern Ireland, the introduction of *New Community Schools* and *Learning Communities* in Scotland and the setting up of specialist *Academies* in England. Finally, the increasing number of *Welsh-medium* and *Gaelic-medium* schools in Wales and Scotland respectively is an indication of the ongoing debate, fuelled by devolution, around issues of national identity, the place of indigenous languages such as Welsh, Scots, Gaelic and Irish in the education system and that of education generally in the process of nation-building.

The first rationalisation move was a result of the 1944 Education Act in England and Wales and the 1947 Education Act in Northern Ireland, which abolished the former division between elementary and higher education and established three phases of education with the first two – primary (5–11) and secondary (11–15, and later 16) – being compulsory. This generally resulted in the construction of new schools as well as the progressive reorganisation of primary and secondary schools in accordance with the new pattern. Currently, in England and Wales most primary schools are maintained by local authorities, and are divided into infant schools (4 or 5–7 year olds), junior schools (7–11) and combined infant and junior schools, which cater for both age groups. In some parts of England, a three-tier system still exists, which can consist of first (5–8), middle (9–14) and then high schools. In Scotland and Northern Ireland, primary schools cover the whole seven years of primary education from Primary 1 to Primary 7 and are funded by the local authority Education or Children's Services departments in Scotland and the Education and Library Boards in Northern Ireland. Some children are educated in the preparatory department of grammar schools in Northern Ireland. Despite the establishment of national schools in the nineteenth century on the principle of non-denomination, Northern Ireland education has developed historically along the line of religious segregation. At primary level, there are three main categories of schools: controlled primary schools, which can be considered to be Protestant schools, voluntary or maintained voluntary primary schools, which can be considered to be Catholic schools, and grammar preparatory schools. In Scotland approximately 18 per cent of children attend 'denominational' schools. Nearly all of these are Roman Catholic and there are no formally designated Protestant schools.

At secondary level, a second rationalisation occurred in England in 1965 with the generalisation of comprehensive schooling mentioned earlier that would cater for all children regardless of their ability. The number of grammar schools and secondary modern schools declined rapidly in the 1970s and 1980s. Currently, there are no grammar schools in Wales and Scotland but there remain some in certain parts of England. Whether at primary or secondary level, the majority of Welsh pupils (97 per cent) attend comprehensive schools. In Scotland and England the figures are 95 per cent and 89 per cent respectively (Croxford 2000). The remaining pupils attend selective schools in the public sector or fee-paying independent schools. One of the main characteristics of secondary schooling in Northern Ireland remains segregation by religion, as mentioned above, but also by ability (its system being selective) and often gender (there remain many single sex schools) (Dunn 1999: 88). Seventy per cent of children aged 11 take the '11+' transfer procedure, which involves tests in mathematics, English and science to gain entry to one of the seventy grammar schools, but fewer than 40 per cent succeed. The others attend one of the 166 free secondary intermediate schools, which again are divided between controlled (including grant-aided integrated schools) and voluntary maintained schools. Following the re-establishment of the Northern Ireland Assembly in 2007, it is possible that there will be significant policy changes in this area.

Croxford has investigated the implementation and impact of compulsory schooling in the UK. She reports that in Scotland 'the change from selective to comprehensive schooling between 1965 and 1975 led to an increase in the average attainment of all pupils but especially those with low prior attainment and girls' (2001: 1). Talking to the Northern Ireland Association for Headteachers in Secondary Schools, Croxford argued that, because Scotland has embraced a comprehensive system more whole-heartedly than England and Northern Ireland, comprehensive education has been more successful in Scotland in reducing social inequality. It has also resulted in a reduction in extremes of low and high pupil attainment, which, she argues, are reinforced by less uniform or more selective schooling provision, such as that currently existing in England and Northern Ireland respectively. She points out, however, that, through parents' choice of school or use of subject specialism, hidden forms of selection can be found in both Scotland and England.

Since the late 1980s, compulsory education in the UK has been characterised by an increasing diversity of provision between its four components. In Northern Ireland, the Department of Education (DENI) has encouraged initiatives to try and reduce religious segregation at school. These have led to the introduction of two curricular themes called *Education for Mutual Understanding* and *Cultural Heritage* in the Northern Ireland curriculum and to the creation of mixed-faith schools, known as *integrated schools*, many of which are now grant-aided.

However, the establishment of *Integrated Community Schools* (ICSs) at national level in Scotland and of *Learning Communities* by Glasgow City are two examples of recent initiatives that seek to encourage the integration of the provision of school education with social work and health education. The aim is to raise children's educational achievement through the improvement of the child's wider social, physical and familial condition. In the case of the ICSs, extra funding is provided to either single schools or clusters of schools to allow the integration and expansion of the range of services offered to young people in disadvantaged areas (SEED 2003). Learning Communities are local clusters of schools situated in parts of Glasgow and typically consist of a secondary school and its associated primaries and pre-5 establishments.

Diversity of provision in the UK is nowhere more marked than in England, where a concern for diversity and parental choice resulted in the introduction of Grant-Maintained (GM) schools and City Technology Colleges in the late 1980s by the then Conservative Government (see Clough *et al.* 1991; Docking 2000a). The changes made to the schooling provision in England differ in their nature from those implemented in the Scottish system, whose 'strong egalitarian and universalistic tenor . . . has proven resistant to attempts to devolve governance to institutions and to use competition to improve performance' (Ozga and Lawn 1999: 228). From the mid-1990s in England, the New Labour government took up the Conservative commitment to diversity whilst reasserting at the same time a somewhat conflicting rationalisation agenda, thereby seeking to introduce 'co-operation within a system designed for competitiveness' (Jackson 2000: 178). The School Standards and Framework Act 1998 renamed all state-maintained schools *Community schools*, *Voluntary* or *Voluntary-aided* schools and *Foundation* schools. The Act effectively abolished the former GM schools which were reintegrated within local authority (LA) control as Foundation schools for the sake of enhancing coherence and co-operation by re-establishing equal funding (if not powers) between all maintained schools.

Raising standards through co-operation and partnership is the main theme of New Labour policies for schools which underpinned initiatives such as the Education Action Zone (EAZ) partnerships, which enabled clusters of schools located in areas of disadvantage to use a number of support initiatives as well as additional funding for three years to improve the quality of their provision (Jackson 2000). The EAZ scheme was itself associated with the Excellence in Cities strategy, one aim of which was to force LAs to co-operate on a range of issues, such as school disaffection, truancy or else catering for gifted and talented pupils. In this aim, LAs and schools could call upon designated centres of excellence, called Beacon Schools, to share good practice with them. They could also benefit from the expanding programme of specialist schools, which the government claims will provide challenging, well-resourced learning environments in nine different curricular and vocational areas. Schools designated by the Department of Education to become Beacon Schools receive additional funding for their work with cluster schools. Likewise, a successful bid to become a specialist school will ensure significant funding (£100,000+) for the school for a period of four years. At the heart of this vast funding campaign is the government's attempt to instigate a partnership culture in the profession through externally imposed and financially rewarded co-operation. The bidding process to gain specialist status and secure extra funding is very competitive, however, and threatens to run counter to the promotion of a genuine partnership between schools. It also raises the question of whether the change of culture initiated by New Labour policies will be sustainable once funding decreases or ceases altogether.

Curriculum

The system of compulsory education in England, Wales and Northern Ireland as we know it today, is the result of the state's unprecedented intervention in education from the late 1980s. It has already been noted above that historically education forms a single system in England and Wales (Green 1997) and, over the last twenty years, the organisation and content of compulsory education in England and Wales has been the object of a significant number of government initiatives aiming at raising standards and allowing the UK to compete in world markets.

Through the 1988 Education Reform Act and the introduction of a National Curriculum the Conservative government effectively took away from the teaching profession their responsibility for deciding what should be taught to pupils of compulsory school age in all state schools in England and Wales. The new statutory document also set out attainment targets for learning and provided a specific framework for the assessment, monitoring and reporting of pupils' learning (see *Assessment*, later in chapter). Similar curricula already existed in other European countries such as France or Germany where education historically played a much more prominent role in the construction of the state, but in England and Wales this initiative was perceived as having 'fundamentally and probably irreversibly transformed the nature of state education' (Bash and Coulby 1991: 1). The curriculum was implemented between 1989 and 1996 in England and Wales and a number of changes were introduced during that time by the Secretary of State in each country. The Qualifications and Curriculum Authority (QCA) in England and the Qualifications, Curriculum and Assessment Authority for Wales (ACCAC) are the statutory bodies responsible for the reviews of curriculum and assessment arrangements in each country. Reviews of the National Curriculum have taken place periodically since its introduction, often leading to adaptations giving more flexibility.

The Education Reform Act 1988 did not apply to Northern Ireland and Scotland, both of which have their own separate curriculum arrangements (see Table 13.2). However, in all four countries

> curricula are formulated in terms of aims and objectives, including 'general teaching requirements' or 'common requirements' and educational cross-curricular themes, programmes of study, targets of attainment and exemplary schemes of work.
>
> (Le Métais *et al.* 2001: 9)

In Northern Ireland, a compulsory school curriculum was established by the Northern Ireland Order 1989 and was introduced into schools in 1990. The order was reviewed in 1993 and 1996 and the responsibility for the curriculum and assessment procedures lies with the Northern Ireland Council for Curriculum, Examinations and Assessment (CCEA). Between the ages of 4 and 16, all pupils attending publicly financed schools follow the Northern Ireland Curriculum and study ten compulsory subjects and six compulsory cross-curricular themes. Those educational themes are not taught separately but woven through the main subjects of the curriculum. Pupils' academic entitlement varies according to the school years which are divided into four Key Stages, as in England and Wales. The NI Curriculum underwent a review early in the century, the process of which originated in a perceived need to increase curriculum *relevance* and to move towards the *development of important life skills* (Smith 2003: 4). The revised framework was implemented from September 2004 onwards (see www.ccea.org. uk). The content of the 14–16 curriculum in particular had been criticised by the

TABLE 13.2 Curriculum arrangements in the UK

Curriculum	ENGLAND	WALES	SCOTLAND	NORTHERN IRELAND
Name and nature	National Curriculum (statutory)	National Curriculum (statutory)	5–14 Guidelines, being replaced by 'A Curriculum for Excellence' 14–16 Standard Grade Curriculum (both advisory)	Northern Ireland Curriculum (compulsory)
Timespan	5 to 16 Four Key Stages KS1: 5 to 7 KS2: 7 to 11 KS3: 11 to 14 KS4: 14 to 16	5 to 16 Four Key Stages Foundation phase: 3 to 7 KS2: 7 to 11 KS3: 11 to 14 KS4: 14 to 16	5 to 14 (no Key Stages) and 14 to 16	4 to 16 Four Key Stages KS1: 4 to 8 KS2: 8 to 11 KS3: 11 to 14 KS4: 14 to 16
Subjects and/ or curricular areas/themes	Core subjects: maths, English, science Fewer compulsory subjects at KS4 Foundation subjects: technology, history, ICT, geography, music, art, physical education and, from KS3, a modern foreign language Other legal requirements: religious education, sex education	Core subjects: maths, English, ICT, science, Welsh Fewer compulsory subjects at KS4 Foundation subjects: technology, history, geography, music, art, physical education, Welsh (in schools where it is not a core subject) and, from KS3, a modern foreign language	Curricular areas (5–12): language, mathematics, environmental studies, expressive arts and physical education, religious and moral education with personal and social development and health education 14 to 16 subjects (12–14): English, mathematics, history, geography, modern studies, science, MFL, art and design, PE, technology, RME, music, drama, and social and personal development, computing	Compulsory subjects: religious education, English, maths, science and technology, creative and expressive studies, language studies (Irish in Irish-medium schools only) Compulsory cross-curricular themes: from KS1: education for mutual understanding, cultural heritage, health education, information technology; from KS3: economic awareness; careers education

CCEA Chief Executive, Gavin Boyd, in 2001 as being 'too rigid, too narrow and too academic, with vocational and technical qualifications often seen as second best' and therefore failing to prepare pupils for the challenge of the twenty-first century (CCEA 2001a). A proposal for a new statutory curriculum at Key Stage 4, *Their Future in Our Hands*, was therefore published in February 2001 and aimed to increase flexibility and move away from a content-led curriculum and towards a more skill-based, broad, balanced and liberal education for 14- to 16-year-olds.

The new arrangements, phased in after September 2003, offer pupils provision for:

- Key skills
- Personal development
- A scientific and technological component
- A creative component
- A work-related component

(CCEA 2001b: 4)

In a similar way to England and Wales, where one major development following the 2000 review was the introduction of *Citizenship* in September 2002, in Northern Ireland it resulted in a proposal to include *Local and Global Citizenship* in the NI Curriculum. In Scotland, Education for Citizenship was one of the five cross-curricular aspects that aim, through the 5–14 programme, to prepare pupils for life in a rapidly changing society.

Scotland, unlike the three other components of the UK, does not have a national curriculum but devised, over the period 1987–93, a non-statutory 5–14 programme, which sets out guidelines for teachers and local authorities on what should be taught to pupils of compulsory education age. The 5–14 curriculum originated in a need for consensus on teaching and learning at compulsory level and for the reconciliation of primary and secondary approaches to the curriculum and particularly the challenge of 'the fresh start' philosophy in the first year of secondary education (Adams 2003; Boyd 1997). Advice on the structure and balance of the 5–14 curriculum was published in 1993 and reviewed in 2000. In Scotland, the underpinning principles of the 5–14 curriculum are reinforced in the reviewed document; these are *progression*, *continuity* and *coherence* – especially so in the transition from primary to secondary education – as well as *balance* and *breadth*. In addition to the non-statutory status of the 5–14 programme, Adams (2003) identifies two main differences from the National Curriculum for England and Wales: the first one is that the Scottish curriculum does not separate the primary and the secondary stages of education and its longer timespan (5–14) aims to encourage continuity of experience. Thus in Scotland, the curriculum and the assessment procedures (see below) reflect a commitment to:

- The importance of continuity in a child's education,
- Children's differing rates of development,
- The importance of avoiding treating each subject as if it were a self-contained entity

(Clark 1997: 37).

Following devolution, however, in 2000 the Scottish Executive defined a list of *National Priorities for Education* and then, in 2005, launched *A Curriculum for Excellence*. The priorities were:

- achievement and attainment;

- framework for learning;

- inclusion and equality;

- values and citizenship;

- learning for life.

The Curriculum for Excellence was based on a commitment that schooling should develop the following four capacities in all pupils:

- successful learners;

- confident individuals;

- responsible citizens;

- effective contributors.

The curriculum is to become more streamlined ('decluttered') and schools and teachers to be given greater responsibility for shaping it within their particular contexts.

By contrast, the National Curriculum for England and Wales is divided into Key Stages 1 and 2 (for primary) and Key Stages 3 and 4 (for secondary). It also makes a distinction between three 'core' subjects, which constitute a prescribed 'basic' entitlement, and six foundation subjects at KS2 plus one at KS3, whereas no core statutory subjects exist in the Scottish document (Adams 2003: 374).

Scottish pupils aged 14 embark on a two-year course of study in which they will generally study seven or eight subjects selected from the Standard Grade curriculum framework. McKinnon and Statham point out that:

> The education of children over 14 is influenced by the fact that Scotland, unlike England, has only one examination board, and so pupils throughout the country who are taking its Standard [Grade] examination follow the same syllabus.
>
> (1999: 171)

The most recent reviews of school curricula in the various parts of the UK all appear to have been an opportunity for the curriculum authorities to articulate what the purpose of education should be for their society. Smith points out that 'the curriculum can still be regarded as the clearest statement by any society on the purpose of education, the values it holds most dear and an expression of what the society strives to be' (2003: 2). Yet this statement was not necessarily made explicit in the curricular documents mentioned previously, which set out a framework for compulsory education in the four countries.

For the first time however, the revised National Curriculum 2000 for England and Wales set out the aims and values of the school curriculum (DfEE/QCA 2000). It also laid down what the purpose of this national framework is:

- to establish a learning entitlement for all pupils, regardless of their socio-economic background, their culture, race and gender and their ability;

- to establish standards for the performance of pupils;

- to promote continuity and coherence of pupils' learning experience;

- to promote public understanding of the work of schools and teachers.

Likewise, the Scottish Guidelines published in 2000 include a previously absent rationale for the 5–14 curriculum, and this was developed further in *A Curriculum for Excellence*. In Northern Ireland, Smith (2003) welcomed the ongoing curriculum review as an opportunity to do just that. All three frameworks link education to the development of the person and of society with clear reference also being made to the economy in the English and Scottish documents. These see teachers and schools as preparing pupils to become *active, productive* and generally *well-rounded adults, workers* and *citizens*. All of the documents stress the importance of promoting the spiritual, and physical development of the child, with an additional emphasis on more traditional aims of the *moral* and *cultural* development of the pupils in the NI Curriculum and the National Curriculum (England and Wales) and on their cognitive (*mental*) development in the English document as opposed to *intellectual* development in Scotland and Northern Ireland. Finally, Le Métais *et al.* point out that 'the curricula in Northern Ireland, Wales and Scotland make explicit links between the subject matter and national heritage' (2001: 14). The impact on pedagogy of the introduction of a National Curriculum in England and Wales is addressed later in this chapter.

Assessment

With the National Curriculum, the 1988 Education Reform Act also introduced a specific framework for assessment of all pupils aged 5 to 16 in all state schools in England and Wales. Each subject had its own set of attainment targets and pupils' progression towards the targets is assessed as part of a national programme of assessment through Standard Assessment Tasks (SATs), which take place at age 7, 11 and 14 in England and Wales, as well as through teacher assessment. Pupils in Wales are assessed in all core subjects by teacher assessment *only* at the end of KS1. At the end of KS2, however, they are assessed by teacher assessment and are also required to sit SATs in core subjects only. In Welsh-medium schools, Welsh language replaces English as a core subject. At the end of KS3 all pupils are assessed in both core and foundation subjects by their teacher and also through SATs.

A new statutory assessment known as *baseline assessment* was introduced in the late 1990s in all four parts of the UK, albeit in different ways. It refers to the assessment of 4- and 5-year-old pupils in one, two or all of the following: reading, writing and personal and social skills. Baseline assessment has been mandatory in England and Wales since 1997, but a new scheme of teacher observation was introduced to replace formal testing from August 2002. In Scotland, assessment generally remains at the discretion of the local authority, and can take the form of external tests or teacher assessment (Croxford 2003: 740–741).

At first sight, assessment arrangements in Northern Ireland are organised in a similar way as in England and Wales. In Northern Ireland, baseline assessment takes place during the first year of compulsory education, age 4, through teacher assessment exclusively, and must be completed by the end of the first primary year. Thereafter, pupils are assessed at the end of each key stage, that is, age 8, 11 and 14. However, pupils are not required to sit end of key stage subject tests at KS1 and KS2 but compulsory assessment takes place in English and mathematics (or in Irish and mathematics in Irish schools) through teacher assessment only. At KS3, assessment then takes the form of both teacher assessment, as well as end of key stage 3 tests in mathematics, English (or Irish) and science. At the end of KS4 (age 16) a number of national qualifications are offered by a range of awarding bodies[2] to pupils in England and Wales, and in Northern Ireland. Most of them take the General Certificate in Secondary Education (GCSE) in which they can choose a range of single general or vocational subjects. The number of subjects to be taken by pupils is not regulated. Short GCSE courses and alternative specialist or vocational qualifications as well as entry level qualifications for pupils who are performing below GCSE level are now available at the end of KS4 in England and Wales and, with some restrictions, in Northern Ireland.[3]

In Scotland, each curricular area of the 5–14 curriculum possesses a set of *Attainment Outcomes*, which are broad competences that pupils are expected to develop. These are divided into strands and attainment targets differentiated in levels. These attainment targets are descriptors of attainment at various stages with A being the lowest level and F the highest one. A pupil's achievement is based on their progress between the levels and they are allowed to move from one level to the next at their own rate, with assessment taking place only when the pupil is deemed to be ready. National testing occurs only in mathematics and English (reading and writing) in Scotland, and even then there is no externally imposed age for testing, as these are used by the teacher to confirm that the pupil has reached a particular level. In practice, however, the tests can present barriers to the pupils' progression given that a teacher cannot report a pupil as having achieved a

---

[2] There are three unitary awarding bodies in England, AQA, EDEXCEL and OCR and one awarding body in respectively Northern Ireland (CCEA), Wales (WJEC) and Scotland (SQA).

[3] www.ucas.ac.uk/candq/ukquals/quals.html,
www.deni.gov.uk/teachers/circulars/latest/dc2003-06.pdf

particular level until they have passed the national test at that level. The validity of the reading and writing tests themselves has been questioned by teachers who feel that they do not reflect the range of curricular outcomes that have to be covered in the course; some English teachers have argued that strands such as 'reading for pleasure' or 'reading aloud' for instance simply cannot be assessed through the kind of assessment instruments used by the tests.

At the end of the last year of compulsory education (S4), pupils take a national Scottish qualification called Standard Grade, which was introduced in the early 1980s following the Dunning Report of 1977. This system of assessment incorporates both internal and external assessment and offers three levels of difficulty called Foundation, General and Credit levels, as a way to ensure certification for all. Pupils typically take seven or eight subjects: in addition to English, mathematics and a modern foreign language, which are compulsory, pupils must choose a social subject (history, geography, modern studies), a scientific subject, a creative and aesthetic subject (art, drama, music or PE) and a technology subject (computing, technological studies, home economics). This is where the principles of breadth and choice conflict, often with some implications on student motivation given that there remains little real margin for choice with three compulsory subjects and then only one possible choice per curricular area.

Pedagogy

'The cultures of teaching are shaped by the contexts of teaching' (Feiman-Nemser and Floden 1986: 515); that is, what is understood as the role of the teacher and the activity of teaching is highly context-dependent. Williams' old humanist strand, such an important part of the early development of schooling in England, is associated with principles of *individualism*, *morality* and *specialism* (McLean 1990). A key characteristic of such *humanism* is that it is anti-rational, and hence it has been suggested that little weight is given in England to 'rational, methodical and systematic knowledge objectives' (Holmes and McLean in McLean 1990: 126). With the principles of *individualism* and *morality* the emphasis in English education is on the whole child and the development of the individual. Traditionally, Scottish secondary education has evolved differently from its English counterpart with rational-encyclopaedic elements and less emphasis on specialism and experience in the learning process (McLean 1995). In his famous book on *The History of Scottish Education*, James Scotland had argued that 'the training of the intellect' was of paramount importance in Scotland and education in the classroom was definitely more teacher-centred than child-centred (cited in Humes and Bryce 2003). For a long time in Scotland it was thought that strong discipline and, if required, corporal punishment were *sine qua non* for effective and productive learning to take place. The 1965 report on *Primary Education in Scotland* brought about more child-centred approaches to teaching and learning and eventually led to the abolition of corporal punishment in 1981 in Scotland, later than many Western European countries but earlier than England and Wales, which waited until 1986. Harrison (1997: 164) points out that in Scotland 'child-centred educational philosophy was adopted more cautiously although perhaps more thoroughly than in England'. If the primary classroom in Scotland aspires to be a more and more 'child-centred, caring place', teaching and learning in the secondary schools remains strongly subject-oriented and examination-oriented, especially so for pupils aged 14–16, although this may change as *A Curriculum for Excellence* is developed and implemented.

The introduction of a National Curriculum in 1988 in England and Wales, and of national frameworks to raise the standards of numeracy and literacy in the primary school in England, have had a significant impact on teachers' work in the classroom as has the setting of performance targets for schools in all four parts of the UK in the late 1990s. The impact of the National Curriculum on teaching and learning in the primary classroom in Wales has been investigated by Cox and Sanders (1994) and in England by Pollard *et al* (1994) and by Croll (1996). The findings for both countries are remarkably similar: teachers and headteachers in both countries are generally positive about the National Curriculum, which, they claim, provides a useful framework for planning and progression (especially throughout key stages 1 and 2) and some clarifications of teaching and learning aims (Cox 2000). Furthermore, it has resulted in an increase in collaboration on curriculum planning within schools and therefore more coherence in pupil experience. Data collection for these studies took place before the first review of the National Curriculum in 1993, which slimmed down its content, and teachers expressed serious misgivings about the overloaded content and the demands placed on them by what they perceived as burdensome procedures for assessment and recording of pupils' learning. The English report stressed the predominance of work in core subjects (English and mathematics particularly) and the lack of flexibility of the framework, which made it difficult for them to adapt their teaching to the children's needs (Cox 2000). Likewise, Le Métais *et al* (2001: 22) report that 'the high profile given to English/Welsh and mathematics through the frameworks in Wales have temporarily reduced the amount of time devoted to [the foundation subjects].' Finally, the Welsh study reported evidence that the organisation of the National Curriculum in a great number of core and non-core separate subjects made it hard for teachers to retain cross-curricular activities in their teaching (Cox and Sanders 1994, quoted in Cox 2000).

With the arrival of New Labour in government in 1997, teaching methods in the primary school were to undergo yet more changes in England with the introduction of methods for teaching literacy and numeracy in the primary schools. The National Strategies for Literacy and Numeracy were originally conceived by the Conservatives, who piloted them shortly before they left office (Docking 2000b). As with several Conservative initiatives, these were taken up and implemented by the Labour government in 1998 and 1999 respectively, as a result of a controversial Ofsted report on the teaching of reading in London boroughs (HMI 1996) and in light of evidence from international studies of pupils' achievements in English and maths, in which English pupils appeared to perform less well than many of their foreign counterparts (Docking 2000a). Primary teachers' teaching of literacy and numeracy was blamed and this justified an unprecedented central intervention into teaching methods. Both strategies aim to set high expectations and challenging targets for pupils, promote active participation and engaging activities, and support teaching and learning. These approaches were subsequently developed into the early stages of secondary school, through the Key Stage 3 Strategy.

Around the same time, the Scottish Office Education and Industry Department launched the Early Intervention Programme (EIP), which aimed to break the link between educational failure and socio-economic disadvantage as acknowledged in a number of reports and research studies (see Fraser *et al.* 2001). This initiative stems from the same concern with social inclusion in Scotland that led to the implementation of the Integrated Community School scheme and of Learning Communities in Glasgow, as mentioned earlier. The choice of a planned intervention from nursery to Primary 3 was advocated in the 1996 Task Force report to the Secretary of State for Scotland as a suitable way to achieve long lasting improvements in pupils' performance (ibid.). The Literacy and Numeracy Strategies in England provide teachers with what can be seen as a rather prescriptive (although non-statutory) approach for the teaching of reading and writing as well as for mathematics. The 'Literacy Hour' effectively provides the teacher with a set teaching plan for reading and writing, in which the lesson is divided into four parts of 10 to 20 minutes each and which combines whole-class teaching and group work. Likewise, teachers are encouraged to allocate 45 to 60 minutes to mathematics teaching every day, using a three-part lesson that consists of an *oral mental starter*, a *main activity* and a *plenary*. The strategies strongly recommend that teachers spend more time on core subjects and that they use more whole-class teaching and questioning and engage the class in interaction.

In contrast with the English initiative, a major characteristic of the Scottish EIP was its flexibility and lack of prescription, with education authorities being expected to 'consider the needs of their area and devise programmes to suit' (SOEID 1999, quoted in Fraser *et al.* 2001: 18). Yet the national evaluation of EIP in Scotland reports a 'remarkable similarity in the teaching methodologies being adopted across the 32 authorities' (Fraser *et al.* 2001: 24). The document reports evidence of significant changes to classroom practice following the implementation of the programme, with an emphasis on phonic-based approaches to reading, more direct teaching of mental arithmetic involving high levels of pupil–teacher interaction, and an increased reliance on whole class teaching generally (ibid.). A number of evaluations of the Literacy and Numeracy Strategies in England have been conducted, among which are some by HMI (Ofsted 2002a,b) and others by an independent team of Canadian researchers (Earl *et al*. 2000, 2001, 2003). The OISE/UT evaluation (Ontario) reports that most of the teachers and headteachers interviewed felt that classroom teaching had improved considerably as a result of the strategies, with greater use of whole-class teaching, more structured lessons and improved planning. Opinions vary, however, on the extent to which pupil learning has improved. In any case, all appear to value the Numeracy Strategy more than its Literacy counterpart in terms of pupil learning and simplicity of implementation.

Following what were considered to be the successes of the National Literacy and Numeracy Strategies in primary schools, non-statutory frameworks for the teaching of English and mathematics at KS3 were introduced in the 2001/2 academic year (KS3 strategy), followed in 2002/3 by similar frameworks for the teaching of science, information and communication technology (ICT) and the foundation subjects at the same level. Little evidence is available at this stage of the impact of the expansion of the original initiatives to the secondary sector and to additional subjects apart from a recent HMI report (Ofsted 2003).

Another initiative that was introduced throughout the UK and had a noticeable impact on teachers' work and pedagogy was the introduction of performance targets for schools, otherwise known as target-setting. Since 1998, benchmarking information based on public examination results and SATs is provided to schools and local authorities by each Department of Education to enable them to set their own targets for improvement, mainly in relation to pupil performance. As with the national frameworks for literacy and numeracy in England and in Scotland mentioned earlier, the driver behind target-setting is governments' concern with raising standards. Yet, whereas the NLS and NNS focus on processes and transaction, the driver behind the introduction of target-setting is more a concern with measurable outcomes. Measurable outcomes are linked to discourses of school *effectiveness*, which are in sharp contrast with initiatives such as EIP, for instance, in which the emphasis is more on school *improvement* through 'achieving changes in practice at both management and classroom level' (Fraser *et al*. 2001: 8). A major concern with target-setting has been that pressure on schools to achieve targets can result in assessment-driven curriculum and pedagogy and the way teachers teach becomes increasingly determined by these initiatives (Fielding 2001; MacGilchrist 2003).

What is clear is that in England

> policies still seem to be based on the belief that standards will not be raised without targets being set and monitored and that teachers, teacher-trainers and education authorities need to be told how to do their work.
>
> (Bines 1998)

Brown (2001) has argued, however, that the same comment can increasingly be made in relation to Scottish policies. The Literacy and Numeracy Strategies and the KS3 strategy have not been implemented outside England. In fact, as Cox (2000) noted, in the very year that the Literacy Strategy was introduced in England, the Welsh Office published its own vision of a much more collaborative approach to raising standards in literacy in its report *National Year of Reading: Getting Ready*, which argues that teachers and policy-makers should work together at improving teaching and learning strategies. Despite some of the improvements in which the national strategies and the centrally manufactured collaboration between LA and schools may result, in light of more genuinely collaborative developments in other parts of the UK, one could argue with Croll (1996) that

> the government may find a partnership model more effective in getting educational change to happen than a model based upon the view of teachers as implementers.
>
> (cited in Cox 2000: 80)

Compulsory education post devolution

> The educational and legislative traditions of England, Wales, and Northern Ireland mean that they share many similarities in terms of educational and curricular structure and terminology. This convergence is reinforced by the fact that pupils from the three nations traditionally take General Certificate of Secondary Education (GCSE) and GCE Advanced Level examinations at age 15–16 and 17–18 respectively. However, the devolution of responsibility for education to the Assemblies, and the emergence of alternative forms of external accreditation of learning, may result in greater divergence over time.
>
> (Le Métais *et al*. 2001: 5)

We have seen some of this diversity in our description of provision for curriculum, assessment and pedagogy. We may also be starting to see some evidence of the smaller parts of the UK leading the way for England. For example, the relaxation of the curriculum in the early years is well under way in Wales, while in Scotland a major review of the secondary curriculum is expected to lead to a less subject-based framework. In England, where teachers and some parents have been calling for such moves, we have begun recently to see similar policy developments.

Changes such as these do nothing to reduce the compulsion of attendance at school, but they may reduce the compulsion on schools and teachers to teach particular content in particular ways. Education is likely to remain high on the political agendas, not least because of the increased recognition of the linkage between economic success and education. With this being the case, we are likely to see continuing debates about the purposes of education, reflecting the continuing struggles between Williams' industrial trainers, public educators and old humanists. Indeed there may well be a fourth key grouping now, which is a global rather than a national force. These might be called the global networkers, who believe that electronic communication is creating a global information society, where national boundaries are becoming increasingly irrelevant. Certainly, there are many aspects of learning and teaching which now make use of the World Wide Web. With economic activity increasingly being organised at transnational level, it would seem essential that future citizens have access to an understanding of these networks and can make full use of them in their learning (see Quicke 1999; Young 1998).

Indeed the very real possibility is raised that, for many young people, more learning will be available through their privately owned technology than is available through formal schooling. Such a scenario could give rise to a very different view of compulsory schooling, where it was seen less as an entitlement and more as an imposition. Of course, such a scenario is also dependent on young people having access to the necessary technology and there must be very real fears that a 'digital divide' will open up between those in the UK who own the technology and those who do not. On the other hand, with careful investment, these new technologies have the potential to expand basic educational provision in a way that could not have been foreseen by those who originally argued for compulsory education.

The other developing agenda, which must call into question a simple view of compulsory education covering the early years of life, is that of lifelong learning. If we are, as is argued, living and working in a society where change is continuing to accelerate, then the idea that compulsory schooling between the ages of 5 and 16 can equip individuals with all of their life's needs is highly dubious. If, on the other hand, the implication of these changes is indeed that individuals will require learning opportunities throughout their lives, then why should these early years receive such priority? Certainly, we may still argue for the acquisition of a range of essential skills during one's childhood, but the promotion of particular forms of knowledge may be far less important than in the past.

Suggested further reading

Compulsory education in Scotland is very well served by the large volume edited by T. Bryce and W. Humes (2003) *Scottish Education*, 2nd edn: *Post Devolution*.

Information on the other constituent parts of the United Kingdom as well as the latest information on Scotland can best be gleaned from the official websites, such as:

The Department for Children, Schools and Families: www.dfes.gov.uk/

The Department of Education, Northern Ireland: www.deni.gov.uk/

Education and Skills (Wales): http://new.wales.gov.uk/topics/educationandskills/?lang=en

Scottish Executive Education Department: www.scotland.gov.uk/Topics/Education/Schools

The Organisation for Economic Cooperation and Development publishes its annual *Education at a Glance* (available from www.oecd.org/document/43/0,3343,en_2649_201185_392515 50_1_1_1_1,00.html), which includes sections on each part of the United Kingdom as well as the UK as a whole, set in international context. Other summary information on the UK and its constituent parts can be obtained from the International Bureau of Education and its *World Data on Education* (available from www.ibe.unesco.org/countries/WDE/WorldDataE.htm).

References

Adams, F. (2003) '5–14: Origins, Development and Implementation', in Bryce, T. G. K. and Humes, W. M. (eds.), *Scottish Education*, 2nd edn: *Post Devolution*. Edinburgh: Edinburgh University Press.

Bash, L. and Coulby, D. (1991) *Contradiction and Conflict: The 1988 Education Act in Action*. London: Cassell.

Bines, H. (1998) 'Hail Zero Intolerance? Opinion', *Times Educational Supplement*. 22 May: 15.

Boyd, B. (1997) 'The Statutory Years of Secondary Education: Change and Progress', in Clark, M. M. and Munn, P. (eds) *Education in Scotland*. London: Routledge.

Brown, S. (2001) 'What is Teaching for?', the General Teaching Council (Scotland) Annual Lecture, 8 May.

Bryce, T. G. K. and Humes, W. M. (eds) *Scottish Education*, 2nd edn: *Post Devolution*. Edinburgh: Edinburgh University Press.

CCEA (2001a) News Release NR/10/01, 22 March. Available at www.ccea.org.uk/press/nr10.01.

CCEA (2001b) *Their Future in Our Hands: Proposals for Key Stage 4, Giving Schools Greater Flexibility on What they Teach 14–16 Year Olds*. Belfast: CCEA.

Clough, N., Lee, V., Menter, I., Trodd, T. and Whitty, G. (1991) 'Restructuring the Education System?', in Bash, L. and Coulby, D. (eds) *The Education Reform Act*. London: Cassell.

Cox, T. (2000) 'The Impact of the National Curriculum upon Primary Education in Wales', in Daugherty, R., Phillips, R. and Rees, G. (eds) *Education Policy-Making in Wales: Explorations in Devolved Governance*. Cardiff: University of Wales Press.

Cox, T. and Sanders, S. (1994) *The Impact of the National Curriculum on the Teaching of 5 Year Olds*. London: Falmer Press.

Croll, P. (1996) 'Practitioners or Policy Makers? Models of Teachers and Educational Change', in Croll, P. (ed.) *Teachers, Pupils and Primary Schooling*. London: Cassell.

Croxford, L. (2000) 'Inequality in Attainment at Age 16: A "Home International" Comparison', CES Briefing No. 19, May. Edinburgh: Centre for Educational Sociology.

Croxford, L. (2001) *Comprehensive Schools in Great Britain: Evidence from Research. A Report to the Northern Ireland Association of Headteachers in Secondary Schools*. Edinburgh: Centre for Educational Sociology.

Croxford, L. (2003) 'Baseline Assessment in Scotland', in Bryce, T. G. K. and Humes, W. M. (eds) *Scottish Education*, 2nd edn: *Post Devolution*. Edinburgh: Edinburgh University Press.

Department for Education and Employment/Qualifications and Curriculum Authority (2000) *Disapplication of the National Curriculum*. London: HMSO.

Department for Education and Skills (2003) *School Attendance – Frequently Asked Questions*. Available at www.dfes.gov.uk/schoolattendance/faq (accessed 6 January 2004).

Docking, J. (ed.) (2000a) *New Labour's Policies for Schools*. London: David Fulton.

Docking, J. (2000b) 'Curriculum Initiatives', in Docking, J. (ed.) *New Labour's Policies for Schools*. London: David Fulton.

Dunn, S. (1999) 'Northern Ireland: Education in a Divided Society', in Phillips, D. (ed.) *The Education Systems of the United Kingdom*. Wallingford: Symposium Books.

Earl, L., Fullan, M., Leithwood, K. and Watson, N. with Jantzi, D., Levin, B. and Torrance, N. (2000) *Watching and Learning: OISE/UT Evaluation of the National Literacy and Numeracy Strategies*. London: DfEE.

Earl, L., Levin, B., Leithwood, K., Fullan, M. and Watson, N. with Torrance, N., Jantzi, D. and Mascall, B. (2001) *Watching and Learning 2: OISE/UT Evaluation of the National Literacy and Numeracy strategies*. London: DfEE.

Earl, L., Watson, N., Levin, B., Leithwood, K., Fullan, M. and Torrance, N. with Jantzi, D., Mascall, B. and Volante, L. (2003) *Watching and Learning 3: Final Report of the External Evaluation of England's National Literacy and Numeracy Strategies*. London: DfEE.

Feiman-Nemser, S. and Floden, R. E. (1986) 'The Cultures of Teaching', in Wittrock, M. C. (ed.) *Handbook of Research on Teaching*, 3rd edn. New York: Macmillan.

Fielding, M. (2001) 'Target Setting, Policy Pathology and Student Perspectives: Learning to Labour in New Times', in Fielding, M. (ed.) *Taking Education Really Seriously: Four Years' Hard Labour*. London: Routledge/Falmer.

Fraser, H., MacDougall, A., Pirne, A. and Croxford, L. (2001) *More than 'an Extra Pair of Hands'?* National Evaluation of the Early Intervention Programme Final Report. Glasgow: SCRE.

Green, A. (1997) *Education, Globalization and the State*. London: Macmillan.

Harris, N. (1993) *Law and Education: Regulations, Consumerism and the Education System*. London: Sweet and Maxwell.

Harrison, C. (1997) 'How Scottish is the Scottish Curriculum: And Does It Matter?', in Clark, M. M. and Munn, P. (eds) *Education in Scotland*. London: Routledge.

Her Majesty's Inspectorate of Schools (HMI) (1996) *The Teaching of Reading in 45 Inner London Primary Schools*. London: Ofsted.

Herman, A. (2001) *The Scottish Enlightenment: The Scots' Invention of the Modern World*. London: Fourth Estate.

Humes, W. and Bryce, T. (2003) 'The Distinctiveness of Scottish Education', in Bryce, T. G. K. and Humes, W. M. (eds) *Scottish Education*, 2nd edn: *Post Devolution*. Edinburgh: Edinburgh University Press.

Jackson, P. (2000) 'Choice, Diversity and Partnerships', in Docking, J. (ed.) *New Labour's Policies for Schools*. London: David Fulton.

Le Métais, J., Andrews, R., Johnson, R. and Spielhofer, T. (2001) *School Curriculum Differences across the UK*. Slough: National Foundation for Educational Research.

MacGilchrist, B. (2003) 'Has School Improvement Passed its Sell-by Date?', Professorial Lecture delivered at the Institute of Education, University of London, 14 May. London: Institute of Education, University of London.

Mackinnon, D. and Statham, J. (1999) *Education in the UK, Facts and Figures*, 3rd edn. Milton Keynes: Open University.

McLean, M. (1990) *Britain and a Single Market Europe*. London: Kogan Page.

McLean, M. (1995) *Educational Traditions Compared: Content, Teaching and Learning in Industrialised Countries*. London: David Fulton.

Office for Standards in Education (2002a) *The National Numeracy Strategy, the First Three Years, 1999–2002*. London: Ofsted.

Office for Standards in Education (2002b) *The National Literacy Strategy, the First Four Years, 1998–2002*. London: Ofsted.

Office for Standards in Education (2003) *The Key Stage Three Strategy, Evaluation of the Second Year*. London: Ofsted.

Ozga, J. and Lawn, M. (1999) 'The Cases of England and Scotland within the United Kingdom,' in Lindblad, S. and Popkewitz, T. (eds) *Educational Governance and Social Integration and Exclusion*. Uppsala: Uppsala University Press.

Paterson, L. (2003) *Scottish Education in the Twentieth Century*. Edinburgh: Edinburgh University Press.

Pollard, A., Broadfoot, P., Croll, P., Osborn, M. and Abbot, D. (1994) *Changing English Primary Schools? The Impact of the ERA at Key Stage One*. London: Cassell.

Quicke, J. (1999) *Curriculum for Life Schools for a Democratic Learning Society*. Buckingham: Open University Press.

Ross, A. (2000) *Curriculum: Construction and Critique*. London: Falmer.

Scottish Executive Education Department (SEED) (2003) *Key Findings from the National Evaluation of the New Community Schools Pilot Programme in Scotland*. Edinburgh: SEED.

Smith, A. (2003) 'Teacher Education and the Northern Ireland Curriculum Review', paper presented at a conference on 'Teacher Education in a Climate of Change' organised by the Department of Education for Northern Ireland and the Department for Employment and Learning, Limavady, 28–29 April.

Williams, R. (1961) *The Long Revolution*. Harmondsworth: Penguin.

Young, M. F. D. (1998) *The Curriculum of the Future: From the 'New Sociology of Education' to a Critical Theory of Learning*. London: Routledge/Falmer.

14

Post-compulsory education

Further and higher education

Catherine Matheson

> Next in importance to freedom and justice is popular education, without which neither freedom nor justice can be permanently maintained.
>
> (James Garfield, 1831–81)

Introduction

UNTIL THE KENNEDY REPORT the term 'further education' seldom seemed to cross politicians' lips, except when mentioned as part of the seamless boundary between further and higher education (Kennedy 1997). Higher education, on the other hand, has increasingly become a major policy issue (Dearing 1997; DfES 2004a; HEFCE 2005). This chapter gives a brief overview of post-school and further education (FE) before focusing mainly on issues related to higher education.

Post-school and further education

This section will briefly examine the historical background to post-school and further education before examining the 14–19 qualifications framework and discussing current issues and future challenges.

Historical overview

In the Victorian era the British ruling class valued individualism, enterprise and *laissez-faire* liberalism and hence saw centralisation and state control as having a corroding influence on the dynamics of individual entrepreneurship. Hence, industrialisation was able to progress rapidly despite a lack of state control over vocational and technical education (Green 1990). However, the need for a more skilled workforce to meet economic challenges led to several Royal Commissions into technical education in the nineteenth century. In the 1880s the independent City and Guilds London Institute for the Advancement of Technical Education and the new polytechnics were established. The Samuelson Commission on Technical Instruction (1884) praised the well-organised continental trade schools, which were well integrated within a secondary education system that offered a superior type of secondary education for those with limited means as opposed to the overlapping and muddled British apprenticeship system (Green 1990). Samuelson paved the way for some important developments took place as a consequence of the Technical Instruction Act (1889) that

> allowed now local councils to set up technical education committees that could be financed by a one penny rate and the 1890 Local Taxation (Whiskey Money) Act provided public funds that could be spent on technical education.
>
> (Green 1990: 299)

Just over a decade later, the Education Act (1902) established Local Education Authorities (LEAs) in England and Wales, among whose duties was the organisation of technical and vocational education. The Act also enabled LEAs to establish Grammar and Junior Technical Schools, giving pupils the choice of an academic or a vocational route after leaving compulsory school at 13. In Scotland the 1918 Education (Scotland) Act created Local Authority Education Departments (rather than Local Education Authorities), among whose duties was organising the provision of technical and vocational education.

Ordinary and Higher National Certificates (ONC and HNC) and Diplomas (OND and HND) were developed in the 1920s to try and address the skills shortage after the First World War.[1] The 1944 Education Act and the 1945 Education (Scotland) Act raised the school leaving age to 15, made provision for technical and other further education and introduced the Ordinary and Higher National Certificates. The Percy Report (1945) set out a radical policy aimed at raising both the provision and the status of a small number of technical colleges that should develop degree-level courses. It also first proposed the creation of a new degree status and practical orientation diploma in technology to equip students for working in industry. The White Paper *Technical Education* (DES 1956) identified a large and rising demand for scientists and engineers as well as technicians and craftsmen. Consequently, it recommended that regional colleges of advanced technology should be created and that the new degree-level Diploma

[1] Ordinary Certificates (ONCs) were awarded after a three-year part-time course at a technical college whereas Higher Certificates (HNCs) were awarded after a further two years. Ordinary and Higher Diplomas (O/HNDs) required two and three years of full time study respectively and were sub-degree qualifications (Evans 2006).

in Technology should be offered as a new alternative route to higher education, as university places were limited.[2] The initiative was successful, as the greatest higher education expansion was in advanced technology colleges (Simon 1991: 119–203). However, the Crowther Report (1959) also highlighted a poor uptake of places in further education by school leavers as more pupils than expected stayed at school beyond the school leaving age of 15. The involvement of employers in technical education was increased with the Industrial Training Act (1964), which led to the formation of the Industrial Training Boards (Central Training Council 1965). These were the forerunners of a series of employer-led organisations including the Manpower Services Commission, the Training Agency and, more recently, Training and Enterprise Councils (Jessup 1991; Keep 1996).

In 2001 new regulations for the inspection of FE provision and the training of FE teachers came into effect in England and Wales (DfES 2001a). The Office for Standards in Education (Ofsted) assumed responsibility together with the Adult Learning Inspectorate (ALI) for the inspection of FE provision, which had previously been undertaken by the funding body Further Education Funding Council (FEFC) (replaced as a funding body by the Learning and Skills Council in 2001). In Scotland, inspection of FE remained in the hands of Her Majesty's Inspectorate of Education (HMIE).

Qualifications framework 14–19

England

With roots in technical and vocal education, the FE sector has a very wide-ranging curriculum: from academic qualifications in the form of GCSEs, A- and AS-levels to a range of ever-expanding vocational courses, especially since the introduction of National Vocational Qualifications (NVQs) in 1986 and General National Vocational Qualifications (GNVQs) in1996. Vocational courses are available in general FE colleges and specialist colleges, as well as in partnership with many employers. These courses include subjects as diverse as science and technology, art and design, business, travel and tourism, catering, construction trades, and hairdressing and beauty. Regulated by the Qualifications and Curriculum Authority (QCA), established in 1997, a National Qualifications Framework (NQF) was established to more easily compare academic and vocational qualifications (Coles 2004).

In December 1997, following the *Review of Qualifications for 16–19 Year Olds* (Dearing 1996) and the subsequent consultation on its recommendations, the government decided that the post-16 curriculum in England was too narrow and

---

[2] In 1956 the National Council for Technical Awards and the National Council for Diplomas in Art and Design were established. They eventually became the Council for National Academic Awards (CNAA) in 1964, which validated most degrees in the public sector until 1991 (Evans 2006).

lacked flexibility. Curriculum 2000 is outlined in *Qualifying for Success* (DfEE 1997). The reforms introduced in September 2000 sought to broaden the curriculum and achieve parity of esteem between academic and vocational qualifications, that is, to encourage young people to study more subjects over two years than had been the case previously, while also helping them to combine academic and vocational study (Ofsted 2001). The Curriculum 2000 reforms fully modularised all A-level programmes and split the qualification into Advanced Subsidiary (AS) and A-level (A2), which carried increased coursework weighting, and also academic and vocational subjects could be combined. The modular approach is deemed to increase the motivation of learners and to provide regular progress checks but, as modules are assessed twice a year in January and June, there is much more time spent on preparation for assessment than previously. The Curriculum 2000 reforms also included a change in the title of Advanced GNVQs to 'Vocational A-levels'[3] and more importantly the introduction of Key Skills. Since many employers thought that young people lacked skills such as ICT, communication, teamwork, self-confidence and willingness to learn, a solution to this problem was to suggest adding Key Skills to the curriculum at age 14 as part of key stage 4 in line with recommendations of *14–19 Opportunity and Excellence* (DfES 2002a) that work-related learning should contribute to the curriculum of all KS4 pupils. Following the Learning and Skills Act in 2001, the Further Education Funding Council and Technology Education Councils were replaced by the Learning and Skills Council (LSC), which assumed responsibility for the planning and funding of FE and government-funded training. The LSC works through a regional network of forty-seven Local Learning and Skills Councils (Evans 2006).

The problems arising from the implementation of Curriculum 2000 prompted the government to commission a wide-ranging review of the whole 14–19 qualifications structure, chaired by Mike Tomlinson. The report concluded that the changes had been implemented too quickly with inadequate piloting and unrealistic demands on candidates and inadequate training of examiners and officers. The report focused on the development of a coherent range of 14–19 learning programmes and on assessment methods and qualification structures (Tomlinson 2002).

Although there have been efforts to harmonise academic and vocational qualifications in terms of parity of esteem and assessment methodology, many of which have been described above, the need for younger pupils to experience vocational subjects has only relatively recently been addressed. A variety of new initiatives have had an impact on the curriculum in FE and schools. Vocational GCSEs became available in 2002 in a range of subjects, including business, engineering, health and social care, and travel and tourism. Each Vocational GCSE consists of three units, is the equivalent of two non-vocational GCSEs and carries

---

[3] These became available as six-unit (Single Award) and twelve-unit (Double Award) qualifications and could be taken with AS and A-level (A2).

a double grade. Assessment is by internally marked and externally moderated tests and assignments. Other available qualifications include BTEC First Diploma and NVQs, which were not previously available to those aged less than 16. Progression to Foundation and Advanced Modern Apprenticeships is also possible in a scheme that includes an extended period of work placement. The Green Paper *14–19: Extending Opportunities, Raising Standards* (DfES 2002b) proposed to formalise the stages at which vocational training enters the curriculum. This means a much more proactive role for the careers service, a modified KS4 curriculum with a core of English, maths, ICT, citizenship, religious education, careers and physical education, and finally the award of a 'Matriculation Diploma' covering Key Skills, vocational and academic qualifications and work-based learning at three levels depending on the qualifications achieved. *Success for All* (DfES 2002c) was the long-term reform programme launched by the government in 2002 to transform the quality and responsiveness of the learning and skills sector in England. The programme recognised the diversity of the FE sector in terms of the learners, learning providers and models of delivery. *Success for All* recommended the need for FE provision to meet national and local skills needs, broaden the curriculum, and improve collaboration between schools, colleges, private training providers and employers (DfES 2002c). *Success for All* also set an agenda to improve literacy and numeracy according to recommendations made in *Skills for Life* (DfES 2001b).

In 2003 the White Paper *21st Century Skills: Realising our Potential* (DfES 2003a) set an agenda for the development of Key Skills, particularly in relation to work-based learning and especially to the Modern Apprenticeship scheme established in 1993. *Principles for Reform of 14–19 Learning Programmes and Qualifications* (DfES 2003b) proposed the incorporation of skills such as numeracy, communication and IT skills, problem-solving, working with others, the ability to respond to change, entrepreneurship, facilitation, ethical competencies, leadership, cultural awareness, customer handling and meta-competencies including instinct and judgment. However, concerns remain about whether Key Skills will fully meet employers' requirements.

An Education Maintenance Allowance (EMA) scheme was introduced in September 2004. The EMA scheme involves paying young people entering Year 12 to remain in further education and to improve their attendance and coursework by means-tested payments of up to £30 per week for up to three years plus a bonus of £100 for remaining on the course and making good progress. Payments are dependent on satisfactory attendance and progress. Piloting the EMA scheme for two years had led to significant improvements in achievement, particularly on vocational courses, and confirmed the effectiveness of the scheme (DfES 2002d).

Scotland

Scotland has its own schools examination system, which comes under the management of the Scottish Qualifications Authority (SQA), which replaced both the Scottish Examination Board (SEB) and the Scottish Vocational Education Council (SCOTVEC) in 1997. SQA is now the single body responsible for all Scottish qualifications other than those offered by universities and professional bodies (i.e. schools, further education colleges, workplaces and education centres). In the summer of 1999 SQA introduced the system of National Qualifications (also known as the Higher Still development programme), which brought together academic and more vocational and work-related subjects.

Higher Grades had been introduced in 1888 as a university entry qualification six decades before A-levels, which were introduced in 1951. Standard Grades replaced O Grades in 1988. Since 1999 Scottish qualifications 16–19 have been completely restructured with the introduction of the Higher Still programme. Previously some pupils aged 16–17 entered did up to five Highers in fifth year while other pupils did Highers in some subjects and various National Certificate modules in others and the remaining pupils did only National Certificate modules in fifth year. Now, all pupils entering fifth year enrol on National Qualifications. Those with Standard Grades 1 and 2 do up to five Highers, which will enable them to take Advanced Highers in the sixth year. Those with Standard Grades 3 or 4, 5 or 6, and no grade do an Intermediate 1, Intermediate 2 or Access Level (1, 2, 3) programme respectively. The new system allows the more academic pupils a progression route to enter higher education while others can climb the qualifications ladder in the way that best suits them.[4] In terms of equivalency with England, the Universities and Colleges Admission Service (UCAS) considers Highers to be worth slightly more than AS-level and Advanced Highers to be equivalent to A-levels.[5]

The new system operates under the Scottish Credit and Qualifications Framework (SCQF), a partnership between the Scottish Qualifications Authority (SQA), the Quality Assurance Agency (QAA) for Higher Education, and Universities UK, which is supported through the Scottish Department for Enterprise, Transport and Lifelong Learning. Unlike England, Scotland has a single awarding body for both vocational and academic education 14–19. Working in partnership with SQA, Scottish higher education institutions (HEIs) have driven the creation of the Scottish Credit and Qualifications Framework. What distinguishes the Scottish SCQF from the English NQF is that it includes all levels of education and training (from Access 1 at SCQG level 1 through Highers at SCQF level 6 to Honours degree at SCQF level 10 and PhD at SCQF level 12).[6] In contrast, the English National Qualifications Framework is separate from the Framework for Higher Education Qualifications.

The Scottish Group Award (SGA) consists of a number of courses and units that

---

[4] All levels consist of three units, each of which counts as a qualification in its own right, and all units beyond Access Level have a terminal examination. See www.sqa.org.uk for more details.

[5] See www.ucas.ac.uk/candq/tariff/tariff0403.doc for more details.

[6] See www.sqa.org.uk for more details.

fit together to make a coherent programme of study. Group Awards are available at six levels of study within the Higher Still programme (from Access Level 2 to Advanced Higher). A Group Award can be gained in one year of full-time study or built up over a longer period of time. Awards are made up of courses, units and external assessments combined to form a group that is recognised by employers, colleges, universities and other providers of education and/or training. It is a benchmark of a student's level of attainment. Examples are science, art and design, and travel and tourism. Not everyone needs to take a Group Award. Programmes of study can involve free-standing courses and units: some students may study four subjects at Higher level that are not interrelated and do not constitute a sufficiently coherent group to be described as a Group Award. There are also *General Awards*, which do not specify mandatory subject content but do have set requirements in terms of the number of courses, units and core skills that must be included, and *Named Awards*, which do specify certain subject requirements as well as a set number of courses, units and core skills.[7]

Current debates and issues

Work-based training and the skills deficit

The current model of work-based training has its roots in a series of initiatives resulting from a response to high youth unemployment in the late 1970s. However, the main criticism of NVQs and SVQs relates to their narrow focus on a range of highly job-specific tasks to the extent that the skills accredited are deemed to be very low and not easily transferred to other occupations (Keep 1996). Having FE and work-based education as separate entities, with the government being responsible for the organisation and funding of the former and employers the latter, has led the UK to do much less well than other countries (Keep 1996). The proportion of young people remaining in education after the school leaving age has been lower than other European countries and UK employers have been willing to employ school-leavers with minimal qualifications (OECD 2001). Half the number of UK workers has vocational qualifications compared with Germany and only 5 per cent of pupils aged 15 are enrolled on vocational programmes compared with 9 per cent in France, 20 per cent in the Netherlands and 30 per cent in Germany (OECD 2002).

Overall, one in four of those who are economically active lacks a qualification, or has qualifications below the equivalent of NVQ level 4 (Campbell 2001). Vocational qualifications overall are in the minority of all qualifications taken in the UK, with half of the economically active population holding academic qualifications (including GCSE, Standard Grade, Higher Grade, O-, AS- and A-level and degrees), whereas only a quarter of the population of England hold

[7] See www.ceg.org.uk/nq/access2/frm-000a.htm for more details.

vocational qualifications (Hodgson and Spours 1999). A key problem in the UK is that the vocational education system is not proactive in response to trends and predictions and tends to react to crises as a result of skills shortages rather than be able to respond to changes in the labour market (Campbell 2001).

Access and widening participation

Inclusiveness and participation have been major themes in FE over the last fifteen years. The Kennedy Report (1997), *Learning Works: Widening Participation in Further Education*, is the report of a committee established in 1994 by FEFC to identify under-represented groups and advise how funding should be arranged to increase participation in post-compulsory education generally and more especially in further education. The Kennedy Report drew attention to the disadvantages of institutions applying marketplace criteria to decisions on their curriculum offer. The report emphasised that non-traditional students were likely to require more support and that additional costs were needed to recruit them and to support them effectively. Strategies were proposed such as frameworks for credit transfer and accumulation, entitlement to support and guidance, universal access to qualifications to NQF Level 3 (SCQF Level 7), embedding widening participation in quality assurance systems and the development of value-added measures in FE (Coles 2004). Although well received by the government, the more radical recommendation of changing the governance of FE institutions in favour of a greater representation from the community was not addressed and not implemented (Parry and Fry 1999).

Looking towards the future

Despite many initiatives designed to provide coherent pathways for young people, whether their strengths lie in academic or vocational subjects, there still remain significant skills shortages and a widely held perception that the current system still favours those with academic strengths, that a significant proportion of the population has taken part in neither vocational nor academic education and that their inclusion holds the key to social and economic prosperity (Coles 2004). The difficulty of having a coherent post-16 curriculum providing equality of opportunity for those having diverse career aspirations was acknowledged in the introduction to the Kennedy Report:

> Further education suffers because of prevailing British attitudes. Not only does there remain a very carefully calibrated hierarchy of worthwhile achievement, which has clearly established routes and which privileges academic success well above any other accomplishment, but there is also an appalling ignorance amongst decision-makers and opinion-formers about what goes on in further education.
>
> (Kennedy 1997: 1)

There is a long history of the academic/vocational divide, but so far, largely from a fear of tarnishing the A-level 'gold standard', there has been relatively little success in achieving parity of esteem between the two routes. However, recently, various initiatives have been introduced to provide greater integration and greater parity of esteem between academic and vocational qualifications and sufficient flexibility to respond to future economic and social challenges (Coles 2004).

In October 2004 *14–19 Curriculum and Qualifications Reform*, the final report of the Working Group on 14–19 Reform led by the former Chief Inspector of Schools, Mike Tomlinson, was published (Tomlinson 2004). The report advised greater inclusion of vocational learning into the current education system. The proposals recommended the development of a diploma that would, over time, bring all existing academic and vocational qualifications within a diploma framework. Under the proposals, young people would study a range of academic and vocational subjects, and would have to satisfy clear national standards in basic skills (written and oral communication, numeracy and ICT). They would also complete an extended project (Tomlinson 2004).

In February 2005 the response to Tomlinson was formalised in the new *14–19 Education and Skills* White Paper, the key points of which were: new functional skills content or acquiring a mastery of functional English and mathematics at the heart of new general (GCSE) Diplomas and specialised Diplomas before leaving education; improving vocational education; stretching all young people and help universities to differentiate between the best candidates; remotivating disengaged learners; and ensuring quality assurance in the delivery of vocational and academic education (DfES 2005a). The White Paper proposed the introduction of new specialised diplomas in fourteen broad sector areas. Employers, through Sector Skills Councils, will lead in their design and higher education institutions will also have an important role to play. The specialised diplomas will replace the current system of around 3,500 separate qualifications and will provide an alternative gateway to higher education and skilled employment. In December 2005 the government published the *14–19 Education and Skills Implementation Plan* to set out how the White Paper was going to be implemented (DfES 2005b). The main points include: a duty on the local authority and the Learning and Skills Council to ensure that there is sufficient provision at local level to meet the needs of 14- to 19-year-olds; a duty on schools to ensure that young people on their roll have access to all the Diplomas available locally; and every area to establish a 14–19 partnership, led by the LA and the LSC, and a prospectus to be drawn up during 2006, which sets out the full range of learning opportunities available to young people locally. The first five specialised diplomas are to be introduced in September 2008 (DfES 2005b).

In March 2005 the government published the White Paper *Skills: Getting on in Business, Getting on at Work*, which builds on the government's first national Skills Strategy, published in July 2003, and sets out proposals and reforms designed to place the employers' needs at the centre of the design and delivery of training (DfES 2005c). In November 2005 *Realising the Potential: A Review of the Future Role of Further Education Colleges* was published (Foster 2005). Key findings include a focus on supplying economically valuable skills, responding to specific local and regional employers' needs and strengthening the voice of the learner. Measures to boost the skills of Britain's workforce were set out in the further education White Paper in March 2006: *Further Education: Raising Skills, Improving Life Chances* (DfES 2006). Proposals included giving greater freedom to colleges that are performing well and taking tougher action on poor quality and on institutions that are classed as failing. A greater role for business, with experts being encouraged to teach, and more partnerships with local industry were among the measures that seek to remedy the skills shortage. FE colleges in England would be able to waive their tuition fees to give young adults between the ages of 19 and 25 a second chance to study for qualifications equivalent to two A-levels. New Adult Learning Grants would also be available to help students with living costs. Funding would furthermore be redirected from failing college courses to those in demand from students and employers, giving top performing colleges the chance to expand while putting poorer performers under threat of closure. New providers could also be brought in to widen the availability of popular courses. The further education White Paper also revealed plans to attract high-fliers into working in further education (DfES 2006).

A government-commissioned investigation into the UK skills deficit, led by Lord Sandy Leitch, which began in 2004 and covered the period up to 2020, underlined that the UK lagged behind competitors and ranked twenty-fourth out of twenty-nine developed nations. The Leitch review of skills, the final report of which was published in December 2006 after an interim report in 2005, called for better skilled workers to ensure the UK remained competitive (Leitch 2005, 2006). Key recommendations included an emphasis on the need for the UK to develop a world-class skills system by setting higher targets; routing public adult education funding through the 'train to gain' scheme and learner accounts; transferring responsibility for qualifications to sector skills councils; and creating a single information, advice and guidance service covering young people and adults (Leitch 2005, 2006).

It is hoped that these reforms will provide sufficient flexibility to respond to future economic and social challenges by providing greater integration and greater parity of esteem between academic and vocational qualifications in order to improve the economic prosperity for this country. However, in their White Paper *14–19 Education and Skills* (DfES 2005a) the government ignored one of Tomlinson's (2004) key recommendations for parity of esteem: the introduction of one overarching 14–19 qualification (at four levels: entry, foundation, intermediate and advanced; building in progression) whereby, as is the case in Scotland, both vocational and academic subjects would be covered within the qualification framework, using A-levels and GCSEs as building blocks for a unified diploma, blending core subjects such as English with specialist learning. Instead, the *14–19 Education and Skills* White Paper proposed the retention of GCSEs and A-levels and the introduction of separate vocational diplomas at three levels (with universities involved in the design of those at level 3), as well as more A-level grades to assist universities to differentiate between students (DfES 2005a).

Higher education

Whereas further education in the UK has a long history of greater or lesser marginalisation, higher education (HE), on the other hand, and especially in the last forty years, has increasingly moved to centre stage. If HE has been firmly at the centre of the political agenda since the 1990s, at the time of writing (July 2007) this is owing in no small part to the controversy over the introduction in 2005 of variable student tuition fees in England, better known as top-up fees, whereby the government had legislated that higher education institutions could impose a fee up to a maximum of £3,000 (Baty 2003). (Tuition fees of £1,000 were first introduced in the UK in 1998 and means-tested maintenance grants were abolished in 1999.)

The present discussion will focus on a historical overview of HE from the nineteenth century followed by examination of the evolution of patterns of participation by key variables (ethnicity, sex, age, geography and social class) and the changes in external structures and in the nature and scope of higher education, focusing on access and widening participation policies, entry requirement and qualifications, changes in the nature of acceptable knowledge, and key differences between the English and Scottish policy contexts.

The nineteenth century

At the beginning of the nineteenth century the British universities were unevenly distributed. England had only two universities, Oxford and Cambridge, while Scotland with only a tenth of the population had four: St Andrews, Glasgow, Edinburgh and Aberdeen. The Scottish universities had seen their student numbers rise sharply in the latter half of the eighteenth century and offered large lectures and a less developed tutorial system than did Oxford and Cambridge (Stephens 1998). The two English universities were far more aristocratic and élitist than their Scottish counterparts and concentrated on a liberal education in the arts and humanities, providing mainly non-vocational courses for residential, as opposed to predominantly local, students. Although the University of Durham, founded in 1832, was based on the Oxford and Cambridge 'aristocratic' model of a collegiate university, University College London, established in 1827, was based on the Scottish model (Bell 2000).

In the second half of the nineteenth century several of the industrial English cities established civic or 'bourgeois' universities, which were locally supported, vocationally orientated, and closely related to and dependent upon local business and industry, with middle-class students living largely at home. Whether aristocratic or bourgeois, university education in the nineteenth and early twentieth centuries was largely a privilege for the fortunate and wealthy, especially in England (Bligh 1990). A notable exception was the University of London, created in 1836, a purely examining body that offered only external degrees until the end of the nineteenth century for courses in technical colleges and other institutions as well as correspondence courses, which thus provided an alternative route of part-time study, distance learning and franchised degrees for non-traditional entrants such as women, mature and working-class students (Stephens 1998). A relatively unknown aspect of higher education is that in the late nineteenth century part-time students constituted the majority outside Oxford, Cambridge and Durham, and residence did not become a dominant feature until the early twentieth century, when the provincial colleges obtained university charters, and more especially after the expansion of HE in the 1960s (Wright 1989).

> In 1883 when a further new university college was opened in Dundee . . . its Principal felt able to claim that the availability of university places per head of population in Scotland at that time was exceeded only in Switzerland.
>
> (Bell 2000: 166)

Scotland's HE experienced significant growth even before the creation of University College Dundee. In the eighteenth century the 'total student population tripled . . . with student numbers at Edinburgh University alone increasing from 400 in 1700 to 2,300 in 1824' (Smith 2000: 311), though few bothered to graduate. As Smith makes clear, the current divide between education and entertainment simply did not exist as we know it now. Indeed, she argues that amusement *and* instruction were major features of at least some Scottish HE and that the instruction was indeed *higher* education. In this way, this eighteenth- and early nineteenth-century idea of what we now call *infotainment* was not a dumbing down of higher education in order for it to appeal to a wider public. As importantly, if not more so, Smith demonstrates that until the full force of the Victorian cult of domesticity began to be felt by Scottish women, there was a major and continued growth in the opportunities afforded to wealthier Scottish women to attend HE courses, estimating that 'there were over 5,000 class enrolments by women at the Andersonian [Institution in Glasgow] alone, between 1796 and 1845' (ibid.: 326). The Andersonian would eventually become a College of Advanced Technology and then finally the University of Strathclyde in 1964 (ibid.).

This 'storming of the citadel' was severely hampered by the growing link from the mid-nineteenth century between university *qualification* and professional employment. Men, it seems, did not mind women educating themselves in the same manner that they minded women seeking prestigious employment. It was only from 1875 in England and 1889 in Scotland that legislation enabled universities to confer degrees on women, though it took until the last quarter of the twentieth century for women in Great Britain to achieve overall parity of numbers with men in higher education (McDermid 2000).

The twentieth century

Evolution of structural and funding changes until Robbins 1963

In the United Kingdom before 1889 the universities were autonomous[8] and relied entirely on student fees, endowments and the support of local communities.[9] In 1889 the government offered £15,000 to help universities and from then on contributions escalated (Bell 2000). A British system of HE was established in 1916 when the Universities Grants Committee (UGC) was created to channel centrally provided public funds to help finance universities. The UGC provided grants rather than payment for services and was only marginally accountable to the state (Smith 1999). In 1988 the UGC was replaced by the Universities Funding Council (UFC), which exerted tighter control on universities, but gave them better incentives to respond to student demand (Booth 1999). In 1966 the public sector institutions that offered degrees and higher national diplomas outside the university sector became autonomous corporate bodies (Pratt 1997) under the control of LEAs in England and local authorities in Scotland and funded by the National Advisory Body for public sector higher education (NAB), before being financed from 1988 to 1992 by central government through the Polytechnics and Colleges Funding Council (PCFC) in England and the Scottish Education Department (SED) in Scotland (Jackson 1999). In 1992, the Further and Higher Education Act 1992 removed the binary divide between universities and public sector institutions. Consequently, the number of universities more than doubled when the public sector institutions became new universities and different national funding councils for HE were established for each of the UK countries (Mackinnon and Statham 1999).

From the Renaissance until the modern age the most insurmountable barriers to HE had been on the grounds of sex and also very often of religious discrimination,

---

[8] In continental Europe universities became completely state-controlled with staff having the status of civil servants and ministries of education being closely involved in determining curriculum content. The norm is that students go as a right to the university of their choice rather than being selected by them.

[9] In the case of Edinburgh, the very first civic university, the town council had a say in its financial and curricular policies. English civic universities followed a similar model since they were established at the initiative of local business and industry élites (Bell 2000).

especially in England when the only universities were Oxford and Cambridge. In the latter half of the nineteenth century the barriers of religion and sex were legally removed, but the financial and hence social class barrier to university education was slower to disappear. At the institutional level the idea of providing scholarships to ease the way for students of limited means developed at a snail's pace. In any case, few scholarships were sufficient to allow a student without other support to attend university, although various discretionary local grants had been available for teacher training since the nineteenth century, especially since the Education Act 1902 that established Local Education Authorities (Schuller *et al.* 1999). Age, whether for men or for women, was not a barrier to higher education insofar as mature students were not excluded from it and had been catered for in considerable numbers by franchised degrees from the University of London and at the provincial colleges that gained university charters in the early twentieth century (Wright 1989).

Another barrier was arguably the consequence of the number of HEIs. By way of comparison, let us note that in 1900 there were seven universities for an English and Welsh population of 23 million, and five for a Scottish population nearly ten times smaller, while the US state of Ohio with the same population of 3 million as Scotland boasted thirty-seven higher education institutions (Miliband 1992). Throughout the twentieth century new HEIs were established to cater for the continual acceleration of full-time undergraduate student numbers. Table 14.1 shows the evolution of full-time student numbers in UK as well as the evolution of the Age Participation Index (API).[10]

In 1987 the API reached 15 per cent, which signalled the passage from an élite to a mass higher education system (Trow 1973). The API more than doubled in 1994 when it reached 32 per cent (Smith 1999: 153). From 1994 to 2000 the growth remained static; it started to increase again in 2001, when the participation rate reached 35 per cent (HEFCE 2005), or, to be more precise, 52 per cent

TABLE 14.1   Age participation index and number of students in the UK 1900–2006

Year	API in %	Undergraduate students in HEIs (rounded up)
1900	0.7	35,000
1950	3.0	140,000
1960	5.0	180,000
1980	12.0	400,000
2001	35.0	1,610,000

Sources: derived from Edwards (1982), HESA (2002), Carpentier (2004) and DfES (2004b).
API: Age Participation Index.

[10] The Age Participation Index (API) for the United Kingdom measures the number of home-domiciled young (aged under 21) initial entrants to full-time and sandwich undergraduate courses expressed as a proportion of the average number of 18- to 19-year-olds in the United Kingdom for that given year (DfES 2004b).

for Scotland and 32 per cent for England (Scottish Executive 2004). In 2001/2 there were 2,086,080 students (of whom 1,610,000 were undergraduate) in 168 British HEIs (Ramsden 2004: 11 and 28). If the number of students doing higher education courses in further education is taken into account (7 per cent of the total number in England and 25 per cent in Scotland) the total number of higher education students was 2,294,165 (Ramsden 2004: 10).

The Robbins Report 1963

Broadly speaking, before the Second World War, university education in the UK had the function of supporting and reproducing a socio-professional élite and universities were attended and staffed mainly by people drawn from the upper middle class. As a consequence of the White Paper *Technical Education* (DES 1956), Diplomas in Technology (Higher National Diplomas) were introduced in some technical colleges to remedy the shortage of both higher education places and scientific and technical skills. Most of the expansion in HE students in the 1950s was in the technical colleges (Simon 1991). A seemingly inevitable consequence of the expansion or universalisation of secondary education would be the growing pressures for higher education places.

In the case of HE the simple question of reducing disparities in participation was for a long time clouded by the substitution of the question of equality of opportunity, a very elastic term and as elusive a philosophical concept as it is a practical target, which has been taken to apply to those able and willing to make use of HE. The concern for equality of opportunity to enter HE began in earnest with the Anderson Report (1960), which recommended the introduction of means-tested mandatory rather than discretionary grants for all full-time HE students to cover maintenance and fees (Schuller *et al.* 1999). The students received maintenance grants and the higher education institutions received fees directly from the Local Education Authorities (LEAs) in England and local authorities (LAs) in Scotland (Longden 2002). The discourse of equality of opportunity culminated with the so-called Robbins meritocratic principle that anyone able to get the necessary qualifications and willing to go should find a place in HE. Having highlighted that the proportion of middle-class children who reach degree-level courses was 'eight times as high as the proportion from working class homes' (Robbins 1963: 46) and had remained unchanged since the 1920s, the Robbins Committee Report, a sociological analysis of the influence of class on access to HE, argued for a massive expansion in the provision of university places within the discourse of equality of opportunity in terms of extending educational opportunity to all those qualified and willing to participate.

Although the Robbins Report (1963) recommended a massive expansion of HE on the grounds of equality of opportunity, the exponential growth (which has so often in Britain been attributed to the Robbins Report) actually started in

1956 and was almost exactly duplicated throughout the individual countries in Europe (Edwards 1982). The API showed a more significant increase *before* the Robbins Report than *after*, as the rate went from 3 per cent in 1950 to 8.5 per cent in 1962, only to reach 12.7 per cent in 1977, 14 per cent in 1987, 20 per cent in 1992 and 34 per cent in 1998. In other words, the age participation rate nearly tripled in the twelve years before Robbins and rose by only about a third in the course of the following fourteen years; twenty-four years after Robbins it had not even doubled.

The 'sharp and internationally synchronous and uniform escalation of higher education post-1955 indicated that a sufficiently powerful change in the international climate of economic and social thinking could trigger off a rapid change in the demand for higher education' (Edwards 1982: 67), especially if the ground had been prepared by raising the school leaving age in the previous decade. Robbins had recommended an expansion of the university sector. However, the creation of new HE provision and the sharp escalation in student numbers from 1956 to 1970 took place in the public sector institutions (polytechnics and technical colleges) that offered degrees and higher national diplomas rather than universities. Between 1965 and 1991 higher education in the public sector grew fivefold. This was about twice the rate of expansion in the universities. By 1992 the public sector awarded more degrees than all the universities together (Jackson 1999).[11] In 1966 the White Paper *A Plan for Polytechnics and Other Colleges* (DES 1966) had introduced two parallel forms of higher education: the binary system of universities and public sector institutions. The public sector institutions were not new. LEAs had long funded technical colleges that offered HE courses. 'What was new was the idea that the public sector should be one of two large pillars supporting higher education' (Jackson 1999: 111).

Evolution of patterns of participation by key variables

The participation of women saw a steady increase from 1971 to 1981, reflecting a trend in the school system with more girls gaining qualifications to enter higher education. The percentage of full-time students in the UK universities was seven men for three women in 1971/2, six men for four women ten years later (Williamson 1986). The number of full-time mature students increased slowly but fairly steadily from 8,500 in 1971/2 to 10,200 in 1979/80; the proportion of mature students, however, fell marginally, although there was a sharp rise in the number of women over 25 and a fall in the proportion of men, especially those aged 21–24 (Squires 1981). Regional participation rate when known variations in social class composition were taken into account showed that Scotland, Wales and the north-west of England were doing better than expected on the basis of social

[11] From 1964 to 1991 public sector degrees were validated and awarded by the Council for National Academic Awards (CNAA) so they would be comparable to university degrees.

class trends, while northern England and East Anglia were doing rather worse (Williamson 1986).

After the Anderson Report (1960) discretionary grants awarded by local authorities were replaced by mandatory income-related grants to full-time students accepted for first degrees. Despite Anderson the implementation of the Robbins recommendations failed to significantly increase the relative participation of working-class students. Hence the removal of the financial barrier did not remove the more entrenched social class divide, perhaps because of the increasing emphasis on residence ever since the early twentieth century and more especially since the early 1960s, or perhaps simply because, although the cost of the post-Robbins expansion was borne by all the taxpayers, the balance of reward favoured those who were already better-off (Williamson 1986). Overall, the expansion in student numbers favoured most those from affluent backgrounds and in the decade 1968–78 the proportion of students from professional and managerial classes expanded even more rapidly (Edwards 1982). However, the public sector accounted for slightly more students from skilled manual, semi-skilled and unskilled backgrounds, but especially more mature students, and above all more students from ethnic minorities. In 1991 students from ethnic minorities represented 14 per cent of the public sector intake while they represented 8 per cent of the intake in the universities (Jackson 1999).

Changes in the nature and scope of higher education

From 1960 onwards the nature and scope of HE changed substantially. Since maintenance grants were available only for full-time courses, many students who did not manage to secure a university place went to the polytechnics (Booth 1999). Consequently, polytechnics became more like universities because the student demand was for degrees in liberal humanities and social sciences (Pratt 1997). At the same time new subjects such as media studies, film and television studies, business studies, sport science and technology management and new ways of learning (group work, peer tutoring, projects) emerged from the polytechnics and conventional subject materials were restructured by the creation of modular courses (Booth 1999). By the 1980s media studies, film and television studies and more generally cultural studies were on offer in universities as well as in the polytechnics (Jackson 1999). Modular courses are now the norm in higher education, which no longer means only a full-time three- to four-year residential narrowly focused learning experience, at the expense of the state and for a socially advantaged élite (Finegold *et al*. 1992: 24). After 1992 the inclusion of professional training courses such as chiropody, nursing, occupational therapy and radiography, previously undertaken as work-based learning and offered at diploma level, further modified the nature and scope of higher education (Thomas 2001).

'Equality of opportunity' is replaced by 'access and widening participation'

After entitlement to secondary schooling became universal[12] the educational discourse shifted from a focus on equality of opportunity for entry to secondary education to a focus on equality of opportunity for entry to HE. The latter discourse was in turn superseded in the late 1970s by the discourse of 'access and widening participation' to HE, which took place against a background of rapidly expanding student numbers and has now become a major policy issue in post-school education in the British context (Fulton 1981, 1989; Parry and Wake 1990; Williams 1997a; Robertson 1997; Dearing 1997; CVCP 1998; DfEE 1998a; DfES 2004a; Scottish Executive 2004; HEFCE 2005 *inter alia*) and worldwide (Halsey 1992, 1993; Davies 1995; Lynch and O'Riordan 1998; Skilbeck and Connell 2000). In the UK and in many industrialised countries:

> the impact of the idea of access has arguably been felt most keenly in the last decade or so [since the mid-1980s] and then in the sectors of, first higher education and then, more recently higher education and training.
>
> (Tight 1996: 131)

Since the early 1990s 'access and widening participation' has thus increasingly become 'the mission for institutions of higher education, defining the character of courses and academic structures, pervading the values of institutions and transforming historic patterns of organisations' (Robertson 1997: 31).

As the concept of access to HE has undeniable political resonances and has to do with who gets educational opportunities and who does not, it is worth bearing in mind that the question of who should have access depends on what HE is for and on the advantages it brings, both for the individual and for society. In the UK the discourse of access and widening participation raises fears about lowering of standards and credential inflation as well as fears that a graduated system of institutions and courses would still privilege an élite (Scott 1995; Williams 1997b).

Because the motivations behind the major policy issue of widening access and increasing participation were the uncertainty caused by the demographic decline and fluctuations of the traditional entry cohort of the 16- to 19-year-olds and a desire to open up opportunities for more and different people, it is useful to examine how the government and funding bodies have approached the issue of access since the mid-1970s.

Two Labour government documents at the end of the 1970s, a 1978 Green Paper *Higher Education into the 1990s: A Discussion Document* (DES/SED 1978) and a 1979 Report *Future Trends in Higher Education* (DES 1979), looked at the impact of

---

[12] The Norwood Report of 1943 led to the 1944 Education Act for England and Wales and the broadly similar 1945 Education (Scotland) Act. These parallel acts gave full and unequivocal access to secondary education for all, free at the point of delivery.

the projections of an increasing 18-year-old population in the early 1980s followed by a rapid decline in the second half of the decade, which would leave the system with considerable spare capacity. The immediate concern was to prevent a too-rapid expansion in the early 1980s while attempting longer-term planning by suggesting measures against a severe pruning of higher education because of a projected demographic fall in the traditional entry cohort. Because of predictions that between 1981 and 1996 the number of people aged between 30 and 44 would increase by about 1.6 million and the number aged over 44 by about 0.3 million, while the number aged between 16 and 29 would decrease by about 0.6 million, the effect of these two government papers was to make many academics and institutions much more aware of the potential of mature student entry because they suggested ways of avoiding the impending fall in student numbers and this for the best of reasons: expansion and equalisation of educational opportunities (Squires 1981).

Indeed, for many, mature students were beginning to be seen as the way to save HE from decline in the 1990s. Although the 1978 Green Paper had suggested that a way of coping with the demographic fall was to increase the number of mature students, especially those from a working-class background, and to further increase the participation of women, there were many obstacles to the effective implementation of these ideas, not least of which was the arrival of a Conservative government in May 1979 led by Prime Minister Margaret Thatcher (Wagner 1989). In the summer of 1981 the Conservative government announced a programme of cuts in public expenditure in the universities that was to reduce their income by about 20 per cent in real terms in the next two years. The government let it be known that the major objective of the squeeze was to reduce the number of students entering HE. The financial disincentive for not meeting target numbers had a rapid effect on institutional behaviour of the universities (Wagner 1989). Because the polytechnics were funded within a local authority system, the impact of reduced unit costs on their institutional finances was not as immediate as it was with the universities. The polytechnics consequently expanded as fast as possible, reasoning that their unit costs would have been even further reduced if other HE institutions had expanded and they had not (Pratt 1997).

The attempted squeeze of higher education provision in the first half of the decade was therefore marked by an unprecedented expansion in student numbers (30 per cent increase) along with reduced unit costs (25 per cent decrease) in the polytechnics and colleges, which saw students denied university places flocking to them (Wagner 1989). In 1984 the funding bodies UGC and NAB each produced two strategy documents as well as a joint statement, which, by stressing 'ability to benefit' from higher education, raised awareness and changed forever the climate for access and continuing education (UGC 1984a, 1984b; NAB 1984a, 1984b; NAB/UGC 1984). The following year came the government's response in the form of a Green Paper, *The Development of Higher Education into the 1990s* (DES

1985), which accepted the 'ability to benefit' as long as it was greater than the costs and not at the expense of standards. Efficiency and a rather élitist concept of quality were underlined (Wagner 1989). The 1987 White Paper *Higher Education: Meeting the Challenge* (DES 1987) nevertheless widened the criteria for entry even further by saying that 'places should be available for all with the necessary qualities [and not qualifications] to benefit from higher education' (DES 1987: 7). In 1989, in a speech at Lancaster University, the Secretary of State for Education and Science urged that the participation rate among the 18-year-olds should double from 15 per cent to reach 30 per cent within the next twenty-five years and that in the later part of the 1990s the expansion of higher education should see an increase in participation from the conventional student age group and from the 'new patterns of recruitment among non-conventional students' (Wagner 1989: 156).

Access courses and alternative routes to higher education

The broad idea of wider access has different ideological roots and is not to be confused with the narrower concept of Access courses designed for mature students without formal qualifications to gain specific entry to further and higher education, which offer an alternative to established examination systems designed for adolescents, whether A-levels or Highers or vocational qualifications. Although some mature students follow the traditional route and return to college or school to study A-levels or Highers, a steadily growing minority of students now enter university via the above-mentioned alternative routes.

Although there had always been older people studying for degrees, the admission of mature students without the conventional entry qualifications was given a boost in the mid-1970s when the grant regulations were changed to make such students, if they were studying full-time, eligible to receive mandatory awards as opposed to awards at the discretion of local education authority. In 1978 the first government recognition of Access courses occurred when the Department of Education and Science asked seven selected local authorities to provide special courses for people who had 'special needs which cannot be met by existing educational arrangements' and who possessed 'valuable experience but lacked the qualifications required' (DES 1978). The 1985 Green Paper welcomed Access courses provided that the challenge of non-standard entry was to maintain a reasonable degree of openness while ensuring that academic rigour and standards were maintained (DES 1985). The 1987 White Paper and subsequent government pronouncements have placed increasing emphasis on extending access and have seen Access courses as playing an important role in it by recognising them as one of three entry routes, the other two being A-levels or Highers and vocational qualifications (DES 1987). Although the number and range of Access courses has grown exponentially since 1978, they are only one of the recognised routes of access to FE and HE for mature students over the age of 21. Access to HE by other alternative routes does also exist and includes long-standing diverse and flexible methods such as examination or assessment, liberal adult education provision, assessment of prior (experiential) learning, probationary enrolment and open entry schemes (Tight 1996).

Over the years Access courses have gained increasing recognition among politicians and others as providing an answer to problems of participation in higher education in the 1990s. Arguably, the more broadly-based Access courses, which offer a closer matching of requirements than A-levels or Highers because they tend to be linked to a particular institution, and which emphasise continuous assessment rather than final examinations, provide an alternative more flexible route while emphasising equality of opportunity (Stowell 1992). Access courses are often perceived by providers and recipients as a form of positive action targeting disadvantaged minority groups and seeking to increase their representation in higher education. Despite this 'access courses have yet to make a major impact upon the social make-up or the assumptions of higher education' (Tight 1996: 132). This particular criticism of Access courses perhaps explains, or is explained by, the fact that they tend to over-emphasise HE as a destination and thus help to sustain traditional perceptions rather than seek to change them (Tight 1996).

The Dearing Report 1997

From 1964 the history of HE has been, along with the discourse of widening access and increasing participation that followed that of equality of opportunity, one of decreased financial commitment and increased control. This is further illustrated by the fact that the whole system of mandatory grants was gradually replaced from 1990 by a part-grant, part-loan scheme (DES 1987).

From 1997 the Labour government has commissioned, responded to and produced reports that emphasised the importance of access and widening participation. The Dearing Report (1997) recommended reducing the disparities in participation for those with the potential to benefit from higher education and also to provide the support necessary to maximise their chances of success. The government responded positively to Dearing in *Higher Education for the New Century: A Response to the Dearing Report* (DfEE 1998b) and also in *The Learning Age: A Renaissance for a New Britain* (DfEE 1998a), in which the government announced it aimed 'to widen access to learning in further, higher and adult education' and 'expand further and higher education to provide for an extra 500,000 young people and adults by 2002' (DfEE 1998a: 5 and 9). The government also set a target of 50 per cent participation for those aged 18–30 by 2010 as well as a target to increase participation amongst traditionally under-represented socio-economic groups (DfEE 1998a). There is an apparent paradox in the government's attitude to access. On the one hand, the government accepted Dearing's recommendation that increasing participation 'must be accompanied by the objective of reducing the disparities in participation in higher education between groups' (Dearing 1997: 101) and admitted that the student support arrangements had not encouraged students from lower socio-economic groups to enter higher education, whether on full-time or part-time courses (DfEE 1998b). On the other hand, Tony Blair's Labour government took things even further in terms of decreased financial commitment by introducing tuition fees in 1998 and in removing maintenance grants in 1999 when loans became available to part-time students for the first time (Woodrow 2001).

The twenty-first century

Balance of relative participation between socio-economic groups still unchanged

Paradoxically, one benefit of the funding squeeze in the 1980s and the shift in funding towards a focus on student numbers has been a greater openness on the part of many institutions to mature, part-time and other 'non-traditional students'. In 1991 a quarter of university entrants were classified as entering via 'non-traditional' routes and in 1995 one third of undergraduate entrants were over 21 (HEFCE 1996). This has in some way reflected the desire of HEIs to maintain numbers during a demographic decline of the traditional cohort, but also reflects some determination to offer new opportunities to previously under-represented groups (Miliband 1992). Although the White Papers of 1987 and 1991 (DES 1987, 1991) talked less about qualifications and more about 'qualities' required to enter HE and stressed flexibility and accessibility, they did not outline specific measures for coherent reform.

Hence, the unprecedented expansion of higher education in the late 1980s and early 1990s most benefited the professional and managerial social classes, women, mature students and some ethnic minorities (Dearing 1997; CVCP 1998). However, neither the expansion nor access and widening participation policies were able to shift the balance of opportunities between most social groups (Dearing 1997; Robertson 1997). Young people from very high-income professional neighbourhoods in exclusive areas have a 75 per cent chance of getting to university; those from middle-class families in owner-occupied suburban semi-detached houses 35 per cent; and those from low-income semi-skilled and unskilled families living in areas of high unemployment 7 per cent (Carvel 1997; HEFCE 1997). In 1998 Baroness Blackstone, the HE minister, even suggested that A-levels were 'too narrow and elitist' and prevented too many young people, especially those from working-class backgrounds, from going on to HE (Clare 1998).

Looking towards the future

At the end of the twentieth century the issue of access to higher education had clearly become a topic at the very core of the government's agenda, especially insofar as the provision of non-standard modes of entry is concerned (Open

University, Access Courses, Accreditation of Prior Experiential Learning and now two-year Foundation Degrees). New ways of funding students and institutions as well as performance indicators have been recently introduced to support not only access and expanding participation, but more specifically widening participation or reducing disparities by attempting to overcome the far wider pattern of social exclusion of less well-off and disadvantaged groups in higher education, especially students from skilled manual, semi-skilled and unskilled social class backgrounds, those from deprived geo-demographic areas, those from under-represented ethnic minority groups, those with learning difficulties and disabled students (Woodrow 2001).

FOUNDATION DEGREES

The closing years of the twentieth century were marked the development of yet another route into higher education, the Foundation Degree, a vocationally focused higher education qualification introduced in September 2001 (DfES 2003c). Foundation Degrees were designed for persons with professional experience wishing to develop their knowledge further. Indeed, in many cases, professional experience and not qualification was the deciding factor in permitting entrance to the course whose length ranged from two to three years part-time. The aim of the Foundation Degree is to increase the number of people qualified at higher technician and associate professional level (DfES 2003c). Possession of the Foundation Degree permits the holder either to enter the final year of an existing undergraduate course or to enter a specially created 'top-up' degree. In the case of Learning Support Assistants or Teaching Assistants, it was commonly intended that the 'top-up' degree be with Qualified Teacher Status. However at the time of writing, the existing one-year top-up degrees do not yet give QTS and a PGCE has to be undertaken afterwards in order for the students to gain QTS status although there do exist some two-year top-up degrees with QTS.[13]

It is too early to say what market value Foundation Degrees will acquire. Neither can we be sure whether holders of 'top-up' degrees will be treated on par with holders of traditional degrees but we need only look to the experience of holders of degrees of the Open University to see what might well occur. It is well documented that for many years following the creation of the Open University in 1970 holders of its degrees were frequently viewed with more than a little suspicion. That they had entered their course with no qualifications was frequently justification enough for this attitude; that they had done the course part-time simply added fuel to the fire. Time will tell if the Foundation Degree follows a similar path. Foundation Degrees are offered in a range of forms and formats by a wide range of institutions. It is too early to evaluate and comment on the influence of Foundation Degrees in the higher education landscape.

[13] See for example www.leedstrinity.ac.uk/dev/registration/chooselevel.asp?route=6.

The first set of performance indicators (PIs) was published in December 1999 by HEFCE on behalf of all four funding councils in the United Kingdom. Performance indicators were access and widening participation especially from socio-economically under-represented groups,[14] non-continuation rates after first year, projected outcomes and efficiencies, and research output. However, PIs differed according to the profile of the institution so that institutions could only be compared with institutions of a similar profile (Thomas 2001). Since 2000, significant statutory developments have required HEIs to adopt more proactive methods to work towards reducing disparities in access and widening participation. These were the Human Rights Act 1998, which came into force in October 2000, the Race Relations (Amendment) Act 2000 and the Special Educational Needs and Disability Act 2001 (SENDA), which came into force in May and September 2002 respectively.

THE HIGHER EDUCATION ACT 2004

In addition to performance indicators and the above statutory developments, the White Paper *The Future of Higher Education* published in January 2003 set out the Government's plans for radical reform in higher education (DfES 2004a). The key proposals were: raising the aspirations of young people through the *Aim Higher* programme; good-quality accessible 'second-chance' routes into higher education; fairer admissions procedures; better benchmarks for institutions to monitor widening participation; reintroducing grants for those from the poorest families; abolishing up-front tuition fees; and allowing universities to set their own fees, which could range from £0 p.a. to £3,000 p.a. if they fulfilled the requirements on access (DfES 2004a).

No acknowledgement was given to the fact that debts running to thousands of pounds may act as a disincentive. However, the introduction of bursaries and the removal of upfront tuition fees will go some way towards reducing barriers to participation. As is the way of many White Papers, much was left unsaid. Hence, in April 2004 DfES published *Widening Participation in Higher Education* (DfES 2004b). This set out the government's proposals for the creation and remit of the Office for Fair Access and its vision for widening participation (DfES 2004c). Attainment is to be raised primarily through the various initiatives aimed at secondary school and at FE:

> There are still significant barriers of aspiration facing young people from non-traditional backgrounds, as well as disabled students and those from some ethnic minority groups.

---

[14] Access performance indicators were: the percentage of students who attended a school or college in the state sector; the percentage whose parents' occupation is classed as skilled manual, semi-skilled, or unskilled; and the percentage whose home area, as denoted by its postcode, is known to have a low proportion of 18- and 19-year-olds in higher education (HEFCE 1999).

59 per cent of a sample of 16–30 year olds from social classes C1, C2, D and E[15] did not plan ever to go to university, and almost half of the sample had never thought about doing a degree. 45 per cent of the sample agreed that 'the student image is not for me'. And aspirations are often set at an early age – one study found that the decision to participate in higher education was made by the age of 14 by the majority of pupils, and some made the decision even earlier.

(DfES 2004a: para. 6.6)

Consequently, the White Paper stated that as the top-up fees were introduced the government was determined to ensure that access to higher education was broadened, not narrowed (DfES 2004b: 2). However, widening access and tuition fees are more likely to be mutually exclusive rather than compatible. Keep and Mayhew (2004: 298) suggest that, given the current social class composition of HE entry, 'there are significant risks that yet greater expansion, unless it is attended by fundamental redistribution of access opportunities, will lead to further declines in social mobility'. Parsons and Bynner (2005) claim that social mobility was greater in 1958 than at the start of the twenty-first century. To safeguard against potential further decline in social mobility, the government has placed on any university in England that wishes to apply fees higher than the basic level (£1,250 in 2006/7) the obligation to enter into an Access Agreement with the Office for Fair Access (OFFA) whereby the university will undertake to produce a plan for access, admissions and student support by means of bursaries.

In July 2004, the Higher Education Bill received the Royal Assent and entered the statute books to become the Higher Education Act 2004. The new grants were offered for the first time in October 2004 and the 'top-up' fees introduced in 2005. Since universities such as Bristol and Cambridge are not going to be launching two-year vocational degree programmes, the significant increase in numbers attending university may not, in itself, do much to widen the overall socio-cultural profile. Meanwhile, the government makes clear that the bulk of the expected increase in student numbers will come through the provision of extra places on two-year Foundation Degree courses. There is a good economic argument for this. Britain needs more skilled technicians (Hindmore 2004).

Despite the new access and widening participation legislation, some socio-economic groups remain under-represented: skilled manual and more especially semi-skilled and unskilled socio-economic groups; men; some ethnic minorities such as African-Caribbean; and disabled students (HEFCE 2005). Although participation of women equalised in 1994 and now women represent nearly 60 per cent of full-time undergraduate students, some previous disparities between men and women nevertheless remain. Men are more attracted to computer sciences,

---

[15] Skilled non-manual, skilled manual, semi-skilled and unskilled.

engineering and technology, physical and mathematical sciences, architecture, building and planning, and less pulled towards education, languages and paramedical subjects (Jary 2001). Mature students are more likely to enter newer universities than traditional universities, especially élite universities. Geographical inequalities are changing and growing. In 2000 the highest young participation rates by real cohorts were found in Scotland with 38.7 per cent, London with 36.4 per cent and the south-east of England with 33.3 per cent. Regional comparisons can be misleading, because participation differentials are sharpest when looking at small areas such as parliamentary constituencies and wards rather than larger geographical areas (HEFCE 2005).

Key differences between higher education in England and in Scotland

Since 1992 HE has been funded along national lines with separate funding councils for England, Wales, Scotland and Northern Ireland. As a consequence there is the likelihood that the already diverse patterns of provision and participation will increase. Unlike the Robbins Report (1963) the Dearing Report (1997) had the advantage of having a separate Scottish Committee (Garrick) to take account of the distinctiveness of Scottish HE. The creation of the Scottish Parliament further shaped the nature, size and direction of Scottish HE in ways that were different from England.

The Scottish HE system contains many features that distinguish it from that of England and the rest of the UK. Some main differences between the English and Scottish HE systems are:

- The four ancient universities[16] developed as community resources and never acquired the social remoteness of Oxford and Cambridge and of those English universities strongly influenced by Oxbridge, which means that localism continues to be important for nearly all Scottish higher education institutions except Stirling and St Andrews (Bell 2000).

- There has been a large number of English academics in Scottish higher education since the 1960s (Paterson 1997) and in some institutions such as Edinburgh and St Andrews nearly a third of students are English, with English 'top-up' fees serving to increase numbers even further (Schofield 2006).

- Scotland has a more uniform and universal system of comprehensive education[17] with later transfer to secondary education and only one year of post-compulsory education before entry to higher education is possible (McPherson et al. 1972).

---

[16] St Andrews, Edinburgh, Glasgow and Aberdeen.
[17] Scottish state education is less diversified than in England thanks to the historical uniformity of the system and early reorganisation to a more completely comprehensive system. Schools

- Scotland has a broader upper secondary curriculum and a broad generalist tradition in higher education derived from a distinctive educational tradition, with a four-year Honours degree course and a three-year Ordinary degree course[18] (McPherson *et al.* 1972).

- The binary divide was less evident than in England since non-university institutions had a distinct purpose in science and technology rather than humanities and social sciences (Bell 2000).

- The Scottish Credit and Qualifications Framework was established as a consequence of partnership between the SQA and Scottish HEIs and includes all levels of education and training including degrees and higher degrees (in contrast, the English NQF is separate from the Framework for Higher Education Qualifications).[19]

- Foundation Degrees do not exist in Scotland and there are no plans for them, but there are clearer progression routes and a better articulation between FE and HE (it is possible to do an HND at an FE college and then move straight into year 2 or 3 of a degree at an HEI) and a larger standardised provision at sub-degree level with a national framework of HNCs and HNDs and a correspondingly large involvement of further education colleges in higher education (Scottish Executive 2001).[20]

- The participation rate is higher in Scotland, at 52 per cent in 2001 as against 35 per cent for England, partly because the proportion of higher education courses in further education was around 30 per cent but only 8 per cent for England (Scottish Executive 2001), which is the consequence of a more seamless transition from school to higher education because of a close articulation between FE and HE.[21] However, 41.5 per cent of Scottish students in higher education institutions are over 25 compared with 44.8 per cent in England (Schuller and Bamford 1999).

---

are less autonomous but the headteacher has gained in decision-making power. Schools were encouraged, rather than required, to implement the 5–14 guidelines, which were introduced gradually and with extensive consultation.

[18] The Ordinary degree is the traditional broad general Scottish degree; in the Faculty of Arts of traditional universities students had to take a first-year philosophy course as a compulsory subject as well as a modern language or English language or mathematics. Honours were introduced in 1889 but only after 1918 did the number of students taking Honours significantly increase. Now very few students take Ordinary degrees in Scotland. In the 1960s, however, many people still took Ordinary degrees and there was a strong correlation between sex and degree taken, with 70 per cent of women taking Ordinary degrees in the humanities and 60 per cent in the sciences (McPherson *et al.* 1972).

[19] See www.sqa.org.uk for more details.

[20] See also www.foundationdegree.org.uk/institutions/faqs_5.shtml.

- Finally, and more importantly, Scotland has had a separate funding council since 1992, no upfront fees and no top-up fees.[22]

To expand on the last point, from 1998 Scottish HEIs have been able to waive tuition fees for part-time undergraduates students who are unemployed or on low incomes and to develop more courses tailored to their needs (SHEFC 1998). Indeed, tuition fees became a key issue for the Scottish Parliament and this coincided with the (re)creation of the said Parliament in 1999. Interestingly, because of intense political pressure by the Liberal Democrats, the Cubie Committee was set up in 1999 not by the Scottish Executive Education Department (SEED) but by the Scottish Parliament itself, thus making the enterprise a more significant one (Mackie 2001). The SEED accepted Cubie's recommendations that bursaries for low-income independent students and for those with additional support needs should be reintroduced. The SEED also accepted that every student would be entitled to student loans, even those from high-income families. Finally the FE system was restructured along Cubie's lines and anomalies between the sectors removed, thus reinforcing the notion of a seamless robe between FE and HE (Mackie 2001).

In practice all the above means that, for students domiciled in Scotland, HE costs less than for students domiciled in England, around £6,000 for a four-year Honours degree course instead of an average of £10,000 for a three-year Honours degree course. The support for students in part-time employment is also better and student retention higher (Mackie 2001). In 2001 the up-front tuition fees of £1,000 per year were replaced by a graduate endowment of £2,000 to be repaid once a graduate earns a salary of around £16,000. Top-up fees, introduced in 2005 in England, do not exist in Scotland, except for students from elsewhere in the UK who come to Scotland to study medicine. The Endowment Scheme is confined to students who are ordinarily resident in Scotland (have lived in Scotland for at least three years). A number of courses are exempt from the Graduate Endowment and up-front fees have to be paid.[23] There are also a number of exempt categories of students for whom higher education has actually become free at the point of delivery.[24]

---

[21] The high participation rate is largely attributed to the funding model, which existed already before the (re)creation of the Scottish Parliament; higher education courses were funded by the Scottish Office Education (and Industry) Department, instead of the Scottish Higher Education Funding Council as was the case for the Higher Education Funding Council in England (Smith and Bocock 1999).

[22] Students from elsewhere in the UK still have to pay fees in Scottish universities, as do Scottish students in English, Welsh and Northern Irish universities, but students from elsewhere in the EU are treated on the same terms as Scottish students (as EU law requires).

However, in June 2007 the Scottish Education Secretary, Fiona Hyslop, told the Scottish Parliament that current and subsequent students would not have to pay the endowment. Scrapping the current £2,289 endowment gained just enough parliamentary backing to go through. British students from outside Scotland but who study there pay £1,700 a year in tuition fees or £2,700 for those studying medicine.

Conclusion

Higher education no longer means only a full-time three- to four-year residential engagement with a narrowly focused learning experience, at the expense of the state. HE has opened new opportunities and diversified its provision and hence arguably met the challenge of the twenty-first century, whereby the right of access to higher education should be available to potential learners throughout their lives. However, many believe that HE itself needs to provide more support for under-represented groups, facilitate a mix-and-match approach and transfer from one institution to another, take courses outside its walls and to the people, use more Accreditation of Prior Experiential Learning (APEL) to select students, and offer courses for professional groups and activities and learning methods for mature students (Thomas 2001). Much has been done and still to has to be done to stimulate demand for higher education from under-represented groups through raising expectations and improving attainment by measures such as community outreach and promotion, information, advice and guidance and development of progression routes. But more needs to be done to change the internal barriers that are personal inhibitions (linked to social class, gender, ethnicity, age) and the public barriers to graduate employment that are sex, ethnicity, age and disability discrimination (Thomas 2001).

Although the changes in higher education since the 1960s, and especially since the late 1980s, were embedded in a discourse, espoused by the access movement, underpinned by an ideology of social justice and equity (Williams 1997b), national policies have nevertheless seemingly tended to be driven by a preference for numerical growth and not by a concern for social justice and equity. In particular, expansion and structural changes and even the recognition of alternative routes have

---

[23] These courses are those preparing for a higher diploma or certificate; postgraduate courses; courses that prepare for a qualification from a professional body; and first degrees in nursing or midwifery.

[24] See the *Graduate Endowment (Scotland) Regulations 2001* and the regulations set out the application of the *Education (Graduate Endowment and Student Support) Act 2001*, which list these as being: over 25 at the start of their course; married prior to the start of the course; having supported themselves out of their own earnings for a total of at least three years prior to the start of the course (para. 4.1); qualifying for an allowance under the Students' Allowances (Scotland) Regulations 1999 by dint of being a lone parent or of being disabled (para. 4.2).

failed to a significant extent to challenge the culture of élitism and consequently how higher education is perceived among the under-represented groups. If the balance of opportunities between most social groups has not markedly changed since Robbins (1963) despite the changes in policy context, this is perhaps because of the inherent tensions and contradictions between the theory and practice of access and widening participation. The key to the contradictions is that, more so in England and less so in Scotland, HE is 'a mass system in its public structures but still an elite system in its private instincts' as many of its practices 'remain rooted in an elite past' (Scott 1995: 2 and 23). Thus, a hierarchy of prestige survives within the HE system in both England and Scotland in terms of institutions and subjects (Jary 2001). This hierarchy of prestige is at its most evident in the persistent socially biased pattern of Oxbridge admissions. In 2000, according to a postcode analysis, 80 per cent of applicants to Cambridge came from the professional and managerial classes, some 46 per cent of entrants were state school applicants and 45 per cent came from the independent sector (Lampl 2000).

Despite wider access to HE, and despite the focus of Parliament in widening access to higher education, UK productivity lags behind other industrialised countries. American and French workers produced 26 per cent and 21 per cent respectively more for every hour worked than British workers (Brennan 2003). Since FE has a greater impact on the whole UK workforce than HE, this means that learners in FE deserve as much support as undergraduates and, since a better skilled workforce is a more productive workforce, this means providing learners and employers with courses that meet their needs. Until now, FE colleges faced many bureaucratic difficulties in offering flexible training and qualifications and especially in gaining funding for them (Brennan 2003), but the Education Act 2004 and various FE-related White Papers have aimed to allow greater flexibility within the FE sector to help increase the skills levels and remedy skills shortages, an outcome that has been desperately needed in the UK for a long time (Hodgson and Spours 1999).

Meanwhile HE in the UK will have to prepare for the outcome of the Bologna Declaration (1999) and ensuing process. The Bologna Declaration is an intergovernmental initiative that aims to create a European Higher Education Area (EHEA) by 2010 and to promote the European system of higher education worldwide. The Bologna Declaration now has forty-five signatory countries (twenty-nine in 1999) and is conducted outside the formal decision-making framework of the European Union. Decision-making needs the consent of all the participating countries. The broad objectives of the Bologna Process are: to remove the obstacles to student mobility across Europe; to enhance the attractiveness of European HE worldwide; to establish a common structure of higher education systems across Europe; and for this common structure to be based on two main cycles, undergraduate and graduate. In its drive to improve the quality of higher education and, in turn, human resources across Europe, the Bologna Process aims to play a key role in delivering stronger, lasting growth and to create more and better employment.[25]

Suggested further reading

Evans (2006) is a good introduction to the history of technical education from the eighteenth century to the present day. It is both clear and comprehensive on policy issues and legislative developments. Barnett (1990) considers the aims of higher education restated in modern terms and discusses conceptual issues, and Smith and Langslow (1999) examine the idea of a university from both a historical and a contemporary perspective. Thomas (2001) is a useful introduction to key issues and factors related to widening participation.

References

Barnett, R. (1990) *The Idea of Higher Education*, Buckingham: Open University Press.

Baty, P. (2003) 'TUC Backlash over Fees Hike', *Times Higher Education Supplement*, 12 September, 2.

Bell, R. (2000) 'Scotland's universities', *Comparative Education*. **36** (2), 163–175.

Bligh, D. (1990) *Higher Education*. London: Cassell.

Bologna Declaration (1999) *The European Higher Education Area*. Joint declaration of the European Ministers of Education convened in Bologna on 19 June 1999. Available at http://aecsite.cramgo.nl/DownloadView.aspx?ses=1820 (accessed 7 December 2007).

Booth, C. (1999) 'The Rise of the New Universities in Britain', in Smith, D. and Langslow, A. K. (eds) *The Idea of a University*. London: Jessica Kingsley.

Brennan, J. (2003) 'Now is the Time to Help People Top Up Their Skills', *The Independent*, 6 November.

Campbell, M. (2001) *Skills in England 2001: The Research Report*. Policy Research Institute: Leeds.

Carpentier, V. (2004) *Historical Statistics on the Funding and Development of the UK University System, 1920–2002*. Data Archives UK. Available at www.data-archive.ac.uk (accessed 7 February 2007).

Carvel, J. (1997) 'University Intake Startlingly Biased towards the Rich', *The Guardian*, 19 April.

Central Training Council (1965) *Central Training Council: Report to the Minister*. London: HMSO.

Clare, J. (1998) 'Universities Told to Make Entry Easier', *Daily Telegraph*, 18 September, 1.

Coles, A. (2004) 'Post-compulsory Education 16–19', in Matheson, D. (ed.) *An Introduction to the Study of Education*, 2nd edn. London: David Fulton.

Committee appointed by the Minister of Education and the Secretary of State for Scotland in June 1958 under the Chairmanship of Sir Colin K. Anderson (1960) *Grants to Students* (The Anderson Report). London: HMSO.

---

[25] See www.ond.vlaanderen.be/hogeronderwijs/bologna/ for more information.

Committee of Vice-Chancellors and Principals (CVCP) (1998) *From Élitism to Inclusion: Good Practice in Widening Access to Higher Education*. Summary Report. London: CVCP.

Crowther, G. (1959) *15 to 18: A Report of the Central Advisory Council (England)*. London: HMSO.

Davies, P. (ed.) (1995) *Adults in Higher Education: International Experiences in Access and Participation*. London: Jessica Kingsley.

Dearing, R. (1996) *Review of Qualifications for 16–19 Year Olds*. London: School Curriculum and Assessment Authority.

Dearing, R. (1997) *Higher Education in the Learning Society*. Report of the National Committee of Inquiry into Higher Education. London: HMSO.

Department for Education and Employment (1997) *Qualifying for Success: a Consultation Paper on the Future of Post-16 Qualifications*. London: DfEE.

Department for Education and Employment (1998a) *The Learning Age: A Renaissance for a New Britain*. London: The Stationery Office.

Department for Education and Employment (1998b) *Higher Education for the 21st Century: Response to the Dearing Report*. London: DfEE.

Department for Education and Skills (2001a) *The Post-16 Education and Training and Inspection Regulations 2001*. London: DfES.

Department for Education and Skills (2001b) *Skills for Life: The National Strategy for Improving Adult Literacy and Numeracy Skills*. London: DfEE.

Department for Education and Skills (2002a) *14–19 Opportunity and Excellence*. London: DfES.

Department for Education and Skills (2002b) *14–19: Extending Opportunities, Raising Standards*. London: DfES

Department for Education and Skills (2002c) *Success for All*. London: DfES.

Department for Education and Skills (2002d) *Implementation of the Education Maintenance Allowance Pilots: The Second Year*. Research Brief 333. London: DfES.

Department for Education and Skills (2003a) *21st Century Skills: Realising our Potential*. London: DfES.

Department for Education and Skills (2003b) *Principles for Reform of 14–19 Learning Programmes and Qualifications*. Working Group on 14–19 Reform. London: DfES.

Department for Education and Skills (2003c) *An Introduction to the Foundation Degree*. London: DfES. Available at www.foundationdegree.org.uk (accessed 5 May 2005).

Department for Education and Skills (2004a) *The Future of Higher Education*. London: The Stationery Office.

Department for Education and Skills (2004b) *Widening Participation in Higher Education*. London: The Stationery Office.

Department for Education and Skills (2004c) *White Paper and the Higher Education Act*. London: The Stationery Office. Available at www.dfes.gov.uk/hegateway/hereform/whitepaperconsultation/index.cfm (accessed 3 March 2005).

Department for Education and Skills (2005a) *14–19 Education and Skills*. London: DfES.

Department for Education and Skills (2005b) *14–19 Education and Skills Implementation Plan*. London: DfES.

Department for Education and Skills (2005c) *Skills: Getting On in Business, Getting On at Work*. London: DfES.

Department for Education and Skills (2006) *Further Education: Raising Skills, Improving Life Chances*. London: DfES.

Department of Education and Science (1956) *Technical Education*. London: HMSO.

Department of Education and Science (1966) *A Plan for Polytechnics and Other Colleges*. London: HMSO.

Department of Education and Science (1978) *Letter of Invitation to Chief Education Officers*. London: DES.

Department of Education and Science (1979) *Future Trends in Higher Education*. London: HMSO.

Department of Education and Science (1985) *The Development of Higher Education into the 1990s*. Cmnd 9524. London: HMSO.

Department of Education and Science (1987) *Higher Education: Meeting the Challenge*. London: HMSO.

Department of Education and Science (1991) *Higher Education: A New Framework*. London: HMSO.

Department of Education and Science and the Scottish Education Department (DES/SED) (1978) *Higher Education into the 1990s: A Discussion Document*. London: HMSO.

Edwards, E. G. (1982) *Higher Education for Everyone*. Nottingham: Spokesman.

Evans, R. (2006) *The History of Technical Education: A Short Introduction*. Cambridge: T Magazine. Available at www.tmag.co.uk/extras/history_of_Technical_Education.pdf (accessed on 7 July 2007).

Finch, J. and Rustin, M. (1986) *A Degree of Choice? Higher Education and the Right to Learn*. Harmondsworth: Penguin.

Finegold, D. *et al.* (eds) (1992) *Higher Education: expansion and reform*. London: Institute for Public Policy Research.

Foster, A. (2005) *Realising the Potential: A Review of the Future Role of Further Education Colleges*. London: DfES.

Fulton, O. (ed.) (1981) *Access to Higher Education*. Guildford: SRHE.

Fulton, O. (ed.) (1989) *Access and Institutional Change*. Milton Keynes: SRHE.

Green, A. (1990) *Education and State Formation: The Rise of Education Systems in England, France and the USA*. Basingstoke: Macmillan Press.

Halsey, A. H. (1992) 'An International Comparison of Access to Higher Education', *Oxford Studies in Comparative Education*. **1** (1), 11–36.

Halsey, A. H. (1993) 'Trends in Access and Equity in Higher Education: Britain in International Perspective', *Oxford Review of Education*. **19** (2), 129–140.

Higher Education Funding Council for England (1996) *Widening Access to Higher Education: A Report by the HEFCE's Advisory Group on Access and Participation*. Executive Summary. Bristol: HEFCE.

Higher Education Funding Council for England (1997) *The Influence of Neighbourhood Type on Participation in Higher Education*. Interim Report. Bristol: HEFCE.

Higher Education Funding Council for England (1999) *Performance Indicators in Higher Education*. Guide 99/66. Bristol: HEFCE.

Higher Education Funding Council for England (2005) *January 2005/03 Research Report: Young Participation in Higher Education*. Bristol: HEFCE. Available at www.hefce.ac.uk/pubs/hefce/2005/05_03/05_03c.pdf (accessed 5 May 2005).

Higher Education Statistical Agency (2002) *Students in Higher Education Institutions 2000/2001*. Cheltenham: Higher Education Statistical Agency.

Hindmore, A. (2004) 'Public Policy, but Domestic Policy Didn't Stop', *Parliamentary Affairs*. **57** (2), 315–328.

Hodgson, A. and Spours, K. (1999) *New Labour? Educational Agenda: Issues and Policies for Education and Training from 14 plus.* London: Kogan Page.

Jackson, R. (1999) 'The Universities, Government and Society', in Smith, D. and Langslow, A. K. (eds) *The Idea of a University.* London: Jessica Kingsley.

Jary, D. (2001) 'Access and Widening Participation', *Higher Education Digest Supplement.* **40** (1), 5.

Jessup, G. (1991) *Outcomes: NVQs and the Emerging Model of Education and Training.* London: Falmer Press.

Keep, E. (1996) 'Missing Presumed Skilled: Training Policy in the UK', in Edwards, R., Sieminski, S. and Zeldin, D. (eds) *Adult Learners, Education and Training.* London: Routledge.

Keep, E. and Mayhew, K. (2004) 'The Economic and Distributional Implications of Current Policies in Higher Education', *Oxford Review of Economic Policy.* **20** (2), 298–314.

Kennedy, H. (1997) *Learning Works: Widening Participation in Further Education.* Coventry: FEFC.

Lampl, P. (2000) 'The Scandal of Bright Children Turned Away by our Top Universities', *The Times*, 10 April.

Leitch, S. (2005) *Skills in the UK: The Long Term Challenge.* Interim Report. London: The Stationery Office.

Leitch, S. (2006) *Prosperity for All in the Global Economy: World Class Skills.* Final Report. London: The Stationery Office.

Longden, B. (2002) 'Funding Policy in Higher Education: Contested Terrain', *Research Papers in Education.* **16** (2), 161–182.

Lynch, K. L. and O'Riordan. C. (1998) 'Inequality in Higher Education: A Study of Class Barriers', *British Journal of Sociology.* **19** (4), 445–478.

McDermid, J. (2000) 'Women and Education', in Purvis, J. (ed.) *Women's History: Britain 1850–1945.* London: Routledge.

Mackie, D. (2001) "How Do Access Policies Compare? England, Northern Ireland, Scotland and Wales', paper presented to the Centre for Higher Education Research and Information Conference 'Access and Retention in Higher Education', London, City University Conference Centre, 18 May.

Mackinnon, D. and Statham, J. (1999) *Education in the UK: Facts and Figures.* London: Hodder and Stoughton.

McPherson, A., Swift, D. and Bernstein, B. (1972) *Eighteen Plus: The Final Selection.* Milton Keynes: Open University Press.

Miliband, D. (1992) 'Introduction: Expansion and Reform', in Finegold, D. *et al.* (eds) *Higher Education, Expansion and Reform.* London: Institute for Public Policy Research.

National Advisory Body (1984a) *Report of Continuing Education Group.* London: NAB.

National Advisory Body (1984b) *A Strategy for Higher Education in the late 1980s and Beyond.* London: NAB.

National Advisory Body and University Grants Committee (1984) *Higher Education and the Needs of Society.* London: National Advisory Board for Public Sector Higher Education/University Grants Committee.

Ofsted (2001) *Curriculum 2000: The First Year of Implementation – September 2000 to July 2001.* London: HMI.

Organisation for Economic Co-operation and Development (2001) *Education Policy Analysis*. Paris: OECD.

Organisation for Economic Co-operation and Development (2002) *Education Policy Analysis*. Paris: OECD.

Parry, G. and Fry, H. (1999) 'Widening Participation in Pursuit of the Learning Society: Kennedy, Dearing and "The Learning Age"', in Hayton, A. (ed.) *Tackling Disaffection and Social Exclusion: Education Perspectives and Policies*. London: Kogan Page.

Parry, G. and Wake, C. (1990) *Access and Alternative Futures for Higher Education*. London: Hodder & Stoughton.

Parsons, S. and Bynner, J. (2005) *Does Numeracy Matter More?* London: NRDC.

Paterson, L. (1997) 'Trends in Participation in Higher Education in Scotland', *Higher Education Quarterly*. **51** (1), 29–48.

Percy, E. (1945) *Higher Technological Education*. London: HMSO.

Pratt, J. (1997) *The Polytechnic Experiment 1965–1992*. Buckingham: SRHE.

Ramsden, B. (2004) *Patterns of Higher Education Institutions in the United Kingdom*. Fourth Report. London: Universities UK.

Robbins, L. C. (1963) *Higher Education*. Report of the Committee of Inquiry into Higher Education. London: HMSO.

Robertson, D. (1997) 'Growth without Equity? Reflections on the Consequences for Social Cohesion of Faltering Progress on Access to Higher Education', *Journal of Access Studies*. **12** (1), 9–31.

Samuelson Royal Commission (1884) *Technical Instruction*. London: HMSO.

Schofield, K. (2006) 'Fee Refugees "Squeezing Out" Scots Students', *The Scotsman*, 26 January.

Schuller, T. and Bamford, C. (1999) *Initial and Continuing Education in Scotland: Divergence, Convergence and Learning Relationships*. Edinburgh: SCRE.

Schuller, T., Raffe, D., Morgan-Klein, B. and Clark, I. (1999) *Part-time Higher Education: Policy, Practice and Experience*. London: Jessica Kingsley.

Scott, P. (1995) *The Meaning of Mass Higher Education*. Buckingham: SRHE.

Scottish Executive (2001) *Participation in Higher Education in Scotland*. Available at www.scotland.gov. uk/stats/educ.htm (accessed 5 May 2005).

Scottish Executive (2004) *Students in Higher Education in Scotland 2002/03*. Edinburgh: Scottish Executive.

Scottish Higher Education Funding Council (1998) *More Opportunities for Part-Time Students in Higher Education*. Edinburgh: SHEFC.

Simon, B. (1991) *Education and the Social Order: British Education since 1944*. London: Lawrence and Wishart.

Skilbeck, M. and Connell, H. (2000) *Access and Equity in Higher Education: An International Perspective on Issues and Strategies*. Dublin: HEA.

Smith, D. (1999) 'The Changing Idea of a University', in Smith, D. and Langslow, A. K. (eds) *The Idea of a University*. London: Jessica Kingsley.

Smith, D. and Bocock, J. (1999) 'Participation and Progression in Mass Higher Education: Policy and FHE Interface', *Journal of Education Policy*. **14** (3), 283–299.

Smith, D. and Langslow, A. K. (eds) (1999) *The Idea of a University*. London: Jessica Kingsley.

Smith, S. J. (2000) 'Retaking the Register: Women's Higher Education in Glasgow and Beyond, *c.* 1796–1845', *Gender and History*. **12** (2), 310–335.

Squires, G. (1981) 'Mature Entry', in Fulton, O. (ed.) *Access to Higher Education*. Guildford: Society for Research into Higher Education.

Stephens, W. B. (1998) *Education in Britain 1750–1914*. London: Palgrave/Macmillan.

Stowell, M. (1992) 'Equal Opportunities, Access and Admissions: Tensions and Issues for Institutional Policy', *Journal of Access Studies*. **7** (2), 164–179.

Thomas, E. (2001) *Widening Participation in Post-compulsory Education*. London: Continuum.

Tight, M. (1996) *Key Concepts in Adult Education and Training*. London: Routledge.

Tomlinson, M. (2002) *Inquiry into A Level Standards: Final Report*. London: DfES.

Tomlinson, M. (2004) *14–19 Curriculum and Qualifications Reform*. London: DfES.

Trow, M. (1973) *Problems in the Transition from Elite to Mass Higher Education*. Berkeley, CA: Carnegie Commission on Higher Education.

University Grants Committee (1984a) *Report of the Continuing Education Working Party*. London: HMSO.

University Grants Committee (1984b) *A Strategy for Higher Education into the 1990s*. London: HMSO.

Wagner, L. (1989) 'National Policy and Institutional Development', in Fulton, O. (ed.) *Access and Institutional Change*. Milton Keynes: SRHE.

Williams, J. (ed.) (1997a) *Negotiating Access to Higher Education: The Discourse of Selectivity and Equity*. Buckingham: SRHE.

Williams, J. (1997b) 'The Discourse of Access: The Legitimation of Selectivity Statistics', in Williams, J. (ed.) *Negotiating Access to Higher Education: The Discourse of Selectivity and Equity*. Buckingham: SRHE.

Williamson, B. (1986) 'Who Has Access?', in Finch, J. and Rustin, M. (eds) *A Degree of Choice? Higher Education and the Right to Learn*. Harmondsworth: Penguin.

Woodrow, M. (2001) 'Are Access Policies and Current Funding Arrangements Compatible?', paper presented to the CHERI Conference Access and Retention in Higher Education, City Conference Centre, London, 18 May.

Wright, P. (1989) 'Access or Exclusion: Some Comments and Future Prospects of Continuing Education in England', *Studies in Higher Education*. **14** (1), 23–40.

15

Lifelong learning

Catherine Matheson and David Matheson

> When planning for a year – sow corn.
> When planning for a decade – plant trees.
> When planning for a lifetime – train and educate people.
> (Kuan Tsu, third century BC)

Introduction

'LEARNING, LIKE BREATHING, IS something everyone does all of the time' (Tight 1996: 21). It is an inevitable part of life that humans learn continuously unless some major physical or psychological trauma interrupts the process. Even when we are asleep, we learn. Indeed, it is increasingly believed that some aspects of learning can even take place in the womb. Babies learn to associate certain rhythmic sounds with a calm, soothing environment and, once born, will respond positively to such sounds being played to them. From cradle to grave, we are acquiring knowledge, skills and attitudes. We pick up incidental bits of information; we are influenced in manners sometimes subtle, sometimes evident. From this it becomes clear that the concept of lifelong learning must concern itself with something more than simply learning throughout life. Otherwise it is a mere tautology and is hence beyond elaboration. Instead it must concern itself with purposeful learning, be this formal, non-formal or informal. We might want to term this education but then there is the other problem of deciding when learning constitutes education and when it does not.

Historical overview

Although there are references in Plato to lifelong education, and Comenius certainly advocated learning throughout the lifespan, adult and lifelong education as we know it in the United Kingdom has its likeliest ancestor in the Mechanics' Institutes of the nineteenth century. In the Mechanics' Institutes, 'workers could improve their basic skills, learn new scientific and technological knowledge and broaden their minds' (Hall 1994: 3), initial job training being done on the job. The notion of broadening the mind is crucial and ties in directly with the goal of the University Extension classes, born as a direct consequence of the growth in the railway system – and the postal service. Tutors would tour the country, armed with cases of books, lodging in cheap hotels, teaching evening classes in just about every university subject imaginable (except the 'professions') to workers who had spent their day toiling in the mines or in factories. The correspondence course, for its part, had been launched in the immediate wake of the introduction of the postage stamp in 1840. Thus, in the course of the eighteenth century we see two distinct forms of learning distant from the institution concerned: on the one hand there is the correspondence course where the learner's only contact with the centre is by post – together with the occasional trip to the centre for examination; on the other there is the Extension class with the tutor travelling sometimes great distances to reach the learners. Interestingly enough, we see both in modern form in that most hi-tech of establishments, the Open University.

The literary aspect of the Extension classes is underlined in the report of the Committee on Distribution of Science and Art Grants (1896) which advised the allocation of additional grants to enable students attending evening science and art classes to gain further literary instruction through University Extension classes. As we shall see shortly, it was through the University Extension classes that one of the mainstays of adult education in the United Kingdom, the Workers' Educational Association, was born.

The late eighteenth and early nineteenth centuries also saw the creation of the model village. Devised by industrialists ostensibly to house the workers and their families, these were constructed at some distance from any centre of population and so quite effectively allowed the owner control over multiple aspects of the inhabitants' lives. We shall briefly discuss two such model villages, New Lanark, near the Falls of the Clyde, and Bourneville, now part of Birmingham. There were many more but not all shared the idea of the benevolent, paternalistic employer.

In 1800 Robert Owen, a Welsh entrepreneur who had made his money in the Manchester cotton trade, arrived in New Lanark to take over management of the cotton mill from his father-in-law, the social reformer David Dale (a director of the Royal Bank of Scotland). Owen realised that he could increase productivity by improving on the already high-quality housing (Kreis 2002) and by educating not just the children of the workers but also the workers themselves (Donnachie 2003). We can speculate on the true motives for this venture but the upshot is clear, as Owen claims in his *A New View of Society* ([1835] 1965) that by education one can give any character one wants to a community. As we saw in Chapter 11 of this volume, Owen established the first nursery school; he also set up his *Institute for the Formation of Character* which was in effect a school and a community centre.

The three lower rooms (in the Institute) will be thrown open for the use of the adult part of the population, who are to be provided with every accommodation requisite to enable them to read, write, account, sew or play, converse or walk about. Two evenings in the week will be appropriated to dancing and music, but on these occasions, every accommodation will be prepared for those who prefer to study or to follow any of the occupations pursued on the other evenings.

(Owen 1816: n.p.)

Following in many respects the social reform trends set by Owen, George Cadbury and his brother Richard constructed Bourneville in 1879 initially for key workers in their chocolate factory, only later expanding it to admit other workers. Like Owen before them, they included a school in the village but George, unlike Robert Owen, was a committed teacher who spent Sunday mornings teaching in the Quaker-run (though secular in its curriculum) Birmingham Adult School. Within the village, the Cadburys operated what might now be termed community education by organising leisure activities for the inhabitants. They were incidentally among the first employers to give their workers free time on Bank Holidays and reputedly the first to make Saturday a half-day, instead of the usual full-day in order to give their workers more time for other activities (Spartacus Educational 2002).

Following its creation by the Rochdale Pioneers in 1844 (Holyoake 1907), the Co-operative Movement formally took education as one of its aims in 1882.

Technical correspondence courses and junior classes were developed during the 1890s and by 1900 over 1,000 students were enrolled for courses, over 500 adults had already taken exams in industrial history, bookkeeping and citizenship and over 900 juniors.

(Co-operative College 2003)

Although the educational mission of the Co-op has waxed and waned over the years it has left a lasting legacy on at least two fronts. One is the continuing existence of the Co-operative College, which 'aims to provide adult and lifelong learning programmes that emphasise co-operative values and principles and be a centre of excellence in training, learning, consultancy and research for the co-operative and mutual sector in the UK and internationally' (Co-operative College 2003). Another is the Workers' Educational Association (WEA).

Marsh (2002) tells us how the founder of the WEA, Albert Mansbridge, had effectively grown up in the Co-operative Movement. Mansbridge then moved on to University Extension classes, where, between 1891 and 1901, he studied a wide range of subjects, and later he became an evening class teacher. However, in the Extension classes Mansfield recognised that they had become a haven for the middle classes. His solution was to found an organisation for the workers, run by the workers. His initial title for the organisation, reflecting the sexism of his age, was the *Association to Promote the Higher Education of Working Men*. This was quickly changed to the *Workers' Educational Association*.

The fortunes of the WEA in England and Wales are somewhat more positive than in Scotland. The WEA became a major provider of adult education in England and Wales while in Scotland it was denied *Responsible Body Status* as a provider of adult education and this made its 'development heavily dependent on collaboration with the universities, local authorities and trade unions' (Duncan 1999: 106).

The University Extension classes for their part grew, developed and changed into a plethora of extra-mural courses, covering almost every subject imaginable until, in the 1990s, much of the subsidy provided to them by local government was withdrawn (Vorhaus 2002). Indeed, from 1979 onwards, market forces had been steadily applied and course fees steadily increased. This is aptly illustrated by the example of a class in Swedish language, which in 1977 cost £2.50; by 2003 it cost £122.50.[1]

Nonetheless, the twentieth century saw the development and perhaps the apotheosis of the notion of lifelong learning. Especially in the period after 1972 (the year that *Learning to Be* – the Faure report – was published by UNESCO), lifelong learning became increasingly a positive term, first among academics and social activists and then among politicians. The problem was that they did not generally mean the same thing. Lifelong learning quickly became an elastic concept, one that basically meant whatever the person using it wanted it to mean, just as long as there was some notion of lifelong and some notion of learning. Lifelong education came into fashion as did terms such as *learning society* and *learning age*. However, whereas the advocates of the concept from the 1970s until the mid-1990s concerned themselves principally with improving quality of life, the political advocates from the mid-1990s onwards seemed more concerned with the economic aspects of lifelong learning. The government Green Paper *The Learning Age: A Renaissance for a New Britain* (DfEE 1998) emphasised above all else that by continuing to seek qualifications – and not merely learning or even education – one increased one's chances of improving one's economic situation. We continue to be forever reminded of the pace of technological change; it would not take a great cynic to believe that there are conscious attempts to make workers feel threatened, and this goes beyond the notion of simply avoiding or removing complacency.

Despite all this, at ground level a locally spawned initiative appeared in a few areas, which directly presented active learning as a lifelong activity. This was the admission of adult learners into secondary schools. While adults were admitted to a rare few secondary schools in England (such as the community schools in Sutton in Ashfield and Milton Keynes), in Scottish urban areas in particular, as a

---

[1] See www.gla.ac.uk:443/departments/adulteducation/index.php?SelectedSubject=Languages&Sel ectedSubheading=Swedish.

direct response to falling school rolls, adults were actively sought, first for leisure classes and later to study for O Grades and Highers. This meant adolescents learning alongside adults while in the school's crèche some of those same pupils might be learning childcare with the children of some of the adults (Matheson 2000). Active learning was thus presented as something that one can do for the full length of one's life.

Before we move on to look at the concept of lifelong learning, we need to spend a moment considering that main target of lifelong learning initiatives, the adult, and examine a few ideas around adults as learners.

A few myths surrounding teachers and learners

Like many other human activities, education in all its various forms has developed its own myths and mythology. Sometimes these have a basis in truth, sometimes not. By way of reorientation, if need be, let us look at a few educational myths and check their validity.

Teachers are old and learners are young is perhaps a view that we maintain from those days in which we were young and our teachers were not so young as us. In other words, we were at school. We were most likely segregated from the rest of the learning population. We learned from our teachers and were blissfully unaware of any learning we might be giving them. Learning was seen as a one-way street, a unidirectional process. Concomitant with this notion are the ideas that *teachers teach only in schools* and *education equals school*. The latter notion clearly denies the educational validity (or even existence) of non-school education, but we dealt in Chapter 1 with some of the difficulties in the use of *school* and *education* as interchangeable terms. The notion that *teachers teach only in schools* is patently ridiculous unless the sharing of knowledge, understanding, skills and attitudes in which teachers outwith school engage is somehow not really teaching. The notion that teachers teach only in schools is further undermined when one considers famous teachers from history. An initial list might well include the following: Confucius, Lao-Tse, Moses, Jesus, Mohammed, Buddha, Plato, Socrates. Every one of them was a teacher of adults and none taught in a school as we know it.

It is commonly believed that *learning gets harder as you get older*. But what evidence is there for this? Anecdotes? Common sense? Or is this just another manifestation of the pro-school bias in the widely held view of what education is? One thing is clear: adults have generally greater demands on their time and energies than do young people. Adults often have higher levels of responsibility. In these senses, there are potentially more distractions for the adult than for the young person. But what do these hurdles tell us about the capacity of an adult to learn? Precisely nothing. At best we can say that adults are better at making excuses, *in believing them* and *in getting them believed* than are young people. Educators with experience of both older and younger learners may like to consider here their own attitudes towards the excuses given by learners for work not being done, and more importantly the different attitudes they manifest towards the older and younger learners who are making the excuses. Perhaps because people view adults and their learning differently from younger people and their learning, they are, we would contend, more likely to accept the excuse of the adult who claims simply to have been 'too busy' than they are to accept, say, an adolescent saying the same. Yet, what evidence do we have for adults actually being more busy than adolescents? This is not to say that there are not busy adults or indolent adolescents but rather to underline the expectation that adults are, per se, busy and more importantly that their excuses are valid since they emanate from an adult.[2]

The making of excuses to one's self and others – and the believing of them by self and others – arguably presents one of the biggest challenges for any so-called learning society – to get potential learners over the hurdle so eloquently expressed by Homer Simpson when his daughter Lisa was starting to learn the saxophone:

> Don't try, Lisa. Trying is the first step to failure.
>
> (*The Simpsons*, season 1, episode 6, 'Moaning Lisa')

Certainly there are some mechanical tasks for which a younger person might well have greater suppleness in the fingers, for example, but beyond these there does not seem to be much of a case for not being able to *teach an old dog new tricks*. Besides, one thing that adults have in greater measure than young people is life experience. Consequently they have a greater context within which to situate their learning.

The concept of lifelong education

The movement towards mass education has gained much momentum over the last 200 years. To attend school as a child for example is now considered the international norm – so much so that Faure felt inclined to write that, between 1960 and 1968, by not being able to attend school 'every year some 2 million or more children (aged between 5 and 14) were denied the right to an education' (Faure *et al.* 1972: 38).

Of course, besides those missed entirely by schooling one must also consider the drop-outs, the school failures (although whether a child fails school or is failed by it is open to conjecture), the unemployed, the misorientated etc. The list is vast of those categories of people for whom the skills and knowledge acquirable at school might be of use. To this must be added the skills and knowledge

---

[2] One of the present writers recalls on one occasion asking an adolescent where his homework was and getting as reply: 'I'm sorry I wasn't able to do it but I had to sit up all night with my dad.' The dad was later revealed to be a heroin addict and the boy (who was very big and strong) would sit up with his stoned father until the latter fell asleep. The son would then carry him to bed and lay him in the recovery position. This could take all night. How many adults could beat that for an excuse? And how many adults would believe this for an excuse?

acquirable outside school that might help an individual to be educated. The result is certainly an enormous mass of people who could benefit physically, mentally or financially from furthering their education and widening their knowledge and understanding.

The background notions in lifelong education as defined by UNESCO are a mixture of old and new. A basis for the idea comes from Erasmus, who wrote: 'We are not born human, we become human or rather . . . we make ourselves human' (Margolin 1981: 172). Compare this with the following quotes used by Faure as 'the major argument in favour of lifelong education'. Lapasade: 'One never ceases to enter life'; and Fromm: 'The individual's entire life is nothing but a process of giving birth to [her/]himself; in truth we are only fully born when we die' (Faure *et al.* 1972: 158).

Despite the span of several centuries the ideas are shades of the same thing. However, there remain problems in defining the concept of lifelong education. For example, according to Dave 'the learning process is the key to all education' (Dave 1972: Concept Characteristic 10) whereas for Faure education is conceived of as a vector – 'the path to learning is irrelevant; only what is learnt or acquired has any importance' (Faure *et al.* 1972: 185). The contradiction between these standpoints is clear but there is also a major contradiction within Faure; in lifelong education the end is, by definition, death. Interim products are deemed irrelevant in some models of education as if it were only what appears as an end-product that counts, and this in a manner worthy of Machiavelli's notion that the end justifies the means. Hence, if we are indeed lifelong learners, then these interim products must be ascribed value, as the end of the learning process (i.e. death) signifies the end of the line. What is learned is in itself an essential part of the process and how it is learned is equally learning in its own right. Therefore, unless the path to learning is seen as part of the learning there is little point in learning at all as the path to learning begins at birth and ends at death. Besides, there is a distinct lack of logic in viewing final products of an educative process (short of death) as identical on the basis only of what has been learned or acquired. If the experience has been different then the product must be also. Faure, however, characteristically hedges his bets by employing the word 'acquire' instead of some stronger term.

According to Gelpi: 'the hypothesis of lifelong education [is] that the educators need not necessarily be professionals' (Gelpi 1979: 19). This is essential for Dave, for whom:

> Lifelong education seeks to view education in its totality. It covers formal, non-formal and informal patterns of education and attempts to articulate all structures and stages of education.
>
> (Dave 1972: 35)

For Skäger, 'lifelong education is not a concept or a thing but a set of basic principles' (Griffin 1983: 156). This effectively says nothing and may even contradict itself, depending on how strong a meaning is taken of concept or principle. Besides, is not a true concept in fact a set of basic principles? Cropley takes an almost equally spurious tack when he writes that 'lifelong education is an orientation, concept or principle, not a tangible thing' (Cropley 1979: 113). Unfortunately Cropley does not define his meaning for 'tangible', upon which his argument hinges. The *Shorter Oxford Dictionary* admits three meanings that encompass both the concrete and the abstract. *Assuming* that Cropley means that lifelong education is not concrete then he agrees with Lengrand, who insists on the indefinable nature of lifelong education remaining forever so:

> Lifelong education is still at the conceptual stage. As with other principles such as freedom, justice and equality, it will doubtless retain indefinitely that certain distance in relation to concrete achievements which is in the nature of concepts.
>
> (Lengrand 1978: 98)

Thus Lengrand places the question 'what is lifelong education?' on almost the same footing as a moral philosopher might put the question 'what is good?' This doubtless raises the philosophical status of lifelong education but does nothing to expedite its implementation, unless of course it can be argued that there is a moral imperative to lifelong education as might be claimed for 'good'.

For De'Ath, lifelong education is of anthropological importance in that it 'could be instrumental in not only preserving all kinds of cultural diversity but also in placing a positive value on individual and collective difference' (De'Ath 1972: 247).

All these writers demonstrate the lack of rigour that Lengrand warns of when he writes: 'the term lifelong education is used haphazardly and loosely in a variety of situations and realities' (Lengrand 1979: 29).

Conceptually there is very little to grasp in the lifelong education debate that consists of anything more than very fine straws or collections of undefined terms and hurrah words such as those used by Cropley and De'Ath above. What there is consists of:

a   an attempt to view education as not confined to school but consisting of purposeful and process learning undertaken wherever and whenever;

b   a view of education as a whole-life activity that ought to be facilitated by the state and in which some may take longer than others to achieve their goals but no-one is deemed a failure.

There are immediate problems with this facilitation, especially when one sees lifelong education as an activity driven by economic need. At this point, and especially where the long-term unemployed are concerned, facilitation may easily turn into compulsion, as we now see in some of the Welfare to Work programmes in the USA, which have been considered for adoption in various European countries.

Lifelong learning at the dawn of the twenty-first century

We live in the era of perhaps the most rapid change known to humanity. The paradigms our parents knew (and with which perhaps we ourselves grew up) are being steadily swept away. Notions such as a job for life are all too clearly obsolete except perhaps for an élite cadre of highly skilled, highly paid workers (Longworth and Davies 1996), while the rest are left with the realisation that in our possibly postmodern world there is a dearth of permanent, decent jobs (Aronowitz and Giroux 1993). Politicians talk about educating the workforce, by which they generally mean training them, while training itself is held up as the great panacea. As an editorial in *The Observer* of 21 July 1996 commented, training is:

> The great palliative of our time. All parties support it and none asks what work there is for the trainees when the training ends. As a policy, it has the immense advantage of being far cheaper than building homes or creating jobs.

Mixed in with this rhetoric is increasing talk about lifelong learning from politicians. The Labour opposition in the UK promised before the 1997 general election that lifelong learning would be the subject of a White Paper (Labour Party 1994) (this being a consultative document leading to a Bill before Parliament) while the then Conservative government (DfEE 1996) contributed to the debate that led to the publication in 1996 of *Learning: The Treasure Within* (Delors *et al*. 1996). Less than one year into office and the promised White Paper had appeared as a Green Paper (DfEE 1998); in other words, merely a consultation document, which need not lead to anything else. The debate goes on but where it will lead to remains to be seen. There persist, however, the conceptual problems with lifelong learning, which show no sign of resolution, except insofar as the liberal aspects of lifelong learning are vanishing from view.

Lifelong learning is what Knapper and Cropley (1985: 20) term 'a utopian idea – an elastic concept which means whatever the person using the term wants it to mean'. As Lengrand (1986: 10) reminds us:

> There is no single centre of thought from which this idea has been disseminated, nor is there a code of propositions that would enable the faithful to be distinguished from the heretics.

Nonetheless, it is a powerful idea, which captures the public imagination and makes it sound as though the interlocutor wants to actually do something positive.

Lifelong learning and school

Strictly speaking, any account of lifelong learning ought to contain an examination, if not of the first learning experiences that a person has, then at least of the first formal learning experiences, such as those that occur in pre-school and in school itself. We have seen earlier some of the influences and effects that can occur in pre-school and school that affect self-esteem and growing self-concept. Influences such as whether one attends pre-school at all, the effect of social class or of one's gender, 'race' and racialisation, the younger learner's needs and the adult's responsibilities in satisfying those needs. School is an undeniably formative influence on a learner's perception of him/herself and also on his/her perception of him/herself as a learner.

It is in school that learners generally have their first introduction to formalised learning strategies. School introduces to learners the essential skills without which all further attempts at purposeful learning are impeded. These basic essential skills are generally held to include for example reading, listening, sifting information. It is worth mentioning in passing, however, that both Freire and Illich[3] question whether reading is such a basic skill as we in the industrialised countries claim it to be. Nonetheless,

Schools . . . have to start a dynamic process through which pupils are progressively weaned off their dependence on teachers and institutions and given the confidence to manage their own learning, co-operating with colleagues, and using a range of resources and learning situations.

(Abbott 1994: 108)

The extent to which schools succeed in this 'weaning' is very much open to debate. In this respect it is worth reflecting on one's own learning from school and judging how much of one's autonomy as a learner is due to influences from school and conversely how much of one's dependency is due to influence from the same source.

Lifelong learning implies by its very nature that learners have become equipped with basic learning skills, that they know how to learn, that they have gained the equipment, the skills and the attitudes needed to pursue their own learning. Learners need to have moved from a dependency stance to one of autonomy, to have developed a sense of self-direction, to have, in the terms of Malcolm Knowles, moved from needing pedagogy to demanding andragogy; in other words, they have to have moved from needing the security that comes from being told what to do, when to do and how to do it to being able to define their own educational

---

[3] Both Illich and Freire began to question the intrinsic value of literacy when they observed in their work in Latin America that the rural poor may have nothing to read and yet their cultures have evident value (Pierre Furter, personal communication).

goals and the pathways to them (Knowles 1998). The question arises of when the learners assume this level of autonomy. One might also ask whether all learners *should* assume such a level and consider some possible ramifications. Let us keep these thoughts at the back of our minds as we continue.

As Howe puts it:

> A person who leaves school ill-equipped with the competencies required for learning independently throughout the remainder of a life is at a severe disadvantage.
>
> (Howe in Claxton 1990: 165)

Much of the literature that appeared in the wake of *Learning to Be* (Faure *et al.* 1972) assumed tacitly or overtly that being properly equipped with learning tools was a necessary condition for lifelong learning. Its starting point is generally that:

> Today no one can hope to amass during his or her youth an initial fund of knowledge which will serve a lifetime. The swift changes taking place in the world call for knowledge to be continuously updated.
>
> (Delors *et al.* 1996: 99)

We witness daily the truth of this statement as we rush forward in technology (and leave many old certainties behind) and in itself it implies a need for schools to instil lifelong learning skills in their pupils. Examples of how dismally schools fail in this task are not hard to find. It is unfortunately true, for example, that the rate of borrowing books from public libraries is in constant decline; employers everywhere complain about how difficult their recruits find mastering new skills; teachers in higher education complain about the declining levels of autonomy they see among their students. We should perhaps take some of these complaints with a small pinch of salt but not dismiss them entirely. Nostalgia is not what it used to be, but nonetheless perceptions breed perceptions on the part of both the observer and the observed, roles that interchange constantly.

Despite this however, anyone who enters a job has to assume that the skills they begin with are almost guaranteed to become outmoded and will require updating or even replacement. Even the most apparently unchanging of occupations are altered by technology and countless others have changed beyond all recognition in the last twenty years while a multitude of other, new professions, particularly relating to information technology, have come into existence.[4]

However, as Stoikov (1975: 114) (and many other writers besides) points out, 'it is usually those who already have a good educational and training background

---

[4] As time goes on, it will be interesting to observe the effect that computer-based communications have on spelling. As anyone who habitually uses e-mail can testify, the smallest mistake in the address and the communication does not go where it is supposed to go. At this point, immense care must be taken. On the other hand, the actual message is often marked by a complete insouciance towards grammar, spelling and syntax.

who volunteer for additional education and training'. In *Learning: The Treasure Within* we find the same message:

> Adults' further participation in educational and cultural activities is related to the level of schooling already received: [so] the more education you have then the more education you want.
>
> (Delors *et al.* 1996: 101)

In other words, it is no new phenomenon that the educated educate themselves the most. If ever there was an argument for wider initial education then this is it. It is also worth noting that Blackledge and Hunt (1985: 170) remind us: 'Educated parents equip their children for a successful career in education.' So if we want formal education to be a real agent for social mobility then we ought to be pressing for adults to increase their level of education in order to encourage their children to increase theirs. In this respect, we find echoes of Paolo Freire and his attempts at teaching literacy. It is well known that Freire despaired of teaching children to read when their parents were illiterate and so he set about teaching their parents, but using materials and learning circumstances that were of relevance to them. As Furter (1999) puts it, he tried to move people from mere literacy to cultural development.

Lifelong learning and economics

In an ideal world, in a true learning society, any person would be free at any time to learn anything that lay within their intellectual capabilities and would feel supported and nurtured in taking such initiatives. Unfortunately simple economics removes this option immediately. All activities, be they formal or non-formal, must be paid for. Each subsidy must be argued for and the formal, initial domain of education clearly and indisputably has first priority. In most countries it would be unthinkable to levy general charges on primary school children, although this is increasingly demanded for some artistic activities; similarly in lower secondary, although paying some fees for upper secondary school is quite common across Europe. Education beyond upper secondary has to play second fiddle; after all it applies to a smaller and smaller proportion of the population. Indeed as we move up the age range of the target population, the greater is the likelihood of fees being applied in one way or another. There are, however, exceptions such as courses aimed at the long-term unemployed, which might be funded at 100 per cent by central government or via unemployment insurance. In this last respect, the challenges laid by the economy are performing exactly as d'Hainaut and Lawton (1981: 37) predict when they say that 'the economy serves as a powerful stimulus to education in general and to lifelong education in particular'. A cynic might say that it gives the government and its agencies something to do with the unemployed. In this light, we might think back to training and the palliative effect that it has.

It is worth bearing in mind that, 'by its very nature, lifelong learning involves a change in the distribution of activities over time and among members of the population, and such a redistribution has implications for the future social structure' (Stoikov 1975: 7). This obliges us to ask the extent to which we, as a society, want to maintain the status quo or whether we want to encourage social development.

If lifelong learning is to become the perceived norm then there is clearly an essential need for major subsidy of those who cannot pay the fees. Otherwise it will serve as further reinforcement of economic stratification as equivalent to cultural stratification. The 'better-off' have access to most culture (by dint of having more cash to pay for it, by generally having more education with which to appreciate it), but should this necessarily be so? Is there not a role for lifelong learning in offering cultural openings to those whose purse-strings cannot usually stretch that far?

However, fine as this is in theory, in practice it means the poorer student having to submit to some kind of means test to decide the fee to be paid. There is also the concomitant problem of over-subsidising learning experiences, since it is all too often the case that when something is perceived (by the consumer) as costing nothing it may be seen as being worth nothing.

For those who can afford courses there are the dire warnings of Ohliger and Dauber that 'concomitant to lifelong education is lifelong students, condemned to perpetual inadequacy' (Cropley 1977: 156). This is a certain problem: how can learners be encouraged to seek purposeful lifelong learning without feeling that their need for learning (for there must be such if they are to seek learning) is witness to a deeper feeling of inadequacy? This is unless a different view of learning need is promoted; one that we might term an ameliorative view of learning, whereby the learning is sought to improve an already 'good' (by whatever terms) situation. This stands in contrast to the deficit model promoted by governments and training providers, in which the message is one of 'train or get left behind' rather than 'learn in order to add to your life'.

However, there is always 'the spectre of uselessness' (Ranson 1998: 255) that hangs over workers feeling insecure in their employment.

Lifelong learning: leisure or education?

This brings us to our next point: is lifelong learning to be a leisure activity or an educational activity? If the former, then s/he who cannot partake of it for whatever reason may not perceive the loss or lack as so great as if it is the latter. The danger is that in attempting to raise the value of lifelong learning its providers, especially to secure funding, may downplay the leisure side, with the concomitant risk of creating a sort of education addict, forever driven from course to course by an insatiable appetite whetted and fuelled by inadequacy. If this became generalised through lifelong learning becoming the perceived norm, then how much more inadequate would be those denied access?

On the other hand, if lifelong learning is perceived as leisure then not only is its social value decreased but it is also seen as nothing more than an optional extra, as a luxury to which only some may be expected to aspire. As a leisure activity, it loses any moral *right* to funding that an educational activity may claim. In this light, we must consider blurring boundaries.

We are used to a society that separates work from play, 'non-work' from 'work' (which often means that activities that do not lead to a wage are diminished in social status terms), and learning from work (although the one may impinge on the other). We are also, perhaps most importantly, used to defining ourselves by our work. If you answer the question as to what you 'do' by describing yourself as 'student in education' then this would probably be considered quite normal. Were you to respond by saying that you enjoy cooking and baking and trying to play jigs and reels on the fiddle, then the one who has asked the question might well look askance. To define oneself by one's work (or pursuits equivalent to work) is acceptable. To define oneself by non-salaried work or by leisure pursuits is not so readily acceptable. This apparent digression reveals its importance when we consider the lack of permanency in many, if not most, jobs. As John White (1997: 71) puts it:

Education for unemployment may become a fixed part of the vocational landscape. In other words, instead of education being conceived as a precursor to work, it may be construed as equally a precursor to non-work, or to leisure, to meaningfully filling one's days.

It is well documented that 'working-class' persons tend to eschew education and training that does not immediately impinge on work or the possibility of obtaining work. Education and training are seen as purely, or least largely, instrumental. What is most easily qualified as intrinsic learning, adult education classes, are dominated by 'middle-class' persons. We have different cultures perceiving education and training according to different terms. This would suggest that, unless lifelong learning is just going to reinforce existing social divisions, it will have to cross the divide between work and leisure. It will have to bridge the cultural and perceptual gaps that exist. How it does so is another question but it is arguable that a change in attitude at the level of the school might help if it abolished the arbitrary divide between work and play, the former being currently seen as serious, the latter frivolous and often confused with fun; in this respect the quote from Montaigne, with which Chapter 11 in the present volume opens, is most appropriate. Our postmodern world seems to strive to break down boundaries. The gaps between education and leisure, work and play, and work and non-work are just a few more to be tackled.

Conclusion

Lifelong learning, lifelong education, the learning society and the learning age have been high on the political agenda for over thirty years. They have built on a long heritage and an ever-increasing literature. Each of the terms can be best construed as a hurrah word. However, each can also mean whatever the interlocutor wishes it to mean. For the present UK government and its immediate predecessors, it means lifelong training. Quality of life, previously a key feature in lifelong learning, now seems to have faded from the discussion. 'Workers require lifelong learning' (*Times Higher Education Supplement* of 19 December 1997), 'Lifelong learning: they're making it work' (*The Independent* of 21 May 1998) and the whole thrust of *The Learning Age: A Renaissance for a New Britain* (DfEE 1998) demonstrate the direction that the rhetoric has taken. However, even in the versions from the 1970s, a number of potentially important elements were missing, namely emotion, moral development and spirituality. These are vaguely subsumed under quality of life but are never actually highlighted. It is almost as if humans were seen as not needing those very parts that are arguably what make them human.

Yet we stand at a moment in time when Western society has lost its old paradigms and, most importantly, lost a large measure of its faith in the future. In this respect, we have an occasion to define the goal of lifelong education in a manner not evident in the 1970s. We have the possibility of moving beyond the present confusion of the hurrah word, and the insecurity that is its undertone, towards placing humans and their feelings at the centre. Let us propose that the aim of lifelong education be to restore and to maintain hope. We can term this *conscientisation* if we wish but with this simple goal in mind we have at our disposal the means of developing a concept that not only hangs together but can be explained to our political masters and to the public at large in terms that are meaningful to them and that stand some chance of loosening purse-strings. Failure to do so will result in lifelong education continuing to be a political buzzword destined to mean whatever an orator wishes it to mean. Failure to actualise lifelong education will mean even more social stratification, more situations where those who have shall receive (in this case education and wealth) while those who have not must content themselves with the droppings from the rich man's table. Otherwise, the last words on lifelong learning will be those of Frank Coffield, who claims that Lifelong Learning died in 2003.

> She was all things to all people. The politicians loved her because in their hands she was so flexible, the practitioners loved her because they could do anything they liked in her name, and the researchers loved her because they made money recording her every twist and turn.
>
> (Coffield 2003: 5)

Suggested further reading

A good point to start in the lifelong learning debate is in Ranson (1998), which presents a wide-ranging series of essays and articles on the topic. *The Learning Age* (DfEE 1998) gives an insight into the manner in which a government interprets the idea. The adult learner is discussed in depth in Knowles (1998), and Tight (1996) offers clear and concise explanations of a number of terms used frequently in the lifelong learning debate. Glendinning (1985) is an interesting account of learning beyond retirement, an area that can only grow as the population ages.

References

Abbott, J. (1994) *Learning Makes Sense*. Letchworth: Education 2000.

Aronowitz, S. and Giroux, H. (1993) *Postmodern Education*. Minneapolis, MN: University of Minnesota Press.

Blackledge, D. and Hunt, B. (1985) *Sociological Interpretations of Education*. London: Routledge.

Claxton, G. (1990) *Teaching to Learn*. London: Cassell.

Coffield, F. (2003) 'Epitaph for the Big L', *Times Education Supplement*, 5 September, p. 5.

Committee on Distribution of Science and Art Grants (1896) *Science and Arts Grants: Report of the Committee Appointed to Inquire into their Distribution, in which is Included a Revised Edition of the Science and Art Directory Embodying the Recommendations of the Committee*. London: HMSO.

Co-operative College (2003) *Background*. Available at www.co-op.ac.uk.

Cropley, A. J. (1977) *Lifelong Education: A Psychological Analysis*. Oxford: Pergamon.

Cropley, A. J. (1979) 'Lifelong Learning: Issues and Questions', in Cropley, A. J. (ed.) *Lifelong Education: A Stocktaking*. Hamburg: UNESCO Institute of Education.

Dave, R. H. (1972) 'Foundations of Lifelong Education: Some Methodological Aspects', in Dave, R. H. (ed.) *Foundations of Lifelong Education*. Oxford: Pergamon.

De'Ath, C. (1972) 'Anthropological and Ecological Foundations of Lifelong Learning', in Dave, R. H. (ed.) *Foundations of Lifelong Education*. Oxford: Pergamon.

Delors, J., Al-Mufti, I., Amagi, I., Carneiro, R., Chung, F., Geremek, B., Gorham, W., Kornhauser, B., Manley, M., Padrón Quero, M., Savané, M.-A., Singh, K., Stavenhagen, R., Won Suhr, M., Nanzhao, Z. (1996) *Education – The Treasure Within*. Paris: UNESCO/HMSO.

DfEE (1996) *Lifetime Learning*. London: HMSO.

DfEE (1998) *The Learning Age: A Renaissance for a New Britain*. London: The Stationery Office.

Donnachie, I. (2003) 'Education in Robert Owen's New Society: The New Lanark Institute and Schools', in *The Encyclopedia of Informal Education*. Available at www.infed.org/thinkers/et-owen.htm (accessed 7 December 2007).

Duncan, R. (1999) 'A Critical History of the Workers' Educational Association in Scotland 1903–1993', in Crowther. J., Martin, I. and Shaw, M. (eds) *Popular Education and Social Movements in Scotland Today*. Leicester: NIACE.

Faure, E., Herrera, F., Kaddowa, A., Lopes, H., Petrovsky, A., Rahnema, M. and Ward, F. (1972) *Learning to Be: The World of Education Today and Tomorrow*. Paris: UNESCO.

Furter, P. (1999) *From Literacy to Cultural Development*. Northampton: Nene University College School of Education Occasional Paper.

Gelpi, E. (1979) *A Future for Lifelong Education*. Manchester: Manchester Monographs.

Glendinning, F. (ed.) (1985) *Educational Gerontology: International Perspectives*. London: Croom Helm.

Griffin, C. (1983) *Curriculum Theory in Adult and Lifelong Education*. Beckenham: Croom Helm.

d'Hainaut, L. and Lawton, D. (1981) 'The Sources of Content Reform Geared to Lifelong Education', in d'Hainaut, L. (coordinator) *Curricula and Lifelong Education – Education on the Move*. Paris: UNESCO.

Hall, V. (1994) *Further Education in the United Kingdom*. London: Collins Educational/Staff College.

Holyoake, G. J. (1907) *Self-Help by the People: The History of the Rochdale Pioneers*. London: Swan Sonnenschein.

Knapper, C. J. and Cropley, A. J. (1985) *Lifelong Learning and Higher Education*. London: Croom Helm.

Knowles, M. (1998) *The Adult Learner*. Houston, TX: Gulf Publishing.

Kreis, S. (2002) 'Robert Owen, 1771–1858'. Available at www.historyguide.org/intellect/owen. html.

Labour Party (1994) *Opening Doors to a Learning Society: A Policy Statement on Education*. London: Labour Party.

Lengrand, P. (1978) *An Introduction to Lifelong Education*. Paris: UNESCO.

Lengrand, P. (1979) 'Prospects of Lifelong Education', in Cropley, A. J. (ed.) *Lifelong Education: A Stocktaking*. Hamburg: UNESCO Institute of Education.

Lengrand, P. (1986) 'Introduction', in Lengrand, P. (ed.) *Areas of Learning Basic to Lifelong Learning*. Oxford: UNESCO/Pergamon.

Longworth, N. and Davies, W. K. (1996) *Lifelong Learning*. London: Kogan Page.

Margolin, J.-C. (1981) 'L'éducation au temps de la Contre-Réforme', in Vial, J. and Mialaret, G. (eds) *Histoire Mondiale de l'Education*. Paris: Presses universitaires de France.

Marsh, C. (2002) 'Mansbridge: A Life'. Available at http://www.wea.org.uk/pdf/Mansbridge.pdf.

Matheson, C. (2000) 'Education in Non-traditional Spaces', in Matheson, C. and Matheson, D. (eds) *Educational Issues in the Learning Age*. London: Continuum.

Owen, R. (1816) 'Address to the Inhabitants of New Lanark'. Available at www.robert-owen.com/quotes.htm.

Owen, R. [1835](1965) *A New View of Society and Report to the County of Lanark*, ed. V. A. C. Gatrell. Harmondsworth: Pelican.

Ranson, S. (ed.) (1998) *Inside the Learning*. London: Cassell.

Spartacus Educational (2002) 'George Cadbury'. Available at www.spartacus.schoolnet.co.uk/REcadbury.htm (accessed 23 September 2007).

Stoikov, V. (1975) *The Economics of Recurrent Education and Training*. Geneva: International Labour Office.

Tight, M. (1996) *Key Concepts in Adult Education and Training*. London: Routledge.

Vorhaus, J. (2002) 'Lifelong Learning and New Educational Order? A Review Article', *Journal of Philosophy of Education*. **36** (1), 119–129.

White, J. (1997) *Education and the End of Work*. London: Cassell.

16

What is educational research?

Changing perspectives

John Nisbet

> A repetition of this experiment with 16,000 or 18,000 more cases is needed before final conclusions should be stated.
>
> (Thorndike 1930)

> Case study is an umbrella term for a family of research methods having in common the decision to focus inquiry round a single instance.
>
> (Adelman *et al.* 1977)

> 'Oh, I can't stand those people,' he said, 'postmodernists or poststructuralists, or whatever they call themselves . . . They think there is no such thing as scientific proof and that science is only one interpretation of the world among others equally valid.'
>   'Well, isn't it?' I said.
>
> (Lodge 2001)

Introduction

These three quotations illustrate different ways in which the concept of educational research has been interpreted over the past century. This chapter reviews the history of educational research in Britain, showing how different styles of research have developed, linked with the function that research is expected to perform. A central theme is the growing acceptance of research in education, which paradoxically, it is suggested, may have had the effect of restricting its scope.

In the late nineteenth century, German scholars began to think in terms of a subject called 'experimental pedagogy', and this set a pattern that was to dominate research in education in the first half of the twentieth century. Educational research, they suggested, should follow the style of research in the physical sciences, using experiments with representative samples to establish fundamental psychological principles of learning and child development, which could then be applied to guide policy and reform practice. In the USA, this idea was taken up actively, particularly the concept of measurement through tests of mental ability and educational attainment. Educational research in Britain reflected both German and American influences in the early years. But a rather different interpretation of educational research developed in the course of the twentieth century. Instead of quantitative studies involving large numbers, mental measurement, standardised tests and statistical analysis, researchers began to use qualitative methods based on intensive case studies of small numbers and sometimes even of a single instance. Quantitative research aimed to produce generalisations: qualitative research gave insights and understanding of the processes in learning and teaching.

The 1960s and 1970s saw massive expansion of educational research. Increased funding led to a pressure for 'relevant' research – which some cynically interpret as limiting research to projects that fit established frames of thought. At the opposite extreme, postmodernist philosophy rejects outright the positivist assumptions in the concept of 'education as a science'. The major change of recent years, however, has been the acceptance of research as a natural and necessary element in educational development, and as an integral part in the professional development of teachers – though that is perhaps more an aspiration than a reality.

Education as a science

The second half of the nineteenth century saw striking advances in science and technology, and the scientific model came to be applied with growing success to medicine, engineering and psychology. Could education too be given a scientific base through research?

Traditionally, educational practice was based on tradition and authority, especially the authority of the Bible or of Aristotle or other classical writers: the validity of an idea was judged by the authority of its source. It was this way of thinking that was challenged in the eighteenth-century period known as the Enlightenment, when authority was replaced by rationality: the validity of an idea was to be judged on the basis of evidence. The concept of basing educational practice on empirical research was taken up in the later years of the nineteenth century: in England in 1877, Francis Galton asserted to the British Association for the Advancement of Science, 'It is now possible to inquire by exact measurement into certain fundamental aspects of mind'; and in Scotland in 1879, Alexander Bain published a treatise with the title *Education as a Science*. But the main thrust of this idea came in Germany. Since philosophers like Kant had dismissed the idea that the mind could be measured, from the 1860s on scholars such as Wundt, Fechner and Helmholtz studied aspects of mental activity that *could* be measured

– reaction time, sensory discrimination, aspects of sensation and perception, and fatigue – studying the senses as an entry to the workings of the mind.

By the first decade of the twentieth century, enough experimental work had been done to enable publication of the first educational research textbooks in Germany and Switzerland, and the influence of textbooks is to define the boundaries and content of a discipline. Because the experimental work described in these early texts had their origin in German laboratories, their basis was largely in psychology and physiology: for example, Wilhelm Lay's *Experimental Didactics: Its Foundations, with Some Considerations of Muscle Sense, Will and Action* (1903); and *Child Psychology and Experimental Pedagogy* (1911) by Edouard Claparède in Geneva. The Introduction to Claparède's text begins:

> That pedagogy ought to be based upon the knowledge of the child, as horticulture is based upon the knowledge of plants, would seem to be an elementary truth. It is, nevertheless, entirely unrecognised by most teachers and nearly all educational authorities.

In USA, the Child Study movement, which was made popular worldwide by Stanley Hall in the 1890s, encouraged parents to make systematic observation and recording of their children's development. Cattell's article 'Mental Tests and Measurement' (1890), and Thorndike's test scales from 1904 onwards established the measurement approach, which dominated educational research in the USA for much of the twentieth century.

Tests and measurements in the USA

American histories of educational research tend to neglect European sources, dating the start of research proper in 1897, when an American researcher, Rice, published the results of his investigations into spelling. He compared class average scores in a spelling test with the amount of time given to spelling in the classroom and found a zero relationship, thus proving 'the futility of the spelling grind', the title of his 1897 paper. Initially, European influence was strong because many American scholars travelled to Germany for their doctoral studies. For example, a major American text in this field, Whipple's *Manual of Mental and Physical Tests*, first published in 1910, reflects in its coverage the influence of Galton (measuring diameter and girth of skull, motor control, strength of grip) and the early German scholars (sensory discrimination, mirror drawing, memory, suggestion), but it also included (at the end) examples from the burgeoning test movement at that time, with tests of reading, arithmetic and spelling.

The leading figure in measurement in these early days was Thorndike, whose doctoral thesis was on learning in animals. Travers (1978) relates how at Harvard Thorndike had to keep his animals in the basement of his professor's house (much to the delight of his children); but the story goes that when Thorndike moved to Columbia University there was no room for the animals and so he turned to research on children instead. Whatever the truth of that, he carried over the laboratory scientist role, that of experimentally exploring basic 'laws of learning', such as the law of effect, later called reinforcement (the importance of reward in learning) and transfer of training (learning in one context is generalised to other contexts – such as learning Latin as a training in logical reasoning – only if common elements are stressed). Thorndike's main contribution, however, was in the construction of tests: together with colleagues, he produced the first standardised attainment tests in 1908, and a handwriting scale in 1909, followed by many others. In 1918, an American *Yearbook* listed 109 standardised tests that were in current use in schools: nearly 900,000 copies of one popular test were used in 1917, and several others had sales of over 100,000 each (Monroe 1918).

The idea of improving the efficiency of teaching by setting standards based on tests seems to recur regularly through the century. The 1908 report of the US Commissioner of Education linked efficiency with testing, and his 1910 report proposed setting standards in terms of test performance. Across the USA Boards of Education began to set up 'Bureaus of Educational Research' (sometimes called 'Bureau of Research and Efficiency'). By 1926, there were 105 such bureaus across the country. But gradually they were abandoned, as they tended to be preoccupied with gathering statistics on test scores with which nothing was done (Nifenecker 1918). Travers' verdict on this short-lived movement was that it 'did little for education, neither clarifying the concept of effectiveness nor making schools more efficient . . . it measured, but did not analyse' (1983: 507).

Research begins to take root

In other countries too, individual scholars were conducting research inquiries and publishing their findings in newly established journals. A fourth edition of Claparède's textbook mentioned above, originally in French and now translated into English, German, Italian, Spanish and Russian, included a new chapter outlining the growth of experimental pedagogy in England, France, Germany, Belgium, Holland and twelve other countries. A feature of the research at this time is that it dealt with issues which are still of interest today; examples from Claparède's text are:

Before learning anything, it is necessary to learn how to learn.

(1911: 57)

How far are the various mental functions independent of each other . . . how far do they reciprocally influence each other? (correlation, factor analysis).

(p. 61)

When we educate a certain function, are we acting upon others at the same time? (transfer of training).

(p. 64)

In England in 1894, an Office of Special Inquiries and Reports had been set up, and its Director, Michael Sadler, pressed the Board of Education (as the equivalent of the Ministry was then called) to establish a national research council, unsuccessfully. Taylor (1972: 4) records an exchange of minutes between Sadler and the Board's Secretary, Morant, which has a surprisingly contemporary ring. Sadler wrote:

> In order that the scientific work of educational inquiry may be searching and fruitful, it must be intellectually independent. Those engaged in it must be free to state whatever they believe to be true, apart from preconsiderations as to what may at the time be thought administratively convenient.

Morant replied in terms that were to be echoed in 1970 by Thatcher and in 1971 in the Rothschild Report:

> It cannot be too clearly impressed upon you that the work of the Office of Special Inquiries and Reports is done and must continue to be done, for the benefit of the Board, at the instance of the Board, and under the direction of the Board

– and Sadler resigned. However, London County Council had its own Inspectors of Schools, and a group of these inspectors carried out numerous experiments and surveys and constructed new tests – especially Winch, who published two books and thirty-eight papers, mostly in American journals, and Ballard, who developed a one-minute reading test standardised on over 22,000 children. (Burt, the most famous of this group, was not appointed until 1915, when he was given explicit responsibility for research.)

In Scotland, Rusk published his *Introduction to Experimental Education* in 1913, acknowledging his debt to Meumann's 1907 text. In 1918 the Educational Institute of Scotland (the teachers' union) set up a Committee on Research, with Boyd as Chair; and Boyd introduced a school-based type of research, with the aim (fifty years before the teacher-researcher movement) of getting teachers actively involved in their own research.

In France, Binet and Simon were studying how to identify mentally handicapped children (as distinct from those educationally backward), and from their work they developed an individual test of intelligence in 1905, which was frequently revised and improved.

In the 1930s in the USA, Terman and Merrill revised the Binet–Simon text extensively to produce a standard version used for the next thirty years. With these tests came a recognition of the wide range of individual differences among children, and the aim of matching instruction to the level of intelligence of the children.

Educational research acquires an identity – and a limited role

By the 1930s, educational research had established a certain degree of respectability and acceptance – 'a certain degree' only, because very few teachers in schools or educational administrators regarded it seriously. Educational research journals grew in number and size, though their readership was almost exclusively members of the academic societies that produced them. Universities set up Departments of Education, but (except in Scotland) these were primarily concerned with teacher training; in England, the Universities of London, Birmingham and Manchester combined this with an active research programme. In 1928 in Scotland, the Educational Institute of Scotland and the Association of Directors of Education had set up the Scottish Council for Research in Education (SCRE), the first such organisation in Europe, but the Scottish Education Department declined to contribute and, as records show (Wake 1984), was wholly sceptical of its value. For the next thirty years, with a staff of only a part-time director and a secretary, SCRE produced a series of significant research publications based largely on the work of academic staff in colleges and universities, but these remained virtually unknown among teachers.

Similar developments were occurring in other European countries as well as in USA, New Zealand and Australia. In Sweden, for example, Torsten Husén and Kjell Harnqvist were leading figures in the empirical, psychologically oriented research that influenced Swedish educational policy in the 1950s and 1960s. Institutes for Educational Research were established in many countries (Norway 1935, Denmark 1954, Finland 1954, the Netherlands 1965).

However, the common attitude to research at this stage in the century was that it was an academic study out of touch with 'real' problems. In fact, important groundwork was done on reading and other elements of the primary school curriculum, but in Europe the secondary school curriculum remained the province of subject specialists. The unreliability of the examination system was also demonstrated in the research of this period, but that tradition was too well established to be affected by mere research evidence. The 'scientific' approach in the early history of educational research, together with its increasing reliance on the sophisticated statistical methods that were being introduced, resulted in educational research being regarded as a specialist activity, 'done by those *outside* the classroom for the benefit of those *outside* the classroom' (Nixon 1981), requiring extended training (much of it statistical and psychological) and with the function of producing theoretical principles to guide teachers and policy-makers.

Until about the 1960s, research was essentially a small-back-room activity. Researchers may have dreamed about reforming the world of education, but it was a long-term aspiration, to be achieved by patient scholarship. There was little expectation that policy-makers, administrators or teachers would be much influenced by, or even interested in, research.

(Nisbet 1984: 3)

This now began to change as the scale of educational research grew and the number of researchers in universities and in specialised units increased dramatically. The role of being the intelligence in the educational system was quite an attractive one for the researchers, even if the system still had only grudging acceptance of the intelligence. By mid-century, researchers had begun to establish this technocratic alliance with the power blocks in education (thus further earning the suspicion of teachers). The 11+ examination, for example, used to select a minority of the year-group for grammar school, relied on standardised tests and statistical analysis that had been validated by research; in this way (though few would have acknowledged it until the mid-1950s) research was used to justify selection as the instrument of a structured society.

Thus, for the researchers, the price of acceptance was the demand that research (or at least, funded research) should be 'relevant'. Relegating research to this instrumental role carries risks: of trivialising, in pursuing volatile educational fashions; of being restrictive, in limiting research within the constraints of existing policy frameworks; of being potentially divisive, creating an élite group of researchers in alliance with authority; and of being ultimately damaging, in that it can leave the researchers wholly dependent on their powerful partner.

This chapter is concerned primarily with experimental research, and not with philosophical or historical research, or to the extensive individual non-funded scholarship in universities – although some of the points apply equally to these fields. Researchers who choose an unpopular or unfashionable line of inquiry are liable to find that they receive no grants and that their papers are not accepted by journals, or, if published, are not widely read or quoted. This restrictive influence of the established orthodoxy is to be found in all science. But the decade of the 1960s in education was to some extent an exception.

The 1960s and 1970s: the new look

The decade of the 1960s was a period of upheaval: it began with major reviews of the educational systems in Britain and major investment in research in the USA to tackle the problem of social disadvantage, and ended with student revolt in France and across the world. Educational research also experienced challenge to its traditional practice.

Rather unexpectedly (at least for the researchers) national governments began to set aside substantial funds for research in education. Between 1964 and 1969, expenditure on educational research in Britain multiplied tenfold; in the USA, expenditure doubled in each year from 1964 through to 1967. An Educational

Research Board was appointed within the Social Science Research Council with funds for projects throughout Britain, and in the Scottish Education Department a Research and Intelligence Unit initiated research programmes and funded research in universities and colleges. Major UK reviews of education were commissioned in these years, Plowden on primary education, Newsom on secondary education and Robbins on higher education, and each of these was accompanied by a substantial research and survey programme. It may be argued that, for the most part, the research findings from these programmes were used to strengthen the case for recommendations that the committee had already reached. This is a limited but wholly valid interpretation of the term, 'research-based policy'. In the absence of adequate evidence, Plowden was frankly prepared to proceed in any case:

> The research evidence so far available is both too sparse and too heavily weighted by studies of special groups of children to be decisively in favour of nursery education for all. We rely, therefore, on the overwhelming evidence of experienced educators.
>
> (DES 1967: para. 303)

It was in these years that educational research began to emerge out of the shadow of the contributory disciplines of psychology and sociology and to develop its own conceptual frameworks, if not actual evidence-based theories. At the same time, a radical change questioned the established experimental style of quantitative statistical research in education. By the 1970s researchers were arguing that qualitative case studies exploring issues in depth with relatively small numbers were more appropriate in education. Quantitative research could show that there were wide ranges of individual differences in every kind of measure but was seldom able to explain the meaning or implications of the findings for everyday contexts: its aim was generalisation for the purposes of prediction and management. Qualitative research, in contrast, aimed at understanding and insight into the complexities of learning and human behaviour (see Stenhouse 1981).

The practice of measurement was also questioned. In-depth interviews were the basis of what are variously called ethnographic, hermeneutic or phenomenological methods. These approach a topic from the perspective of the interviewee rather than within a framework decided in advance by the researcher. Phenomenography (Entwistle 1981) has its roots in the philosophy of phenomenology, which opposes the positivism or naturalism inherent in contemporary science and technology – the standard scientific approach to knowledge by formulating hypotheses and designing experimental procedures to test these – on the grounds that this finds (or negates) only what the researcher is looking for, whereas the open-ended methods of phenomenography produce data for formulating new interpretive constructs. This approach focuses on awareness or 'encountering', and accepts the role of description in how we perceive situations and how we interpret or 'understand' them. Thus, from the interview transcripts, the researcher derives interpretive categories: for example, the way students speak about their reading and understanding leads to the categorisation of 'deep' and 'surface' learning. Recognising the subjectivity involved, the interpretation must be fully supported by excerpts from what has been said.

Two related innovations about this time introduced new perceptions of educational research, action research and the teacher-researcher movement. Following the Plowden Report in 1967, which had proposed 'positive discrimination' for schools in areas of social deprivation, a large-scale programme of five projects in England and one in Scotland was launched in that year, called the Educational Priority Areas (or EPA) projects, which aimed to combine action to improve conditions with research to identify how best to achieve this. The report, *Educational Priority* (1972), defines this 'novel type of research . . . [as] small-scale intervention in the functioning of the real world . . . and the close examination of the effects of such interventions' (p. 165). Action and research have different aims and values:

> Research values concepts such as precision, control, replication and attempts to generalise from the observation of specific events. Administrative action . . . translates generalisation into specific instances.
>
> (ibid.)

But in action research those who initiate action also conduct research that directs actions in a developing programme of reform.

Nixon, in *A Teacher's Guide to Action Research* (1981), applies this to the concept of the 'teacher-researcher': 'The case for action research may be stated briefly. By investigating and reflecting upon their own practice teachers may increase their understanding of the classroom' (p. 6).

The teacher-researcher concept was developed in another major project begun in 1967, the Schools Council Humanities Project directed by Stenhouse. The Humanities Project produced materials for the discussion of controversial issues (such as racial prejudice), but an integral part was evaluation by the teachers themselves both to define the research problem and to initiate research to guide subsequent action.

> [This] marks a radical departure from the traditionalist view of research as a specialist activity, the results of which teachers apply rather than create. . . The teacher as a researcher movement, with its focus on the practical educational problems arising from particular situations, and with the aim of illuminating such situations for those involved, offers an alternative.
>
> (Elliott 1981: 1)

The teacher-researcher movement was taken up and given support by both BERA and SERA (the British and the Scottish Educational Research Associations), but it remained a minority group with relatively little published output. In recent years the concept has been incorporated in professional development, and more widely in networking systems, with research now seen as a professional activity for teachers as well as (or instead of) for specialist researchers.

The postmodernist movement goes much further than this in challenging the instrumental view of research, arguing that reality is a social construction.

> Postmodernism abandons the enlightenment ambitions of unity, certainty and predictability, because many aspects of life are ephemeral, if not completely unpredictable. . . . The metaphor of chaos questions progressive betterment, questions the idea that the quality of life has improved. It seeks to understand, but not to reconcile, divisions. . . . Those who write from a postmodern perspective tend to question the value of rationality, to reject grand theory, to favour local knowledge over systemic understanding, to eschew large-scale studies, and to view the world as an indeterminate place beyond coherent description. . . . [It is] a requiem for the passing of the modernist quest for certainty, predictability, and the hoped-for advancement of knowledge and society-at-large.
>
> (Constas 1998)

This extreme standpoint takes us back to the nineteenth-century arguments about whether scientific procedures can be fruitfully applied in the field of educational inquiry. At least, it requires us to examine more thoughtfully the positivist assumption that there are 'correct' answers to educational issues, which can be discovered by experiment and observation, that there is a reality that may not be immediately obvious but can eventually be discovered (or uncovered) by research if enough effort is put into it.

These were fundamental changes in our perception of what educational research is and what its function should be. Many still hold to the older interpretation, in which the function of research is *instrumental*, that is, it is of value in so far as it can be used to solve problems or guide policy. Empirical research of this kind has been fuelled by the need for predictability. Policy-makers, said Stenhouse (1981) 'seek the reassurance of certainty to ameliorate the agony of responsibility'. The perspective of the 'new look' was quite different. At the conclusion of the 1972 EPA report, Halsey wrote:

> The co-operation of research in policy formation has to develop 'organically' rather than 'mechanically'. Action research is unlikely ever to yield neat and definite prescriptions from field-tested plans. What it offers is an aid to intelligent decision-making, not a substitute for it. Research brings relevant information rather than uniquely exclusive conclusions.
>
> (1972: 178–179)

There is a variety of acceptable forms of research, which corresponds to the variety of functions that research is seen to perform: to provide answers to problems, to guide policy, to provide insights and understanding, to establish fundamental principles of learning. Can these different styles of research co-exist? They must, for, if they are treated as separate, the academic becomes marginal and the practical is superficial.

But there is an inherent danger when we try to integrate the academic with the practical. Practical forms of research, linked to issues arising in current policy and provision, will tend to be given priority over theoretical and long-term studies, which often prove eventually more important in that they bring about fundamental changes of attitude and understanding. Today the modern state uses research as an integral instrument of government. If as researchers we go along with the demands of immediate policy issues, we have access to funds and influence – but at a price. For this is a Faustian bargain, as it risks losing autonomy and missing out on basic issues.

Underlying this tension between the applied and the theoretical approaches to research, there is a more fundamental contrast, illustrated by the Greek historian Thucydides. He complained that, among his contemporaries, the ability to understand a question from all sides meant that one was totally unfit for action. There is a sense that worthwhile research must start from a position of uncertainty, and uncertainty is difficult to reconcile with action and decision. Two contemporary European scholars, Husén and Kogan (1984), relate this to the issue of government funding of research in these terms:

> Can national authorities sponsor the generation of uncertainty? Policy makers foreclose on issues . . . . Social science can keep open the space.

What has been described so far is the trend in the later decades of the twentieth century to move away from the experimental paradigm, whether through qualitative case studies, action research, the teacher-researcher movement or (at the extreme) postmodernism. At the same time, however, a quite different trend can be seen in the increasing recognition of educational research as an integral element in policy and practice. Where research is being funded by government or public authorities, there is an expectation (or even a demand) that research should be oriented to the requirements of the 'users' or 'consumers' of research. The concept of 'users' is characteristic, in implying that research is done in one place by one group, and then transferred to another group in another place to be put to use. The terms, 'users' and 'consumers', implicitly accept an *instrumental* function for research in education. On this view, good research is research that can be used, or that identifies 'What works', the title of a best-selling American book on current research. Evaluation and data-gathering studies are more likely to attract funding than theoretical analyses that aim at insights into problems, the *enlightenment* function of research. The emergence of this very different trend is best illustrated by events in Britain from 1970 on.

As government funding for research increased, the inevitable consequence was a demand by ministers for a greater say in how the funds were to be spent. Margaret Thatcher, then Secretary of State for Education and Science, declared in a speech to the National Foundation for Educational Research in 1970:

> There was clearly only one direction that the Department's research policy could sensibly take. It had to move from a basis of patronage – the rather passive support of ideas which were essentially other people's, related to problems which were often of other people's choosing – to a basis of commission. This meant the active initiation of work by the Department on problems of its own choosing, within a timetable and procedure which were relevant to its needs.

This view was quickly taken up in a review of government research funding in 1971 by Lord Rothschild, who produced the crude 'customer–contractor principle': the customer (government department) says what s/he wants; the contractor (researcher) does it (if s/he can); and the customer pays. A response from the Social Science Research Council at the time questioned whether following the 'customer's' priorities was best for the advancement of knowledge:

> It is not so much a matter of an ordered hierarchy of priorities, as a process of grasping at opportunities presented by an almost accidental coagulation of interest among a group of able research workers around a chosen problem in order to shift a frontier of knowledge forward.

The words 'an almost accidental coagulation of interest' are a good description of what happens in research but, in the spirit of the times, they were hardly likely to persuade. Later, however, there has been fuller recognition of the importance of theoretical studies that contribute to the underlying disciplines in education – in Britain, especially in programmes such as the Teaching and Learning Research Programme supported by the Economic and Social Research Council (ESRC). Even the Minister for Education, David Blunkett, in a speech to the Council of ESRC in February 2000, expressed the point in words that could never have been accepted twenty years earlier:

> There must be a place for the fundamental 'blue skies' research which thinks the unthinkable. We need researchers who can challenge fundamental assumptions and orthodoxies, and this may well have big policy effects much further down the road.

The nature and function of research in education

This review of the historical development of educational research has not dealt with the actual research topics that were favoured at different times: in the early stages, psychological studies of transfer of training and of fatigue in learning; then, the use of tests in selection and the reliability of examinations; in mid-century, sociological aspects such as the influence of home environment; and later a much richer variety of topics, as different styles of research came to be accepted. Instead, the chapter has focused on the concept of research in education – what it is, how it was done and what its function should be – showing how this concept has changed over the past 100 years. At the risk of oversimplification, this can be portrayed as a series of phases, each with different perceptions of research and different implications for the contribution that research may make to education.

1   Initially, research was seen as primarily an academic activity: its contribution to school practice and policy issues was essentially theoretical and long-term.

2   Later, research came to be viewed as the work of experts and specialists, to be used, where appropriate, by teachers and administrators; the profitable business of test construction (involving complex statistical procedures) was a feature of this period.

3   From the 1960s on, educational research came to be accepted as a discipline in its own right, with its own distinctive procedures and literature; a greatly expanded research activity has extended to cover a wide range of issues.

This third phase has brought research into closer partnership with policy and practice, though in differing ways. Increased funding has given those who commission research a claim to greater say in the design, and sometimes also in the management, of a project and the dissemination of findings. At the same time, the teacher-researcher movement, which initially aimed to support teachers in carrying out research studies themselves, has developed into something more fundamental: a view of research as a key element in a professional approach, a mode of working to be adopted by all in facing up to problems, whether in policy-making or in school-based projects to pilot new curriculum initiatives. In summary, the role of researcher has moved from academic theorist in phase 1, through expert consultant in phase 2, to reflective practitioner in phase 3.

We are now perhaps moving into a fourth phase, in which research has an even more important role, the concept of education as an evidence-based profession. Large-scale projects, centrally funded, now accompany policy initiatives, though we have yet to see how far they actually influence development and practice.

The broadened interpretation of research is the main achievement of recent years: in a word, research has become accessible. Primary school children working on their projects speak of doing research, and we can only hope that they do not subsequently come to regard research as a remote and inaccessible style of working limited to a small élite of specialists. However, it would be wrong to impose a dimension of value on the three phases outlined above: they are essentially a dimension of involvement. All three approaches to researching have their place. There are still some who hold that the underlying contribution of the academic theorist is in the long term the most influential and the most important. Also the need for specialist expertise, and for research that is rigorous and highly skilled, must be acknowledged, for there is a danger of devaluing research if it is too lightly treated as something that anyone can do. A Senior Chief Inspector in England in 1976 complained:

> People say they have done some research when they really mean they have stopped to think for three minutes.
>
> (Nisbet and Broadfoot 1980: 2)

But research has become part of every professional role today, and in education one task of professional development is to weave a research element into the expertise of teachers, leading them to adopt at a personal level the self-questioning approach that leads to reflection and understanding, and from there into action.

Suggested further reading

To get a feeling for the early history of educational research, the best method is to browse in the basement of a university library through the first issues of education journals such as the *Journal of Experimental Pedagogy* (1911), which became the *British Journal of Educational Psychology* in 1931. The American history is told by R. M. W. Travers in chapter 1 of the fourth edition of *An Introduction to Educational Research* (1978). A short history of educational research in Europe by G. de Landsheere is reprinted as chapter 1 of *Educational Research: Current Issues,* edited by M. Hammersley (1993), an Open University textbook that includes thirteen other journal reprints on developments throughout the twentieth century. J. Ruddock and D. McIntyre, *Challenges for Educational Research* (1998), covers a range of current issues in educational research, summarised in the *Report of a BERA Colloquium, Educational Policy and Research* (British Educational Research Association 2003). If you wish to explore phenomenology or postmodernism, try www.phenomenology.org or www.as.ua.edu/ant/Faculty/murphy/436/pomo.htm or investigate the Blackwell Companions series of books on philosophy.

References

Adelman, C., Jenkins, D. and Kemmis, S. (1977) 'Re-thinking Case Study: Notes from the Second Cambridge Conference', *Cambridge Journal of Education.* **6**, 139–150.

Bain, A. (1879) *Education as a Science.* London: Kegan, Trench & Trubner.

British Educational Research Association (2003) *Report of a BERA Colloquium, Educational Policy and Research.* Macclesfield: British Educational Research Association.

Cattell, J. M. (1890) 'Mental Tests and Measurement', *Mind.* **15**, 373–381.

Claparède, E. (1911) *Child Psychology and Experimental Pedagogy,* 4th edn, English translation. London: Edward Arnold.

Constas, M. (1998) 'The Changing Nature of Educational Research and a Critique of Postmodernism', *Educational Researcher*. **27** (2), 26–32.

Department of Education and Science (DES) (1967) *Children and their Primary Schools* (the Plowden Report). London: HMSO.

Elliott, J. (1981) 'Foreword', in Nixon, J. *A Teachers' Guide to Action Research: Evaluation, Enquiry and Development in the Classroom.* London: Grant McIntyre.

Entwistle, N. (1981) *Styles of Learning and Teaching.* Chichester: Wiley.

Halsey, A. H. (1972) *Educational Priority*, Vol. 1. London: HMSO.

Hammersley, M. (ed.) (1993) *Educational Research: Current Issues.* Buckingham: Open University Press.

Husén, T. and Kogan, M. (eds) (1984) *Educational Research and Policy: How do they Relate?* Oxford: Pergamon Press.

Lay, W. (1903) *Experimental Didactics: Its Foundations with Some Considerations of Muscle Sense, Will and Action.* Leipzig: O. Nemnich.

Lodge, D. (2001) *Thinks. . .* London: Secker & Warburg.

Monroe, W. S. (1918) 'Existing Tests and Standards', in *The 17th Yearbook of the National Society for the Study of Education* (Part 2). Bloomington, IL: Public School Publishing Co.

Nifenecker, E. A. (1918) 'Bureaus of Research in City School Systems', in *The 17th Yearbook of the National Society for the Study of Education* (Part 2). Bloomington, IL: Public School Publishing Co.

Nisbet, J. (1984) 'The Changing Scene', in Dockrell, W. B. (ed.) *An Attitude of Mind: 25 Years of Educational Research in Scotland.* Edinburgh: Scottish Council for Research in Education.

Nisbet, J. and Broadfoot, P. (1980) *The Impact of Research on Policy and Practice in Education.* Aberdeen: Aberdeen University Press.

Nixon, J. (1981) *A Teachers' Guide to Action Research: Evaluation, Enquiry and Development in the Classroom.* London: Grant McIntyre.

Rice, J. M. (1897) 'The Futility of the Spelling Grind', *Forum.* **23**, 163–172.

Rothschild Report (1971) *A Framework for Government Research and Development.* London: HMSO.

Ruddock, J. and McIntyre, D. (1998) *Challenges for Educational Research.* London: Paul Chapman.

Rusk, R. R. (1913) *Introduction to Experimental Education.* London: Longmans Green.

Stenhouse, L. (1981) 'What Counts as Educational Research?', *British Journal of Educational Studies.* **29**, 103–114.

Taylor, W. (1972) 'Retrospect and Prospect in Educational Research', *Educational Research.* **15**, 3–7.

Thatcher, M. (1970) Speech to the National Foundation for Educational Research, London. Quoted in *The Guardian*, 2 December.

Thorndike, E. L. (1930) Fictitious quotation in Wodehouse, H. 'Discernment of the Disciplinary Value of Studies', *British Journal of Educational Psychology.* **1** (1), 41–47.

Travers, R. M. W. (1978) *An Introduction to Educational Research*, 4th edn. New York: Collier Macmillan Publishers.

Travers, R. M. W. (1983) *How Research Has Changed American Schools.* Kalamazoo, MI: Collier Macmillan.

Wake, R. (1984) *Events Antecedent to the Founding of the Scottish Council for Research in Education.* MEd thesis, University of Edinburgh.

Whipple, G. M. (1910) *Manual of Mental and Physical Tests.* Baltimore, MD: Warwick & York.

17

Afterword

Now that I have read about education, how do I write about it?

David Matheson

Introduction

EACH CHAPTER IN THIS book has introduced you to a different aspect of education, with of course some overlap between certain of the chapters. However, reading about the topic is only part of the academic journey. Another, very important, part consists of writing about it. What follows aims to show you how to research an academic essay, how to structure it and then how to write it. The chapter ends with a section on argumentation and the various errors one can make (which are often employed by mistake, carelessly or in an attempt to argue in a less than rigorous manner). The same tools can of course be used to research and write an oral presentation, although there you will have to give some attention to visual aids such as PowerPoint.

This chapter is the fruit of helping students over many years and seeing where they can run into problems in writing essays. It is also the fruit of my own experience of writing and of developing as a writer, of remembering where I have had difficulties and how I resolved them. There is of course no such thing as a recipe for an essay. Every essay is (or should be) unique. For this reason, what I am offering here is guidance, which, like everything else in this book, you should examine critically. Decide for yourself whether it makes sense. Does the advice offered here agree with your experience? Are the arguments sound? If so, why? If not, why not? When you ask these questions and others like them, you are beginning the journey towards academic creation: you are analysing the prose that is before you. This is something you always have to do in academic writing and it is analysis that makes academic writing stand out from mere description.[1]

---

[1] Description is always necessary but it is inappropriate for academic writing to consist only of that.

Essay-writing: some pointers

This section is in two parts: part 1 deals with the build-up to writing the essay and gives guidance on carrying out research. Part 2 deals with what to do when you come to put pen to paper or fingers to keyboard. You may very well find some of the statements blindingly obvious. However, sometimes even the most obvious needs to be said since things sometimes only *become* blindingly obvious when they are said.

Part 1 Preparing the ground

And the question is . . .

IF YOU ARE TACKLING A SET QUESTION

Read the question carefully and thoroughly and make sure that you understand what is being asked of you. It is all too common for students to write very good essays that do not tackle the question as posed. Answer the question as it is actually asked, not as you think it ought to have been asked.

IF YOU ARE SETTING YOUR OWN QUESTION

Read the module/course guide very carefully and ensure that your proposed question is relevant to what you are meant to be doing. Seek advice from your tutor. Read the assessment criteria for the essay to see what you will be judged against. At the end of writing each draft, look back and check whether you have answered your question. If you have not, depending on how your course is organised, you may be able to change the question so that it fits the essay.

Plan ahead

This means several things. First, plan when you are going to start work on your research for the essay. Plan when you are going to write that all-important first draft. Plan when you are going to revise your essay. Plan when you are going to have the final draft ready. Perhaps most importantly: *plan what you are going to put in the essay.* An essay, like all creative writing, has to have a beginning, a middle and an end.

> The White Rabbit put on his spectacles. 'Where shall I begin, please your Majesty?' he asked. 'Begin at the beginning,' the King said, very gravely, 'and go on till you come to the end: then stop.'
>
> (Carroll 1886: chapter XII)

The beginning lays out what you are going to say; the middle says it; the end tells the reader what you have said, what conclusions you have drawn. Put another way, the beginning sets the context, the middle gives the content and the end gives closure. Imagine reading a story that started in the middle and assumed that you knew all the characters; or a story that stopped dead, with no ending.[2] Neither of these is very satisfying. Your essay is, in effect, a story; it needs a narrative structure and it needs to take the reader from one place to another. This is why your plan needs to show clearly where you are starting and where you are finishing. But do remember that, at this stage, it is a plan. Nothing more. It is there to remind you of what you are going to write and it lets you see if you have a clear idea of where you are trying to go and how you will know when you get there. But remember: a plan is not carved in tablets of stone. A plan is just what it says it is. It is a series of ideas that you believe, at the time of writing them, will lead to a successful and satisfying essay. If you find that a part of your plan becomes redundant then jettison it.

Plans can easily become over-ambitious and I personally have seen essay plans that would have taken a tome the size of *War and Peace* to realise, so strive to keep the plan short and workable. Your plan does not commit you to anything. What it does is to give your thoughts a focus and a direction which show a promising avenue to follow. You can modify it at any time during the writing process.

Whatever the final size and shape of your plan, make sure that it flows logically from one point on to the next.

It can help to discuss the essay topic with a friend, just to see if you both have the same understanding of the question.

Research for an essay is critical

Even if your thoughts are entirely original then you lend credibility to them by showing how they are distinguished from previous writings.

Research can open your mind to possibilities that you have not yet considered. *But* do make sure you note your findings so that you can use the most salient parts in the actual writing of your essay. There are many methods for doing this. Popular with adult learners especially is underlining lines of text. This is not recommended for library books. In fact, it is to be seriously discouraged. Annotating library texts can make them unreadable for other library users and usually renders them useless for blind and partially sighted users who rely on scanners and text recognition software.

Putting flags on especially relevant pages is also popular but note on the flag the

---

[2] To get the idea, take any fairy story and imagine what it would be like to read it to a child but without 'Once upon a time . . .' Then imagine what it would be like without the ending. In either case, the story is lost and the person to whom you are reading the story is left a bit befuddled.

page number and what it was on the page that was so appealing. In this way, if you drop the book and your flags fall out then all is not lost and also you have a rapid means of finding out again what it was that interested you in the first place.

My preferred method used to be to make jottings in a notebook. This is more time-consuming than the other two methods listed but it had, for me, the crucial advantage of still being available to me when the book had gone back to the library (I still have occasion to use notes that I made over two decades ago). My jottings always started with the full bibliographical data on the book and then I would use either direct quotes (if they are fairly short) or non-quotes (i.e. paraphrasing the gist of what the writer has said). It is essential to note the page number, even for indirect quotes, just in case you ever need to see the setting for your quotation.

Nowadays I prefer to take my notes directly onto a computer, but using the same method as I did with my old notebooks. Advantages are manifest, such as not having to rewrite everything, but there are negatives that are easily overlooked: working from notes already word-processed lends itself to over-use of cutting and pasting and with this comes the real danger of not actually reading precisely what you are copying. Rather one may read what one *thinks* one is copying, rather than what is actually on the page.

Of course, if you are sufficiently clued up then you may wish to use a bibliographical referencing program such as *Endnote* or *Reference Manager*. The principal use of these programs comes when one has to use the same source material for different outputs and these outputs require different forms of referencing. Endnote and Reference Manager are worth trying out but be warned: there are those who swear by such programs and those who swear at them.

Every method has its good points and bad points and there are certainly others I have not listed. Nonetheless it is critical that you find a method of retaining your research findings so that you can refer to them again at a later date.

Deciding which books to read is a sticky problem

If you can get the books on the reading list then fine. Otherwise, take a look at the ones on the library shelf that are to either side of where your chosen book ought to be. Think creatively. Think laterally (read Edward de Bono's *Lateral Thinking!*). Think around the topic. Use the index at the back of books. Check the table of contents. Use the reference list(s) in the book. These may seem like statements of the obvious but I continue to be amazed at how many people I encounter who do not do them.

Using the Web

With the unbelievable amount of material available online, it is easy to be tempted into viewing the Web as being all one needs for academic writing. Be aware that, although there is much of great value on the Web (e.g. online refereed journals and well-established databases) there is also much that is nonsense. There are no controls whatever on material that gets on to the Web so there may be no indication of the academic validity of anything you may find there. A classic example of this is Wikipedia,[3] whose quality ranges enormously. But all the better Wikipedia articles are referenced, which means that you have other, perhaps peer-reviewed, sources to check. Use these rather than the Wikipedia entry itself.

Check the journals

Academic journals will give you material that is much more up to date than books tend to. *But* don't assume that just because something is old it is useless. Neither should you assume that newness means value. There is old nonsense and new nonsense. All of it is still nonsense. Equally there are texts dating back sometimes thousands of years (such as those of Plato and Aristotle) that are relevant and valuable in many education essays. Just that the text is old tells you nothing of the relevancy of the writing.

Part 2 Writing the essay

How to avoid getting low marks

POOR EXPRESSION AND VAGUENESS

Poor expression and vagueness are invariably the result of haste. There do exist rare individuals who can sit down and write a good essay in one go, but these individuals are either unusually talented or writing about a topic they have been immersed in for a long time. The rest of us take several attempts and we take time over the thinking about the essay and the writing of it. Simply put, for most people, it takes time to crystallise a good argument. You need to take time to immerse yourself in the literature, focusing on the topic you are going to write about and then to mull it over for a little while. A first plan needs to follow shortly afterwards. Get down on paper some ideas of what you are thinking about writing and keep reading and mulling. Remember, the cure for writer's cramp is writer's block and the only to get writing down on paper is, funnily enough, to write.

Often, the most difficult part of writing any essay is making a start. You should aim to write a first paragraph at the first opportunity that you have after choosing your essay title – once you have done some initial reading and thinking. Managing this will normally make you more receptive to relevant ideas, and it becomes easier to read round a topic purposefully. This first paragraph need only be your plan put

---

[3] At the time of writing (September 2007), Wikipedia is trying to improve its quality control procedures, following complaints of political editing of various articles, which either lionised or demonised their subjects.

into continuous prose, rather than bullet points. After all, your opening paragraph should only tell the reader what the essay is about. This said, by the time you have finished the rest of the essay, you will probably have revised this first paragraph several times and it is often said by writers that the opening paragraph is the last one to be finalised.

Take the time to write the first draft of the essay as soon as you can after the title has been selected. The more you write, the more you can write and the better focused your reading is going to be. The first draft should be reread and once you have put right its most obvious errors, try to leave it unread for at least a week, before you return to it. This way you will read it with fresh eyes, almost as if it had been written by someone else, and not only will you be more aware of the mistakes that remain and the parts that don't work, you will also be more aware of the parts that are well written.

The aim is do what is known as an iterative process: you return to the essay several times and each time you make adjustments to it. This is what each writer in this book has done with his/her chapter. Between iterations, you need to leave the essay and do more reading of journal articles and chapters from books that have some bearing on the argument you are making or that discuss your topic. As you go back and forth to the essay, your readings are much more likely to make sense since you are seeing them in the context of your own work.

As a final check, someone apart from you should read through the completed essay to check that it is clearly written and that there are no major grammatical or spelling errors. Students might well work in pairs for this purpose. Everyone can write gibberish; everyone can miss out letters, words or even whole sentences – and anyone can depend on the sometimes dubious results put out by the spellcheckers that are part of most word-processing programs. When we write, we know what we *want* to say. We can all, however, become blind to what we have actually written.

MUDDLING TENSES, SAYING WHAT YOU FEEL AND WHICH VOICE TO USE

Novice academic writers (and not uncommonly more experienced ones too) can tie themselves in knots over which tense to use when they refer to a piece of writing. Should one say, for example, Winch and Gingell (1999) *term* Education an essentially contested concept or that they *termed* it an essentially contested concept? After all, it was some years ago that they made their claim.

There are two ways of approaching this. One is to always use the past tense since the claim was made in the past, which makes sense. The other is to always use the present tense since the claim is made every time you read it in their book. The essential point here is to decide which way to use (and your course tutors may have their preferences, so check with them) and stick to it – rigidly and without exception!

In conversation, it is common for people to liberally mix opinions and arguments for which they have evidence. They will assert (i.e. say things without evidence) and they will argue (i.e. say things with evidence based on facts they cite or on the logical flow of the argument). In conversation, opinions abound and they are often prefaced by terms such as *I feel* or *I believe*. Problems can arise when this conversational looseness is carried over into essays.

Using terms such as *I feel* or *I believe* reduce what you are saying to the level of an opinion and nothing more. Saying *I feel because* . . . gives a reason for your opinion so why not drop *I feel* entirely and just present your reasons?

The exception to this comes when you are writing a reflective essay in which you examine your experience. In this case, what you feel and what you believe are important because you are being reflective. However, don't forget to compare what you thought or felt with what the literature says. That way you show whether others have experienced similar sentiments to yours.

This brings us to another bone of contention in essay-writing: which voice to use. The tradition in scientific circles is generally to avoid using the first person singular. In social sciences, such as Education, writers frequently use the first person and say *I* if they are solo writers or *we* only if there is more than one of them. Some of those from a scientific background will use a passive voice and, rather than writing *I will show that* . . ., they say *it will be shown that* . . . . In addition there are those who write *the writer will show that* . . . . Although some of these styles can seem bit awkward, fundamentally it does not matter which one you use (unless your course tutors say otherwise). What is important is to pick one and to stick to it. Don't be *I* in one line, *we* in the next and *the writer* in the one after that. If you do switch voices, then you may well confuse your reader, if not actually annoy them.

IRRELEVANCE AND POOR ARGUMENT

Irrelevance and poor argument are often the result of students not thinking through what is demanded by the topic or title set. It always helps to write as a first paragraph an explanation in your own words of what the assignment set is actually asking, and how a response will be framed. Any difficult terms in the title/question should be defined briefly in your own words, but not by quoting a dictionary, since dictionaries only give the immediate *definition* of a word, not its sense or its implications, unless that is all is needed. Other sorts of introductions ('setting the scene' etc.) should in general be avoided, unless you are specifically asked to provide a background to the essay. The main principle of a good Education essay is that it answers a question directly and in the most economic way (i.e. with no lengthy digressions).

Other impediments to good argument are unnecessary repetition and unsupported generalisations or assertions. Examples of unsupported generalisations or assertions would be when a writer states, without giving reasons for his/ her beliefs: 'Comprehensive schools have failed, and should be abandoned'; or 'Progressive methods of teaching are unstructured and do not work.' In fact, an acceptable argument may well only make a few major points, which amount to saying that comprehensive schools have failed or that progressive teaching methods do not work. But, in making these, an essay marshals *evidence* in favour of the *argument* and deals with as many possible criticisms of it as possible. The force of a case will, therefore, lie in the illustrations and examples made, clarifying main points, and the other sorts of evidence (e.g. taken from references) used. So, where important points are repeated, they are repeated so that a different criticism can be dealt with, or a different example given to strengthen the argument.

In sum, a good argument is not necessarily one that makes many points, but one in which the key points are well supported and criticisms of them are well met. A good essay structure therefore would be as follows:

1   A first paragraph that interprets the question set in the student's own words and defines main terms.

2   A clear summary of the student's answer to the question set, indicating which parts of the answer need clarification (with examples, evidence etc.) and what sorts of criticisms of the answer need to be faced.

3   A step-by-step discussion of the answer (already summarised). This discussion will be in two parts – first, providing examples and other sorts of evidence supporting the case, and, second, stating and dealing with criticisms of it.

4   A restatement of the answer to the question set, indicating the extent to which it might still be questioned in the light of criticisms, and any further problems with it that have been thrown up by examples and illustrations.

POOR REFERENCING

In any academic essay, a reasonable selection of writers who have commented on the topic being discussed must be referred to and named. When they are named, the date of a publication on the topic must also be cited. What follows shows how the Harvard style does this:

Kelly (1981) argues that educational curricula should . . .

Peters (1966) believes that . . .

Whenever a writer is named, the date of a relevant publication should normally follow immediately. This writer and the text cited should then, always, appear in the bibliography or list of references at the end of the essay. When a writer's work is cited by another writer, both texts should be indicated in the essay and appear if possible in the bibliography, as follows:

(in essay text)   Piaget and Inhelder (1969, cited Bee, 1992) write that. . .

(in references)   Piaget, J. and Inhelder, B. (1969) *The Psychology of the Child,* New York: Basic Books, cited: Bee, H. (1992) *Child Development*, 3rd edn, London: HarperCollins.

When a point made in an essay is not self-evidently true, it must be argued through (on the basis of a student's own ideas and experiences) and/or be supported by a writer who also makes the same or an equivalent point.

So, for example, a student might write: 'humiliation and harassment continue to be used as a method of teaching in medicine.' This is not self-evidently true (in other words it might, in fact, not be true). Some writers who have found it to be true need to be cited. Therefore, the sentence could read: 'research has shown that humiliation and harassment continue to be used as a method of clinical teaching (Lempp and Seale 2004; Musselman *et al.* 2005)'. Notice that two articles are referred to (which adds credibility to your claim) and that no page number is given as the sentence is not a direct quote.

Lempp and Seale (2004) and Musselman *et al.* (2005) are then listed in the essay's bibliography. The titles of texts are *not* included in the body of the essay, only in the bibliography, unless you have a special reason for giving the title (as I have done later when I refer to Anthony Flew's 1975 book *Thinking about Thinking*, which I want to emphasise as an important text). With this system (the 'Harvard' system), footnotes are usually not needed, except perhaps to mention a point deriving from the argument but not directly relevant to the direction being taken. Examples can be found in the journals. It is worth bearing in mind that footnotes tend to be read, but endnotes are not read to anywhere near the same extent.

Quotations should be as short as possible (a sentence is often quite long enough). The page of a text from where the quotation is taken should be stated following the quotation, as follows:

For example, Bruner (1963) says 'any subject can be taught effectively in some intellectually honest form to any child at any stage of development' (p. 33).

Where a quotation exceeds about two lines, it should usually be written as a separate indented paragraph.

There are literally thousands of referencing styles and the list is growing. Unless there is a course requirement to use a particular style, then the style you adopt does not matter. What is important is that you use a referencing style and that you are consistent in your use of it.

How to get high marks

WRITE CLEAR, WELL-SUPPORTED, RELEVANT ARGUMENTS

High marks for essays are obtained by students writing clear, well-supported arguments that deal directly with the topic or question set. Arguments are likely to be clear if they are expressed in students' own words, using simple, non-technical language. There are no right answers[4] in Education, but there are better or worse presented arguments. Students may well decide to make a case that is different from that provided by a tutor in a lecture. Tutors are usually pleased to be disagreed with. The quality of the argument will depend on how good the reasons are that support it, and the quality of the evidence cited. Students should not be afraid to state, clearly, their own reasons for believing a particular point of view, but they must support those reasons with examples and references. Examples may well be taken from students' own experiences. Providing these are expressed convincingly, they count as real evidence. The crucial matter will be how well these experiences fit into the general case being made.

A good example would be a student's citing of his/her own experiences of being a dyslexic in higher education to argue a view that some forms of academic support for dyslexic people are more effective than others. Provided these experiences are described clearly, in ways a reader can recognise as valid (that is, other people might well have had the same experiences in similar circumstances), they are acceptable. However, a single experience does not make an argument; such an experience will always need further support (usually from books and articles, though more examples and illustrations can help). Students must also recognise positions opposing their own and make some attempt to explain why they do not accept these.

GOOD REFERENCING

Perhaps the single most important feature of a good essay is the quality of its referencing. It is not difficult to find support for most arguments in books and articles on the library shelves, though students will need to browse for a time in order to find these. An easy way of achieving this is to remove potentially relevant texts from the shelves and check through indices (usually at the end) or contents pages to find the appropriate section. It is not necessary to read much of a book in order to cite it in an essay. Students may well find only one paragraph in a text relevant to their essay topic: it is still legitimate to cite the whole book as a reference. Books and journal articles relevant to topics on education can be

---

[4] This is not to suggest there are not correct and incorrect ways of executing tasks, which clearly there often are. Rather it is to suggest that there are multiple interpretations of the same scenario, whereby different arguments may lead to different conclusions. On a basic level, there are many ways to hold a pencil but not all of them will allow you to write legibly, if at all.

found not only in the Education section of the library but also in most parts of any library: you should not be afraid to cite texts from Psychology, Sociology, Philosophy, Literature, Linguistics, History, Geography, Law etc. in support of their arguments. The more support that can be stated, taken from a variety of (reasonably up-to-date or acknowledged classic) texts, the better.

It is very important not to be enslaved by course booklists. These are almost always indicative only and, in any case, books listed are usually quickly borrowed by the first students to arrive at a library. Tutors are always pleased to find books and articles referred to that they themselves have not yet discovered. To say that a booklist is indicative means that there are many other books that could have been listed, but have not been, through lack of space. Tutors are not especially looking in essays for references to set books, although, where these are easily obtained, it is expected that students will, where relevant, refer to them. Tutors are, more obviously, looking for references to *appropriate* texts. There are very many chapters and articles that are appropriate texts for essays in education and far from all of them appear in books and journals with the word *education* in the title.

You need to become aware of the wealth of material available through online databases, whether public domain (such as ERIC and the British Education Index) or restricted access (for which you may need an *Athens* username and password, for which you need to speak to your librarian). Higher education institutions subscribe to refereed journals and most of these can usually be accessed online (though you will usually need a username and password from the librarian in order to do this).

Research is where the Internet can really come into its own and open you up to a range of sources you might otherwise not consider. You need to think of a set of *keywords* to search for using either a general search engine or the search facility that most journal publishers provide on their home page.

However, bear in mind the warning about the Web given above: there is a lot of stuff on it; a lot of this is of great worth but an awful lot more is guff. You should also bear in mind that some of the abstract services demand payment by credit card; but, before you rush off and pay for access, check that your library does not already subscribe to the source concerned. If you are going to pay, try to find out whether what you are paying for is actually worthwhile and whether it is worth, to you, the charge being asked.

Be warned: not all sites that request payment are secure. Data is regularly intercepted on the Web by unscrupulous characters and used for unscrupulous ends.

A GOOD ARGUMENT RELIES ON ITS EVIDENCE

Evidence will be of several kinds:

a   An appropriate book, or journal article, properly referred to, provides a form of evidence. This has been discussed extensively above.

b Policy documents, Acts of Parliament, Statutory Orders, Green Papers, White Papers etc.

c Material from archives.

d Students' own experiences are a form of evidence. Again, this has been discussed above.

e Empirical research evidence. Where students discover that some research has been carried out that supports (or opposes) the point being made, this may well be discussed at some length (though beware of padding out an essay by simply describing a long research project). It is not always easy to find research evidence to support an educational argument, so students should not worry unduly if they do not discover much. It is, by contrast, relatively easy to discover writers who (for whatever reason) support one point of view or another.

f A reasoned argument is a form of evidence. Usually, the reasons supporting a point of view will relate to a, b, c, d or e above.

NOTE

The word *proof* should not be used in an Education essay, unless you are using the term in a mathematical sense.[5] Important educational positions are never proved. We simply provide evidence for them. This is because education is based upon the study of human beings, and we rarely (if ever) *prove* anything about people. The rare exception would be where you turned to a physical science such as Biology for evidence, where (possibly) some physical law has been proved that reflects upon an educational idea. This is so remote a possibility that students are best advised not to use the word *proof* even here, but simply to discuss the biological evidence as good (valid) evidence. In short, you should attempt to introduce the word *evidence* (with accompanying ideas) at key points in their essays since a sound argument *indicates* what *appears* to be true. It does not prove anything. This is a crucial concept. You should work to eliminate words such as *prove, proof* etc.

It is also essential to get clear in your head, and hence in your writing, that there are several kinds of *theory* (see Chapter 3 in the present volume for a detailed discussion of the nature of theory). The simplest sort is the basic personal theory, which is really just a notion based on some personal experience: e.g. 'every time I leave my umbrella at home, it rains.' There is actually no causal link between the two phenomena but superficially there may appear to be. On a more serious level, we have *descriptive* and *prescriptive* theories. A descriptive theory is a scientific theory. An example is the Theory of Evolution (strictly speaking, it should be *theories* since

---

[5] The mathematical use of the word *prove* is somewhat dodgy as what is meant is that a proposition has been demonstrated to be true, subject to a long list of caveats that may or may not be explicitly stated. Outside of most mathematics, *prove* is frequently used to mean that it has been shown that there is the greatest likelihood that the proposition is true.

there are a few different ones). There is no absolute proof that evolution ever happened; rather there is strong evidence that, out of all the possible ways for the biosphere to have got to where it is at this moment, the most likely is through an evolutionary process. The scientific theory of this kind describes what likely happened. 'If I drop a stone in the Earth's gravitational field, it will fall' is an illustration of the Theory of Gravity. Where you can repeat an experiment and always get the same result, then a theory may become a Law. It never gets proved as such but it just happens to be true every time it is tested.

In social sciences, theories tend to be prescriptive. In other words, the theorist sets out various conditions and argues that, if these are fulfilled, then a particular result will ensue. I might argue that if private schools were abolished then greater social cohesion should result. This would be a simple example of a prescriptive theory. The strength of the theory would be dependent on the evidence given to back up my claim.

ANALYTICAL RATHER THAN DESCRIPTIVE

Descriptive arguments are those in which points made are not supported by reasons and/or explanations. Few ideas in education are so straightforward that they do not need explanation. As a simple example, students might believe that it is obvious that learning occurs best in happy places, and that teachers should be kind to their learners. But writers such as Gramsci (Entwistle 1980) thought that the best learning occurs when learners work hard (pleasure is irrelevant) and that formal learning should be viewed just like a job of work. Other people, such as some of the more aggressive teachers in my primary school in the 1960s, held onto the belief that people will learn best in order to avoid pain or punishment and so dispensed physical punishment with liberal abandon. It can also be argued that the end justifies the means and that the path taken to learning is irrelevant. All that counts is the learning thus acquired. This opens the debate over process versus product.

So anyone proposing that learners should be in happy places to do their learning would need to justify such a proposal and would need to counter the arguments that are opposed to happy places being where learning happens best or according to which happiness is irrelevant in learning.

ORIGINALITY, UNIQUENESS

Originality is usually stated as the key to being awarded the highest attainable essay grades. In fact, students do not have to be exceptionally able to produce arguments with a degree of originality. Obviously, it is unlikely that any idea will be wholly original, but it may be markedly different from currently accepted ideas. The secret of expressing such a (relatively) original point of view is, first, to try to understand what the current views are, then to deliberately fashion an argument that shows a recognition of these before arriving at a deviant position. This position may be difficult to sustain, but by expressing it students will come to a better understanding of current views.

For example, it is easy to see from the figures available from the Higher Education Statistical Agency[6] that few applicants to medical school come from social classes 4 and 5. This problem is usually located in the relatively low rate of academic success generally enjoyed by pupils in schools where social classes 4 and 5[7] predominate; or in the aspirations that teachers in such schools have for their pupils with regard to school examinations and thence further or higher education, so that they work to create self-fulfilling prophecies of social reproduction. An alternative argument might recognise these two standpoints but recognise also that many pupils from such schools do in fact attain the levels required for medical school but do not make the application. It might consider the tendency for humans to feel most comfortable in surroundings where they see people like themselves (by whatever criteria). Thus it might argue that the root cause for the low level of applicants from social classes 4 and 5 is in the image potential applicants have of higher education in general and medical school in particular (see Kamali *et al.* 2005; Heathfield and Wakeford 1994). Considering such an argument side by side with the others might lead to some new insights into educational issues, which might then engender ideas for remediation or rectification.

NOTE

A synthesis of ideas, produced from a student's own individual point of view, can sometimes reveal a new insight. It is only by writing down a set of ideas that we discover whether or not it is worth expressing. Usually, the best essays arise through students taking risks, trying to fashion some novel case, rather than through students playing safe and trying to write the argument they believe that their tutors want.

Argumentation

 means recognising that your opinion needs to be backed up with, for example, reference to evidence from elsewhere. There are, however, a number of what are termed sophistical devices (after the Ancient Greek Sophists, who were paid to write speeches and convincing arguments, especially for people who were going to appear in court). What follows is a list of such rhetorical devices. It is not exhaustive but rather indicative of the kinds of ways that logic can escape from an argument. If you listen to politicians, you may well notice much use of such devices. Be careful, though: there are occasions when the use of some of these devices can be legitimate.

[6] www.hesa.ac.uk/index.php/content/view/455/141/ (accessed 29 September 2007).
[7] Semi-skilled manual and unskilled manual respectively.

Ad hominem

> Would you buy a used car from this man?
> (1968 US presidential campaign poster showing Richard Nixon, nicknamed *Tricky Dicky*
> and reputed to be economical with the truth.)

Argumentum ad hominem is used to reduce the value of a person's argument or stance by being derogatory about the person. An example of this occurred in 2003 when the then Conservative leader, Ian Duncan Smith, referred in a speech to the Conservative party conference to Charles Kennedy's alleged drinking habits as a means of attacking the Lib Dems' policies. That Kennedy turned out to have a very real drinking problem is immaterial. In fact several of the UK's more illustrious prime ministers have also had a drinking problem.[8]

Ad antiquitatem (appeal to antiquity)

'We have always done things this way so we must be right.' This asserts that just because something is old then it is valuable/correct/justified.

Ad crumenam (appeal to money)

'Microsoft must be good, otherwise they would not have got so rich.'

Ad lazarum (appeal to poverty)

This assumes that to be poor is to be virtuous by dint of being poor.

Ad nauseam

This asserts that the more often something is heard then the more true it becomes. This is frequently seen in the generation of 'truth' by the media. For example, bird flu, which has killed very few people and for which there is no evidence that it will go on to kill many more, has filled many column inches in the press and has become a perceived threat through being talked about. There is also the case of the measles-mumps-rubella triple vaccine, of which a very limited trial using dubious methodology and a tiny sample was picked up by the media and taken as the truth.[9]

The converse of ad nauseam is also true: the New Orleans floods of 2005 were

---

[8] Winston Churchill was apparently told by Lady Astor one evening at a reception: *Winston, you're drunk.* Without missing a beat, Churchill is said to have replied, *My dear, you're ugly but in the morning I shall be sober.*

[9] See Wakefield *et al.* (1998) for the original paper that set off the storm and whose evidence base was very weak indeed and certainly far too small to be generalisable, and www.mmrthefacts.nhs.uk/library/research.php for a lengthy list of research papers debunking its claims.

seen as more of a disaster than the Kashmiri earthquake of the same year since the former received enormously more coverage in the media than did the latter. The former killed fewer than 1,000 people; the latter killed at least 50,000 people. See Miller *et al.* (1998) for an explanation of how ad nauseam and its converse work with the broadcast and print media.

Appeal to authority

This is fine if the authority is legitimate for the topic under discussion. It becomes fallacious when the authority has little or nothing to do with the topic. See for example Enoch Powell's use of Virgil ('Like the Roman, I see the Tiber foaming with much blood') in an attempt to add legitimacy to his argument when he attacked immigration into the UK in his famous 'rivers of blood' speech in 1968.[10]

Appeal to common sense

'Common sense is a set of prejudices acquired before the age of eighteen' (Albert Einstein). What is common sense for you might be complete anathema to me. Common knowledge is equally fraught since what I commonly know might be alien to you. Both common sense and common knowledge are cultural constructs.

Appeal to the emotion of pity

This is fallacious when it is used to distract from the substance of the argument and to distract from relevant evidence (e.g. 'Don't hit me; I'm just a poor person'). It can, when properly used, be quite legitimate and arguably can have echoes of Aristotle's idea that we should treat equals equally and treat unequals unequally.

Appeal to novelty

A new thing is better than an old thing *because* it is new. This reasoning is used (fallaciously) to justify not considering older, but still relevant, sources of material for essays.

Appeal to popularity

'The people are always right.' 'Capital punishment is justified because the people approve of it.' This is one of the greatest failings of Utilitarianism, which took as its bedrock the aim of pursuing the greatest happiness of the greatest number.

---

[10] The text of this speech is available at www.martinfrost.ws/htmlfiles/rivers_blood2.html (accessed 29 September 2007). It employs one sophistical device after another.

Appeal to threat

This is a common way to end discussions in some pubs. It is legitimate when some sort of sanction may be employed and is commonly used in discussions between employers and unions.

Argument from ignorance

There are two types and they go like this:

1   This proposition is not known to be true, therefore it is false.
2   This proposition is not known to be false, therefore it is true.

It is legitimate to use this in courts of law, where one side or the other must establish its case *beyond reasonable doubt* in criminal courts or *on balance of probabilities* in civil courts. In both cases, if a proposition is not established to be true (or false) then it is deemed to be false (or true).

Fallacy of many questions

'Are you still beating your wife, Mr Smith? Please answer yes or no' is the classic of this genre. Whether the respondent answers yes or no, he will admit to having a wife, and having beaten her at some time in the past. Thus, these facts are *presupposed* by the question and, if it has not been agreed upon by the speakers before, the question is improper, and the fallacy of many questions has been committed. There are presuppositions built into the question. The only answers are to ask that the question be broken down into smaller questions or to reply 'none of the above.'

No true Scotsman

This term was coined by Anthony Flew in his 1975 book *Thinking about Thinking*. It refers to a form of argument in which rebuttal of the opening statement leads to a revision of that statement, with the aim of the proponent never being 'proved' wrong. It is more than simply refining the proposition (which is usually a valid procedure), as it is dependent on an *ad hoc* change to shore up the assertion. So:

A   No Scotsman puts sugar on his porridge.
B   Angus is a Scotsman and he puts sugar on his porridge.
A   Then he can't be a *true* Scotsman.

Over-generalisation

This is the basis of stereotyping in which one takes a limited experience and generalises it to an entire population (or country or ethnic group or whatever). This is commonly done when a person uses limited data and applies them, without justification, to a much larger population or group.

Question-begging

Assuming to be true that which remains to be shown. This is not the same as the mundane use of the term, which means simply to suggest a question. In the philosophical sense, question-begging links propositions without showing why (or how) they are linked. A typical one is to claim that raising the price of fuel will reduce global warming. It has to be shown that there is a link between fuel prices, fuel consumption and global warming. Without these links being demonstrated, questions are begged. A category of question-begging founds the argument on its conclusion and is known as *circular argument,* an example (with thanks to Andrew R. Davidson, the copy-editor of this edition) being 'The charges of physical abuse are absolutely untrue, because the police would never do something like that.'

Slippery slope

This is also the 'thin end of the wedge'. It is used by libertarians to fend off such initiatives as identity cards. It is used by other groups to protest against such phenomena as immigration. Fundamentally, slippery slope depends on extrapolation from the situation we are in now to one that has yet to come to pass. Its legitimacy is variable since it requires certain prophetic powers, though these may be based on past experiences. However, such inductive reasoning depends on the past being a valid indicator of the future. This it may or may not be. Nonetheless, 'those who cannot learn from history are doomed to repeat it' (George Santayana[11]).

Stereotyping

This links in with (at least) ad hominem and over-generalisation. Individuals are ascribed to groups and certain traits are ascribed to those groups. Examples include the depiction of, for example, the Scots in most popular TV drama as thugs, drunks, thick, psychopaths and so on. This is not to say there are none of those in Scotland but by applying stereotypes there is the creation of the expectation that all Scots are like that. Stereotyping is never justified in arguments.

This list is a taster of sophistical devices. It is neither exhaustive nor complete. Try to find some more!

[11] Available from www.wisdomquotes.com/cat_history.html (accessed 29 September 2007).

Conclusion

Essay-writing is a skill. Like any skill, it can be learned. Like any skill, some people find it easier to learn to do well than do others. However, like any skill, it gets better with practice and the only way to practise writing essays is to write essays. This is where the iterative process is so useful: you revisit the same essay several times and in effect have several bites at the cherry. You get to practise your writing skills more times than if you just dashed off your essay in one hectic night of writing. Following the essay-writing pointers will strengthen and develop your writing skills. Paying attention to the various sophistical devices and knowing how to recognise them and how to see when they are being used illegitimately will strengthen not only your writing but also your analytical skills.

Good luck and enjoy the journey.

References

Bee, H. (1992) *Child Development*, 3rd edn. Glasgow: HarperCollins.

de Bono, Edward (1973) *Lateral Thinking*. Harmondsworth: Penguin.

Bruner, J. S. (1963) *The Process of Education*. New York: Vintage Books.

Carroll, L. (1886) *Alice's Adventures in Wonderland*. London: Macmillan.

Entwistle, H. (1980) *Antonio Gramsci: Conservative Schooling for Radical Politics*. London: Routledge.

Flew, A. (1975) *Thinking about Thinking, or Do I Sincerely Want to be Right?* Glasgow: Fontana.

Heathfield, M. and Wakeford, N. (1994) *They Always Eat Green Apples*. Lancaster: Unit for Innovation in Higher Education.

Kamali, A. W., Nicholson, S. and Wood, D. F. (2005) 'A Model for Widening Access into Medicine and Dentistry: The SAMDA-BL Project', *Medical Education*. **39** (9), 918–925.

Kelly, A. V. (1981) *The Curriculum: Theory and Practice*. London: Harper Row.

Lempp, H. and Seale, C. (2004) 'The Hidden Curriculum in Undergraduate Medical Education: Qualitative Study of Medical Students' Perceptions of Teaching', *British Medical Journal*. **329** (7469): 770–773. Available at doi: 10.1136/bmj.329.7469.770.

Miller, D., Katzinger, J. and Beharrel, P. (1998) *The Circuit of Mass Communication*. London: SAGE.

Musselman, L. J., MacRae, H. M., Reznick, R. K. and Lingard, L. A. (2005) ' "You Learn Better under the Gun": Intimidation and Harassment in Surgical Education', *Medical Education*. **39**, 926–934.

Peters, R. S. (1966) *Ethics and Education*. London: Allen and Unwin.

Piaget, J. and Inhelder, B. (1969) *The Psychology of the Child*. New York: Basic Books, cited: Bee, H. (1992) *Child Development*, 3rd edn. Glasgow: HarperCollins.

Wakefield, A. J., Murch, S. H., Anthony, A., Linnell, J., Casson, D. M., Malik, M., Berelowitz, M., Dhillon, A. P., Thomson, M. A., Harvey, P., Valentine, A., Davies, S. E. and Walker-Smith, J. A. (1998) 'Ileal-lymphoid-nodular Hyperplasia, Non-specific Colitis, and Pervasive Developmental Disorder in Children', *The Lancet*. **351**, 637–641.

Winch, C. and Gingell, J. (1999) *Key Concepts in the Philosophy of Education*. London: Routledge.

Index

Lightning Source UK Ltd.
Milton Keynes UK
UKOW06f0105170913

217328UK00017B/595/P